The Afghans

THE PEOPLES OF ASIA

General Editor
Morris Rossabi

...e in this series comprises a complete history, from
...present, of the people under consideration. Written
...eologists, historians and anthropologists, the books
...a wide, multi-disciplinary readership, as well as to
the general reader.

PUBLISHED

...ATION

The Afghans

Willem Vogelsang

A John Wiley & Sons, Ltd., Publication

This paperback edition first published 2008
© 2008 Willem Vogelsang

Edition history: Blackwell Publishing Ltd (hardback, 2002)

Blackwell Publishing was acquired by John Wiley & Sons in February 2007. Blackwell's publishing program has been merged with Wiley's global Scientific, Technical, and Medical business to form Wiley-Blackwell.

Registered Office
John Wiley & Sons Ltd, The Atrium, Southern Gate, Chichester, West Sussex, PO19 8SQ, United Kingdom

Editorial Offices
350 Main Street, Malden, MA 02148-5020, USA
9600 Garsington Road, Oxford, OX4 2DQ, UK
The Atrium, Southern Gate, Chichester, West Sussex, PO19 8SQ, UK

For details of our global editorial offices, for customer services, and for information about how to apply for permission to reuse the copyright material in this book please see our website at www.wiley.com/wiley-blackwell.

Library of Congress Cataloging-in-Publication Data

Vogelsang, Willem.
  The Afghans / Willem Vogelsang
  p. cm.—(The peoples of Asia)
  Includes bibliographical references and index.
ISBN 978-1-4051-8243-0 (pb : alk paper)
  1. Afghanistan—History. I. Title. II. Series
DS358.V64 2002
958.1—dc21

                    2001000332

A catalogue record for this book is available from the British Library.

Set in 10.5 on 12pt by SNP Best-set Typesetter Ltd., Hong Kong
Printed in Singapore by C.O.S. Printers Pte Ltd

01 2008

Contents

Illustrations

Figures

Maps

Preface to the Updated Paperback Edition

The hardback edition of this book was completed a few months before 9/11. The fall of the Taliban and massive Western presence in Afghanistan led to a flood of books and articles being published on the subject. Archaeological work in the country was also started up again, with large-scale surveys in the west of the country, and limited excavations in the north, and in and around Kabul. The National Museum of Afghanistan, in Kabul, was heavily damaged during the civil war and many of its objects destroyed or looted. Nowadays the building has been brought back to its former glory and numerous objects have been restored or returned. The famous Tillya Tepe hoard of gold objects, discovered in 1978 and 1979 by the Soviet excavator Viktor Sarianidi in North Afghanistan, was miraculously preserved, together with many other priceless Afghan treasures, in the vaults of the Presidential Palace. This collection is now touring the world and attracting thousands of visitors.

Diplomats and military who are currently involved in the affairs of Afghanistan are slowly realising that defeating the Taliban regime was relatively easy, but trying to bring peace and stability is another matter. They have found that knowledge and appreciation of local history and culture are indispensable for the success of their work and for understanding local actors. When Zawahiri, the number two of al-Qaida, sometime in 2006 told the British military in Helmand province that there would not be a second Dr Brydon, few people knew who he was referring to. Most Afghans, however, understood the reference very well. Zawahiri was talking about the famous retreat from Kabul in the winter of 1842. Some 16,000 men and women of the British garrison in Kabul (located close to the place where you will now find the headquarters of the ISAF forces) were forced to withdraw to British India. Dr Brydon was the only man who reached the East Afghan town of Jalalabad. All others had been killed, taken hostage, or just died of the cold. History is important in Afghanistan, and if you do not speak the language of history, communication is very difficult.

When I wrote this book in the 1990s, few people around me had any idea what I was working on, and many kindly suggested that perhaps I should do something more useful. After 9/11, I found myself in a maelstrom of political and military developments, and some very interesting and exciting visits to the country, in various capacities. My first visit after the fall of the Taliban was in the spring and summer of 2002, when I travelled by myself all over the country and visited some archaeological sites that I had not seen for years. My last visit, until now, was only a few weeks ago. This time I stayed in Kabul, and it was clear that travelling to the south was far too dangerous. It hurts me to see, each time I visit the country, how the optimism of the Afghans of 2002 is slowly turning into disillusionment. It also hurts to hear foreign diplomats and military (when talking in private!) talk about a certain inevitability of the downward spiralling security situation in the country. Future historians should study how the situation of 2002, with the Taliban completely defeated and a local population fully willing to welcome outside assistance, has changed such that the country is apparently rapidly sliding into a new civil war. A general inability to come to grips with Afghan culture and Afghan and regional history will certainly be among some of the points that will be mentioned.

Willem Vogelsang, 8 December 2007

Preface to the 2002 Edition

The terrorist attacks on New York and Washington on 11 September 2001 caused the deaths of thousands of people and indescribable misery for their families. They also brought Afghanistan back into the limelight. For years Afghanistan had been virtually forgotten. It was a country few knew anything about, except perhaps for the fact that Afghan women had to cover themselves up completely in a *chadari* so that their presence would not tempt their pious men folk to more worldly thoughts. Islam was seen to have gone crazy in 'Far-away-istan'. With hindsight, we should have paid more attention.

The terrible events of 11 September brought the people of Afghanistan into contact with a rapidly changing world in which global developments affect even those who live and die in the secluded valleys of the Indo-Iranian borderlands. Many Afghans felt that playing host and protecting a foreigner, even one of the world's most wanted terrorists, demonstrated an Afghan sense of hospitality and they regarded it as a purely Afghan affair. However, Osama bin Laden had not retreated to Afghanistan to help the Afghans. He was there, primarily, to fight those he considered infidels anywhere he could hit them. His presence in Afghanistan thus affected the rest of the world. And it drew retribution upon the Afghans.

The Taliban members had been brought up in refugee camps surrounded by brutal civil war. They were educated by religious teachers steeped in dogma who preached an extremely strict interpretation of Islamic law. The Taliban are therefore very different from the traditional Afghan leaders I worked and travelled with when their country was occupied by the Soviet Union. One of these greybeards once told me: 'One half of the Koran is fine, the other half we write ourselves'. The Taliban, however, see things in a different light. They show a narrow-minded religious and political parochialism that astounds and at times frightens those looking on. Their attitude towards women and their cynical exploitation of the opium trade have led to their country losing all the prestige it had acquired when it defeated the Soviet Union. Their subsequent alliance with international terrorist groups has placed them beyond the pale. After the aeroplanes hit the World Trade Center, the Taliban were confronted with an extremely angry outside world that stretched far beyond the borders of their own small villages, let alone their country.

The Taliban came to power when Afghanistan had lost all vestiges of a state. By 1992 most bureaucrats and educated groups with an interest in the State of Afghanistan had either been killed or lured to the West. The Taliban used Islam to impose peace upon the mosaic of religious and ethnic entities that characterizes the country, with disastrous effects. If there is something to learn from the present crisis it is perhaps the sad fact that a massive brain-drain from a poor and undeveloped country like Afghanistan may plunge the country into a deeper crisis, with horrendous effects not only for the country itself but also for the rest of the world. Afghanistan has now become a prime example of 'the failure of political Islam'. Perhaps the time has come for the moderate, traditional leaders of the peoples of Afghanistan to raise their voices.

In the present book I hope to show something of the dramatic history of the country, ever confronted by influences and immigrants from the west, north and east. Calling Afghanistan the 'Crossroads of Civilizations' has become a cliché, but there is no denying that the lands of Afghanistan always constituted an area through which passed individuals and peoples from Central Asia, the Middle East and the Indian subcontinent on their way to acquire prestige, wealth, conquest or religious converts. Such influences were rarely peaceful and they mark the country's history as particularly bloody.

I would like to thank Professor Morris Rossabi for stimulating me to write this book, and Gillian, Jan Hendrik and Robert for their endurance and for the many marvellous trips we made together through the East.

Willem Vogelsang, Leiden, 1 October 2001

The transcription of Arabic names follows in the main that of the *Encyclopaedia of Islam*. For Chinese names I am indebted to Mark Leenhouts (Leiden University) for adjusting them all to the Pinyin system. It should be noted that many of the sounds starting with 'j' may originally refer to a 'k' sound.

1

Up and Down the Hindu Kush

The Hindu Kush rises high above the plains and valleys of Afghanistan. Over the millennia these majestic mountains have looked down upon peaceful farmers and wandering pastoralists, upon the armies of Alexander the Great and Chingiz-Khan, upon traders and pilgrims, and in recent years upon multitudes of desparate foreign diplomats who have tried to bring peace to this war-torn country. Whatever these men and women accomplished in Afghanistan, not far off there always loomed the towering height of the Hindu Kush. Thousands of years ago the ancient Iranians called this range the *upâ'ri saêna*, or (*kôf-i*) *apârsên*, '(the mountains) above the falcon', or in other words, 'mountains that rise higher than a bird can fly'.[1] In the late first millennium BC, the Greeks correspondingly used the name of the *Paropanisadae* to indicate the plains that stretch immediately southeast of the mountains, around the modern capital of Kabul.[2] The Classical name probably derives from Iranian *para-upa'risaêna*, which should mean something like 'the land which lies beyond the *upa'risaêna*' and thus indicating a name given by people who lived on the other, northern side of the mountains. In the early seventh century of the modern era, the Chinese Buddhist pilgrim Xuanzang, while travelling through Afghanistan on his way from China to the Indian subcontinent and back again, used the name of *Poluoxina* to describe the mountains north of Kabul.[3] The appellation recalls the Old Iranian name, and in his *Records* the

1 The identity of the (Old Iranian, Avestan) *Saêna Mᵊrᵊγa* ('Saena bird', eagle, falcon?) remains unknown. In later Iranian mythology it is referred to as the *Simurgh* (Middle Persian *Sênmurv*); compare Bartholomae 1904:398 and Monchi-Zadeh 1975:128.
2 A western offshoot of the Hindu Kush, north and northeast of Herat, is still known as the Paropamisus Range by western geographers.
3 Translation of the *Si-Yu-Ki, Buddhist Records of the Western World*, by Samuel Beal (1884: II, 286).

Illustration 1   *Group of Afghan Mujahedin, summer 1982 (photograph: author).*

pilgrim unwittingly illustrates this point by telling that '[t]he very birds that fly in their wheeling flight cannot mount alone this point, but go afoot across the height and then fly downwards'.

The Hindu Kush is an offshoot of the Himalayas. In its widest sense the name covers much of the rugged centre and northeast of Afghanistan. The mountains affect the country's climate, the quality of its soil, the availability of water and its routes of communication. In this way, the Hindu Kush constitutes a constant factor in the life of the people who make a living along its flanks and in the surrounding plains. It is a difficult life, in a harsh and often cruel environment, with cold winters and hot summers. In some areas there is plenty of water, while other places receive hardly any precipitation at all. Sometimes, as at the time of writing this book, it does not rain for years on end, causing immense suffering and great overall damage. The average life expectancy for Afghan men and women is consequently very low; the CIA factbook for the year 2000 gives an estimate of 45.88 years.[4]

Although producing relatively little and forcing people into a constant struggle against the environment, the country is also singularly unique and full of potential, which is mainly due to its geographical position. The people of Afghanistan live along one of the most important high roads of Asia (Ill. 1). Their country constitutes the con-

4   CIA factbook www.odci.gov/cia/publications/factbook/geos/af.html

necting link between the steppes and deserts of Central Asia, the vast expanses of the Middle East and Iran, and the lush plains and sweltering heat of the Indian subcontinent. Throughout history, immigrants from neighbouring lands moved into and across the mountains and passes of Afghanistan, traversing the country from all sides. They all left their traces, and their descendants, and thus created the mosaic of ethnic groups that characterizes the country's present population.

Contacts with the outside world, however, were never one-sided. Time and again, the hardened men from Afghanistan moved from their mountains down into the surrounding plains and deserts, for grazing, trade or plunder. They defeated kingdoms and founded empires. In this way, the history of the people of Afghanistan is also the history of those who live beyond its modern borders.

Against this environmental and geographical backdrop, the people of Afghanistan have woven a web of shared customs, beliefs, and techniques, and with a comparable outlook on life. This web justifies the writing of a book on the history of the Afghans as a single group distinct from neighbouring peoples, even if the name 'Afghan' really only applies to one of the peoples that inhabit the country. These are the Pashtuns, who for centuries have constituted the dominant ethnic group of Afghanistan and who live mainly in the south and east of the country and in neighbouring Pakistan. It also means that in order to understand the people of Afghanistan and their history, it is necessary to know something about the physical environment that made the Afghans into what they are now.

Present-day Afghanistan

The modern Islamic State of Afghanistan (*Dawlat-i Islâmi-yi Afghânistân*)[5] is a landlocked country of 647,500 square km (Map 1) and is therefore somewhat larger than France.[6] In the south and east, over a distance of 2,430 km, it borders on Pakistan. In the northeast, high in the mountains, it shares a very short boundary (76 km) with China. Two northern neighbouring countries are Tajikistan (1,206 km) and Uzbekistan (137 km). In the northwest lies Turkmenistan (744 km), and to the west Afghanistan is bounded by the Islamic Republic of Iran (936 km). Estimates of Afghanistan's present population are notoriously vague. In 1978, experts accepted a figure

---

5 The Taliban movement, presently in control of most of the country including the capital Kabul, describes the country as the Islamic Emirate of Afghanistan.
6 CIA factbook.

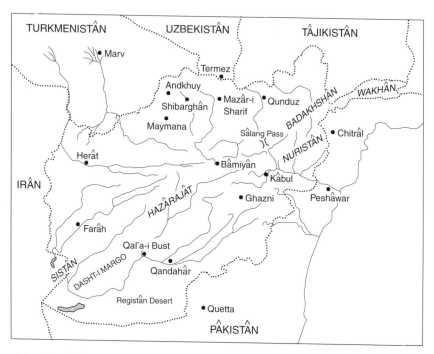

Map 1 *The main cities and districts of Afghanistan.*

of some fifteen million. Following the communist coup of 27 April 1978, and especially after the invasion of the country by Soviet forces at Christmas 1979, some five million refugees fled the country. Hundreds of thousands died during the war (Ill. 2), which continued after the Soviet withdrawal that was completed on 15 February 1989. The number of refugees who have since then returned to their country is unknown, nor are there clear figures of new refugees trying to escape the internecine wars that dominate modern politics. The CIA factbook for 2000 gives estimates of some 1,200,000 Afghans still remaining in Pakistan, and some 1,400,000 in Iran. Yet what is clear is that in spite of all the upheaval, the population of Afghanistan has in fact increased considerably and estimates indicate a figure of almost 26 million for mid-2000. However, reliable information and figures are absent and the present description of Afghanistan and its population is therefore mainly based on the pre-1979 situation.

Almost all of the modern frontiers of Afghanistan were formally defined and acknowledged in the late nineteenth century. Most of the

Illustration 2 *Two Afghan Mujahedin on their way from Ghazni to Hazarajat, summer 1982 (photograph: author).*

borders were not pegged out along clear geographical features, or on the basis of long-accepted historical traditions. Instead, political and military considerations by the superpowers of those days determined the course of the frontiers. Hence, in the days when European powers controlled most of the globe, British and Russian boundary commissions traversed this part of the world in order to mark Afghanistan's outer contours. They intentionally separated the British possessions in the Indian subcontinent from the Russian conquests in Central

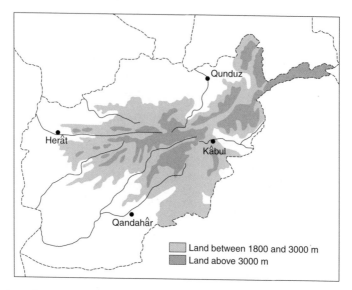

Map 2   *The mountains of Afghanistan.*

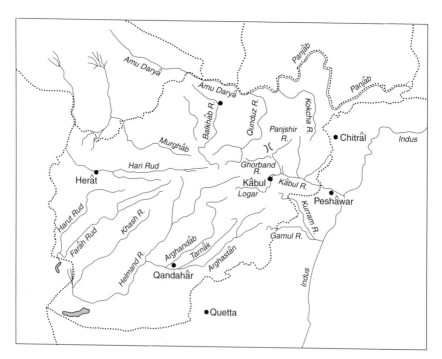

Map 3   *The main rivers of Afghanistan.*

Asia.[7] These were the years of the Great Game between Russia and England, so well described by Rudyard Kipling in his book, *Kim*. In those years, the state of Afghanistan under Amir 'Abd al-Rahman Khan (*r*. 1880–1901) was eventually acknowledged, not as an independent country, but as a buffer state within the British sphere of influence. It was formed to prevent any British soldier from directly facing his Russian opponent. For this reason, the borders of modern Afghanistan often cut straight through traditional tribal lands. This is especially the case in the east, where the lands of the Pashtuns are divided by the so-called Durand line of 1893.[8] Elsewhere, in the southwest, the borderline defined in 1872 and again in 1904,[9] splits up an isolated area of potentially fertile lands (Sistan) between Afghanistan and Iran. Only in the northeast does the modern border follow a plain geographical feature, namely the Panj river (the Panjab) and its continuation, the Amu Darya (the Oxus of Classical authors).[10]

The Hindu Kush Mountains

The Hindu Kush mountains cover most of the northeastern and central parts of the country (Map 2). It extends in a southwestern direction from a mountain knot in the far northeast, where the modern borders of Afghanistan meet those of Tajikistan, China and Pakistan. This mountain knot is generally known as the Qara Qorum (Turk. 'Black Rubble') and by itself constitutes the most northwestern limit of the Himalaya Range. Here the mountains are extremely high, rising to altitudes of over 7,000 metres. Further southwest and down towards Central Afghanistan the mountains slowly diminish in height, but the adjoining Kuh-i Baba Range, to the west of the capital Kabul, is still more than 5,000 metres high.[11]

---

7   Compare Hungerford Holdich (1901; 1910). Another interesting account is by C. C. Davies 1932. For the so-called Great Game, see especially the books by Peter Hopkirk.

8   Named after Sir Henry Mortimer Durand (1850–1924), at that time Foreign Secretary of the Government of (British) India (1884–94).

9   In September 1904, the Persians and Afghans were made to accept the lines drawn by Colonel A. H. McMahon. The lines of 1904 mostly follow those of 1872, drawn by General Sir Frederic Goldsmid (see Hamilton 1906). The distribution of the water of the Hilmand river remained a problem, which was only solved in 1973 with the Hilmand Water Treaty, which was ratified by the Afghan government in 1977.

10   The Classical name of the Oxus lives on in that of the Wakhsh river, a tributary of the Panj/Amu Darya. The confluence of these rivers actually marks the place where the Panj river changes its name and becomes the Amu Darya. See B. Spuler in the *Enc. Isl.* (Amu Darya).

11   The Shah Fuladi peak rises to a height of 5,158 metres.

Illustration 3   *The lakes of Band-i Amir in Central Afghanistan (photo-graph: author, summer 1978).*

The mountains of the Kuh-i Baba and its offshoots mark the origin of most of Afghanistan's major rivers (Ill. 3).[12] These are the Surkhab (or Qunduz river), the Balkhab, the Hari Rud, the Hilmand, the Arghandab, and the Kabul rivers (Map 3). The Surkhab or Qunduz river flows north past the city of Qunduz towards the Amu Darya. The Balkhab, somewhat further to the west, also descends north and flows towards and past Balkh, ancient Bactra, but its waters are drained off and evaporate before they reach the Amu Darya. The Hari Rud goes west and passes the town of Herat and then turns north (as the Tajand river) to empty into the Qara Qum desert of modern Turkmenistan. The Hilmand flows southwest through the deserts of Southwest Afghanistan until it empties its waters in the depression of Sistan. This is the so-called Hilmand Hamun, which also receives the waters of a number of minor rivers that descend down the mountains of Central Afghanistan, including the Khash Rud, the Farah Rud and the Harut Rud. Occasionally the Hilmand Hamun overflows and its excess water then flows via the Shilagh channel southwards towards another large depression nearby, called the Gud-i Zirah. The main contributary of the Hilmand is the Arghandab, which also originates near the Kuh-i Baba range and

12   Compare a passage in the Iranian (Middle Persian) *Bundahishn* (ed. Anklesaria 87,11–88.3), in which it is stated that the *Hêtomand, Harêw, Marw* and *Balkh* originate in the *Apârsên* mountains.

flows east of the Hilmand, passes the town of Qandahar (Pashto: Kandahar) in the south of the country and then joins the Hilmand at the ancient site of (Qalʿa-i) Bust. The Kabul river proceeds east, past the city of Kabul, and after receiving the waters of a series of tributaries flows towards the Indus.

All of these mountains, which separate the north of the country from the south, are generally known, since at least the early fourteenth century, as the Hindu Kush ('Hindu-killer'). The Moroccan traveller Ibn Battuta (AD 1304–77), who visited this part of the world in the early 1330s, tells us '[t]he mountain is called Hindu Kush, which means "Slayer of Indians", because the slave boys and girls who are brought from India die there in large numbers as a result of the extreme cold and the quantity of snow'.[13]

The name of the Hindu Kush, however, should only really be applied to that part of the mountains that rises immediately north of Kabul. Here the mountain range is at its narrowest and allows for traffic to proceed via either of a series of passes.[14] In fact, the name was perhaps originally only used for one of these thoroughfares, although we do not know which one. At present, the main pass across the Hindu Kush is the Salang Pass and Tunnel. It directly connects the north of the country with the south and the country's capital, Kabul. The modern road crosses the mountains at a height of 3,363 metres. Built under Soviet supervision between 1956 and 1964 it replaced a lengthy and circuitous route west of Kabul via the Shibar Pass, close to the Bamiyan Valley.[15] Another, but at present much less frequented route between north and south leads east of the Salang, through the Panjshir valley.[16]

13   Ibn Battuta III 84. Translation by Routledge 1929:178. The name may also be a corruption of *Hindu Kuh* (Mountain of Hindu). Compare Dupree 1980:1.

14   Compare Grötzbach 1990:240–141. Babur, the Mughal conqueror of India in the early sixteenth century, lists seven passes of the Hindu Kush (*Bâburnâme*, trans. by Beveridge 1922:204–5).

15   Traditionally there were two main routes from Kabul to Bamiyan. The first goes north from Kabul and turns to the west along the Ghorband river and crosses the Shibar Pass (2,987 m). The other route leads west from Kabul and crosses two passes, namely the Unay Pass (3,354 m) and the Hajigak (3,567 m) or Iraq Pass (3,963 m). From the Bamiyan valley, the ancient road proceeds north via the Aq Ribat Pass (3,117 m) and the Dandan Shikan Pass (2,744 m). A modern track, built with the help of German engineers and opened in 1933, leads north from just west of the Shibar Pass, along the Bamiyan river, to Doab-i Mekhzarin and hence down into the plains of North Afghanistan.

16   This route crosses the mountains via the Khawak Pass. Traditionally (but without any evidence) this is the route thought to have been followed by Alexander the Great in the spring of 329 BC when he led his army from the Kabul valley across the mountains to the north (compare Wood 1997:142–4).

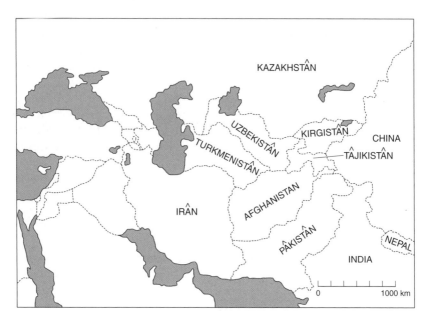

Map 4   *Afghanistan in Southwest Asia.*

Afghanistan's Position in Southwest Asia

The modern state of Afghanistan and the adjoining foothills of
Pakistan constitute the eastern part of the Iranian Plateau (Map 4).
This highland zone extends from the Zagros Range in the west
(along the modern Iran–Iraq border) to the banks of the Indus river
in the east. It forms the connecting link between the Near East,
Central Asia and the Indian subcontinent and throughout history
it has been the thoroughfare for migrants from Central Asia in the
north to the Near East in the southwest or the Indian subcontinent
in the southeast.

The easiest route from the deserts and semi-deserts of South
Central Asia onto the Iranian Plateau leads via a gap in the mountain chain that bounds the Iranian Plateau in the north. This break
lies between the cities of Mashhad in modern Northeast Iran and
Herat in West Afghanistan. The north–south route via the so-called
Herat corridor links up with the two major east–west roads that tra-
verse the Plateau. The course of these two routes is determined by
the availability of food and water. Huge deserts, namely the Dasht-i
Kavir in the north and the adjoining Dasht-i Lut in the south,
dominate the centre of modern Iran and the Iranian Plateau. These
wastelands constitute an enormous barrier and consequently any

east–west traffic either has to proceed north or south of these empty expanses.

The northern route passes along the small strip of inhabitable land between the central deserts of Iran and the Elburz Mountains, which form the northern part of the mountain ring that surrounds the Plateau. This northern route leads from the west, past modern Tehran, to the city of Mashhad. From here the traveller may continue to Central Asia and the ancient towns of Bukhara, Samarqand and places beyond. This is the historical Silk Road and also the course of a modern railway link. From Mashhad, a secondary route leads southeast to Afghanistan, in particular to the old staging post of Herat. Leaving this ancient place the traveller may continue to northern Afghanistan and hence cross the Hindu Kush to Kabul and the valley of the Indus. He may also go south, towards the province of Sistan, along the Iran/Pakistan/Afghanistan border, or southeast towards the city of Qandahar. From Qandahar the traveller continues eastwards towards the Middle Indus valley, or northeastwards, towards Ghazni and the Kabul valley.

The southern route across the Iranian Plateau leads from southern Iran to the drainage basin of the Hilmand River in Sistan. From here, it proceeds via Qandahar to the Indus valley in the east, or the Kabul plain in the northeast. Another southern overland route, which bypasses Afghanistan to the south, leads through Iranian and Pakistani Baluchistan. The importance of this particular route has always been minimal because of the harsh conditions along the way. Alexander the Great followed this route in the opposite direction, thereby almost losing his life and his army.[17]

Before the age of mechanized transport, travelling across the Iranian Plateau usually was an undertaking that took weeks or even months. Until comparatively recently, wheeled transport was virtually unknown. Horses, camels, donkeys and ponies provided the main means of transport. The average distance covered by a caravan amounted to about 35 km per day, depending upon the terrain. The maximum daily distance for small groups of horse riders was about 60 km.[18] The distance between Kabul and Qandahar, some 500 km, took some fifteen days. Large army groups travelled even more slowly. In the summer of 1880, a large British military column covered the distance between Kabul and Qandahar in twenty days, which, it should be added, was regarded as being extremely fast.[19]

17   Arrian, *Anabasis Alexandri* VI 21ff.
18   In the nineteenth century, Baluch robbers on camels could ride up to 120 km or more per day (Marvin 1885:354).
19   The famous march of General Sir Frederick Roberts (1832–1914) in August 1880, during the Second Anglo-Afghan War.

The Natural Environment

Afghanistan forms part of an arid, semi-desert belt of lands that extends across much of the Iranian Plateau.[20] Dry, hot summers and cold winters with much snow are permanent features. In the winter, snow covers most of the mountains from about 1,800 metres upwards. In March the snow begins to melt and the rivers rise. The rivers in Afghanistan therefore carry the maximum amount of water during the spring, causing occasional floodings. Apart from these constant features, the climatic variations in Afghanistan are enormous, not in the least because the north of the country lies open to the cold winds from Central Asia, while the lands southeast of the mountains are affected by the Indian monsoon. Precipitation ranges from an annual average of 75 mm in the extremely dry southwest of the country to 213 mm in Mazar-i Sharif (the main city of North Afghanistan), 328 mm in the eastern town of Ghazni, and an excessive 1,150 mm high up in the Salang Pass.[21]

The vegetation of the country is equally diverse. In the east, around the modern town of Jalalabad at an altitude of 552 metres, the vegetation is subtropical, even allowing for some palm trees. Some 100 km to the west, much higher up along the Kabul valley but still south of the Hindu Kush mountains, vegetation is very different. Kabul itself lies at an altitude of 1,803 metres and here the trees include the oak, walnut, alder, ash and juniper. North of the mountains, the sand and loess covered lands support steppe vegetation and, if properly watered, yield rich agricultural crops. In South and West Afghanistan vegetation is minimal. Here the landscape is dominated by the so-called *dasht*, the stony desert which is typical for much of the Iranian Plateau,[22] or by sandy wastes (the *reg*), as for instance the Registan desert of South Afghanistan.[23]

Forests used to be found in the extreme east of the country, along the borders with Pakistan, but recent unchecked deforestation has changed all this. The forests of the Panjshir valley, still known in the Middle Ages, have also disappeared. Large forests can still be found in the more secluded districts of Nuristan, northeast of modern Kabul.

20   For the climate and vegetation of Afghanistan, see Dupree 1980:3ff.; Humlum 1959; Kraus 1975:32ff.
21   Compare Rathjens 1975:41.
22   Defined by Fisher 1968:93 as: 'relatively firm and dry desert, composed of generally small and compacted rock fragments: pebbles, flints, or, most often, silts.'
23   A *rig* or *reg* refers to finer deposits, usually of sand, which may be in regular dune formation or irregularly deposited as a variable sheet (Fisher 1968:93).

Wildlife in Afghanistan is limited.[24] Tigers, which used to roam the banks of the Amu Darya, the shores of the inland lakes of Sistan and until very recently the foothills around Jalalabad in the east, have disappeared. So have the lions.[25] However, eagles, foxes, gazelles, hyenas, jackals and wolves can still be found. Wild asses and wild boars were known until very recent times. High up in the Qara Qorum and Hindu Kush there are snow leopards, wild goats, as for instance the markhor and the ibex, and wild sheep (including the argali or Marco Polo sheep).

Throughout history, Afghanistan has been a supplier of coveted minerals.[26] Famous are the deposits of lapis lazuli (*Fârsi*: *Lâjaward* or *Lâjward*) near Sar-i Sang in the valley of the Kokcha river, in the northeast of the country.[27] Recently, lapis lazuli has also been reported from the Chagai hills west of Quetta along the Afghan/Pakistan border.[28] Lapis is found at only a few places on earth, and the Afghan mines, and in particular those in Badakhshan, seem to have been exploited from a very early date onwards. From the late fourth millennium BC, this semi-precious stone was exported to the surrounding lands, as far as Egypt. Equally important are the copper deposits at many places in the country, especially in the Logar valley south of Kabul; at some places southwest of Herat; along the Arghandab river north of Qandahar, and near Andarab north of the Panjshir valley. Also important, especially for the production of bronze, are the tin deposits to the southwest of Herat. Gold is found near Muqqur, northeast of Qandahar, and in the rivers of Badakhshan. Huge deposits of iron ore are found near the Hajigak Pass, west of Kabul. The natural gas reserves from near Shibarghan and Sar-i Pul, in the northwest of the country, were exploited since the late 1960s for export to the north.

Agriculture and Nomadism

Only about 12 per cent of the total surface of Afghanistan is cultivated. Of this total, some 20 per cent is suitable for dry farming.

24 Compare Elphinstone 1815:141–5.
25 Marco Polo, ed. Latham 1958:75, refers to their presence in medieval North Afghanistan.
26 Compare Grötzbach 1990:52–5. The famous Balas rubies, named after the land of Badakhshan, do in fact derive from the neighbouring district of Shughnan, along the right bank of the Panj river, outside Afghan Badakhshan (compare Marco Polo, ed. Latham 1958:76).
27 Herrmann 1968; Potts 1994:199–208. See also Marco Polo, ed. Latham 1958:77.
28 Compare Potts 1994:210.

These lands produce mainly wheat and barley.[29] The rest of cultivable land must be irrigated. Even considering the fact that the population of Afghanistan is relatively small, shortage of land is therefore a major problem. Throughout the country the people have for millennia tried to increase the extent of cultivable land by digging canals and, since the first millennium BC, constructing huge networks of underground tunnels, the so-called *ka(h)rez* or *qanât*.[30]

Most of the cultivated land lies in the southeast, in and around the Qandahar oasis; in the east, in the Kabul valley and around Jalalabad; in the north, around Qunduz and Mazar-i Sharif, and in the west, in the valley of the Hari Rud, around the town of Herat. These are the lands traditionally known for their high agricultural production. In the past, large-scale irrigation networks in Sistan and in the northeast of the country created other centres of human activity, but these have since been destroyed or fallen in disrepair.

Animal husbandry is also widely practised. Sheep, goats and chicken are found in almost every village in the country. The immediate neighbourhood of the villages, however, does not always provide enough food for the animals, and many people move with their herds into the mountains for summer pasturage. Some of them lead the life of full-time pastoralists, always on the move with their herds. Such annual migrations make it possible for the people of Afghanistan to exploit the pastures high up in the mountains and it is yet another way for the Afghans to increase the produce of their land.

Each spring, the nomads and semi-nomads move their herds into the mountains of Central Afghanistan. In the autumn they return to their villages or winter camps. The winter quarters are found in the arid steppes of the southwest and west; in the plains of North Afghanistan; and in the low-lying, warm and monsoon-affected districts along the Pakistan border in the east and southeast of the country. In the southwest and west of the country the nomads are predominantly Durrani Pashtuns, although they are joined by Pashtun Ghaljis, another Pashtun tribal confederacy, who have adopted many aspects of the Durranis, and by other ethnic groups, including Baluch and Aymaqs. Those who winter in the north are often Özbeks and others, including Durrani Pashtuns. The latter are the descendants of those who were forcibly moved from the south in the late nineteenth century. In the west, the nomads are generally Ghalji Pashtuns.

---

29 Dupree 1980:43.
30 *Qanât* is the Arabic name used in Iran and (western) Afghanistan; *karez* or *kahrez* is the Pashto word.

In 1979, the number of nomads in Afghanistan was estimated at about one to two million people.[31] Most of these are Pashtuns and Baluch. The nomads and semi-nomads, generally called *Kuchi*[32] in Afghanistan, mostly keep sheep and goats. The produce of the animals (meat, dairy products, hair and wool) is exchanged or sold in order to purchase grain, vegetables, fruit and other products of settled life. In this way, an extensive network of exchange has developed along the routes annually followed by the nomads and semi-nomads. The merchant *Powindah* (Ghalji) Pashtuns[33] used to move annually from the Afghanistan mountains to the valley of the Indus and hence deep into India. These long-distance migrations were stopped in the early 1960s when the border between Afghanistan and Pakistan was closed. In recent decades, migrations inside Afghanistan continue, although trucks are now often being used to move lifestock and family from one place to the other.

In Afghanistan, the Pashtun and Baluch nomads from the south generally live in black goat hair tents, while most of the non-Pashtun nomads and semi-nomads from the north, following a Central Asian tradition, live in yurts.[34] These are circular and framed constructions covered with felt.[35] They are portable, normally provided with a domed roof, and are extremely strong. Its basic structure is a lattice framework that constitutes the wall; woolen bands are bound around the wall to keep it together. Their survival into the future is open to question, for they are expensive and take much time to set up, and before the late 1970s their use in Afghanistan was already dwindling.

---

31 Grötzbach 1990:57. For the nomads of Afghanistan, see the many studies by Klaus Ferdinand and by N. and R. Tapper. See also Jentsch 1973, Glatzer 1977 and Pedersen 1994.
32 The *Fârsi* word *Kuch* refers to a wandering tribe (and robbers).
33 *Powal* is the Pashto verb for 'to graze'. See also Persian *puyidan*, 'to wander', 'to trot.'
34 A more precise term is *Khergâh* (Dari) or *Uy* (Özbek).
35 For these dwellings, see especially the study by Szabo and Barfield 1991.

2

The Peoples of Afghanistan

Throughout history many ethnic groups have settled in Afghanistan. They came from the west, from the east, from the south and especially from the steppes and deserts of Central Asia to the north. In a recent study of the ethnic groups of Afghanistan, some 55 ethnic names are listed.[1] On the basis of their language these peoples can be roughly divided into Iranian (especially the Baluch, Pashtuns and Tajiks), Turkic (mainly the Türkmen and Özbeks) and others. It should be realized, however, that language is not always a clear-cut ethnic marker. The Hazaras from Central Afghanistan, for instance, nowadays speak (Iranian) Persian (*Fârsi* or Dari), but are in the main clearly of Turco-Mongolian origin.

The Pashtuns

In general terms, the mountains of Central and Northeast Afghanistan separate the Pashtun-dominated south of the country from the non-Pashtun groups in the north. The Pashtuns have traditionally been the Afghans *par excellence*, all the other ethnic groups of Afghanistan carrying another name. They also form the largest part of the population, some 40 to 50 per cent. Thus, as late as the nineteenth century, the name of Afghanistan was still being used only to describe the habitat of the Pashtuns, along both sides of the Durand line, while the west and north of modern Afghanistan were generally known as Khurasan and (Lesser) Turkestan respectively.[2]

The Pashtuns, in India and Pakistan generally known as the Pathans, constitute a distinct ethnic group that by the year 2000

1 See Orywal 1986.
2 For the use of the name of Afghan, Afghanistan etc., compare Mousavi 1998:1ff.

numbered some 20 million people.[3] They now live in approximately equal numbers along both sides of the Afghanistan/Pakistan border. The Pashtun lands cover a roughly triangular area that stretches in a straight west–east line from Southwest Afghanistan to the Middle Indus Valley, and up north along the Indus river to the Swat valley in modern Pakistan. The Hindu Kush mountains constitute the north-western border. Peshawar in North Pakistan and Qandahar in South Afghanistan are traditionally the main urban centres of the Pashtuns.

The Pashtuns speak Pashto, or Pakhto, which is an Iranian language and thus related to Persian (*Fârsi*), Kurdish, Baluchi and so forth.[4] Together with Persian, which is called *Dari* in Afghanistan, it is one of the two official languages of the country. The origin of the name of the Pashtuns, and of their language, is a moot point.[5] It is only securely known from the late medieval period onwards, although the name has been tentatively linked to that of the *Pasianoi* mentioned in Classical sources.[6] According to the texts this group formed part of a huge wave of mainly Iranian Scythian invaders that infiltrated from the north onto the eastern parts of the Iranian Plateau in the late second century BC. However, this identification cannot as yet be substantiated.

The origin of the name of the Afghans is equally problematic. It is not of Pashto origin.[7] It is therefore more than likely that outsiders used this name to describe some of the peoples of the Indo-Iranian borderlands, who may or may not have been Pashtuns. The name perhaps occurs in Varaha Mihira's *Bṛhat-Saṃhitâ*, a Sanskrit work from the Indian subcontinent of the early sixth century, under the ethnic appellation of the *Avagânâs*.[8] The identification of this name, however, is still disputed, and so is that of the *Abojian* which is found in the travelogue of the Chinese pilgrim Xuanzang from the early seventh century.[9]

The first reliable reference to the name of the Afghans dates to the tenth century. In the *Hudud al-ʿÂlam*, an anonymous Persian work from the late tenth century, reference is made to 'Saul, a pleasant

3   For a bibliography of the Pashtuns, see Orywal 1986:20–1.
4   The two names Pashto and Pakhto reflect the two main dialects of the language. Pashto (the 'soft' dialect) is spoken in the south, while Pakhto (the 'hard' dialect) is found in the north. Peshawar in modern Pakistan is, correspondingly, locally known as Pekhawar. Compare Caroe 1958:xvi–xvii.
5   Compare Morgenstierne 1940 and 1979:29 and Brandenstein and Mayrhofer 1964:138.
6   Bailey 1993:10.
7   Morgenstierne 1979:28.
8   *Bẓhat-Saṃhitâ* XI 61 and XVI 38.
9   A district with this name was apparently located somewhere in the borderlands between Afghanistan and Pakistan (*The Life of Hiuen-Tsiang*, trans. Beal 1911:193).

village on a mountain. In it live Afghans.'[10] This village was, according to the text, probably located near Gardiz, east of Ghazni. The book also tells about a village near modern Jalalabad where the local king used to have many Hindu, Muslim and Afghan wives. From the time of Mahmud of Ghazni, at the end of the tenth century AD, references to Afghans become more frequent. The Afghans of his day are generally located in the borderlands between Iran and the Indian subcontinent. The most explicit mentioning of the Afghans is found in al-Biruni's *Ta'rikh al-Hind* (eleventh century AD).[11] Here it is said that various tribes of Afghans lived in the mountains in the west of India. Al-Biruni adds that they were savage people and he describes them as Hindus.

Ibn Battuta, the thirteenth-century traveller from Morocco whom I referred to before in connection with the Hindu Kush, writes about the 'Persians called Afghans' who lived between Ghazni and the Indus plains.[12] He adds that their principal mountain is called the 'Kuh Sulayman', thus recalling an old tradition among the Pashtuns that their original habitat is located near the Kuh-i Sulayman mountains, east of Qandahar.[13]

Looking for the origin of the Pashtuns and the Afghans is something like exploring the source of the Amazon. Is there one specific beginning? And are the Pashtuns originally identical with the Afghans? Although the Pashtuns nowadays constitute a clear ethnic group with their own language and culture, there is no evidence whatsoever that all modern Pashtuns share the same ethnic origins. In fact it is highly unlikely.[14] There are still pockets of non-Pashtun groups in lands otherwise completely dominated by Pashtuns and the Pashtuns are slowly engulfing these people, culturally and linguistically. This process must have been going on for centuries. Ethnicity is not a static phenomenon and many people in the borderlands at some stage in their history may have accepted 'Pashtunhood' and adopted Pashto as their language. The opposite development also took place, whereby Pashtun groups lost their 'Pashtunhood'. A modern example of 'fusion' may be the southern groups of the (non-Pashtun) Taymani and Maliki Aymaq in West Afghanistan, who feel affiliated to the Pashtuns and have adopted Qandahari Pashtun culture and language.[15] On the other hand, 'fission' may be indicated by the Persian

10   *Hudud al-ʿÂlam*, trans. Minorsky 1937:91.
11   Trans. Sachau 1888; 1910: I,1,208.
12   Ibn Battuta, trans. Routledge 1929:180.
13   Elphinstone (1815:151) tells about the Pashtuns that the 'Árabs call them Solimaunee'.
14   Compare Janata 1987:212 and Spain 1985:39.
15   They are known for their typical black tents that resemble that of the Pashtuns (Szabo and Barfield 1991:48–50).

speaking (Pashtun) Nurzay Durranis in Southwest Afghanistan, who feel more related to non-Pashtun groups.[16] In nineteenth-century literature there are, within the same context, frequent references to the non-Pashtun background of certain 'Pasthun' tribes. Mountstuart Elphinstone tells of the Nasir Ghaljis, a tribe of wandering *Kuchis* or Powindahs who live along the Afghanistan/Pakistan border. According to him: 'The Hotukees [Hotaki Ghaljis] say that the Naussers have been their Humsauyahs [clients], but not their kindred: some even represent them as sprung from the Beloches [Baluchis]; and though they speak Pushtoo, and strenuously maintain their descent from the Afghauns, their features and appearance certainly indicate a race distinct from that nation.'[17]

Pashto

An important aspect of Pashtunhood is the language. Pashto/Pakhto belongs to the family of Iranian languages. These were introduced to the Iranian Plateau by people from South Central Asia from the second millennium BC onwards. Pashto is not the only Iranian language, and probably also not the first, to be spoken south of the mountains. We know this, because in the midst of Pashtun land there are, apart from the ubiquitous Persian speaking Tajiks, still small pockets of people who speak other Iranian languages. These can be found in the Logar valley south of Kabul (at least up to 1978) and near Kaniguram (Waziristan) in Pakistan. These people speak Ormuri. They call themselves Barakis, and this name also occurs in the early sixteenth-century biography of Babur, the founder of the Mughal dynasty of India, who spent much time in the borderlands in preparation of his invasion of the subcontinent.[18] In addition, north of Kabul, there are people speaking Paraci.[19] Paraci and Ormuri are two related Iranian languages, which in the past were spoken by far more people in a much larger area. They were pushed aside and driven away to isolated valleys by those who spoke another language, including the Pashtuns.

16   See Roy 1990:111 for the affiliation of Persian speaking Nurzay with the (mainly Tajik) *Jam'iyyat-i Islâmi* resistance organization in the war against the Soviet Union. Their Pashto speaking kinsmen sided with another (Pashtun) organization.
17   Elphinstone 1815:461. See also Janata 1987 for the apparently non-Pashtun background of the Jajis and Turis.
18   *Bâburnâma*, trans. Beveridge 1922:207; 220 and Elphinstone 1815:315. See also Orywal 1986:63–4. Their total number in the Logar valley in 1980 was estimated at 2,000 to 5,000 (Ethnologue Data Base). Caroe 1958:191 refers to three villages southeast of Peshawar called Upper, Middle and Nether Urmar.
19   See Orywal 1986:61–2. Paraci is listed by Babur as one of the eleven (!) languages of the Kabul area (trans. Beveridge 1922:207).

While Paraci and Ormuri are generally classed as South, or Southeast Iranian languages, Pashto is generally held to belong to the so-called Northeast Iranian branch.[20] If this classification is correct, it would mean that at some time in history the Pashto language of South Afghanistan and Pakistan was introduced from north of the mountains. Over the centuries Pashto subsequently replaced other Iranian tongues that had been introduced to the area at an earlier time.[21] This replacement, which was a long process and is in fact still continuing, is likely to have run parallel to the development of the Pashtuns as a nation.

The Pashtun Tribal Structure

The Pashtuns nowadays constitute a clearly recognizable ethnic group. They are themselves keenly aware of their distinctive character, their common background, their own language and culture and their land. They are at the same time split up in many lineages, clans, tribes and confederacies of tribes.[22] It is not surprising therefore that their society has often been described as typically tribal. Furthermore, Pashtun society is generally regarded as a particular example of a so-called segmentary lineage organization. Such a structure is based on descent groups whereby the various units, such as nuclear families, sub-clans, clans, tribes and confederations of tribes, together constitute some sort of abstract pyramid with the (eponymous) ancestor placed on top. To a large degree, Pashtun society very well answers this model. The Pashtuns all know exactly where they belong within the pyramid of kinship relationships. The social orientation of a Pashtun is directed towards his particular place in this system, and more often than not political and military strife between the Pashtuns, or between Pashtuns and others, is linked to the kinship relationships between and among the contestants.

However, the model of the segmentary lineage organization suggests a static, permanent structure and places very strong emphasis on descent. It excludes other factors that affect the position of the individual and the structure of his group and make Pashtun society

20   The Northeast Iranian languages (Morgenstierne 1958:167ff.) include the so-called Pamir languages of Badakhshan, and (vestiges of) other Iranian languages spoken in South Central Asia.
21   Compare the position of the Tajiks who for ages used to live in and around Urgun in East Afghanistan, and used to be called Fermali or Furmuli and who were engaged in iron working (Elphinstone 1815:315; Bellew 1891:126; Janata 1975).
22   For the following discussion I am much indebted to Christine Noelle's masterly work (1997, esp. pp. 125ff.).

into a far more dynamic entity. Economic and ecological circumstances are very important, and so are more individual aspects, such as personal honour. Tribal relationships are generally regarded as patrilineal, but in fact relationships via the female line also play an essential role. There is also the position of outsiders within the tribe, including holy men and groups of people subjugated by the (Pashtun) dominant group. Very important is the relationship with neighbouring groups, and especially with neighbouring states. Powerful neighbours may appoint tribal leaders, who otherwise are not much more than village headmen, as representatives of their realm. They may provide these headmen with large subsidies and subsequently increase the tribal leaders' influence within their own group, thereby disrupting its basically equalitarian structure. The same breaking down of traditional relationships may occur when the group comes into contact with other outsiders, such as traders, armies, nomads and others.

The Pashtun Family Tree

In the early seventeenth century, a Pashtun from North India called Khwaja Niʿmat Allah described the tribal structure and origin of Pashtun society in his work, the *Makhzan-i Afghâni*.[23] Although it undoubtedly contains information on the ethnogenesis of the Pashtuns, this genealogy should not be read as a sound historical source that indicates how the Pashtuns came into being as a distinct ethnic group. Instead, it should be used as a source of information, from the seventeenth century or earlier, for the way in which the Pashtuns saw themselves as a group.

Niʿmat Allah differentiates between four main groups of Pashtuns. These are the descendants of the three sons of the putative ancestor of all Pashtuns, Qays ʿAbd al-Rashid Pathan, plus another, fourth group. The putative ancestor himself descended, according to traditional genealogies, from King Sarul (Saul), the Jewish king. The allegedly Jewish ancestry of the Pashtuns was a subject always hotly debated in Pashtun tea houses![24]

The three sons of Qays ʿAbd al-Rashid Pathan were named Sarban, Bitan and Ghurghusht (although there are many variants of these names). Most important of these, at least in the eyes of Niʿmat Allah, was Sarban. He was the eldest son. His descendants, via his son

---

23 Compare Caroe 1958 and Glatzer 1977:107–18. Another genealogy of the Pashtuns is contained in the *Hayât-i Afghâni*, by Hayat Khan.
24 Caroe 1958:1–7.

Sharkhbun, are mainly found in South Afghanistan, and via his other son Kharshbun, in the Peshawar Valley. Those in the west include the Abdalis, who since the mid-eighteenth century are called the Durranis. Those in the east include the Yusufzay, who live north of Peshawar, and many other tribes in the same area.

The relationship between the descendants of Sharkhbun and Kharshbun is of great interest. If Ni'mat Allah is correct, this would indicate historical connections. In this context the spread of another group, namely the offspring of a man called Kasi, is also important. Kasi was another descendant of Kharshbun, the son of Sarban. Kasi's descendants include the Shinwaris, who nowadays live in the Jalalabad area west of Peshawar. But they also include two other tribes who live far to the south, in the Quetta region southeast of Qandahar, namely the Kasis themselves and the Ketrans.

The descendants of the second brother, (Shaykh) Bitan, constitute the second branch of the Pashtuns. Ni'mat Allah tells that Bitan's daughter, called Bibi Mato, married an outsider with the name of Shah Husayn of Ghur (an area in Central Afghanistan). From this marriage derives, among others, the large confederacy of the Ghaljis (Ghilzay)[25] and other tribes, living in the lands between Ghazni in Afghanistan and the Indus river in Pakistan. The Ghaljis themselves descend, according to Ni'mat Allah, from a son of Bibi Mato and Shah Husayn, who was conceived before they were married. Whatever really happened, Ni'mat Allah seems to have held a low opinion about this branch and especially about the Ghaljis!

The third brother, Ghurghusht, became the ancestor of a number of tribes that are spread throughout the land of the Pashtuns. The largest of these are the Kakars, who live in the unproductive lands north of Quetta, in modern Pakistan. Another group of the same branch is that of the Safis, who live far away from the Kakars in an area northeast of Kabul. If these groups are related, and there is no reason to doubt it, this would again, as in the case of the Durranis and Yusufzay, indicate large-scale migrations of the Pashtuns. Since the lands in and around Kabul are known in the main to have been inhabited, as they still are, by non-Pashto speaking people, the presence of the Safis in this area is clearly intrusive and they may well originate from the far south, from near the Kakars.

There is a fourth branch of Pashtuns. They are the descendants of Karran or Karlan. The native genealogists do not agree as to whether he was a foundling adopted by Qays, or whether he belonged to one of the three branches. Whatever, Karlan is the ancestor of most of

25 The name Ghilzay is the Persianized form of the name they give themselves: *Ghalji* (sg. *Ghaljai*).

the Pashtun groups that live in modern Pakistan and in particular in the rather inaccessible lands south of the Peshawar Valley. They include the Afridis, the Khataks, the Mangals, the Waziris, the Bangash, the Mahsuds, and many others. Their low status in the genealogy clearly reflects their isolated position; not many people in northern India in the early seventeenth century had ever heard of them.

Pashtun Migrations

The supposed relationship between the Abdalis/Durranis of South Afghanistan and the Yusufzay and others from the Peshawar valley and beyond would indicate that at some time in their history these groups were living in close proximity. The spread of the Kasi tribes and the descendants of Ghurghusht would reflect the same situation. There are in fact written records, apparently based on oral tradition, that tell about the move, sometime in the fifteenth and sixteenth centuries, of Pashtun groups from South Afghanistan, via the Kabul valley, to the plains of Peshawar and beyond.[26] A Pashtun migration from the Qandahar area towards the west, to the lands of South and West Afghanistan, is even more recent. This migration is supported by historical evidence and dates to the seventeenth and eighteenth centuries.[27] Those settling in these parts were Abdalis/Durranis, descendants of Sharkhbun.

The migrations of the Pashtuns, it should be realized, continue to the present day, with groups of Pashtuns pushing other people out of the way, as for instance in Hazarajat in Central Afghanistan; in the Jalalabad area in East Afghanistan, and in the lands north of Peshawar. Furthermore, the lands immediately south of the Hindu Kush passes, in the Kabul valley, were only (partly) occupied by Pashtuns in relatively recent years. Kabul has never been a Pashtun town. All this would indicate that the speakers of Pashto at some moment in their history were concentrated in modern Southeast Afghanistan or, even more likely, in the neighbouring districts of Pakistan.[28]

The picture that emerges is an initial spread of the Pashtuns from the Sulayman mountain valleys of the Afghan/Pakistan borderlands,

26 Caroe 1958:168ff. and Elphinstone 1815:330f.
27 Compare Noelle 1997:233.
28 Traditionally the Sulayman mountains in Pakistan (east of Qandahar) are listed as the homeland of the Pashtuns (compare Morgenstierne 1979:29). The Sulayman Range is called *Da Kase Khar* in Pashto; compare the name of *Kâsh* that is given to the Pashtuns by the Ormuris of Kaniguram, and the name of the tribe of the Kasis who live near Quetta in Pakistan.

into the plains of Southeast and East Afghanistan.[29] This move was followed by a migration of large groups of Pashtuns along the Qandahar–Kabul route to the north, and hence to the east, into the Peshawar valley. According to various sources, this last migration took place sometime before the beginning of the sixteenth century. Other groups moved from the Qandahar area to the west and north-west, towards Sistan and Herat. It seems at this place pointless to speculate as to the reasons behind these large-scale migrations. There may have been political or natural causes, or both. Furthermore, it is safe to assume that even before these migrations started, some of the Pashtuns annually moved with their herds into the Afghanistan mountains and thus became acquainted with the conditions in this part of the world.

Whatever the reasons behind these migrations, the arrival and subsequent rise to power of large groups of Pashtuns in the vast plains of South and East Afghanistan brought about important political and social changes. The influence of the urban centres and their mainly Tajik (Persian-speaking) population had to give way to the countryside and its new Pashtun settlers. Moreover, the Pashtuns themselves, deriving from the poor and secluded valleys of the borderlands, suddenly found themselves in the wide and relatively productive plains south and east of the Afghan mountains. If the advent of the Pashtuns brought about great changes to the local population, it also caused great changes in the living conditions of the Pashtuns themselves.

Pashtun Life

The Pashtuns are generally known for their sense of independence, equality, their personal honour or *nang* (*Fârsi*: 'honour') and their militancy. Their code of honour, the *Pashtunwâli* (or *Pakhtunwâli*), has been the subject of many studies.[30] Its main aspects relate to hospitality (*malmastiyâ*), asylum (*nanawâtay*), revenge (*badal*) and so forth. Equality of all adult male members of the group is, at least in theory, one of the key-principles of Pashtun life. Basically, any grown-up man of sufficient experience is allowed a vote in the tribal meeting, the *Jirga*. Of course some men, often the Khans, wield more power in the meeting than others. Yet, the power of the Khan is never secure. It is based primarily on his personal qualities, rather than on any feeling of loyalty as towards the hierarchy.[31] Of course the situation

29 See also Elphinstone 1815:396, who tells that the Abdalis/Durranis may derive from the east.
30 Compare Steul 1981. See also Adamec 1997:251–2 and Edwards 1996.
31 Compare Olesen 1995:29.

is nowhere exactly identical. In certain areas, as for instance among the mountains and in the secluded valleys along the Afghanistan/Pakistan border, the 'ideals' of Pashtunhood and its emphasis on equality are still very strong. In other areas, as for instance among the Durranis and Ghaljis in South and East Afghanistan, the tribal leaders have for centuries built up much wealth and power. They could do so partly because of the space and relative fertility of the land, and partly because of the location of their group along a major east–west route between Iran and India. The ideals however of Pashtunhood are still recognized by most of the Pashto speakers.

There is another important difference between the Pashtuns living in the plains of Afghanistan and those who live further to the east, among the borderland mountains. The Durranis and most of the Ghaljis from the plains are spread over large stretches of land, and their various tribes, sub-tribes and clans are often living intermixed with each other, often within the same villages.[32] In the borderlands, where the terrain is in general far more accentuated than the plains of South and Southeast Afghanistan, the tribal groups tend to be living separately. This means that ambitious Pashtun leaders in Afghanistan need to seek alliances, and are trained to do so, among Pashtuns from different descent groups. They cannot rely on their own direct kinsmen because they live dispersed over such a large area. In this way Pashtun leaders from the Durranis or the Ghaljis may at some time, as for instance in the early eighteenth century, start to control many groups of Pashtuns from different kinship groups. Pashtun leaders from modern Pakistan may achieve a strong position within their own group and in their own area, but will meet great difficulties in acquiring a position among Pashtuns from a different region.

All of the Pashtuns in Afghanistan and Pakistan are Muslims, and almost all of them belong to the Sunni branch, which is one of the two main divisions of Islam. The exception are a number of Pashtun groups that live south of Jalalabad and Peshawar, namely the Turis and, for some of their members, the Orakzay and the Bangash.[33] They are Shi'ites, belonging to the second large branch of Islam.[34]

Pashtun women in Pakistan and especially in Afghanistan still wear a *burqaʿ* (or *chadri*), which is a garment that covers the head and

---

32   This process is also found among the Pashtun nomads, whereby many Ghaljis from among the Hotaki, Tarakki and Tokhi tribes have joined the Durranis who have their winter camps in the southwest and west of the country (compare N. Tapper 1974:131).

33   The Sayyids of Tirah, southwest of Peshawar, are also reported to be Shi'ites (*Enc. Isl.*, 'Afghanistan').

34   For a possible connection to the Rawshaniyya movement in the sixteenth century, see Caroe 1958:200–4.

body of the wearer, including her face. The garment includes a rectangular piece of netting over the eyes to allow the wearer to see. Underneath she wears trousers and a long-sleeved dress. Pashtun men are also easily recognized by their costume, which usually consists of loose, baggy trousers, a long shirt and a waistcoat. They also like to wear open sandals. Many Pashtuns still wear a turban (*lungi*), with one end characteristically hanging loose across the shoulder. The turban is nowadays especially worn in Taliban-controlled areas, where the men often wear a turban of black cloth with thin white stripes. Elsewhere, the Chitrali cap (*pawkul*) is becoming more and more popular.

The Pashtuns of Afghanistan

The Pashtuns of Afghanistan are nowadays concentrated in the southeast, east and southwest of the country. The two main groups in the country are the tribal confederacies of the Durranis and the Ghaljis. Both of them are predominantly sedentary.

The first, formerly known as the Abdalis, live in the south and southwest, with Qandahar as their main centre. They are subdivided into several tribes. Some of these, namely the putative descendants of someone called Zirak, are the Popalzay, ʿAlikozay, Barakzay and Achakzay.[35] Another group of tribes is that of the alleged descendants of Panjpao, namely the Nurzay, ʿAlizay and Ishaqzay.[36] The Popalzay and Barakzay are traditionally the most important of the Abdalis/Durranis. One of the Popalzay clans, the Sadozay, provided Afghanistan with its royal dynasty from the mid-eighteenth to the beginning of the eighteenth century. The Barakzay succeeded the Popalzay as king-makers, and their leaders ruled Afghanistan until 1978.

Kinsmen of the Abdalis/Durranis are the Spin Tarins and Tor Tarins, who both live east of Qandahar, in modern Pakistan, and the Sheranis, who live close to the Tarins, in the Sulayman mountains. The distribution of these groups again illustrates the probability that the Abdalis/Durranis, and perhaps all Pashtuns, originate in the same area, close to the Sulayman mountains in modern Pakistan.

The Ghaljis live in the east of the country, with the town of Ghazni as their focal point. According to Niʿmat Allah they are closely related to a number of Pashtun tribes that now live further to the east, as far

---

35 The Achakzay were separated from the Barakzay in the mid-eighteenth century by Ahmad Shah Durrani (Noelle 1997:226, 230).
36 The Achakzay, Nurzay and Ishaqzay are, or were at least until very recent times, for the greater part nomadic.

as the west bank of the Indus. The number of Ghaljis in Afghanistan presently amounts to twice that of the Durranis. They inhabit an area that lies roughly between Kabul in the north and Qandahar in the south, and between the mountains of Central Afghanistan to the west and the Afghanistan/Pakistan borders to the east. Their spread to the west, into the mountains, is of relatively recent date, and around 1800 Ghazni was still a town inhabited and surrounded by Tajiks and Hazaras, as, in fact, it for the greater part still is.[37] As in the case of the Durranis, the Ghaljis thus also represent an east to west drive of the Pashtuns.

The Ghalji confederacy includes a number of tribes. Traditionally they are divided into the Turan (to the south) and Burhan (to the north).[38] The Turan include the Nasir, Kharoti, Hotaki and Tokhi Ghaljis. The Tokhis live to the south of Muqqur, some 100 km southwest of Ghazni. The famous fortress of Qal'at-i Ghilzay, 138 km north of Qandahar, lies in the centre of their lands and is consequently also known as Qal'at-i Tokhi. To the east of the Tokhis live the Hotaki Ghaljis. They formed the driving force behind the Afghan conquest of Iran in the early eighteenth century, as will be discussed later in this book. The Kharotis live even further to the east, along the banks of the upper Gumal river, close to the Pakistan border. The Nasir Ghaljis are mostly *Kuchis* who used to travel down into the Indus valley for the winter.[39] This stopped in the early 1960s when the border with Pakistan was closed.

The Burhan include the Sulayman Khel, 'Ali Khel and the Tarakkis. The latter live around Muqqur, southwest of Ghazni. The Powindahs, who used to travel between India and Afghanistan before the borders were closed around 1960, were mostly Sulayman Khel. An important sub-group of the Sulayman Khel are the Ahmadzay, who live between Gardiz and Jalalabad. They are generally wealthy people who before the war were closely linked to the Durrani rulers of the country.

To the east of the Ghaljis, along the borders with Pakistan, live a number of Pashtun groups that belong to the Karlan branch. They include the Khugianis, who live south of Jalalabad; the Jajis, further to the south;[40] and a number of groups that live in the district of Paktya (along the Pakistan border). These are the Muqbils, Mangals, Jadrans, Tanis, Khostwals and Waziris. All of these groups are closely related to their kinsmen from east of the Durand line, in present-day Pakistan.

---

37 Elphinstone 1815:433.
38 Compare Elphinstone 1815:437.
39 Elphinstone 1815:457–61.
40 For the Jajis, see Janata 1987.

Relatively recent is the expansion of Pashtuns to the north of the country. These migrations mostly date to the 1880s and later when Amir ʿAbd al-Rahman Khan forced many Pashtun groups hostile to his rule to settle in North Afghanistan.[41] By 1979 they formed a size-able part of the population, especially in the northwest and in the Baghlan-Qunduz area north of the Salang Pass. They are generally called 'Qandaharis', after the name of the main urban centre in South Afghanistan.

The Turkic Ethnic Groups

The largest among the Turkic ethnic groups in North Afghanistan are the Özbeks.[42] They can easily be recognized. The women wear trousers, long-sleeved dresses and a headscarf, and often these gar-ments are made out of brightly coloured *ikat*.[43] The men wear long, striped and buttonless *ikat* coats with long sleeves, held in place by sashes or belts, which they combine with high leather boots. On their head they have a small turban. They are relative newcomers in this part of the world, having settled here from the late fifteenth century onwards. In Afghanistan they nowadays count some 1.6 million people (2000 estimate).[44] They are ethnically, linguistically and cul-turally closely related to the Özbeks in neighbouring Uzbekistan and adjacent lands. As in the case of the Pashtuns and many other ethnic groups in Afghanistan, the Özbeks are grouped into tribes and clans, including the Qataghan from the Qunduz area, but this structure does not play as important a role as with the Pashtuns.[45]

The Özbeks are Sunni Muslims. Their name is derived, so it is claimed, from that of Özbek Khan, who in the early fourteenth century was one of the leaders of the Golden Horde of the Mongols in Russia and West Central Asia. In the fifteenth century the Özbeks occupied much of the land between the (Lower) Volga and the Aral Sea. They soon moved south, towards the Iranian Plateau. They occupied the famous cities of Samarqand and Bukhara and moved further south, only to be stopped from conquering Iran by the rising

41   Compare Glatzer 1977.
42   For a bibliography of the Özbeks in Afghanistan, see Orywal 1986:24–5. See especially Naby 1984.
43   *Ikat* is a term from Indonesia that describes a process whereby a pattern is resist-dyed on the warp, weft, or both, before weaving (Burnham 1980:72).
44   CIA Factbook.
45   Compare the name of the pre-1964 province of Qataghan along the Qunduz river.

power of the Safawids under Shah Isma'il (battle near Marw, AD 1510). However, the Özbeks remained in control of Samarqand, Bukhara, Khiva and much of northern Afghanistan. Other Özbeks arrived in the north of Afghanistan from the late nineteenth century onwards and especially after the Russian Revolution. These are known as the *muhâjerin* (refugees) and as such they are distinguished from the autochthonous Özbeks.

Other Turkic groups include the Türkmen (or Turcoman), who nowadays live for the greater part in the northwest of the country, close to the modern republic of Turkmenistan.[46] The traditional clothing of the Türkmen consists of a shirt, baggy trousers and a long, buttonless coat that overlaps at the front and is kept in place with a sash or belt. Their headgear consists of a turban or the famous shaggy hat. Women's clothing includes a red, silk dress and trousers, over which they wear, inside the house, a short-sleeved coat. Outside of the house the women wear long-sleeved coats of various types. The most characteristic and famous part of women's clothing is the headgear, which could be up to half a metre in height. Nowadays most Türkmen women wear headscarves. A conspicuous feature of traditional Türkmen dress is the quantity of silver jewellery worn by the women. Brides used to wear between five to seven kilos of silver!

The Türkmen apparently originate from among the Ghuzz or Oghuz Turkic tribes that in the late first millennium AD moved from Central Asia towards the Iranian Plateau, although their exact lineage remains unknown. What is known is that their direct ancestors used to live along the eastern littoral of the Caspian Sea and moved east towards the banks of the Amu Darya and towards the Marw oasis from the sixteenth century onwards. Their language belongs to the so-called West Turkic languages, which also include modern Turkish, and is different from the East Turkic languages spoken by the other Turkic groups of Central Asia.

The Türkmen in Afghanistan mainly belong to the tribes of the Ersari and Tekke, but also other Türkmen tribes are represented. For the greater part descendants of refugees from the north and northwest after the Russian Revolution, they are particularly known for their carpet weaving and for their Karakul (Persian lamb) skins. Their number is some half million (1995 estimate).[47] Like the Özbeks they are Sunni Muslims.

---

46   For a bibliography of the Türkmen in Afghanistan, see Orywal 1986:28. For the Türkmen in general, see Kalter 1984.
47   Ethnologue Data Base.

The Tajiks

There are a large number of people in Afghanistan who speak a dialect of Iranian Persian (*Fârsi*), generally called *Dari*.[48] Among these are the Tajiks (*Tâjik*), who live mainly in the large cities and in the northeast of the country. They represent one of the oldest strata of the Afghan population. In earlier days, the name Tajik was used by (Özbek) nomads to indicate the local population (mostly *Fârsi* speaking) of the lands they had conquered in South Central Asia and northern Afghanistan.[49] Since then it has become restricted to the Sunnite, sedentary and Persian-speaking people of Afghanistan and neighbouring lands (as for instance in Tajikistan). In recent years, however, the name of Tajik is more and more being used to indicate all non-Pashtun, Persian-speaking peoples of Afghanistan, comparable to the Pashtun custom to call all Persian speakers *Fârsiwân*. However, the Persian speakers in the west of the country usually carry other ethnic names (see below), and the Farsiwan 'proper' are Shi'ites who live in the west of the country, in and near Herat.[50] The 'real' Tajiks of Afghanistan mainly live in the northeast of the country, although it should be realized that they prefer to be known by their place of origin (Panjshiri, Badakhshani) and regard the word Tajik as derogatory.

The Mountain Tajiks and the Isma'ilis

The Tajiks are often linked, although without much reason, to the so-called Mountain Tajiks (also called the Pamiris or Ghalchas), who live in the extreme northeast of the country and beyond, and include the Wakhanis and others.[51] They form rather secluded communities who speak a set of Northeast Iranian languages.[52] Apart from their

---

48   *Fârsi* (the word is the Arabized form of *Pârsi*) is derived from the spoken form of Middle Persian, generally called *Pârsi-yi dari*. The origin of the word *dari* is still unclear. Generally it is thought to be related to the word for the royal court, Persian *dari*. Dari is the lingua franca of Afghanistan.

49   Compare Orywal 1986:22. Originally, the name *tâzi* was used by the Iranians to indicate the (Islamic) Arabs. Later the Turkic-speaking groups used the term to denote all Muslims (Arabian and Iranian). However, see also C. E. Bosworth's contribution 'Tâdjik' in *Enc. Isl.*

50   Orywal 1986:49–50.

51   Orywal 1986:46–9.

52   Languages spoken in the northeast of Afghanistan include Wakhi, spoken in the Wakhan corridor; Shughni (Shughnani; spoken in Shughnan); Roshani (north of Shughnan); Ishkashimi (in and around Ishkashim); Sanglechi (along the Sanglech;

language, they are also characterized by their faith, since they are predominantly Isma'ilis. These constitute a branch of the Shi'a (the so-called *Ismâ'iliyya* branch), which is different from the main section of the Shi'a (the so-called *Imâmiyya*), which is prevalent in modern Iran.

All Shi'ites denounce the succession of 'Ali bin Abi Talib, Muhammad's cousin and son-in-law, by the founder of the Umayyad dynasty, Caliph Mu'awiya, in AD 661. Instead they regard 'Ali's sons Hasan and Husayn, and their descendants, as the true successors of Muhammad. When one of these descendants, Imam Ja'far as-Sadiq,[53] died in AD 765, he was succeeded by his son, Imam Musa al-Qazim. However, Ja'far had earlier appointed another son, called Isma'il, as his heir, but the latter died before his father. The group that did not accept the imamate of Musa al-Qazim, but instead regarded Isma'il, and in particular his son Muhammad as the true heirs, later developed into the Isma'ili branch of the Shi'ites. The others accepted Musa al-Qazim and his successors, until the eleventh imam, Hasan al-'Askari, who died in AD 874. He was reported to have had a son, the twelfth imam, who had withdrawn from the world and was believed to return when the proper time had come. This belief in the Hidden Imam is one of the hallmarks of the Imami, or Twelver Shi'ites. The Isma'ilis, to the contrary, and especially those living in Badakhshan, believe in an unbroken line of imams, continuing to the present time.

The Badakhshanis belong to a particular branch of the *Ismâ'iliyya*, namely that of the Nizaris (*Nizâriyya*).[54] They split off from the main branch in the late eleventh and early twelfth centuries following a leadership dispute. The Nizaris became particularly known for their early leaders or imams, namely the Lords of Alamut, a mountain fortress west of modern Tehran. In the European west, the lord of Alamut was better known as the Old Man of the Mountain.[55] The imams of Alamut were, rightly or not, infamous for their policy of assassinating their opponents. When in AD 1256 Alamut was taken by the Mongol ruler, Hülegü, the Nizari imams consequently lost most of their power. At present the Nizari Isma'ilis are led by their

and Yidgha-Munjani (or Munji; spoken in the Munjan valley and in Chitral, Pakistan). Other languages belonging to this group are Yazgulami (in modern Tajikistan), and Wanchi (*idem*; now extinct). Across the border with China, another language (Sarikoli) used to be spoken until recent times.

53 The sixth imam of the Imami Shi'ites, and the fifth imam of the Isma'ilis (who do not regard 'Ali as imam).

54 For the Badakhshani Isma'ilis, see also Van den Berg 1997.

55 Marco Polo (trans. Latham 1958:70–3) correspondingly refers to the Sheikh of the Mountain, called Alaodin.

Living Imam, Agha Khan IV (Shah Karim al-Husayni), who claims descent from the imams of Alamut.[56] His adherents regard him as the forty-ninth imam in an unbroken line from ʿAli and his son Hasan.[57]

Ismaʿili Shiʿa was reputedly introduced to Badakhshan in the eleventh century by the poet and author Nasir-i Khusraw, who is still highly revered as *pir* (spiritual guide) among the Badakhshanis.[58] His tomb may be visited along the upper reaches of the Kokcha river at the site of Yamgan, southeast of Fayzabad, the capital of Badakhshan. Ismaʿili Shiʿa differs in many aspects from the *Imâmiyya*. Apart from the absence of a Hidden Imam and the presence of a Living Imam (in this case the Agha Khan), the Nizari Ismaʿilis also regard ʿAli bin Abi Talib, Muhammad's son-in-law and cousin, almost as important as Muhammad himself. While Muhammad is the one who proclaimed the message of God, it was ʿAli, according to them, who interpreted the message. Furthermore, the Ismaʿilis emphasize an esoteric inter-pretation of the divine message and they consequently have several stages of initiation. Outward appearance is not regarded as essential. This would explain the rather relaxed attitude of the Ismaʿilis as regards the rules and regulations prevalent among the Sunnites and Imami Shiʿites.

The Nuristanis

Another major group in Afghanistan is that of the Nuristanis.[59] Because of their languages and their culture, all very different from that of their neighbours, they have been the subject of extensive studies. They live in the secluded mountains northeast of Kabul and south of the Hindu Kush watershed, between the Alingar river to the west and the Kunar river to the east. The district is called Nuristan ('Land of the Light'), but before its conquest by Amir ʿAbd al-Rahman Khan in the winter of 1895/6 it was known (to outsiders)

56　He is the grandson of Agha Khan III (1877–1957), who reorganized the Nizari community. The titel of *Âghâ Khân* (or *Âqâ Khân*) was given to his ancestor, Hasan ʿAli Shah Mahallati by the Qajar king, Fath ʿAli Shah (r. 1797–1834), who also gave him a daughter in marriage.

57　They regard him as the *Khodâ-yi zinda*, 'living god', and the *Imâm-i Zamân* or *Imâm-i hâziru'l-waqt*, the 'Imam of the (present) era'.

58　He originated from eastern Iran and in his career as missionary (*dâʿi*) acted on behalf of the (Ismaʿili) Fatimid rulers of Egypt.

59　Literature on Nuristan is extensive. Compare Jettmar 1974; Klimburg and Janata 1990. Still very informative is Robertson 1896. See also Elphinstone 1815:617–28. For a bibliography and short survey, see Orywal 1986:51–4.

as Kafiristan ('Land of the Infidels'), because of the non-Islamic religion of its people.[60]

Outsiders used to regard the Kafirs as robbers, murderers, wine drinkers and fire-worshippers. Alexander Burnes, who travelled from Peshawar to Kabul in the early 1830s, added that the 'Kaffirs appear to be a most barbarous people, eaters of bears and monkeys, and fighting with arrows, and scalping their enemies'.[61] He furthermore described them as the aborigines of Afghanistan and added that the Kafirs were supposed to descend from Alexander the Great. Mountstuart Elphinstone, writing about 'Caufiristaun' in 1815, likewise told that they resembled the Greeks and were 'celebrated for their beauty and European complexion, worshipped idols, drank wine in silver cups or vases, used chairs and tables, and spoke a language unknown to their neighbours'.[62]

The number of Nuristanis from before 1979 was generally reckoned to be some 100,000.[63] They speak a variety of related languages. These so-called Kafiri languages belong to the Indo-Iranian language family and are thus related to the Indo-Aryan (including Hindi) and Iranian languages (as e.g. *Fârsi*, Baluchi, Pashto). The Kafiri languages probably constitute a third branch, being neither specifically Indo-Aryan nor Iranian.[64]

Relatively little is known about the culture of the Kafirs from before the time that they were forced to adopt Islam. Their society was tribal and oligarchal. The position of women was low, and polygamy was the norm. Poor kinsmen tended to look after the herds. There were also artisans, who formed a separate class, and then there were slaves. These were mostly captives from the wars that were fought among the Kafirs themselves and against the Muslims living along the fringes of Kafiristan. The Kafirs also had a strong sense of what was 'clean' and 'unclean', and they followed a complicated system of rules to separate the two. The pre-Islamic religious rituals of the Kafirs, although insufficiently known, are of particular interest. The drinking of wine, the sacrifice of animals, the presence of priests and singers of hymns, and the use of a sacrificial fire all suggest a close relationship to the ancient religion of the Indo-Iranians. The

60   From Arabic *kâfir*, 'infidel'. This name ('Capherstam') also occurs in a travelogue of the Jesuit priest Benedict Goës, who in the early seventeenth century travelled from India, via Peshawar and modern Afghanistan, to China (compare Sykes 1940:308).

61   Burnes 1834, II:211; see also I:165–6.

62   Elphinstone 1815:617.

63   Ethnologue Data Base.

64   Morgenstierne 1979:25.

names of some of the Kafir gods also recall Indo-Iranian deities, as for instance that of the main god of the Kafirs, called Imra, Mara or Yamrai. This name recalls Indo-Iranian Yama or Yima, the Lord of the Underworld. Another god in this context is that of Indr, whose name is related to that of Indo-Iranian Indra.[65] Next to the many gods and goddesses, there were also demons and spirits that needed propitiating.

Linguists recognize four (or five) separate Kafiri tongues, namely Kati, Prasun, Waigali (and Gambiri) and Ashkun. The various languages also reflect socio-political and cultural differences between their speakers. For instance, the Kati speakers used mainly to wear black coloured clothes (and were therefore often called, in Persian, *siyâh-push*; Pashto *Torkâfir*, 'wearers of black'), the others white coloured garments (the *safid-push*; Pashto *Spinkâfir*, 'wearers of white'). Kati is spoken in the northwest and especially in the northeast of Nuristan. The language often functions as the *lingua franca* of the region, and shortly after the Marxist takeover it was recognized as one of the official languages of Afghanistan. The centre of the Kati speakers, and of Nuristan in general, is the village of Kamgrom (Kamdesh), which is located in the Bashgal valley. Here the British doctor (Sir) George Scott Robertson spent much time during his year-long visit to the Kafirs in 1890/1891. This visit resulted in the famous book *The Kafirs of the Hindu-Kush*, which was published in 1896, in the same year that the Kafirs were defeated by the Afghans and forced to adopt Islam.

Kati speakers, similar to most of the other Kafirs, used to form a fairly egalitarian society, at least for those who were 'free'. There were, however, men of authority, and among the Kati speakers this resulted in some sort of oligarchy of influential clans. Among them, further prestige could be acquired by killing an enemy and by giving lavish feasts. Descent remained important, however, and from among the Kati groups derive the few extant, huge wooden statues of ancestors, either men or women, who are depicted sitting or standing, or, in the case of men, even riding a horse. Most of these statues were destroyed following the advent of Islam, but some of them have survived in ethnological collections throughout the world.

Another language is Prasun. It is spoken by a small group of people in a secluded valley with Kati speakers to the east and west. The valley used to constitute the religious centre of Kafiristan. Here, at Kushteki, there stood one of the few religious buildings of the area,

---

65 Indr was known as the deity that introduced wine-making. In Indo-Aryan literature Indra is known for his ability to drink huge amounts of (equally intoxicating) *Soma*.

dedicated to Mara (Imra), the main deity of the Kafirs. The Prasun speakers were primarily concerned with religion. As in the case of the Kati speakers, they were led by a small group of people whose position was fairly secure. There were no carved statues of ancestors. Instead all energy was spent on the production of statues of the gods.

South of the Prasun speakers there are Nuristanis who speak Waigali (and closely related Gambiri) and Ashkun. Together they form a large group. Of all the Nuristanis, the Waigali and Ashkun speakers traditionally maintained the closest contacts with the people living in the Kabul valley to the south. These contacts were not always peaceful, and the Waigali and Ashkun speakers therefore developed a fairly martial culture in which fame could be acquired by killing enemies. In this way, their society was the most egalitarian, and the carving of woodwork was directed at the living, rather than the ancestors or the gods.

The Baluch and Brahuis

Another Iranian-speaking group, living in the southwest of the country and in neighbouring parts of Pakistan and Iran, are the Baluch.[66] They speak a Northwest Iranian language, Baluchi. Most of them are now sedentary and all of them are Sunnis. They seem to descend from people who moved from the north to the southeast of the Iranian Plateau during the Middle Ages. They are first mentioned in Islamic sources from the tenth century. Sometime later they moved further from present-day Southeast Iran into modern Pakistani Baluchistan. Their name also appears in Firdawsi's *Shâh-nâme* (early eleventh century). Large number of Baluch tribesmen settled in Sistan by the end of the eighteenth century, following the fall of the Iranian Zand dynasty.[67]

In 1979, according to estimates, there were some 200,000 Baluch in the country. In 1996, their number in Pakistan was estimated at one million.[68] Often living together with them are the Brahuis, who speak a Dravidian language akin to the languages spoken in South India, such as Tamil and Malayalam.[69] Their number in Afghanistan, prior to 1979, was estimated at about 20,000, but this figure is controversial. The Brahuis used to dominate a large extent of land. The

66   See Orywal 1986:35–8. Compare Morgenstierne 1958:169–200.
67   Compare Tate 1910:93ff.
68   According to the Ethnologue Data Base.
69   For the Brahuis, see Orywal 1986:37–8.

so-called Brahui confederation was established in the seventeenth century, and by the mid-eighteenth century it comprized almost all of eastern Baluchistan, including the modern port of Karachi. It was led by Brahuis and included the many Baluch tribes of the area. The confederation collapsed by the early nineteenth century and in 1876 a treaty was signed which made it into a British protectorate. Its main centre is the town of Kalat, south of Quetta.

The Hazaras

The Hazaras of Central Afghanistan speak Persian (*Fârsi, Hazâragi*), but are clearly of Mongolian origin which shows by their Turco-Mongoloid features.[70] Their number is estimated at about 1.5 million (1989 figures).[71] They inhabit the poor lands in the mountains of Central Afghanistan, generally called Hazarajat.[72] Their name derives from Persian *hazâr*, 'thousand', and probably refers to a (Mongol) military contingent (Mongol *ming*). The Hazaras used to occupy a much larger area, including large tracks to the east and south of their present habitat. However, following their defeat at the hands of Amir ʿAbd al-Rahman Khan during a war that lasted for some years (1890–3), the Pashtuns drove them higher up into the mountains. Most of the Hazaras are Imami Shiʿites and are in relatively close contact with their co-religionists in Iran and Iraq.[73] There are also Ismaʿili Hazaras, who live in the northeast of Hazarajat in separation from the Imami Hazaras.

The Hazaras are grouped into tribes and clans, traditionally headed by a *Mir* or *Beg*, but there is no overall genealogy and the tribal organization is far less important than with the Pashtuns. They are traditionally led by 'outsiders', namely *Sâdât* (singular: *Sayyid*), who claim descent from Muhammad.[74] Those who have enjoyed a religious education, receive the title of *Shaykh*. The recent war, however, has changed the structure of Hazara society, and most power now lies with newly emerged religious leaders and the officials of political parties, the most important of which is the *Hizb-i Wahdat-i Islâmi*.

70 A recent study on the Hazaras is by Mousavi 1998. For a bibliography, see Orywal 1986:26–7.
71 Ethnologue Data Base.
72 Being the Arabic plural form of *Hazâra*. Now often also called Hazaristan.
73 Their conversion from Sunnism to Shi'ism appears to date back to Safawid times (sixteenth–eighteenth centuries AD).
74 Kopecky 1982.

The Aymaq

The Aymaq of West Central Afghanistan form another Persian speaking group.[75] They represent the Persian-speaking, Sunni nomads and semi-nomads of West Afghanistan and their number in Afghanistan in 1993 was estimated at more than 400,000.[76] This group of people is made up of the Chahar ('four') Aymaq, which includes four tribes (the Jamshidis,[77] Aymaq Hazaras, Firuzkuhis[78] and Taymanis).[79] Together with the Taymuris[80] and some other groups (the so-called *Aymaq-i digar*, 'other Aymaq')[81] they constitute a relatively distinct group in the western foothills of the Central Afghan highlands. They are generally semi-nomads, and especially the Firuzkuhis are known for the conical felt yurts in which they live.

The Taymuris live northwest of Herat. The Jamshidis live further to the west, in and around the modern town of Kushk, north of Herat. The Aymaq Hazaras, who live northeast of Herat, are ethnically related to the Hazaras in Central Afghanistan, but they are Sunnites and not Shi'ites. Their urban centre at present is Qal'a-i Naw. Finally, the Firuzkuhis live along the upper course of the Hari Rud river, east of Herat. The Taymanis, some of whom have adopted a Pashtun-style black tent, live south of the Firuzkuhis.

Minor Ethnic Groups

Other, minor ethnic groups that have settled in Afghanistan include Mongols, Arabs, Qizilbash and many others. There are also various groups that originate in the Indian subcontinent, or at least ethnically closely related to the people of India and Pakistan. The oldest of these are probably the speakers of Dardic (Indo-Aryan) languages, includ-

75   For this group, see Orywal 1986:29–34, and especially Centlivres 1976.
76   Ethnologue Data Base.
77   The Jamshidis claim descend from Jamshid (compare Avestan *Yima Khshaêta*, the Lord of the Underworld) and they sometimes call themselves also Kayanis (compare the legendary Kayanian, Kavyan dynasty of ancient Iranian tradition).
78   For this group, see Mandersloot 1971. According to their own traditions, they originate from Firuzkuh east of Tehran, whence they were taken to the Herat area by Timur (also known as Tamerlane), in the late fifteenth century.
79   The composition of the Aymaq is still disputed. The Aymaq Hazaras are sometimes excluded from the Chahar Aymaq, and the Taymuris are sometimes added. Elphinstone (1815:480) lists the four tribes of the *Chahaur Oeemauk* as the *Teimunees*, *Hazaurehs*, *Teimoories*, and *Zoories*.
80   Also called the Sunni Hazaras. For the Taymuris, see Singer 1982.
81   Including the Zuris, Malikis, Mishmast and Tahiris.

ing Pasha'i.[82] The Pasha'i speakers live along the western and south-ern fringes of Nuristan and are nowadays also known as *Dihgân* or *Kohistâni*. Many of them are Shi'ites, and accordingly known as *'Ali-Ilâhis*. Marco Polo in the 1270s may refer to them and their 'Indian' character:[83]

> Ten days' journey south of Badakhshan is a country called Pashai. The inhabitants, who have brown skins and speak a language of their own, are idolators. They are adepts in enchantment and diabolic arts. The men wear ear-rings and brooches of gold and silver and pearls and pre-cious stones in profusion. They are very crafty folk and artful in their own way. The climate is very hot. The stock diet is flesh and rice.

The Pasha'i speakers may in fact have arrived here from the east at a very early date, if they did not settle here immediately after the Indo-Aryan migrations from north of the Hindu Kush in the second millennium BC. They inhabit an area that stretches from close to the Salang Pass north of Kabul,[84] south and eastwards along the fringes of the mountains of Nuristan, to the banks of the Kunar river north of Jalalabad. Their number was estimated in 1982 at more than 100,000.[85] From their habitat in the side-valleys along the Kabul river it is clear that they used to live in a much larger area, and that in the course of time they were pushed out of the plains between Kabul and Jalalabad, mainly by Pashtun immigrants. This process is still continuing.

Another Dardic (Indo-Aryan) language, now (almost) extinct, is Tirahi, which used to be spoken in some villages south of Jalalabad by people who apparently had been pushed out of Tirah (further south, on the other side of the Safed Koh) by Pashtuns (the Afridis).[86]

The number of Mongols in Afghanistan is extremely limited.[87] The Ethnologue Data Base lists a few thousand people, with only some 200 or less speakers of Mogholi. They live, or used to live, in various villages south of Herat in West Afghanistan.

In North Afghanistan there are said to be some communities of Arabs, speaking Arabic.[88] They regard themselves as descendants of the Arab colonists from the early years of the Islamic conquest.

---

82   Orywal 1986:54–6. See also Kieffer, in Orywal 1986, and Elphinstone 1815:319.
83   Marco Polo, ed. Latham 1958:78.
84   They may even have lived at some time in the Panjshir valley (Morgenstierne, in Jettmar 1974:4).
85   According to Ethnologue Data Base.
86   Orywal 1986:62–3.
87   Orywal 1986:42–3.
88   For an extensive study of the Arabs of Afghanistan, see Barfield 1981. See also Orywal 1986:39–40. Compare Elphinstone 1815:322.

However, they are more probably descendants of Arabs who were forcibly settled in or near Samarqand in the time of Timur (fourteenth century).[89]

The Qizilbash live in the main cities of Afghanistan, mainly in Kabul.[90] They are the descendants of Turkic troops stationed in Kabul in the eighteenth century by the Iranian king Nadir Shah or his successors.[91] Their name ('red heads') refers to the scarlet or crimson headgear with twelve panels (for the twelve imams of Shi'ite Islam), which the Türkmen supporters of the Safawids in the late fifteenth to the early eighteenth centuries used to wear. They have generally held important administrative posts in the country. Their number nowadays is estimated at some 30,000.[92] They speak Persian and are (Imami-) Shi'ites.

89   Adamec 1997:42.
90   Orywal 1986:59–60.
91   J. B. Fraser 1828; Noelle 1997:25–6.
92   Adamec 1997:265.

3

The Early Years

When in 1978/9 war broke out in Afghanistan, local archaeological research was still in its infancy and only a limited number of sites had been subject to controlled digging.[1] A small number of excavation reports and general surveys have since been published, but to date archaeological knowledge about the prehistory and protohistory of the country, from before *c.*500 BC, still remains slim. Moreover, the interpretation of excavated objects from any site in the world, especially from prehistory when written documentation is absent, is always extremely difficult. Excavated items provide very little direct historical information and basically they only tell something about the material culture of the items' users and producers. They seldom give direct information about the history of these people, their language, their social organization and other aspects of their lifes.

Yet, the material culture of the people living in what is now Afghanistan in the faraway past, as brought to light by archaeology, shows a number of patterns that are found again throughout the later history of the country. These include a continuous cross-fertilization between local traditions and outside influences. They also show a strong relationship between East and Southeast Afghanistan on the one hand and the hilly tracks along the Indus in modern Pakistan on the other, all of this area roughly corresponding to the habitat of the modern Pashtuns. It is also clear that the northern parts of Afghanistan formed part of a much wider cultural horizon that included lands to the north and northwest, in present-day Tajikistan, Uzbekistan and Turkmenistan. There are also indications of northern influence on the lands south of the Hindu Kush. Also interesting is the position of Sistan in Southwest Afghanistan, where from ear-

1 Compare Brentjes 1983, Sarianidi 1977, and Shaffer 1978:71–186. A comprehensive and extremely useful survey is by Ball 1982.

liest times influences can be detected from the north and the east, and especially from the (Iranian) west.

The Chalcolithic

Following the end of the last Ice Age, people soon learnt to domesticate animals and to cultivate plants for food production. This is generally called the Neolithic Revolution. By the mid-sixth millennium BC, food crops are being cultivated across most of the Iranian Plateau, including modern Afghanistan.[2] By this time, stone was still the basic material for tool production. This changed with the introduction of metal, and primarily that of copper and bronze, and hence archaeologists often differentiate between a Copper Age (Chalcolithic) and a subsequent Bronze Age, although such a periodization is often somewhat arbitrary.[3] On the Iranian Plateau, the Chalcolithic is dated to a period between approximately 5500 and 3000 BC. The Bronze Age continued to the second half of the second millennium BC, which marks the beginning of the Iron Age.

During the Chalcolithic, food production on the Plateau increased, with a concurrent growth of the population. At the end, by c.3000 BC, proto-urban settlements had developed all over the Plateau. This process intensified in the succeeding Bronze Age, and by the early and mid-third millennium BC various settlements had grown into small urban centres that were based on craft specialization, inter-regional trade and the exploitation and domination of the surrounding countryside. These centres were located in the small, often isolated enclaves and oases of productive land that dot the Iranian countryside. In this respect, the development on the Plateau was rather different from that in the fertile plains of Mesopotamia and in the Indus Valley, where roughly at the same time (third millennium BC) much larger political entities developed, based on a much larger extent of productive land.

The most important Chalcolithic and Bronze Age site in South Afghanistan, as known to date, is Mundigak.[4] The site lies some 35 km northwest of modern Qandahar along the Kushk-i Nakhud Rud, a tributary of the Arghandab river, and it was discovered in 1951 by French archaeologists. It occupies a strategic position along one of the routes that lead from the mountainous lands in the north

2   For Neolithic and earlier sites in Afghanistan, see Shaffer 1978:71–90.
3   Bronze is an alloy of copper and tin. Low-tin bronze was used in Afghanistan as early as the sixth millennium BC (Shaffer 1978:89).
4   The excavation report is by Casal 1961. See also Shaffer 1978:71–186; Allchin and Allchin 1982:133ff. For an extensive bibliography, see Ball 1982: No. 743.

to the fertile and extensive Qandahar plains in the south. The Qandahar oasis itself forms a bottleneck for any traffic between east and west, since it is bounded to the north by the mountains of Central Afghanistan and to the south by the inhospitable Registan Desert.[5] Here various rivers from the northeast and east (including the Tarnak and the Arghas(t)an) flow into the Arghandab river, which itself empties into the Hilmand some 130 km further west. The plentiful supply of water and its strategic position have made the Qandahar oasis into one of the most important districts of the country, and the Mundigak site represents its oldest permanent settlement known to date.

The excavators of Mundigak distinguished seven main periods of occupation, of which Periods I–IV are Chalcolithic and Bronze Age in date. The subsequent Period V marks a sharp decrease in the extent of habitation at the site and is attributed to the (early) second millennium BC. Periods VI and VII belong to the (developed) Iron Age and yielded pottery that is comparable to the ceramics found in the lowest levels of nearby Old Qandahar (and dated to the early and mid-first millennium BC).[6]

The lowest levels of Mundigak did not provide any evidence of building activities. They probably represent the campsite of nomads or semi-nomads, and are generally dated to the early fourth millennium BC. In slightly later levels, still within Period I as distinguished by the excavators, simple houses were brought to light that were built of *pakhsa* (pressed tiered mud) and crude brick. Pottery found in and around the houses includes wheelmade wares often with painted decorations. It was also noticed that copper implements were widely used from the very beginning. It is also from this Period that the first lapis lazuli beads were attested. These finds might indicate, as traditionally assumed, contacts with the famous lapis lazuli mines in Badakhshan, but should perhaps more logically be linked to the newly discovered lapis seams in the nearby Chagai hills. The excavators also found a figurine of a humped bull (the zebu, or *Bos Indicus*), an animal which is well-known from more humid lands, such as the neighbouring Indian subcontinent.

In Period II, dated roughly to the mid-fourth millennium BC, the pottery shows some regression in quality, and it is often handmade and undecorated. On the other hand, the houses were well-built (with deeper foundations) and generally larger in size than during Period I. Other finds from Period II include sling stones, stone arrow points, copper artefacts, cone-shaped spindle whorls, bone awls, alabaster

5 Called the Arachosian Corridor by A. J. Toynbee (1961:53–6).
6 For this site, see Ball 1982: No. 522; MacNicoll and Ball 1996; Helms 1997.

vases and beads of lapis lazuli. The French archaeologists also discovered the first example of a stone stamp (or button) seal. Such seals, which were used to indicate ownership or provenance, belong to a tradition that in the fourth millennium spread all over the Iranian Plateau.[7]

The finds from Mundigak Periods I–II are thus not an isolated phenomenon, but should be placed within a much broader context of developments all over the Plateau and beyond. Particularly close parallels in material culture were found in the hilly tracks to the east, as for instance in the Quetta valley, Pakistan. This area lies some 200 km southeast of Mundigak, at the northwestern entrance to the strategic Bolan Pass that descends into the Indus Valley. One of the sites here is Kili Gul Muhammad.[8] The so-called Kili Gul Muhammad pottery (wheelmade black-on-red slipped ware) is very akin to some of the ceramics from the early levels at Mundigak and at the same time is strongly reminiscent of the so-called Togau black-on-red ware from South Baluchistan.[9] Also interesting is the polychrome painted pottery of the so-called Kechi Beg tradition, which at Mundigak occurs in later levels of Period I and which is also known from the Quetta Valley.

There is another important site, which lies some 150 km southeast of Quetta.[10] This is the large settlement of Mehrgarh, discovered by French archaeologists in the early 1970s and excavated between 1974 and 1986. It is strategically located along the edge of the Indus valley and close to the southeastern entrance to the Bolan Pass. Here the earliest levels, dating to the seventh millennium, yielded evidence of a pre-ceramic society with housing structures. The people cultivated wheat, barley and dates and they kept humped bulls and other cattle. The excavators also found the bones of sheep and goats. From a later period, from around 5500 BC, there is evidence for the use of cotton. From this time, there are also the first indications for the production of pottery.

At Mehrgarh, copper artefacts make their appearance in Period III (mid-fifth to mid-fourth millennia BC). Some of the wheelmade pottery from this time belongs to the Kili Gul Muhammad/Togau horizon, which would locate this phase in the development of Mehrgarh within the same broad context as Mundigak I–II in South Afghanistan.

7 Stamp seals are known from many other Chalcolithic sites on the Iranian Plateau, as e.g. Sialk III and Tepe Hisar Ib-c. (Tosi et al. 1992:199).
8 The site is located some three km from Quetta City; see esp. Fairservis 1975:136ff.
9 Togau ware is described by Fairservis 1975:156.
10 See Jarrige 1987.

Long-distance trade is indicated at Mehrgarh by the frequent find, from the beginning, of lapis lazuli, turquoise, agate, mother-of-pearl and conch shells. The importance of these finds in relation to Mundigak is the fact that apparently at a very early date, in the seventh millennium BC, trade or exchange networks existed between sites on the Iranian Plateau and places in and close to the Indus valley (Mehrgarh). These networks, as far as can be reconstructed at present, included the exchange of semi-precious stones. The turquoise perhaps derives from modern Northeast Iran,[11] and lapis lazuli originates from Badakhshan or the Chagai hills.

The Early Bronze Age

The excavated items from the next phase in Mundigak's history, Period III, are comparable to finds from the nearby site of Sa'id Qal'a.[12] The pertinent levels at the two sites date back approximately to the period between 3500 and 2800 BC.[13] The French archaeologists at Mundigak discovered many copper and bronze utensils, including a bronze shaft-hole axe and adze, and large numbers of crude female figurines. They also found square and circular compartmented stamp seals, often made of steatite. The cone-shaped spindle whorls of Periods I–II are replaced by disk-shaped examples.

The ceramic assemblage, now mainly consisting of decorated wheelmade wares, includes the so-called Quetta ware, named after the nearby district in Pakistan where it was first discovered. Quetta ware is a striking and boldly decorated type of pottery of red-buff colour, with a light slip, and decorated with black (or red) designs. Apart from this Quetta ware, the ceramics from Mundigak III include other wares that are commonly found in the Quetta valley and neighbouring lands. In fact, the similarities between the ceramics from Mundigak and Sa'id Qal'a on the one hand, and the site of Damb Sadaat (II) in the Quetta Valley on the other, are so obvious that the archaeologist, Jim Shaffer, speaks of a single cultural complex.[14]

Comparative material to the 'Quetta ware' is known from among the ceramics of the so-called Namazga III assemblage, which was brought to light much further in the north, in modern Turkmenistan and which is generally dated to the second half of the fourth millen-

---

11   Turquoise is found west of modern Mashhad, in northeast Iran. Compare Ferrier 1857:106–7. It was also found in the Qyzyl Qum desert of South Central Asia (compare Potts 1994:195).
12   For a bibliography, see Ball 1982: No. 968.
13   Compare Shaffer 1978:115.
14   Shaffer 1978:173.

nium BC.[15] The Namazga sequence is concentrated in the foothills along the Kopet Dagh mountains, southeast and northwest of modern Ashkhabad, the capital of modern Turkmenistan. In the Namazga III period, people started to move west from the centre of the Namazga lands and they colonized the oasis of the Tajand river (the Hari Rud), to the west of the Marw oasis and just northwest of Afghanistan. Here they developed what is generally known as the Geoksyur culture, named after the type site in the oasis. One of the characteristics of the Geoksyur culture is the use of buff pottery with a buff slib, decorated with polychrome (black and red) motifs. These motifs are strikingly similar to those shown on the Quetta ware. In addition, the seated female figurines found in large quantities in the Tajand oasis recall comparable figurines from Saʿid Qalʿa and sites further east in the borderlands.

Another interesting parallel, although at present insufficiently studied, is that of funerary customs. In the Geoksyur oasis multiple burials were found in circular tombs made of mud brick (the so-called *tholoi*). Comparable graves were found at Mundigak, in the later levels of Period III. Here, stone-lined chists contained collective burials of (parts of) corpses, some of which had been excarnated elsewhere. In earlier levels from the same Period, the dead were buried in simple contracted burials.

The origins of the so-called Quetta ware and associated traditions are still a matter of debate. Sarianidi suggests that the main stimulus passed from north to south. He postulates that newcomers from the west settled in the hitherto virginal lands along the lower course of the Tajand river and developed their own distinctive type of pottery. When the river shifted its course and the lands could no longer be properly irrigated, they moved on, towards the south via the Herat corridor, onto the Iranian Plateau and the Quetta valley.[16] The French archaeologist Jarrige, however, suggests that contacts between Turkmenistan and the south went both ways and that the available evidence would suggest the presence of extensive networks of contacts.[17] Although this observation is basically correct, the intrusive character of the Quetta ware and associated traditions in South Afghanistan and the Quetta area is evident and it is therefore likely that the Quetta ware has its origins among northern traditions. It is unlikely, however, that its distribution to the south was merely caused by the shifting of a river course. Something more substantial may have occurred in the late fourth millennium, as for instance population pressure from the

15   Kohl 1984:214–15.
16   Sarianidi 1998:23.
17   Jarrige 1987a.

steppes of Central Asia, which would be the first recorded instance of a feature that dominates the whole history of the eastern part of the Iranian Plateau. Whatever the case, it may be assumed that the carriers of the 'Quetta ware culture' brought with them more than an idea of how to make striking looking pottery. They probably also introduced a particular type of female figurines and perhaps a distinctive funerary custom. Since these aspects were apparently so widely and easily adopted by local craftsmen at Mundigak and in the Quetta valley, the same people from the far north probably also introduced other, and hitherto unknown cultural characteristics. If later historical developments are anything to go by, the people from the Tajand and neighbouring regions also became the dominant class among the autochthonous population of Mundigak and the Quetta valley. All this is impossible to prove, but pressure from the north upon the oasis settlements of the Iranian Plateau is a constant feature in the history of the area, and there is no reason to assume that this feature is limited to the historical period.

Sites in modern Sistan, in modern Southwest Afghanistan or beyond, provide further information. The most famous Bronze Age site in Iranian Sistan is that of Shahr-i Sokhta ('Burnt Town'), excavated by Italian archaeologists in the late 1960s and 1970s.[18] The huge site, which was occupied throughout the third millennium BC, is marked by large amounts of worked and non-worked stone and semi-precious stone: alabaster, carnelian, chalcedony, lapis lazuli, steatite and turquoise. The Italian archaeologists distinguish four main periods of occupation, of which the earliest, Period I (dated to between *c.*3200 and 2800 BC), was roughly contemporary with Mundigak III. The designs on some of the pottery are reminiscent of the pottery from Namazga III (Geoksyur oasis) and the Quetta ware from Mundigak and the Quetta Valley.[19] Shahr-i Sokhta has also yielded evidence for the presence of *tholoi*. The tombs were mostly used for multiple burials, and are either circular or square in shape. Of further interest was the find of a catacomb grave. This type of grave is well known in Central Asia, but whether or not there is a direct link remains a moot point.[20] In view of the other information discussed above, however, a northern origin is very well possible.

Shahr-i Sokhta, apart from showing links to lands to the north and east, also belongs to another cultural horizon, namely that of

18   See Tosi 1969 and Lamberg-Karlovsky and Tosi, 1973. For prehistoric Sistan, see also Tosi 1983.
19   Compare Biscione 1973.
20   Tosi, Maleu Shahmirzadi and Joyenda 1992 (1996):213–14.

the Elamite and Mesopotamian world. Direct links between Shahr-i Sokhta and Mesopotamia are indicated by the find at the Sistani site (Period I) of a Proto-Elamite tablet and a number of sealings of Uruk/Jemdet Nasr type, which are well known from Mesopotamia and dated to *c.*3000 BC. One of the sites that in this respect are of particular importance is Tepe Yahya, which lies some 450 km to the west of Sistan, in modern Iran. From levels belonging to Period IVC at Tepe Yahya, 27 Proto-Elamite tablets were unearthed, together with cylinder seals, Jemdet Nasr polychrome pottery and bevelled rim bowls, all indicative of close links with late fourth millennium Elam and Mesopotamia.[21]

The Middle Bronze Age

Mundigak IV dates to the late first half and the middle of the third millennium BC. In the preceding period (Mundigak III), as discussed above, the Arghandab valley in South Afghanistan was connected with semi-urban sites all over the Plateau and beyond. Trade networks had developed that were linked to the procurement of lapis lazuli and other semi-precious stones. It is furthermore probable that in the late fourth millennium groups of people migrated from Turkmenistan in the north, via South Afghanistan, to the fringes of the Indus valley. Finally, by that time, Elamite and Mesopotamian influences had reached east as far as Sistan along the Iran/Afghanistan border. All in all, the foundations were laid for the rapid development that took place in the succeeding Middle Bronze Age.

Mundigak IV started with the levelling of preceding structures and the construction of a platform. A monumental building was erected on top and one of its walls was adorned or strengthened with a colonnade. Archaeologists also discovered the remains of (apparently) defensive walls with rectangular bastions that surrounded the site. Of great interest, but hitherto unexplained, are the structures that were found on top of a nearby hill. These structures, which possibly had a religious function, include whitewashed rooms with benches and centrally positioned hearths. Period IV in fact marks Mundigak's transition from a village to a major urban centre. Its size increased dramatically, from 6/8 ha in Period III to 55/60 ha in Period IV, although it should be noted that not all the area was inhabited. This development was not restricted to Mundigak. The same building

---

21 On the Plateau, similar tablets and other evidence for contacts with Elam were recovered from Tepe Sialk IV, near Kashan; Tall-i Iblis V; and Tepe Hisar II.

activities occurred at Damb Sadaat (Period III) in the Quetta Valley, and at Mehrgarh, Period VII, where a large mudbrick platform was erected.

Period IV of Mundigak yielded many stone compartmented stamp seals and a spiral-headed bronze pin. There are plenty of alabaster vessels and other stone vessels with geometric designs. This type of vessel is found all over the Plateau, and also in the Indus valley and in Mesopotamia. A general decline is noticeable in the production of female figurines, although examples were found in the early phases of this period of the so-called 'Zhob Mother Goddess', a type of female figurine that is also widely found further east, in modern Pakistan (e.g. Mehrgarh VII). There is also a decline in the amount of painted pottery, although it should be noted that in the early levels of Period IV pottery decorated with zoomorphic motifs was found.

The finds from Mundigak IV and settlements to the east recall comparable discoveries from sites further west, in Sistan. To the archaeologists studying the material culture of Shahr-i Sokhta, Mundigak, Damb Sadaat and a number of neighbouring sites, the parallels in material culture are very strong and the whole assemblage has accordingly been dubbed the 'Hilmand Civilization'.[22] Periods II and III of the huge site of Shahr-i Sokhta yielded black-on-buff and black-on-red wares, anthropomorphic and theriomorphic figurines and evidence for the wide-spread use of compartmented stamp seals. In Period III (as at Mundigak IV), there is a sharp reduction in painted wares. The 'monumental architecture' of Mundigak IV can be compared to the urban character of Shahr-i Sokhta. As at Mundigak, the size of the site increased considerably, from about 15/17 ha in Period I to approximately 150 ha in Period III.[23] Huge amounts of finished and unfinished stone artefacts and other remains were found. It is clear that the site acted as a production centre for the whole area, and perhaps also for lands much further to the east or west. Trade may indeed have been one of the major factors in the rise of these early urban centres of the Hilmand Civilization,[24] although ethnic differentiation, related to a possible influx of newcomers from the north in the Mundigak III period, may also have been a contributing factor. In this way, the growing contacts with the outside world, as so often in the history of Afghanistan, led to the further economic development and social and ethnic stratification of the people living on the Plateau.

22   Lamberg-Karlovsky and Tosi 1973:26.
23   See Tosi, Malek Shahmirzadi and Joyenda 1992 (1996):204.
24   The importance of trade for the emergence of the Middle Bronze Age cultures on the Plateau was particularly emphasized by Ph. Kohl in various of his studies. Compare also Potts 1994.

The Indus Civilization

One of the most famous finds from Mundigak derives from the later levels of Period IV. It is a white calcite head of a man with his hair bound in a fillet.[25] This item is one of the few objects from Mundigak and the Hilmand Civilization that show close parallels to the artistic repertoire of the so-called Indus Civilization.[26] This highly evolved culture flourished in the Indus valley and the northeastern parts of the Iranian Plateau in the second half of the third millennium BC. Its emergence should thus be placed at the same time or somewhat later than that of the Hilmand Civilization, and the calcite head would indicate that at least the later phases of Mundigak Period IV were contemporary with some stage in the development of the Indus Civilization.

The Indus Civilization was only properly brought to light from the 1920s onwards. It is characterized by an evolved degree of planning and by a high standardization of various aspects of material culture. It covered a huge area of land, including the Panjab (with its main site of Harappa) and the lower Indus Valley (including the huge town of Mohenjo Daro) and the coastal regions of western India and southern Pakistan. Towns and villages were built according to a uniform plan. The houses were constructed of burnt brick and the towns were fortified and provided with public drainage systems and wells. The people used a uniform system of weights and measures. Characteristic are the wheelmade, painted vessels, which were mass-produced and examples of which are found everywhere. Archaeologists have also discovered large numbers of rectangular seal-stones that are engraved with inscriptions in a non-alphabetic and hitherto undeciphered script.[27] Subsistence was based on the cultivation of cereals and pulses, together with dates and other products. Livestock included sheep, goats, cattle (especially the zebu), pigs, cats and dogs. Camels, probably two-humped, were also kept, at least by the so-called Mature Harappan period. The remains of horses are only known from the latest phases, well into the second millennium.

---

25 It was exhibited in the Kabul Museum. Its whereabouts at present are unknown.
26 Literature about the Indus Civilization is enormous. Compare *Vergessene Städte am Indus. Frühe Kulturen in Pakistan vom 8. bis 2. Jahrtausend*, Mainz am Rhein 1987.
27 The script, which ran from right to left, may reflect a Dravidian language. The inscriptions are generally found on the stone seals and hardly ever count more than 20 characters. Recently, a large inscription of some 400 characters was discovered at the Indian site of Dholavira.

Contacts were established with the Persian Gulf, Mesopotamia and the Iranian Plateau. Mesopotamian sources relate to extensive overseas contacts, throughout the second half of the third millennium, with the lands of Dilmun, Magan and Meluhha. While Dilmun and Magan were located in or near to the Persian Gulf, the land of Meluhha probably represents the Indus delta. It was known as a source of ivory, various types of wood, and metals, such as copper, gold and tin. Lapis lazuli and carnelian are also mentioned, which would indicate that Meluhha was an intermediate station in the trade of various products from the Iranian Plateau.

The exploitation by the people of the Indus Civilization of resources in what is now Afghanistan was dramatically illustrated in the late 1970s. Along the Amu Darya, close to its confluence with the Kokcha river in Badakhshan, a number of Indus Civilization sites were brought to light. One of these, the two ha site of Shortughai, was excavated by French archaeologists between 1977 and 1979.[28] The place was probably linked to the trade of semi-precious materials, including lapis lazuli, which are found in nearby Badakhshan. The finds from Shortughai include all the characteristics of the Indus sites: bricks with the same size as in the Indus valley; pottery, including those with depictions of the very 'Indian' peacock; and a seal with the engraving of an, equally 'Indian', rhinoceros. A survey of the environment of the site showed the remains of a canal that dates to the same period and which led water from the Kokcha river (some 20 km from Shortughai) to the lands around the site.

While Shortughai shows clear evidence of the extent of the Indus Civilization onto the extreme northeastern parts of the Plateau, there are hardly any indications, bar the calcite head, as to the influence of the Indus Civilization in the southeast of Afghanistan. In fact, the Hilmand Civilization came to an end around this time. The settlement of Mehrgarh (Period VII) was deserted in the mid-third millennium, while a nearby settlement, Nausharo, showed a clear continuity from a Mehrgarh Period VII occupation to a next phase that showed all the characteristics of the Indus Civilization. Further onto the Plateau, in the Quetta Valley, the site of Damb Sadaat was deserted, also around the mid-third millennium BC. As for Mundigak, it should be noted that the calcite head was found in the later levels of Period IV. These later phases of Period IV at Mundigak, generally dated to the second half of the third millennium, mark a period of decline and much of the site was eventually deserted. A similar

---

28   This is only one of the sites in the region that date to the third millennium BC. For a bibliography of Shortughai, see Ball 1982: No. 1089. See also Francfort 1989; Gentelle 1989; Lyonnet 1997.

development took place at Shahr-i Sokhta in Sistan, which shrunk to a small settlement of some six ha. In sum, it is clear that the Hilmand Civilization came to an end in the second half of the third millennium, while the Indus Civilization was still flourishing.

The same general collapse took place in Turkmenistan, although apparently somewhat later than in South Afghanistan. The Namazga sequence reached its zenith in the late third millennium in the so-called Namazga V period. During those years, contacts were maintained with the Indus valley and with Mesopotamia. This was also the time of the Indus Civilization occupation of Shortughai in Badakhshan. The Namazga sites yielded ample evidence of the influence of the Indus Civilization: beads, figurines and pottery all testify to the extent of the trade networks that crossed the Plateau in the second half of the third millennium BC. It is therefore very attractive to suggest that the decline of the Hilmand Civilization was, apart from other as yet unknown factors, caused by a general abandonment of the southern trade route via modern South Afghanistan. Instead contacts were maintained by a more northern land route and by a much more southern, overseas exchange network.

Strikingly absent from the archaeological record is most of northern Afghanistan, between Shortughai to the east and the Namazga lands to the west. By the mid-third millennium, there were, as far as is known to date, no substantial settlements in the plains of the north, either belonging to the Namazga sequence or to the Indus Civilization. It may very well be, however, that archaeological data are as yet insufficient. The discovery of the so-called Fullol hoard at Khush tepe, in Baghlan province north of the Salang Pass, may indicate that northern Afghanistan was not the virginal land it appears to have been.[29] At this site, in 1966, a collection of gold and silver vessels was discovered, which show definite parallels in decoration to Mesopotamian objects and to items from south of the Hindu Kush, although the date of this hoard is still unknown. It should perhaps be related to the so-called Bactria-Margiana Archaeological Complex (BMAC), which emerged in northern Afghanistan in the late third millennium, but the hoard may also be of a slightly earlier date, in which case it would indicate the extent of western and southern traditions into this region. Considering the importance of Badakhshan for the trade in semi-precious stones, this would be very well possible. But even if this is the case, the northern plains apparently remained uncolonized. The reason may be the fact that the deltas of the various rivers that descend down the Hindu Kush into the plains

---

29 Ball 1982: No. 582. See also N. H. Dupree et al. 1974:9–10, for the Fullol hoard as exhibited in the Kabul Museum.

of North Afghanistan were very difficult to canalize and to use for large-scale irrigation. This only happened in the late third millennium with the rise of the BMAC, but by that time the Hilmand Civilization in South Afghanistan had disappeared and the Namazga sequence of Turkmenistan and the Indus Civilization of the eastern plains were in decline.

4

The Advent of the Indo-Iranian Speaking Peoples

From the late second millennium BC onwards, indirect accounts have been transmitted, from both India and Iran, which testify to the arrival of large numbers of new immigrants on the Iranian Plateau and in the Indian subcontinent.[1] The immigrants introduced new languages and cultures, and they were destined to mould the region's history until the present day. Much of their early history is hypothetical and based on circumstantial evidence, since ancient migrants generally did not leave behind written statements as to their identity and their language; neither did they tend to record their ancient history. What is clear from the archaeological record discussed in the preceding chapter is that they arrived in lands that had gone through a period of gradual development and, at certain places, subsequent decline. This process included the emergence of proto-urban centres with craft specialization and extensive networks of contacts with other settlements on the Plateau, and also with cities beyond, in Elam and Mesopotamia to the west, and in the Indus valley to the east.

The evidence for their presence is mainly based on the circumstance that the newcomers brought with them the Indo-Iranian languages. These tongues are still, to this day, the dominant languages in Iran, Afghanistan and the Indian subcontinent and they constitute a branch of the large Indo-European language family. Following the *communis opinio*, the speakers of proto-Indo-European originated somewhere in the steppes of South Russia and the Ukraine between the fifth and third millennia BC. The earliest Indo-Iranian records from India date roughly to the late-second millennium BC. These are the hymns contained in the *Rig Veda*. It may thus safely be assumed that the Indo-Iranian speaking peoples separated themselves from those speaking other Indo-European languages long before the mid-

---

1 For a fairly up-to-date account of the Indo-Europeans and their languages, see Mallory 1989. See also the various issues of the *Journal of Indo-European Studies*.

second millennium BC. But how did they get to the Plateau and the Indian subcontinent?

From South Russia to the Iranian Plateau and India, there are three possible routes. They lead (a) via southeastern Europe and across modern Turkey, (b) directly across the Caucasus between the Black Sea and the Caspian Sea, and (c) across the Ural mountains and along the various oases of South Central Asia, east of the Caspian. The western route, across modern Turkey, seems most unlikely, although recently reintroduced as a possibility by the Russian archaeologist Sarianidi on the basis of the archaeological record.[2] The routes across the Caucasus are also an unlikely option, since the Caucasus is not an easy mountain range to pass in great numbers and the historical record from later centuries shows that it was hardly ever used for large-scale migrations from north to south.[3] The third option, a route east of the Caspian, therefore seems most likely. From later centuries we know that this passage was used time and again by people from the north to migrate to the Iranian Plateau.

On their way to the Plateau, the Indo-Iranian speaking peoples thus at some time in their history crossed the Urals from west to east and entered the steppes north of the Aral Sea in what is now Kazakhstan. Some of them subsequently moved south, along the age-old routes that connect Central Asia with the Iranian Plateau. The routes all lead to present-day North Afghanistan and the northern flanks of the Iranian Plateau. From there they moved further south, via the gap in the mountains between Mashhad and Herat, and via the Hindu Kush passes further to the east. We simply do not know which of these routes was taken by the Indo-Iranians. At some time in their wanderings they probably used both and probably a number of minor ones as well, but in all cases the Indo-Iranian migrants first came into contact with the peoples living north of the mountains, including the lands of modern North Afghanistan, before ascending the Plateau.

Indo-European and Indo-Iranian

The Indo-European language family is strictly speaking a linguistic phenomenon. Apart from Indo-Iranian it encompasses Armenian, Greek, the Italic languages (among others, Latin), Germanic (with English, German and Dutch), Celtic, Balto-Slavonic (including

2   Sarianidi 1998. This possibility was adequately refuted by Mallory, in Sarianidi 1998:180ff.
3   Compare Diakonoff 1985:49ff.

Russian). It also encompasses lesser-known language families such as Anatolian (including Hittite), the Illyrian languages (including Albanian) and Tokharian (from the extreme western parts of China). The oldest traces of Indo-European date to the early and mid-second millennium BC. These are the cuneiform records of the Hittites in Anatolia, the Greek of the Mycenaeans (Linear B) and the Vedic Sanskrit of Northwest India.

Etymological studies of the Indo-European languages have revealed certain common words that shed light on the ancient so-called proto-Indo-European culture. These words indicate that the people practised agriculture and were accompanied by domesticized animals (including the horse). They made pottery, wove their clothes and other textiles, and their means of transport included wheeled vehicles. These aspects indicate that the proto-Indo-Europeans were still living together in roughly the same area by at least the early sixth millennium BC, but probably later.[4] This is roughly the time of the Secondary Products Revolution, as defined by Andrew Sherratt.[5] The term refers to the use of cattle for milk production and traction; that of sheep and goats for wool and milk, and to uses of plants other than direct consumption.

The term Indo-Iranian is coined after its two main sub-branches, namely Indo-Aryan and Iranian. At present it includes the Indian (Indo-Aryan) languages (including Hindi, Bengali, Naipali),[6] and the Iranian languages, which embrace modern Persian, Kurdish, Pashto, Baluchi, and many other tongues.[7] The Kafiri languages from Nuristan are also Indo-Iranian, but they apparently constitute a separate, third branch, being neither specifically Indo-Aryan nor Iranian. From their present distribution it can be concluded that the Indo-Aryans preceded the Iranians. The first passed through modern Afghanistan before descending into the Indian subcontinent. They were followed, or pushed from behind, by their Iranian kinsmen who eventually remained on the Iranian Plateau. The Iranian migrations onto the Plateau must have started by at least the late second millennium, since Assyrian sources from the late ninth century BC refer to the land of *Madai* and *Parsuash* (Classical Media and Persia). These districts

---

4   This does not mean that the proto-Indo-Europeans necessarily formed a culturally and linguistically homogeneous group.
5   Sherratt 1981.
6   These are the so-called Modern Indo-Aryan (Indian) languages. They find their origins in the so-called Prakrit or Middle Indian languages (as for instance Gandhari and Pali). In turn these derive from the Old Indian languages (Vedic and Sanskrit).
7   These are the New Iranian languages. There are also Middle Iranian languages, as for instance Middle Persian, Sogdian, Bactrian, etc. Old Iranian languages include Avestan and Old Persian.

were located in and beyond the Zagros mountains, east of the Mesopotamian plains. It is likely that the people living there were the ancestors of the Medes and Persians, the two West Iranian tribal confederacies that would dominate the Plateau for many centuries to come.[8]

From the fact that the Indo-Iranians occupied much of the Iranian Plateau and northern India it is safe to conclude that whatever routes they followed, they came in large numbers and more or less pushed the autochthonous population out of the way. The Indo-Iranian wanderings were indeed a dramatic occurrence, the first of the documented large-scale migrations of people from Central Asia onto the Plateau and beyond. In centuries to come they would be followed by Scythians, Huns, Turks, Mongols and Özbeks.

The (Indo-)Iranian speaking groups are also the people who eventually gave their name to the land of Iran (and to *Ariana* Afghan Airlines[9]). They called themselves *Arya*,[10] and in the (Old Iranian) Avesta of the Zoroastrians the people call their land *A'ryânâm Vaêjah* (*Erân Vêz* in Middle Persian), 'Expanse of the Aryans', or **A'ryânâm Kshathra* (*Erân Shahr*), 'Realm of the Aryans'. Among the ancient Iranians, the name was used to denote a kinship level above that of the confederacies of tribes (Persians, Medes), but clearly separating them from the (in Avestan) *ana'rya* ('non-aryans'; compare Greek *Anariákai*).[11] In other words, the Iranians were at the time that they coined these phrases still very well aware that they belonged to one nation. A good example of the self-identification of the Iranians is given by the Persian Achaemenid king, Darius (*r.* 522–486 BC), in some of his texts (DNa; DSe), where he tells 'I am Darius the Great King . . . son of Hystaspes, an Achaemenian, a Persian, son of a Persian, an Aryan, having Aryan lineage.'[12] In Classical works we correspondingly find the name of *Ariane*, obviously coined after the

8   Compare Brandenstein and Mayrhofer 1964:1–4.

9   The 'Aryan' background of Afghanistan was probably introduced in Afghanistan in the 1930s when Germany had become an important partner of the country and set up, among other things, the first regular air link with Europe (Kabul to Berlin). Before that time, the Pashtuns were more inclined to link their origins to the Bani Israel (Caroe 1958:3ff.; Elphinstone 1815:154–7). Compare also the royal palace in Kabul that used to be guarded by sentries with German helmets and swastikas (according to Levi 1984:32).

10   In Sanskrit *ârya*; in Avestan *a'rya*; in Old Persian *ariya*. The word may be linked to that for 'man' (compare Greek *anér*; and the Latin name Nero; see Lecoq 1997:33).

11   Herodotus (*Historiae* VII 62 [hereafter *Hist.*]) tells that the Medes used to be called 'Arioí; he also refers to another group of the Medes, the 'Arizantoí (*idem* I 101).

12   Trans. Kent 1953:138.

Iranian word, which the Greeks used to describe a large part of the Iranian Plateau, including modern-day Afghanistan.[13]

The Steppe Bronze Age

At some time long before the mid-second millennium BC, the Indo-Iranians moved from the Indo-European *Heimat* in the west to the steppes east of the Urals, before moving south to the Iranian Plateau. To understand something about the Indo-Iranians before they arrived in Afghanistan it is useful to see whether they can be traced in Central Asia. In recent years, archaeological investigations have indeed shed some light on the material culture of the people living there in the fourth, third and second millennia BC.

Recent archaeological discussions on the early history of Central Asia agree that by at least the late fourth or early third millennium BC pastoralists had spread from west of the Urals to as far east as the Yenisei and the Mongolian mountains in the east. These pastoralists, probably of Indo-European and in particular Indo-Iranian stock, made extensive use of the horse, also for riding.[14] The influence from the west is seen in the parallels between the so-called Yamnaya Culture from west of the Urals and the Afanasievo Culture from east of the mountains. The Yamnaya Culture is generally dated from the middle of the fourth to the late third millennia BC.[15] Its name derives from the fact that the people buried their dead in pits or shafts (*yamna*), often covered with a burial mound or *kurgan*. The corpses were laid down with flexed legs and were covered with ochre. Grave-goods include pottery and livestock. Only a few settlements have been found,[16] thus indicating that the people of the Yamnaya Culture were predominantly nomadic pastoralists, constantly moving with their herds across the steppes. The people raised goats and sheep, but they also had horses, pigs and cattle. They rode their horses, but they also used wagons, both four and two-wheeled, although it is not clear whether they were drawn by oxen or horses.

The carriers of the Yamnaya Culture seem to have spread to the east, giving the impetus to the establishment of the aforementioned Afanasievo Culture, by at least the turn of the fourth/third millennia

---

13 Strabo XV 2.8.
14 At the fourth/third millennia BC site of Boatai, in Kazakhstan, 99 per cent of the animal bones were of horses (Christian 1998:85).
15 Its origins are generally placed in the preceding Srednyi Stog and Khvalynsk cultures.
16 The largest site being Mikhailovka, of some 1.5 ha.

BC. One of the best known centres of the Afanasievo Culture lies in the Minusinsk area, near modern Krasnoyarsk, but comparable remains have been found all over northern Kazakhstan. The material culture of the 'Afanasievo' people was very similar to that of the Yamnaya Culture. Again, since only a few settlements have been found, the people were probably predominantly nomadic pastoralists who moved their herds over large distances. As in the case of the Yamnaya Culture, the excavated skeletons indicate that the people of the Afanasievo Culture were almost certainly of Europoid origin.

Dating from the mid-third millennium, Russian archaeologists indicate great changes all over the steppe belt. West of the Urals, this is the time of the Srubnaya (timber grave) Culture. East of the Urals, it is that of the Andronovo Culture. As in earlier centuries, the material culture from west and east of the Urals is very similar. On both sides of the mountains there are more settlements than before and these are more often than not fortified. It seems in general that people become more sedentary, although pastoralism is still widespread. Horses become more important, and at the site of Sintashta, near Magnitogorsk just east of the Urals, horse burials were found together with the remains of two-wheeled carts, or 'chariots'.[17] These burials date to c.2000 BC or earlier. By that time kurgans rose in large numbers above the flat landscape, no doubt the resting-places of the chiefs.

In recent years, a large number of mummies and other finds have been unearthed in the extreme east of the Eurasian steppe belt, namely in the Uyghur Autonomous Region, in the northwest of modern China, close to modern Kazakhstan. These mummies date to a period from about 2000 BC onwards and many of them show strong Europoid features. They were buried with few grave goods, and what has survived in many cases was their woollen clothing.[18] Another interesting feature are the carefully bundled twigs of ephedra found in many of the graves.[19] Ephedra has for long been one of the possibilities for the identification of the *Haoma/Soma* plant, which was used for the preparation of the sacred hallucinogenic drink of the Indo-Iranians. There is no way in which we can definitely identify the ancient people from western China with Iranians or Indo-Iranians.[20] Yet, whatever their cultural and linguistic background, they lived in close proximity to those generally associated with the Steppe Bronze Age cultures discussed above. These in their turn are likely candidates

17   Compare Anthony and Vinogradov 1995.
18   Barber 1999.
19   Ibid., pp. 159f.
20   They might also have been the ancestors of those who in the first millennium AD left their traces in texts written in (equally Indo-European) Tokharian A and B.

for the forebears or kinsmen of the Indo-Iranians who around the mid-second millennium BC invaded the Iranian Plateau.

The Indo-Aryans

The oldest written sources in Indo-Iranian are the ancient Vedic texts from India; parts of the Avesta, the holy book of the Zoroastrians, from Iran; and certain cuneiform texts from the Middle East which relate to the Mitanni.

The Vedas are composed in an ancient form of Sanskrit, which itself marks an early stage in the development of many modern Indian languages. The Vedic texts from India, and especially its oldest part, the *Rig Veda*, approximately date to the second half of the second millennium BC or slightly later. Its geographical horizon is limited to the northwest of the Indian subcontinent, approximately equivalent to modern northern Pakistan. Only in later Vedic texts, and later Sanskrit literature, do we find a shift further south-eastward of the cultural centre of the Indians, towards the plains of the Ganges and Yamuna.

The *Rig Veda* lists various names of rivers that can be identified with existing names and rivers in the borderlands of Afghanistan and Pakistan. There are references to the *Gomati* (perhaps the Gumal river in the borderlands), *Kubhâ* (Kabul), *Suvastu* (Swat, north of Peshawar), the *Sindhu* (Indus).[21] Another interesting name is that of *Gandhâri*, which can directly be linked to the name of Gandhara, which is known from later Indian sources, and from Classical texts. It was the name used for the district around modern Peshawar and ancient Taxila, in northern Pakistan. From the texts it is evident that the people speaking Vedic were relative newcomers in the Indian subcontinent. They talk about wars, apparently with the autochthonous population of the land, and they refer to their chariots, which played an important role in their rituals.

On the basis of the geographical horizon of the Vedic texts, and their language, it is safe to assume that the ancestors of those who composed these ancient texts originated from outside of the northwestern parts of the subcontinent, from the northern side of the mountains of Afghanistan. At some time during their wanderings, the Indo-Aryans must therefore have resided, however briefly, in what is now Afghanistan, before they moved down into the Indus valley. In the process it is more than likely that some of them remained behind, perhaps north of the mountains, but more than likely to the south

21   Compare Stein 1917.

of the mountains, as for instance in the Kabul valley and in the Afghanistan/Pakistan borderlands.[22]

Near Eastern Sources

The Indian subcontinent is not the only place where evidence of the earliest Indo-Iranians has been found. Cuneiform records from the Near East have yielded a few words and names that are clearly Indo-Iranian, and probably Indo-Aryan in origin.[23] These words were used among the Mitanni of northern Syria. The Mitanni apparently constituted the ruling class of the local Hurrite (non-Indo-Iranian, Caucasian) population of the area. The Hurrites, and their Mitanni, derived from the east and northeast, from the Iranian Plateau. Around the middle of the second millennium BC they established a vast realm and maintained close contacts with the Hittites on the Anatolian Plateau and with the Egyptians in the Nile Valley. At that time, they were known for their expertise in horse training and chariot manufacture. The chariots now in the Egyptian Museum, Cairo, originally from the tomb of Tutankhamun, may well derive from the Mitanni. Various items in Tutankhamun's wardrobe, namely one of his tunics, an accompanying hip-wrap, a pair of sandals, his gauntlets and perhaps even his socks, have also been attributed a Mitanni origin or at least Mitanni inspiration.[24]

One of the sources on Mitanni horse training is the still extant so-called Manual of Kikkuli. It includes technical terms that clearly show the Mitanni's close linguistic affinity to Indo-Iranian, and in particular to Indo-Aryan.[25] In addition, the names of Mitanni gods included in a Hittite text from c.1380 BC show links to the Indo-Iranian, and in particular the Indo-Aryan pantheon. The gods include *Mi-it-ra* (compare Indo-Aryan Mitra), *Aru-na* (Varuna),[26] *In-da-ra* (Indra) and the *Na-sa-at-tiya* (Nasatyas).[27]

The information about the Mitanni seems to indicate that their Indo-Iranian component was Indo-Aryan, rather than Iranian.[28] It

---

22   This point was discussed in detail by Burrow 1973.
23   For the Mitanni, see Kammenhuber 1968 and Mayrhofer 1966, 1974. Whether or not the words are Indo-Aryan, compare Diakonoff 1993.
24   For these chariots, see Littauer and Crouwel 1985. For Tutankhamun's wardrobe, see Vogelsang-Eastwood 1999.
25   For these and other words, see Harmatta 1992 (1996):372–3.
26   This reading is disputed. See Diakonoff 1993.
27   These names occur in a treaty text between the Mitanni Sattiwazza (or Matiwaza) and the Hittite king Suppiluliumas I.
28   See especially Mayrhofer 1966.

should be clear, however, that the words and names used by the Mitanni do not prove that any stratum of Mitanni society actually spoke Indo-Aryan. Even the apparently Indo-Aryan names of some of the Mitanni kings do not prove that they spoke Indo-Aryan, or that their ancestors ever did. The least that can be inferred is that the Hurrites/Mitanni had somehow been in contact (directly or indirectly) with Indo-Aryan groups. These introduced them, among other things, to the manufacture of chariots and the tactics of chariot warfare, horse training, and the names of some deities. It also means that these contacts were established before the Indo-Aryans disappeared from the Plateau and were replaced by a second wave of Indo-Iranians, namely the Iranians themselves. Considering the date of the Mitanni, it can thus be concluded that the interaction between the Hurrites/Mitanni on the one hand and the Indo-Aryans on the other took place sometime in the first half of the second millennium at the latest.

Before the Indo-Iranians

In Afghanistan and the rest of the East Iranian world, immigrants from the north thus eventually replaced the autochthonous population. The newcomers spoke an Indo-Iranian language, either Indo-Aryan or, at a later date, Iranian. It is also likely that they, or at least some of them, arrived on the Plateau by the mid-second millennium BC at the latest. The world described in the oldest sources (*Vedas* and *Avesta*) is one of people primarily concerned with animal husbandry. Such a world would correspond well with what we know from archaeological research in Central Asia. It does not tally with the urban culture, its evolved craft specialization and long-distance trade that flourished on the Plateau during much of the third millennium. Some of the newcomers or their ancestors may of course have been in contact with the sedentary world of the Iranian Plateau for some time, but the bulk of the Indo-Iranians clearly remained virtually aloof from developments in the oases of South Central Asia and Afghanistan. It is therefore likely that they arrived in the lands along the Hindu Kush sometime between the late third and the mid-second millennium BC, and moved on relatively quickly. Who exactly were the people who lived in Afghanistan before the tidal wave of Indo-Iranian speaking peoples?

There are, in fact, still some people left in Afghanistan who speak a non-Indo-European language that may have been spoken in the area before the arrival of the new immigrants. In the south, and in neighbouring Pakistan, there is a group of people that speak Brahui. This language belongs to the Dravidian family of languages that is widely found in South India. Serious arguments have furthermore been brought forward that link Brahui and the Dravidian languages in general, to the language of the ancient Elamites from South and Southwest Iran.[29] If so, it would mean that in the years before *c.*2000 BC people speaking a Dravidian/Elamite language populated much of the Iranian Plateau.[30] Such a hypothesis is not as far-fetched as it seems. Elamite influence on the cultures and economy of the Iranian Plateau in the third millennium BC has been discussed above, and in the next chapter we will see that this influence continued well into the early second millennium. These contacts were perhaps stimulated by a linguistic relationship. If correct, it would mean that subsequent developments on the Iranian Plateau were very similar to what happened in the Indian subcontinent from the early first millennium BC onwards. Here the Indo-Aryan speakers slowly pushed the Dravidian speakers to the south. The same probably happened on the Plateau, and the Brahui were the only Dravidian speakers to remain, hidden in their secluded and barren valleys of East Baluchistan.[31]

Zarathustra

If to date little is known about the Indo-Aryans in Afghanistan, our information about the Iranians who followed in their wake is also disappointingly meagre.[32] Our main source is the *Avesta*.[33] This is the common name for a collection of texts, some of them of great antiquity, that are all that is left of a much larger corpus collected in the time of the Sasanian kings of Iran, sometime between AD 300 and 600. These texts form the holy book of the Zoroastrians or the Parsis as they are known in India, who are the followers of the prophet Zoroaster, called Zarathustra by the Iranians.

Zarathustra is the priest whose name is mentioned in the oldest part of the *Avesta*, in the so-called *Gâthâs*. He describes himself as a priest (*zaotar*) and tells about the revelation he received from Ahura Mazda, 'Lord Wisdom'. The religion revealed by Ahura Mazda differentiates between Good and Evil, or the Truth and the Lie. Good is represented by Ahura Mazda and his *Amesha Spenta*s ('immortal

---

29   Compare McAlpin 1981.
30   It has often been suggested that the people of the Indus Civilization spoke a language related to Dravidian/Elamite.
31   For a different hypothesis as to the origins of the Brahui, see Elfenbein 1987.
32   For Zoroastrianism, see e.g. Boyce 1975/1989; 1982; 1991; Varenne 1996.
33   The name Avesta is derived from Middle Persian *Apastâk*, '(basic) text' or 'injunction'.

holy ones'), together with some other, minor deities. Evil is represented by Angra Mainyu and a host of minor demons (*daevas*). Ahura Mazda created the world in order to establish a battleground to defeat Angra Mainyu. Man is asked to join the side of Truth and to fight against the Lie. Man thus has a moral choice. In the end, Truth will overcome the Lie and the world will be returned to its pristine state, without all the pollution counter-created by Evil, such as the mountains on the originally flat earth, the salt in the sea, etc.

The date of Zarathustra, his homeland, and even his existence are still disputed. Some date him to the second millennium BC. Others prefer a more recent date, sometime around 600 BC. It cannot be denied that the language of the *Gâthâs*, which is generally classed as an East Iranian language, is still very closely related to that of the oldest part of the Vedic literature, the *Rig Veda*. It is hardly likely that both texts are separated in time by many centuries. It could therefore be argued that at least the language of Zarathustra dates back to roughly the same time as that of the Vedic texts, namely to approximately the late second millennium BC.

Another question is the homeland of Zarathustra. The Avesta contains many names of places that can be located in Eastern Iran, and in particular in modern Afghanistan (see below). However, these passages are of a later date and do not prove that Zarathustra lived in the same area. Traditionally Zarathustra's name is connected to that of Bactria, the ancient name for the northern parts of modern Afghanistan. This identification is partly based on the identity of Vishtaspa, the patron of Zarathustra mentioned in the Avesta. His name reappears in the Old Persian texts of the Achaemenid Period as that of the father of King Darius (*r.* 522–486 BC), and that of many other people of rank who either officially or not were linked to Bactria. However, all this is rather speculative. Zarathustra is also sometimes linked to Azarbayjan in Northwest Iran, obviously because of the close link between the people who developed this identification, and their own homeland, namely Azarbayjan. The same could apply to Bactria; it may have been the place where the priests or others who spread the religion of Zarathustra originated, or at least the area that they regarded as most important.

To understand something more about the date and homeland of the Iranian prophet, it should first of all be realized that his world, like that of the Vedic priests that composed the *Rig Veda*, is one of cattle breeders. There are no urban centres and in the *Gâthâs* there are no references to faraway countries. If it is accepted that Zarathustra's language dates to approximately the late second millennium and that Zarathustra used a language that in his time was not archaic and not only used by priests, he should be dated to about that time. It may also be assumed that he lived somewhere in the east or north-east of the Iranian world, in a region that was dominated by Irani-ans who lived on animal husbandry, without contacts with urbanized life. Does this description fit Afghanistan and neighbouring lands of the second millennium? To answer this question, we have to turn in the next chapter to the archaeological record from ancient Bactria and Margiana.

Iranian Culture and Religion

Before trying to further pinpoint the arrival of the Indo-Iranians and the date of Zarathustra, it is necessary to emphasize one particular aspect of the Indo-Iranian cultures. This relates to the close similar-ities in religious life. Although the religion of Zarathustra is monothe-istic, this does not mean that other gods are not included in the Zoroastrian pantheon. Most of the gods of Zarathustra are also found among the Indo-Aryan deities. They include Indra, Mithra (Mitra), Verethraghna (compare the Vedic demon *Vrtra*), Naŋhaitya (Nasatyas), and others. In fact, the religion of Zarathustra is closely related to that of the Indo-Aryans who settled in the Indian subcon-tinent. Close parallels are the prominent position of the daily ritual of libations and prayers. In these, water and fire play a dominant role. Larger rituals include the use of *haoma* (Iranian) or *soma* (Sanskrit). This was a drink made of a plant or mushroom. It was hallucino-genic and made of a plant or fungus that grew in the mountains. At an early date it was replaced in India by another plant. In Iran, the Zoroastrians to the present day use the ephedra, called *hum* in many Iranian languages.[34] This identification would perhaps link the early Indo-Iranians to the occurrence of carefully bundled twigs of ephedra found in graves in the Uyghur Autonomous Region, near modern Ürümchi. Such bundles are also reminiscent of the bundles of twigs carried by the Zoroastrian priests (Avestan *barᵊsman-*) and the sacrificial grass used by their Indo-Aryan counterparts (Sanskrit *barhis-*).[35]

A most interesting phenomenon is the fact that in the Avesta the demons who support Angra Mainyu are called *daeva*, which in Indo-Aryan literature is the normal word for the gods (*deva*). One of these *daeva* demons is Indra, who in the Rig Vedic pantheon is one of the main deities. Zarathustra, or his predecessors, seems consciously to

---

34   Stein 1931; The name *Umân* or *Ume* (compare Old Iranian *Haoma*) in Pashto refers to the Ephedra plant. Compare Boyce 1975:157ff.
35   Boyce 1975/1989:167.

have opposed the structure of the Iranian pantheon to that which of old was prevalent among the Indo-Iranians and which continued to be upheld by the Indo-Aryans. In the later parts of the Avesta, the *daevas* and their activities are accentuated by the use of verbs and nouns that are clearly derogatory. Whether all this was instigated on purpose by Zarathustra and his followers in order to differentiate his religion from that of the Indo-Aryans who in his time still lived on the Plateau, as suggested by the British Indologist Burrow, remains an attractive, but controversial hypothesis.[36]

Whether Burrow was correct or not, it is apparent that in Zarathustra's time, and for centuries thereafter, there was no clear dividing line between 'Iranians' and 'Indians'. Their languages were still mutually understandable, and their religions and the rest of their culture were still comparable. The transition from *Irânshahr* to *Hindustân* was obviously very gradual, with Iranians and Indians living in close proximity to each other. In the later history of the area there are various references to this situation. For instance, in the Persian Achaemenid period, around 500 BC, people of obviously Indian origin were living in the hilly tracks immediately east of Qandahar. The 'anti-daevic' stance taken in the *Avesta*, which seems such a deliberate act, may thus well have been based on the wish on the side of the Zoroastrians to differentiate themselves from Indo-Aryans and others who lived so closely nearby.

36 Burrow 1973.

5

Archaeology and the Indo-Iranians

Sometime in the second millennium BC, people speaking Indo-Iranian languages settled and passed through the lands of what is now called Afghanistan. The Indo-Aryans came first, in the first half or middle of the second millennium, later followed by the Iranians. The first would move on, albeit not without affecting the ancestors of the Mitanni in northern Syria; the latter were to stay. Both the Indo-Aryans and the Iranians migrated in large numbers and their impact, once it reached its climax, must have been dramatic.

In the past it was often suggested that these new immigrants were responsible for the decline of the Indus Civilization, which collapsed around the beginning of the second millennium. The end of the Hilmand Civilization and that of the Namazga sequence in the late third millennium have also been attributed to them. Others have linked the arrival of the Indo-Iranians to the spread in northern Iran of handmade, painted pottery that marks the start of the Iron Age in the second half of the second millennium. Until relatively recently, it was impossible to find firm evidence for any of these suggestions, but new archaeological research in northern Afghanistan and neighbouring lands has shed new light on this fascinating problem.

While settled life in South Afghanistan declined in the late third millennium BC, a period of rapid growth took place in North Afghanistan. The first evidence of this development came to light in the late 1970s, when certain plundered objects from the north were sold in Kabul. These included various items that recalled the artistic work from Elam and Mesopotamia. On stylistic grounds, the objects were dated to the turn of the third to second millennium BC.[1] Soon, similar finds were brought to light in the Marw oasis, Turkmenistan, and at various sites in adjoining North Afghanistan.[2]

1 Compare the various publications by P. Amiet.
2 For a discussion of Bronze Age sites in North Afghanistan, see especially Kohl 1984:159ff. and Sarianidi 1986; 1998.

The Bactria-Margiana Archaeological Complex

Between 1969 and 1979, Soviet archaeologists engaged in large-scale excavations and archaeological surveys in North Afghanistan. They soon discovered a number of sites that provided close parallels to the objects that shortly before had been introduced to the Kabul bazaar.[3] Some of the major sites were brought to light in the Dashli oasis, north of modern Aqcha and not far from ancient Bactra (Balkh).[4] Dashli 3, the main site of the oasis, includes an almost rectangular structure (88 × 84 metres along its sides), generally called 'the palace', and nearby another rectangular building ('the temple'), which inside contained a smaller, circular structure.

The 'palace' consists of a courtyard (40 × 38 metres) and a series of uniformly built rooms along its four sides. The other building is a rectangular, walled enclosure of some 130 × 150 metres, which housed a circular structure of about 36 metres in diameter. Excavations inside this round building yielded traces of fires and burnt animal bones. Nine rectangular towers protected its outer walls. Around this structure, and still within the outer walls of the 'temple', there were three concentric rings of buildings. The excavator, Viktor Sarianidi, suggested that a religious community used the site, and that the inner, circular building was used as a temple.[5] Ceramics, metal objects and stone tools accompanied a number of human burials within the round structure. The bodies were buried in a flexed position with the head towards the north. There were also, according to the excavator, a number of cenotaphs or empty graves, filled with pottery. Whatever its precise purpose, the building certainly fulfilled an important function in the daily life of the oasis inhabitants. Radiocarbon dates of finds from this oasis indicate that Dashli 3 was occupied sometime between the late third and the early second millennium BC.[6]

Another site nearby is Dashli 1. This place may be of a slightly later date than Dashli 3 and represents a rectangular site of 99 × 85 metres. The walls, built of sun-dried bricks, were strengthened by semi-circular towers, very different from the pilasters and rectangular towers of Dashli 3. Originally the walls of Dashli 1 rose to a height of some eight metres. Inside there was a complex of buildings.

---

3 For the Bactria-Margiana Archaeological Complex, see in particular Hiebert 1993; 1994 and Sarianidi 1998.
4 Ball 1982: No. 257.
5 Sarianidi 1986:61.
6 Hiebert 1993.

It is important to realize that the finds in Bactria have no substantial local antecedents. They are also very different from the finds in South Afghanistan, as for instance at Mundigak. The closest parallels to the finds in Bactria derive from the nearby Marw district, ancient Margiana, in modern Turkmenistan. In fact, the correspondences are so evident that archaeologists have started to describe this culture as the Bactria-Margiana Archaeological Complex (BMAC).

Parallels from Margiana

Margiana itself seems to have been settled in the preceding Namazga V Period. This was the time that the Indus Civilization was strongest and established outlying trading posts across the Hindu Kush at sites such as Shortughai in Northeast Afghanistan. Namazga V pottery was found at various places in Margiana and indicates the direct antecedents of the BMAC as brought to light in this area.[7] An early BMAC settlement is that of Kelleli 4, which consists of a square fortification of 125 metres. Its outer walls are provided by rectangular towers. Another important, early BMAC settlement with large-scale buildings is that of Gonur 1, which eventually extended over an area of at least 20 ha.[8] It includes a square fortress (80 metres) to the north and apparently a religious structure, measuring $c.120 \times 120$ metres, to the south. As at Kelleli 4 and Dashli 3, the defensive walls of the citadel have rectangular towers, while those of the 'temple', perhaps of later date, are circular.

Another spectacular BMAC site in Margiana is that of Togolok 21, which includes a rectangular structure of 140×100 metres. Semicircular towers strengthen its outer walls and in the middle rises a rectangular temple (?) complex.[9] Yet another site is the settlement of Taip I, which consists of a square fortress with the usual circular towers, surrounded by a settlement.

In general, the major sites in Margiana are grouped into a number of oases, all dominated by a 'capital'. The oldest group, that of Kelleli, lies in the north, while the youngest, that of Takhirbai, lies in the south. In between lie the oases of Taip, Gonur, Togolok, and others. Cultivation of the area thus seems to have slowly shifted from north to south.

---

7   Hiebert 1993:138.
8   For a description of the site, see Sarianidi 1998:83–9.
9   For a full description of the site of Togolok 21, see Sarianidi 1998:90–103.

In Margiana, the wheelmade pottery continues some earlier (Namazga V) forms, but there are also new traditions, including ceramics that are handmade with incised ornamentation. This type of pottery is usually held to indicate influences from the steppes further to the north, and it seems to increase in popularity in the later phases of BMAC.[10] New are also the large amounts of stone seals (or amulets) of the so-called Murghab style, which are flat and usually square in shape. Most of them are made of steatite. They carry figurines on both sides and have a hole for a cord. The figurines generally depict wild animals, but there are also examples showing a hero-type male figure holding two wild animals, recalling the Mesopotamian Gilgamesh epic. The seals belong to the tradition of stamp seals that was prevalent on the Plateau from the fourth millennium onwards, but their execution is very different. Related to these objects are metal (copper or bronze) compartmented seals, with a loop-handle on the reverse side.

Other 'new' objects include vessels with sculptured rims, the so-called ritual vessels; stone maces with twisted bands; pins with heads shaped like squeezed fists; ceremonial axes; footed alabaster vases; composite statuettes; stone kidney-shaped vessels, miniature columns and stone sceptres. The repertoire also includes cylinder seals, underlining the links with Mesopotamia where this type of seal was used for millennia.

Of particular interest are the earthenware containers from Togolok 21 and other sites in Margiana, which apparently contained remains of Ephedra. This plant has long been tentatively identified with the ancient *Haoma* or *Soma*, the sacred drink of the Indo-Iranians that is widely mentioned in their ancient sources. This has led the excavator of the site, Viktor Sarianidi, to link the Bactria-Margiana Archaeological Complex to the arrival in this area of Indo-Raniam speaking peoples.[11]

In spite of the very close parallels between the BMAC material culture in Margiana and in Bactria, one important difference is noteworthy. This relates to the almost total absence in Bactria of anthropomorphic figurines.[12] In Turkmenistan districts further to the west, during the Early and Middle Bronze Ages, these figurines had been very popular. This fact is of great interest, both as to the relative chronology of the BMAC settlements and to the nature of the BMAC as a whole. In this respect, it should be noted that in Margiana the

10 Compare Masson 1992 (1996).
11 Sarianidi 1998.
12 They are known from Jarkutan, north of the Amu Darya. Compare Sarianidi 1998:139.

anthropomorphic figurines only seem to occur in the earlier settlements, and they are absent from the later sites within the BMAC, as for instance in the Takhirbai oasis. The use of the figurines thus reflects a tradition that originated in the Early and Middle Bronze Ages in lands further west, and which was discontinued during the period of development of the BMAC (Late Bronze Age).

The Setting of BMAC

In Bactria and Margiana, the settlements of the BMAC reflect a new type of social organization, settled in virginal or near-virginal lands. The urban centres of the Hilmand Civilization and of the Namazga sequence had grown organically through a process of craft specialization and the development of exchange networks over large distances. The settlements of the BMAC in northern Afghanistan, to the contrary, suggest a form of large-scale colonization. The fortresses and temples fulfilled a local function and the BMAC sites controlled the local countryside. Furthermore, the extent of this fairly homogeneous culture over such a large extent of land, and continuing over several centuries, indicates a close and enduring interrelationship.

At a time that the Hilmand Civilization and the Namazga sequence came to an end, in the second half of the third millennium BC, the people of the BMAC seem to have found new lands and a new way to exploit their environment. Their cultivation of virginal and near-virginal lands in Margiana and northern Afghanistan would indicate that they had mastered advanced techniques of large-scale irrigation. Their main means of subsistence was no longer the production of goods for the international market. They were more or less self-sufficient. This does not mean that they did not maintain any contacts with the outside world.[13] It does mean that their economy was not dependent upon these contacts. Hence probably the success of the BMAC, and the reasons behind the decline of the Hilmand Civilization and the Namazga sequence. These cultures had been absorbed into a large-scale exchange network that covered the whole Plateau between the Indus and the Tigris. When exchange halted, for whatever reason, the major settlements in South Afghanistan, Eastern Iran and Turkmenistan received a blow from which they never recovered. The new settlements in ancient Margiana and Bactria, unaffected by these changes, continued to thrive.

---

13 Sarianidi has clearly demonstrated that many aspects of the material culture of the BMAC were strongly influenced by Mesopotamia and Elam.

Outside Contacts

BMAC settlements are not only found in North Afghanistan and ancient Margiana. An important site north of the Amu Darya is that of Sapalli Tepe, excavated by A. Askarov between 1969 and 1974.[14] It lies some five km north of the Amu Darya and about 70 km west of Termez. The earliest levels include a square fortress of 82 metres along its sides, with circular towers indicating a relatively late date in the development of BMAC. The pottery from the site is comparable to the wares from the BMAC complex. The sites of Sapalli and nearby Jarkutan, however, also revealed their own, highly interesting characteristics. At Sapalli the dead were buried in catacombs inside the settlement, often beneath the houses, and almost 200 burials were found. Men were laid down on their right side, while women were on their left. Noteworthy are the many weapons found in the tombs, both at Sapalli and at Jarkutan. Radiocarbon dates place the BMAC levels at Sapalli Tepe around 1750 BC.[15]

Jarkutan itself is a large site, covering more than 100 ha. It lies some 60 km north of the Amu Darya and the ancient town of Termez. The settlement includes a number of large building complexes, including a citadel of three ha which houses a palace (?) and a number of large buildings. There are also a temple, living quarters and a necropolis that contained more than a thousand skeletons. There are traces of ancient canals all over the site.

Typical BMAC items have also been found in lands far beyond. Miniature columns of a type well known in Margiana and Bactria were recovered in Pakistan, namely in Quetta[16] and at nearby Sibi.[17] At Mehrgarh (Period VIII), other objects of BMAC nature were brought to light.[18] The columns are also known from the foothills of the Kopet Dagh near Ashkhabad and at the site of Tepe Hissar in North Iran (Period III). Examples of the 'ritual vessels' with sculptured rim, which are well known from Margiana and Bactria, were found in Baluchistan: Sir Aurel Stein discovered a rim of a 'ritual vessel' in the cemetery of Kulli, in (Pakistani) Baluchistan.[19] At the same site he also found a 'miniature column'.[20] Nearby, at the site of

---

14 For a description of the site, see Masson 1992 (1996):343ff. and Sarianidi 1998:83–9.
15 Hiebert 1993:148.
16 Jarrige and Hassan 1989.
17 Santoni 1984. The cemetery included cenotaphs. The grave goods, apart from the miniature columns, included other objects reminiscent of BMAC.
18 Santoni 1984; Jarrige 1987.
19 Stein 1931, pl. XXXI.
20 Stein 1931, pl. XI.

Mehi, he discovered other objects that recall the material culture of
BMAC.[21] Another place where BMAC-related objects were found is
that of Shahdad in East Iran, near Kirman.[22]

The above finds indicate that BMAC, however self-sufficient, did
not remain limited to Margiana and Bactria. Specimens of its material culture found their way to the north, to the south and to the west.
Thus, in the late third and early second millennia, at a time that the
Hilmand Civilization had collapsed and the Namazga sequence and
Indus Civilization were in decline, contacts across the Plateau were
maintained. Full-scale BMAC sites, however, have to date not been
found anywhere in East Iran or South Afghanistan, and it appears
that BMAC remained linked to the newly discovered productivity
of the northern oases. So who were the people introducing BMAC
objects in the lands of Baluchistan, along the Indus valley, and in
the steppes south of the Iranian deserts? Some of them no doubt
were linked up with the exchange network that had been built up
in previous centuries and that is represented in the many objects
of obviously Mesopotamian origin found at the BMAC sites. But
there must have been others, taking BMAC objects to remote places
along the barren Makran coast, or depositing them in tombs in the
Quetta valley. Were these traders? Or were there other people
involved?

Chronology

Russian archaeologists date BMAC to a period between the late third
and the end of the second millennium BC.[23] Other archaeologists tend
to restrict the BMAC to a period between *c.*2000 and 1500 BC.[24]
Important in this respect is the site of Shortughai. Its early levels
belong to the Indus Civilization and date to the late third millennium.
On top, however, levels have been brought to light which relate to
BMAC. The finds from these levels can specifically be compared to
finds from later BMAC sites, such as Jarkutan. It thus seems that
Shortughai was included in the BMAC horizon at a relatively later
stage in the BMAC's development, and that this stage was not much
later than the beginning of the second millennium. It also means that
the earlier (Indus Civilization) levels of Shortughai were more or less
contemporary with the earlier phases of the BMAC.

21 Stein 1931, pl. VIII.
22 Hakemi 1972; Hakemi and Sajjedi 1988.
23 Sarianidi 1998:76–8.
24 Hiebert 1993:136–48.

The latest of the BMAC levels at Shortughai are attributed by radiocarbon dating to about 1600 BC. Of further relevance to the date of the end of the BMAC are the finds at the site of Yaz. This place, in ancient Margiana, belongs to the Iron Age and has yielded items and architecture that are totally different from that of the preceding BMAC sites. A radiocarbon date for Yaz Period I gives a period between *c.*1500 and 1300 BC.[25] It is therefore likely that the latest BMAC levels in Margiana, in the Takhirbai oasis, date to a period between *c.*1700 and 1500 BC. In general, BMAC may thus be dated to a period between the late-third and the mid-second millennium BC.

It is tempting, however, to date the earliest phases of BMAC even earlier. The Elamite-style silver pinhead (originally a seal) from Gonur, so proudly illustrated on the cover of Sarianidi's study of 1998, closely resembles a similar depiction on a silver vase from near Persepolis in Southwest Iran that is securely dated to *c.*2200 BC.[26]

BMAC and the Indo-Iranians

So who were the people of the BMAC? Were they Indo-Iranians? The answer would appear to be negative. The sedentary culture of the BMAC people does not tally with the culture of the Indo-Iranians as known to us from their own records. But still we know, or at least we think we know, that sometime during the first half or middle of the second millennium Indo-Iranians (and in particular Indo-Aryans) settled in, or at least passed through the lands of the BMAC. Are there any traces of these immigrants at all?

Important discoveries have recently been made further east from Bactria, in southern Tajikistan.[27] Here, during the second millennium BC, nomadism seems to have become more popular. Archaeological research shows a mixture of influences from the west (BMAC), and from the Andronovo steppe cultures of the north. The northern influence includes types of handmade pottery with incised decoration and other objects, including metal knives with curved-back tops, which have a clear Central Asian origin. At various sites, tumuli have been identified reminiscent of Andronovo-type burials. In the tombs, remains were found of dogs, camels and horses, clearly reminiscent of the northern Steppe Bronze Age.[28]

25   Hiebert 1993.
26   Klochkov 1998.
27   Compare Masson 1992 (1996):337–56 and Litvinsky and P'yankova 1992 (1996).
28   Compare P'yankova 1992 (1996).

Similar tumuli were recorded from the so-called Wakhsh culture sites, along the Wakhsh river, also in modern Tajikistan. The tumuli measure between two and fourteen metres in diameter. Corpses were inhumed, the men mostly along their right side; the women generally along their left. A similar feature was found at the nearby BMAC site of Sapalli. Pottery from the tombs is mostly handmade. Along the nearby Kafirnigan river, near Bishkent, corpses were buried, on their right or left side according to their sex, but also with small fires set in square hearths for men, and circular ones for women. Most of the pottery is handmade. At the site of Tulkhar, a group of graves was found with the remains of cremated bodies. Other traces of crema-tion are known from the Steppe Bronze Age cemetery of Tash Tepe north of the Syr Darya.[29]

The parallel use of inhumation and cremation is also found south of the Hindu Kush, among the remains of the so-called Gandhara Grave Culture, which is generally dated to the second and early first millennia BC.[30] The people of this Culture, which spread all over the lower valley of the Kabul river and up north into the Swat valley and beyond, may well have been related to the Indo-Iranians or to the Indo-Aryans in particular, as often surmized. To corroborate this point, the Indo-Aryan *Rig Veda* indicates that the ancient Indians practised both cremation and inhumation.[31]

Influences from the northern steppes are not only found in Tajik-istan and Uzbekistan. Russian archaeologists have reported the find of Timber Grave (Srubnaya) tombs along the Kopet Dagh mountain range east of the Caspian and the so-called Tazabagyab Culture (first half of the second millennium BC) from the lower Amu Darya is also reported to show clear links to the Timber Grave culture.[32]

In ancient Margiana, at the site of Takhirbai 3, next to the 'normal' interments of the BMAC, there were traces of partial cremation. In addition, some of the inhumations showed an anthropological type that is similar to that found among the Andronovo cultures from the north.[33] The Russian archaeologist, Masson, draws attention to the appearance in the Takhirbai oasis of the swastika as a motif on pottery,[34] the same motif that is also found in some of the tombs of the Tulkhar cemetery. What is important to realize is that the Takhir-bai oasis is one of the 'younger' BMAC oases in Margiana and Sar-ianidi classes it among the latest of the BMAC settlements in the area.

29   Masson 1992 (1996):350.
30   Compare Dani 1992 (1996).
31   Compare Allchin and Allchin 1982:307.
32   Masson 1992 (1996):350. For its date, see Kohl 1984:230.
33   Masson 1992 (1996):351.
34   Ibid.

The same relatively late date as compared to the BMAC period should be given to the tombs and related sites in Tajikistan, which often contain ceramics or other finds that link up with the later phases of the Sapalli BMAC levels.

Symbiosis and Decline

In conclusion, archaeological research has brought to light the emergence by the late third millennium of a highly developed culture in the Marw oasis and in ancient Bactria. There can be no doubt that BMAC flourished because of its organizational and technical success in increasing the agricultural production of the land. BMAC was a colonizing society. For those who lived in the Marw oasis, the Bactrian plains constituted the 'wild east', a land full of potential, but as yet still uncultivated. Chiefs resided in citadels that dominated the surrounding countryside. Close contacts with Elam and Mesopotamia cannot be denied, but there is no reason to assume that BMAC was a mere offshoot of Near Eastern Civilization. The finds in Margiana clearly show that the BMAC is a development of the Middle Bronze Age cultures that flourished in the third millennium in lands to the west, in modern Turkmenistan.

Yet contacts with the west were strong. Of great interest was the find at Gonur of a potsherd with what appear to be signs of Proto-Elamite B Linear script, dating to the late third millennium BC.[35] This would indicate that, by that time, the BMAC developed independently, but within the much wider world of exchange networks that stretched from the Near East, via the Iranian Plateau to the Indus valley. This would again indicate that BMAC emerged at the time that the Indus Civilization and the Elamite and Mesopotamian Civilizations were still flourishing. It would also strengthen the hypothesis that at that time Elamite was the main language being used and spoken on the Plateau.

From the materials discussed above it has also become clear that BMAC developed first in the Marw oasis and then spread to North Afghanistan and beyond. In the earliest BMAC sites in the Marw oasis, the persistence of local traditions is still evident. At the BMAC sites in North Afghanistan, the continuation of traditions from Turkmenistan, like the use of anthropomorphic figurines, is almost absent. What is found in association with the later phases of the BMAC is a growing mass of evidence that points at contacts with northern lands, with the steppe cultures of Central Asia, since long associated with

35 Compare Klochkov 1998.

the Indo-Iranians. This would indicate an initial symbiosis between Indo-Iranian pastoralists from the north and the sedentary, non-Indo-Iranian BMAC population from the south. This symbiosis expressed itself in various forms. Funerary practices would indicate that some Indo-Iranians settled among the sedentary population. Incised, hand-made pottery also refers to contacts with the north. The local people may also have adopted certain rituals, including the use of Ephedra. For all we know, some of the people of BMAC even adopted Indo-Iranian names, as in the case of the Mitanni who by *c.*1500 BC appear in the Near East. The use of horses and chariots may at the end have given the Indo-Iranians the edge to subdue at least some of the oasis settlements. In fact, some horses' bones have been found at Kelleli, Taip and Takhirbai, and there may also be a representation of a chariot.[36] In all, the military nature of many of the BMAC sites does indicate a less than peaceful environment.

Symbiosis does not mean that both groups were living separately from each other, with some sort of demarcation line in between. The BMAC people certainly exchanged their products with the Indo-Iranians living nearby, and vice versa. BMAC settlements populated by non-Indo-Iranians may have been built in lands further north, towards Sogdia in modern Kazakhstan. At the same time, Indo-Iranian pastoralists will have moved south, into and past the lands of the BMAC, in search of new pastures and booty. Some of them probably moved into the Hindu Kush mountains for the summer, as modern Afghans still tend to do. Other minor groups moved further south and southeast, towards the Indus valley, thus paving the way for their kinsmen who soon would follow *en masse* in their wake. Examples of BMAC material culture thus found their way to the Quetta valley and Baluchistan.

Whatever the specific ramifications we will probably never under-stand, there probably was, for some time, a situation of equilibrium. Symbiosis implies exchange between two parties. When at some stage one of the parties becomes too strong or too weak, the symbiosis is disrupted. In Margiana and Bactria this happened in the late first half of the second millennium BC when pressure from the north upon the oasis settlements of the BMAC simply became too strong for the sedentary population to resist. There was no longer any exchange. The Indo-Iranians who had been in constant contact with BMAC were themselves swept aside by their kinsmen who pushed from

36　Perhaps the famous cylinder seal from Tepe Hisar, Period III B, depicts a chariot. See especially Ghirshman 1977. Compare also the figurines of horse riders (?) from Pirak, southeast of the Bolan Pass in modern Pakistan, which date from the late first half of the second millennium onwards (Jarrige and Santoni 1979).

behind. Masses of Indo-Iranians settled and passed through the lands that formerly had been inhabited by the BMAC people, without adopting any of their characteristics. It was a matter of numbers. When the Indo-Aryans eventually arrived in the northwest of the Indian subcontinent, their knowledge of the BMAC culture was almost nil. Only recent archaeological research has brought this great civilization from northern Afghanistan back to life.

The Iron Age

After the mid-second millennium BC, the BMAC sites in Afghanistan and adjacent lands were replaced by a number of settlements that are traditionally attributed to the Iron Age, although at first iron constitutes a very scarce product.[37] If the BMAC settlements were dominated by the pre-Indo-Iranian population of the area, the Iron Age sites are likely to have been populated in the main by people speaking an Indo-Iranian language.

One of the 'type-sites' for the Early Iron Age in this part of the world is Yaz Depe in ancient Margiana. Radiocarbon dating indicates that the early phases of Yaz Depe should be attributed to a period between *c*.1500–1300 BC. In the mid-1950s the Soviet archaeologist V. M. Masson excavated at Yaz Depe a citadel of about one ha.[38] It was built on top of a platform of six metres high, surrounded by a fair-sized settlement (together with the citadel measuring some 16 ha). The excavator distinguished three main periods of occupation, the oldest of which (Period I) is associated with the erection of the platform and the citadel. In this period handmade wares, often painted, predominate. In the succeeding periods (Yaz II–III) wheelmade wares become more popular and cylindrical-conical vessels make their appearance. In Yaz II, the first iron implements were found. From later levels (Yaz III), bronze arrowheads with three wings were recovered.

The relationship with the remains of the BMAC levels is still not clear. The Russian archaeologist, Sarianidi, tells that Yaz I pottery was found in the latest levels of the BMAC sites,[39] and at Togolok 1 in Margiana the BMAC levels were covered by materials that belong to the (late) Yaz 1 Period.[40] There is also the evident shift of settlements from north to south, which already started in the Bronze Age.

---

37   For an introduction and discussion of the finds, see Kohl 1984:193–200 and Askarov 1992 (1996).
38   Masson 1959.
39   Sarianidi 1993:20.
40   Sarianidi and Koshelenko 1985:181.

Later settlements are likely to be found south and upstream along the Murghab, the main river of Margiana. Yaz Depe lies to the south-west of the Takhirbai oase, which marks the last stage of the BMAC in the area.

It is clear from the Yaz levels that its remains belong to a different culture. The sites of the Yaz 1 group are in general smaller than those of BMAC. The coarse handmade pottery, sometimes with simple geometric motifs, marks a clear break with the wheelmade, undecorated wares of BMAC. There are no terracotta figurines and no seals or amulets. In addition, the construction of the platforms is different from the architectural traditions of BMAC. The archaeologist Askarov consequently holds the opinion that the handmade pottery of the Early Iron Age is the result of an amalgamation of two traditions, namely that of the local population and that of the Steppe Bronze Age from the north.[41]

In North Afghanistan, there are a number of settlements that have yielded materials very similar to the finds from Yaz Depe. The most important of these is Tilla Tepe. It is located some five km north of Shibarghan, in modern Jawzjan province, in the northwest of the country.[42] The site consists of a man-made platform, rectangular, of some six metres high. The platform measures 36×28 metres. It was made of rectangular mudbricks and surrounded by a wall with circular towers. The pottery associated with the building of this platform includes handmade and wheelmade wares. Sarianidi distinguishes two succeeding periods. He is inclined to date the building of the platform to a period between *c.*1000 and 800 BC. Period II, dated by Sarianidi to *c.*800–600 BC, is characterized by an increased popularity of wheelmade pottery, including some black polished wares of unknown origin. In Period III (according to the excavator dating to the Persian Achaemenid period, *c.*600–400 BC), handmade wares are almost totally absent.

To date, Yaz 1-related sites are known roughly from an area between west of Ashkhabad, the modern capital of Turkmenistan, to beyond Tashqurghan in North Afghanistan.[43] The dating of the Yaz sequence remains a moot point, since there are only a few radiocarbon datings. For Yaz Depe there is a date of *c.*1400 BC.[44] For the Early Iron Age levels of Kuchuk Tepe in Uzbekistan a date is given of *c.*1100 BC,[45] and for Tilla Tepe, in North Afghanistan, there is a

41   Askarov 1992 (1996):453.
42   Ball 1982: No. 1192; Kohl 1984:199; Sarianidi 1972; 1986:85–8; 1989.
43   Compare Ball 1982: Vol. II, map 59, on p. 475.
44   Hiebert 1993:144.
45   Kohl 1984:236.

date of *c*.1000 BC.[46] However, the different techniques of calibrating the radiocarbon dates are misleading and the last two dates may be too young. A beginning of the Early Iron Age in this part of the world sometime in the second half of the second millennium BC seems most likely.

If the BMAC was carried in the main by non-Indo-Iranian speaking people, there can hardly be any doubt that the succeeding Iron Age represents the domination of the countryside by a different group of people. In view of the material culture of the early Iron Age sites in the region and the history of northern pressure upon the BMAC in previous centuries, there can hardly be any doubt as to the identity of the newcomers. They must have belonged to the Indo-Iranian Steppe Bronze Age. But did the people who built the citadels that by the late second millennium dotted the Bactrian landscape speak an Indo-Aryan or an Iranian language? To answer this question we can only speculate. The Indo-Aryans had penetrated into the Indian subcontinent by the late-second millennium. The same group had influenced the ancestors of the Mitanni by the late first half of the second millennium, at the latest. The presence of Indo-Aryans in northern Afghanistan would therefore have partly coincided with the BMAC. If Indo-Aryan-speaking people inhabited the Iron Age citadels, they probably belonged to a group that had stayed behind while their kinsmen moved to India, which is of course very well possible. On the other hand, we know that by the late ninth century, Persians and Medes were living in western Iran.[47] Both of these groups, as we know very well from various sources, spoke an Iranian language. Both groups would therefore have arrived in this region before the mid-ninth century BC. They came from the northeast, from the steppes and deserts east of the Caspian and the foothills along the northern edges of the Iranian Plateau. Pastoral tribes may move very quickly; however, it is still safe to suggest that the ancestors of the Persians and Medes were already living in Eastern Iran by the late second millennium. In the second half of the second millennium, when the Iron Age citadels were built, northern Afghanistan was therefore probably dominated by small groups of Indo-Aryans who had not moved across the Hindu Kush. They were progressively being pushed out of the way by their Iranian-speaking kinsmen arriving from the north. Both groups, it should be repeated, were linguistically and culturally closely related, and they may hardly have

46   Kohl 1984:199.
47   As made clear by Assyrian sources (compare Brandenstein and Mayrhofer 1964:1–2).

regarded the other as being 'different'. The process of Iranization of the Iranian Plateau took a long time and was not completed in historical times. Indeed, the Indo-Aryan speaking Pasha'i speakers in the Kabul valley represent a pre-Iranian, Indo-Aryan speaking stratum along the extreme eastern edges of the Plateau. The people from Kafiristan/Nuristan northeast of Kabul are another example.

6

Scythian Horsemen

The majestic ruins of ancient Persepolis, the capital of the Persian Achaemenids, rise up along the edge of a bleak plain in Southwest Iran. The buildings date to the mid-first millennium BC. Around that time, the lands of faraway Afghanistan had recently been incorporated into the Persian Empire. The ruins attract thousands of tourists. Most of them admire the beautiful reliefs that are placed along the northern and eastern facades of the famous Apadana palace of Darius the Great (r. 522–486 BC). The reliefs show groups of delegates from all parts of the realm, all the men being dressed in their own local apparel and all being led before the king.[1] They offer symbolic gifts and in this way show their loyalty and that of their subjects. The inscriptions at Persepolis give the names of the delegates' homelands, and thus we know that some of them actually derived from what is now called Afghanistan (Fig. 1). They come from ancient Bactria, in the north of the country; from Areia, around Herat in the west; from Drangiana, which is modern Sistan in the southwest; from Arachosia around modern Qandahar. There are also Indian delegates from the borderlands, who are clad in loincloths and sandals. Some of the 'Afghan' delegations bring a Bactrian (two-humped) camel, others present metal vases or a leopard skin. What is striking is that many of the delegates wear an outfit and weapons that are very reminiscent of those associated with the famous and contemporary Scythians from the Ukraine and South Russia.

The Scythians are best known for their golden artefacts and their tumuli (*kurgan*s), which generally date to the early second half of the first millennium BC, roughly from the same time as the Persepolis reliefs.[2] The objects from the tombs include beautiful representations

---

1 For a discussion of the costume and weaponry as depicted in the reliefs, see Vogelsang 1992b:135ff.
2 For the Scythians, compare Rolle 1980.

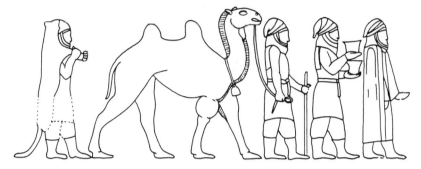

Figure 1   *Delegation of Eastern Iranian subjects of the Persian Achaemenid kings, as taken from the Persepolis Apadana*

of the Scythians themselves, which show them dressed in trousers, tunics and a *bashlyq* that covers their head, chin and neck. They have long, uncurled hair and a similar beard and they are carrying an *akinakes* (short sword) and a *gorytos* (bow-and-arrow case). Their bow is of the composite type, short but extremely powerful. All these aspects of daily life are not only found on Scythian objects, but also on depictions of Scythians made by Greek and Iranian craftsmen. If the almost identically dressed and armed delegates from Afghanistan also are Scythians, how did they end up in Afghanistan in the mid-first century BC?

Bactrians in Assyria

Around 400 BC, a Greek physician named Ctesias resided at the court of the Persian Achaemenid king, Artaxerxes II (*r*. 404–359 BC). There he heard stories about the history of the Persians and other peoples. On this basis he wrote a long account, the *Persica*, only fragments of which survive.[3] In his book he tells about the rise of the Iranian Medes from West Iran, the predecessors of the Persian Achaemenids. He in particular informs his readers that when the Medes were about to take the Assyrian capital of Nineveh, they were attacked in the back by the Bactrians.

This particular passage has puzzled many people. It is clear from other sources that Ctesias refers to the rise of the Median realm in modern West Iran and the fall of the Assyrian Empire in Mesopotamia in the late seventh century BC. However, historians

3   For Ctesias, see Auberger 1991.

have never taken Ctesias's reference to the Bactrians very seriously, mainly because the greater part of the information contained in the *Persica* is, to say the least, rather fantastic. Yet, as will be outlined below, this particular mentioning of the Bactrians, from the ancient province of Bactria in modern North Afghanistan, does indeed mirror an important episode in the history of Afghanistan and the rest of the Iranian Plateau. It is also closely linked to the apparel of the delegates from Afghanistan in the Persepolis reliefs.

Ctesias's narrative, but without a reference to Bactrians, is comparable to a much better known story told by the Greek historian, Herodotus, who wrote in the mid-fifth century BC. In Book Four of his *Historiae*, Herodotus gives a long account of the Scythians from the Ukraine and South Russia and he starts this narrative with a story about their origins.[4] He tells how they derived from Central Asia and that they were driven away by another people, the Massagetae, who pushed them across a river, called the Araxes. The Scythians subsequently fled to the land of the Cimmerians and in turn drove them across the Caucasus to Anatolia in modern East Turkey. The Scythians, in pursuit, also crossed the Caucasus, but inadvertently they took a different route, much further to the east, and soon found themselves on the Iranian Plateau, in the land of the Medes. The Scythians, according to Herodotus, thereupon defeated the Medes, who were just about to take the Assyrian capital, Nineveh. For 28 years, continues Herodotus, the Scythians dominated the Medes and all of Asia, until the Median king, Cyaxares, invited the Scythian leaders for a meal and had them all killed. The surviving Scythians subsequently moved north, across the Caucasus, and back to the steppes of the present-day Ukraine.

The Cimmerians and Scythians in the Near East

Herodotus's story about the Scythians and Cimmerians is supported by contemporary Near Eastern sources. From the late eighth century BC, the ancient civilizations in the plains of Syria and Mesopotamia were confronted with a new and aggressive foe from the northern and eastern mountains. The Assyrians and Babylonians refer to them as the *Gimirr(â)i* and the *Ishguzâi* (*Ashguzâi*), names which clearly reflect the Greek names of the Cimmerians and Scythians. The Near

---

4 Herodotus, *Historiae* IV 1ff (hereafter *Hist.*); see also ibid. I 103–4; VI 84; VII 20. For the Mesopotamian sources, compare Kristensen 1988; Salvini 1995; Zawadzki 1988. For the Scythians and Cimmerians in the Near East, compare Khazanov 1984. In general, see Diakonoff 1985.

Eastern sources agree that the Cimmerians and Scythians were horse riding bowmen who, in the late eighth and seventh centuries BC, spread terror throughout the Near East. In the Bible, the *Ashkenaz* (Scythians) and their horses are described as the terrifying opponents of the Babylonians (Jer. 51.27).[5] Jeremiah probably refers to them when he says (Jer. 6.23):

> Behold, a people is coming from the north country, a great nation is stirring from the farthest parts of the earth. They lay hold on bow and spear, they are cruel and have no mercy, the sound of them is like the roaring sea; they ride upon horses, set in array as a man for battle, against you, O daughter of Zion!

The first Near Eastern kingdom to meet the newcomers, according to written documents, was that of the Urartians.[6] They lived in modern eastern Turkey and northwestern Iran and to the north and northeast of the Mesopotamian plains.[7] That first encounter, in which the *Gimirri* and the Urartian king Rusa II were involved, occurred around 714 BC. Soon afterwards the annals of the Neo-Assyrian Empire mention the *Ishguzâi*. According to the Assyrians, the *Ishguzâi* lived in the northern Zagros, to the east and northeast of Mesopotamia.

In ancient Near Eastern and Greek sources, the names of the *Gimirri* and *Ishguzâi* are often interchanged. A good example is the trilingual text of the Behistun inscription of the Persian Achaemenid king, Darius.[8] The text dates to early in his reign, around 520 BC, and contains a list of provinces that formed part of the Empire. The list includes, in the Old Persian version, the name of *Saka* (the Persian name for the Scythians). The Akkadian version of the same text refers in this instance to the *Gimirri*.[9] The ancient Jews accordingly regarded the Scythians and Cimmerians as kinsmen. In Genesis (10.2–3), Ashkenaz (the Scythians) is called the son of Gomer (the Cimmerians).[10]

It is furthermore clear, from some of the names of the Scythian and Cimmerian invaders, that the ruling elite of the newcomers, if not all of them, spoke an Iranian language.[11] The etymology of the name Scythian, or *Saka*, has accordingly been sought in Indo-Iranian. The

---

5 Jeremiah 1:13–14; 4:6; Ezekiel 38:6. See Hyatt 1940 and Wilke 1913.
6 Luckenbill 1926: Nos. 137–9.
7 For the Urartians, compare Salvini 1995.
8 For this text, see Kent 1953; for a bibliography, Vogelsang 1998:195.
9 Vogelsang 1992b:102.
10 Dhorme 1932.
11 Compare Diakonoff 1985:94–5.

British linguist Sir Harold Bailey suggested that the word was an adjective based on the verb *sak-*, 'be strong'.[12] Whether this etymology is correct or not, the Scythians and Cimmerians clearly constituted a branch of the Iranian speaking world that originated in Central Asia. From the fact that Classical and Near Eastern sources indicate a distinction between the Medes and Persians on the one hand and the Scythians on the other, it is furthermore evident that the Scythians moved onto the Plateau after the Persians and Medes.

The Origins of the Scythians

The Near Eastern sources do not provide any information as to the exact origins of the Scythians and Cimmerians, apart from the fact that by the mid-seventh century they were found throughout the Zagros and in much of modern Turkey. We are therefore left with Herodotus' story. Traditionally, his account has been interpreted as referring to migration routes that lead from east to west across the Ural Mountains and down south across the modern Caucasus, between the Black Sea and the Caspian. However, there are a number of objections to this identification. First of all, the Caucasus has seldom been used as an important thoroughfare for large-scale migrations. The mountains constitute a formidable barrier and even the routes directly along the coast of the Black Sea and Caspian respectively are difficult to negotiate. Secondly, Herodotus's knowledge of the Iranian Plateau was extremely limited. It is clear from his writings that he did not have a clue as to the geography of the lands east and north of Mesopotamia. His reference to the Caucasus therefore does not necessarily refer to the modern Caucasus. Even two centuries later, in the time of Alexander the Great, the name of the Caucasus was used by the Greeks and Macedonians for the whole range of mountains from Armenia in the west, via the Elburz, to the mountains of Afghanistan in the east. The famous city of *Alexandria sub Caucaso* lay just north of modern Kabul. Thirdly, the Massagetae mentioned in Herodotus's story were also Scythians, according to Herodotus himself (*Hist.* I 201), and in later Greek sources the name of the Massagetae was used for a people that lived in the northeast of the Persian Achaemenid Empire, near ancient Choresmia south of the Aral Sea. If the Massagetae pushed any people out of the way, it is likely that they would force them across the Syr Darya or Amu Darya and towards the Iranian Plateau. The conclusion is that Herodotus's story about the Scythian migrations should be reinter-

12 Bailey 1958:133.

preted. They did not cross the Caucasus between the Black Sea and the Caspian, but instead they moved onto the Plateau from the northeast, and in doing so they migrated along the same routes as were used by their Iranian kinsmen who preceded them.

The Scythian Revolution

The Scythians and Cimmerians make their appearance in Near Eastern written sources in the late eighth century BC. The sources locate them in the mountains and valleys north and east of Syria and Mesopotamia. If it is accepted that these peoples had an eastern origin, it is likely that by at least the mid-eighth century BC they had settled in the fertile plains of West and Northwest Iran, mainly in modern Azarbayjan. These plains are traditionally the halting place and pastureland for nomads from the east. The Turks from Central Asia settled here in the Middle Ages before advancing to the west (and conquering what came to be called 'Turkey'), and also the Mongols established their base here in the thirteenth century. Before the mid-eighth century BC therefore, the Scythians, or at least some of them, had moved from South Central Asia, via North Afghanistan and Northeast Iran, to their new habitat in Azarbayjan.[13] Others apparently moved west, across the Urals, to the Ukraine, where Classical sources locate them in the mid-first millennium BC. This means that by the first quarter of the first millennium BC (or earlier), much of northern Iran and parts of modern Afghanistan were populated by a people that originated from the steppes of Central Asia and were related to earlier waves of Iranians and Indo-Aryans. Who were these Scythians?

The so-called Scythian Revolution started at the end of the second millennium.[14] It originated, as it now evident, in eastern Kazakhstan and adjacent regions in Central Asia among people speaking a (Northeast) Iranian language. They were people whose ancestors had remained behind when their kinsmen moved south towards the Iranian Plateau. The Revolution was marked by a new wave of 'extreme' pastoralism, namely a development towards almost total dependence on animal husbandry. In the typical conditions of Central Asia this meant that the people had to move round with their herds

13 Compare also the occurrence of Bactrian camels in Assyria by the mid-eighth century BC. They were brought as tribute from northeast of Mesopotamia, and depicted on the obelisk of Shalmanasar II. For early attestations of the Bactrian camel in the Near East, see Bulliet 1975:36, 62–4, 156–60.
14 For the Central Asian developments, see Christian 1998:99–162 and Davis-Kimball 1995.

during the full time of the year. This process coincided with a growing use of the horse for riding. The mobility of the Central Asian nomads subsequently increased considerably and new waves of migrations followed. Many of the typically 'Scythian' attributes made their appearance around this time: the sinew compound bow, the earliest specimens of which, as far as we know, date to the ninth century; the short sword (*akinakes*); the typical artistic products of the Scythians, executed in the so-called animal-style, and so forth. This can be combined with other aspects that in later centuries are linked to the Scythians. These include their dress and general appearance: their wearing of trousers, eminently suitable for horse-riding[15]; the long coat with empty sleeves (*kandys*)[16]; the *bashlyq* covering their head and neck, and so forth.

The Spread of the Scythians

By the late sixth century BC, the Persian Achaemenids indicate the presence of Scythian and Scythian related groups in a wide belt in the north of their Empire and beyond. The Persians called the Scythians by the name of the Sakas.[17] They identified them in the European northwest of their Empire with the name of the *Sakâ Paradrayâ* ('the Sakas Across the Sea'). They also located them in the northeast, in South Central Asia, as for instance the *Sakâ Tigraxaudâ* ('the Sakas with the Pointed Caps') and the *Sakâ Haumavargâ* ('the Haoma-using Sakas'). In the reliefs, these groups are all depicted wearing the typical Scythian dress. The interesting thing, alluded to at the beginning of this chapter, is that other groups, not directly known as Scythians, wear the same type of costume. These are the peoples from the lands that according to Greek and Near Eastern sources had been invaded centuries before by the Cimmerians and Scythians: Cappadocia (eastern Turkey), Armenia and Media. But peoples from areas much further east, lands now within the modern borders of Afghanistan and beyond, also wear the same type of costume.

Furthermore, the Greek historiographer Herodotus tells that in the fifth century BC, the people from Gandhara, which lies in the Kabul

15 Compare the so-called Cherchen Man, now in the Ürümchi Museum. This mummy is dated to about 1000 BC. He wears a shirt, trousers, leggings and boots (Barber 1999).

16 For the history and Central Asian origin of this remarkable piece of garment, see Gervers-Molnar 1973.

17 Compare Pliny VI 50 and Herodotus, *Historiae* VII 64. The word Saka should be seen as the singular of the (plural) *Skuta. See also Szemerenyi 1980.

valley and further east, were using Scythian weaponry.[18] In fact, he says that they were wearing 'Bactrian' arms. Since it is clear that the Bactrians from North Afghanistan were dressed in Scythian apparel and armed with Scythian weapons, this would show that to Herodotus and his sources, the term 'Bactrian' was used in a much wider context, indicating 'Scythian'. Here there is of course the link between the Bactrians of Ctesias and the Scythians of Herodotus. The two writers, probably without realizing it, used different sources to describe the same people, namely the Scythians from the east.

The spread of Scythian costume and armoury thus covered a wide belt of lands in the north of the Persian Achaemenid Empire. This is attested to in the Persepolis reliefs and in the *Historiae* of Herodotus.[19] The belt stretched from Cappadocia in modern East Turkey, via Armenia and Media, to the lands of the east, including Parthia around modern Ashkhabad; Areia around modern Herat; Bactria in North Afghanistan; Sogdia around modern Bukhara and Samarqand, and Choresmia south of the Aral Sea.[20] But also the delegates in the Persepolis reliefs from Drangiana in Southwest Afghanistan and from Arachosia in South Afghanistan wear Scythian clothing. Finally, on the basis of Herodotus's testimony, the use of Scythian weaponry even seems to have reached, by at least the fifth century, across the Hindu Kush mountains into the Kabul valley and beyond.

Herodotus and the Persepolis reliefs oppose the Scythian belt in the north of the Iranian Plateau to a 'southern' belt, although the dividing line of course was not very clear-cut. This southern belt included most of the (equally Iranian) Persian confederacy in South-west Iran and many others generally known as the Paktyans by Herodotus. The original costume and weaponry of the Persians were very unlike that of the Scythians and related groups in the north. In war the Persians used to be, principally, footsoldiers, holding long lances, huge shields and longbows. As for the Paktyans, Herodotus uses this name when he describes the outfit of some of the contingents of the Persian Achaemenid army (*Hist.* VII 61ff.) from the south and southeast of the Plateau. The interesting feature is that these include hitherto unknown peoples from South and East Afghanistan. They were the Parikanians, who lived in or near ancient Arachosia (around modern Qandahar),[21] but also the Caspians and the Paktyans themselves. The two last mentioned groups cannot be satisfactorily

18　Herodotus, *Hist.* VII 66.
19　Compare the roster of Xerxes's army against Greece: *Hist.* VII 61ff.
20　Strabo (XI 11) tells that the Sogdians and Bactrians in earlier times did not differ much from the (Scythian) nomads in their customs and modes of life.
21　Vogelsang 1992b:197–8.

identified, but there are sufficient grounds to suggest that they lived in the east of modern Afghanistan or nearby.[22]

The main feature that emerges is that the 'northern' Scythian belt as distinguished on the basis of the Persepolis reliefs, seems to partly overlap in South and East Afghanistan with the 'southern' Paktyan group described by Herodotus. The same problem occurs when we look at the outfit and weaponry of the people from Cappadocia (modern East Turkey) and Armenia. The Persepolis reliefs indicate a Scythian costume, while Herodotus describes something completely different (*Hist.* VII 72–73). The answer to this problem is relatively simple. The delegates depicted at Persepolis reflect the ruling elite of their district, which was Scythian, while the army contingents described by Herodotus are likely to describe the levies drawn from the autochthonous population. The important point to realize is that the Scythianization on the Plateau was a process. Some areas and groups of people were more influenced by the northern newcomers than others. In some areas large numbers of Scythians constituted the ruling class; in other areas they lived in harmony with the autochthonous population without exercizing a strong influence on local culture. In yet other parts of the Plateau, as for instance in the south and extreme east, the influence of the Scythians may at first have been minimal.

As for Afghanistan, all this would mean that by *c.*500 BC the north of the country was far more 'Scythianized' than the south and southeast. This is also shown on the so-called Darius Statue, which was found at Susa in Southwest Iran in 1972.[23] On the left and right hand side of the pedestal that carries a statue of Darius the Great, there are rows of delegates from the various provinces of the Persian Achaemenid Empire. The delegates are dressed in local wear and their place of origin is written underneath. The point is that the delegate from *Harauvatish* (Arachosia, around modern Qandahar) is shown wearing a long, airy dress, very different from the Scythian costume that the Arachosian delegates wear in the Persepolis reliefs, and very different from the Scythian dress worn by other delegates on the same statue.

In other words, by about 500 BC we can, hypothetically, distinguish four ethnic strata in what is now modern Afghanistan: the Scythian newcomers; a pre-Scythian Iranian population; Indo-Aryan speaking groups; and the remnants of the pre-Indo-Iranian autochthonous population. In most areas the Scythians, being the latest to arrive with superior strength and mobility, constituted the

---

22 Vogelsang 1992b:189ff.
23 Vogelsang 1992b:104–5; 143–5.

ruling class. They certainly did so in the north, in what was called Bactria. Their relationship with the pre-Scythian, but equally Iranian local population of the area is difficult to gauge, but a process of amalgamation is likely. The development in West Iran among the Medes may be illustrative, as I will discuss below. The Indo-Aryan groups resided along the eastern fringes of the Plateau, and the 'Iranization' of their lands was now combined with a growing influence from the side of the Scythian rulers. This is probably what occurred in the Kabul valley and ancient Gandhara. As to the non-Indo-Iranian autochthonous population, there is no evidence whatsoever, unlesss we try to find them among some of the hitherto unexplained names of ethnic groups that are found in Iranian and Classical sources, but all identifications would be highly speculative.

The Scythians and the Medes

The symbiosis between the Scythian newcomers and the equally Iranian, local population on the Plateau is illustrated by Herodotus. He tells how the Medes in what is now West Iran used to send their sons to the Scythians in order to learn to shoot the bow and to speak the (Scythian) language (*Hist.* I 73). Near Eastern sources from the seventh century, before the fall of the Assyrian Empire, confirm that at that time in the western mountains of the Iranian Plateau the Scythians were closely involved in the affairs of ancient Media. This involvement was not only militarily or political. As is clear from Herodotus's account, the Scythians also affected other aspects of Median culture. Interesting are, again, the reliefs at Persepolis, the Persian Achaemenid capital. They show the Medes wearing typically Scythian riding costume, including trousers, tunic and *bashlyq*, and carrying an *akinakes* and the *gorytos*. In this way, they are clearly differentiated from the Persians, who are in the main shown wearing the traditional Near Eastern long gowns and carrying the traditional Near Eastern weapons.

As in Afghanistan, it is impossible to indicate a clear dividing line between the Scythianized north and the non-Scythianized south. Scythianization, as said before, was a process that affected groups irrespective of their ethnic origin. Most Medes appear to have adopted Scythian dress and weaponry, but this does not mean that all of them did, or that all the Medes adopted Scythian culture to the same degree. The same applies to the Persians. Most of them resisted the northern influence, but some may well have accepted aspects of it.

In 550 BC the Persians under Cyrus the Great defeated their erst-while masters, the Medes. They inherited an empire that stretched from Cappadocia in the far northwest, to Parthia and Hyrcania in modern Northeast Iran, and perhaps even further east. All of these lands had been overrun by the Scythians and Cimmerians in preceding years and from the late seventh century BC been brought under control of the Scythianized Medes from their capital, Ecbatana, modern Hamadan. In this way the realm of the Medes should be described as a Scythian empire. The Persians, for the greater part still unaffected by the process of Scythianization, suddenly found themselves in control of a huge extent of land that was dominated by Scythians or people who had been strongly influenced by them. The Persians suddenly constituted the ruling minority in a world for the greater part dominated by trouser-wearing and horse-riding bowmen whose origins lay in the far northeast. If the Persians were to keep their empire, they somehow had to cope with this dichotomy on the Plateau before their Persian–Scythian Empire fell apart. Here the seeds were sown for a widening gap among the people on the Plateau which would open dangerously after the death of Cyrus the Great in 530 BC. It would set up Medes against Persians, but also Medes against Medes, and Persians against Persians. It would also oppose North Afghanistan against South Afghanistan. The climax would come when Cambyses, Cyrus's son and sucessor, died in 522 BC.

Oldest Geographical References

An important document has survived from the first half of the first millennium BC, and therefore approximately from the time that the Scythians from the north immigrated onto the Plateau.[24] It is included in the Zoroastrian Avesta, in a section called the *Vidêvdât* (Av. *vi.daêva.dâta*, 'Law against the Daevas'). The first chapter (*fargêrd*) of the *Vidêvdât* contains a list of sixteen lands that, according to the text, were created by the Zoroastrian main deity, Ahura Mazda. It includes the oldest unequivocal references to the land of Afghanistan.

The list starts with the mythical land of *A^iryân^ðm Vaêjah*, 'the expanse of the Aryans', and ends with a reference to the land along the *Ra_ηhâ*, a mythical river the name of which is also found in ancient Indian sources (compare Skt. *Rasâ*). There are no references whatsoever to the Medes or the Persians, thus suggesting that the list was composed and used in a period before the rise of the Medes around 650 BC.

24 For this section, see also Vogelsang 2000.

The sixteen lands of the *Vidêvdât* are located in a wide semi-circle around the Central Mountains of Afghanistan. The list starts in *A^{i}ryân$^{\partial}$m Vaêjah*, the location of which remains a moot point. It probably represents a mythical land somewhere in the far north. The list continues with the land of ancient Sogdia (around Bukhara and Samarqand). It then goes down, via Bactria, Margiana and Areia towards Sistan in Southwest Afghanistan. Then it lists some lands in modern South Afghanistan (including Arachosia around Qandahar), and it ends with a number of lands that are located east of the mountains as far as the Indus Valley.

Some of the names contained in the list simply cannot yet be identified, but others are well known from later sources, Persian Achaemenid or Greek. For instance, the name of *Bâxδi*, which appears as the fourth name in the list, can be identified with the district of Classical Bactria, around modern Balkh in North Afghanistan. *Haro^{i}va*, which appears as the sixth name, can be linked to Classical Areia. Its name can still be recognized in that of modern Herat, and in that of the river of the region, the Hari Rud. *Nisâya*, which is listed as number five, is reported in the text as being located between *Mo^{u}ru* (ancient Margiana, modern Marw) and *Bâxδi* (no. 4). This probably means that it lay along one of the routes connecting the two, in modern Northwest Afghanistan. The name of *Harax^{v}a^{i}ti*, which takes the tenth place in the list, can be related to that of the Persian Achaemenid district of *Harauvatish* (Old Persian), the Arachosia of Classical authors, around ancient and modern Qandahar. The name of the *Haêtumant* (no. 11) can be linked to that of the Classical Etymandrus river, the modern Hilmand.

Another district of Afghanistan that can perhaps be identified is that of *Xn$^{\partial}$nta* (no. 9), which is called the land of the *V$^{\partial}$hrkânas*. The latter name is strongly reminiscent of that of the Classical province of Hyrcania (Old Persian *Varkâna-*), modern Gurgan, to the southeast of the Caspian Sea. *Xn$^{\partial}$nta* has therefore in the past commonly been identified with Hyrcania.[25] This traditional identification, however, is open to doubt, if only since all the other names of the list seem to belong to the eastern part of the Iranian world. And since the name of *Xn$^{\partial}$nta* proceeds that of *Harax^{v}a^{i}ti* and *Haêtumant*, it is apparent that *Xn$^{\partial}$nta* was located somewhere in southern Afghanistan. [26] Such a location is supported by further evidence. The name of the *V$^{\partial}$hrkânas* can be compared with that of the Parikani-

---

25 Monchi-Zadeh 1975:124–6.
26 As done by Gnoli (1977: Pl. 1), who identifies the region with modern Urgun in Southeast Afghanistan. See also the remarks by Morgenstiere, in Gnoli 1980:235, note to page 39, line 5.

ans who are listed by Herodotus in his taxation list of the Persian Achaemenid Empire.[27] These Parikanians lived somewhere in the southeast of the Iranian Plateau.[28] The same name can also be linked to the *Barrikana* listed in the (Elamite) Persepolis Fortification Tablets[29] from the time of the Achaemenid king Darius, and the (Aramaic) *prkn* mentioned on the so-called Haoma utensils from Persepolis.[30] Both names denote districts that were located close to Arachosia.

The above data would show that the composer and audience of the *Vidêvdât* list regarded most of the lands surrounding the Hindu Kush mountains as part of their 'Aryan' *koine*. Since they put the name of *A'ryân[ə]m Vaêjah* on top of the list, before Sogdia, it is equally evident that they held the opinion that their original homeland was located north of ancient Sogdia, along or beyond the modern Syr Darya. All this means, firstly, that by the first half of the first millennium people who shared a common religious background populated much of Eastern Iran. Secondly, that these people were aware of the supposed fact that sometime in their history they had immigrated from the north.

If an attempt is made to put the above observations into an historical context, a link with the Iranians of the late second and the Scythians of the early first millennium BC is obvious. Indeed, the Scythians appear to constitute the best option, since they were the last to infiltrate the Plateau sometime in the early first millennium. This does not mean that Zarathustra was one of the Scythians who swept across Iran. That is even unlikely, since there is no evidence whatsoever that the Scythians from the Eurasian steppes were Zoroastrians. What it does mean, is that the composer of the *Vidêvdât* list and his audience identified their own background, or that of their (Scythian) rulers, with the man who had revealed their adopted religion.[31] To them, Zarathustra used to live and work in the lands far to the north where they, or their rulers, originated.

This notion of a northern origin does not stand alone. Herodotus's story about the Massagetae, the Scythians and the Cimmerians is one

---

27   Herodotus, *Hist.* III 89ff.
28   This identification is all the more likely since Herodotus (*Hist.* III 92) lists a second group of Parikanians, who almost certainly represent the Hyrcanians from southeast of the Caspian.
29   Vogelsang 1985:82–7; 1992:165–6.
30   Bowman 1970.
31   Compare the Pashtuns who claim descent from early Arab warriors (Caroe 1958:3ff), and various groups high in the mountains of Afghanistan who, according to nineteenth century ethnographers, used to claim descent from Alexander the Great (Burnes 1834: II, pp. 214–19).

of many. These stories probably reflect legends told by the Scythians themselves, and there are frequent references to their eastern origin, far away in the steppes of Central Asia.[32] The stories tell about migrations forced upon them by their neighbours, who in turn were compelled to migrate by their neighbours. Herodotus also tells about the burial of Scythian kings, from north of the Black Sea, in lands far to the east.[33] If the Scythians from the Black Sea area transmitted stories about their eastern origin, there is no reason to assume that the Scythians that arrived in Eastern Iran did not remember their place of origin. To them, $A^i ryân^o m$ *Vaêjah* was their homeland, far in the north, beyond the banks of the Syr Darya.

Whatever the case, by the first half of the first millennium BC some of the Scythian rulers of Eastern Iran and (northern) Afghanistan had adopted Zoroastrianism. By the same time other Scythians had migrated to the west, where they became known as the Scythians and the Cimmerians. To the ancient Greeks, the Scythians were also known as the Bactrians, after the name of the most important province in the Persian Achaemenid East. The opening up of the Iranian world, as brought about by the Scythian migrations, undoubtedly contributed to the spread of the religion of Zarathustra to the west. Traces of Zoroastrianism, as found in the Classical period in Cappadocia and lands further west,[34] thus may date back to a period much older than the Persian Achaemenid empire.

Iranian, and probably Zoroastrian priests depicted in West and East Iran since the mid-first millennium BC, are recognized by their Scythian dress.[35] Furthermore, depictions of the ancient Indo-Iranian god Mitra who was adopted by the Romans throughout their Empire, show a young god wearing a so-called Phrygian cap. This cap is no other that the Scythian *bashlyq* complete with side-flaps that protect the cheeks and mouth.[36] The Scythians, in short, contributed far more to Near Eastern culture than cavalry tactics, short swords and trousers. They constituted the vehicle for the spread of Zoroastrianism and possibly also that of the worship of Mitra, from Afghanistan and Eastern Iran to the rest of the Iranian world and far beyond.

---

32 Compare the story of Aristeas (Herodotus IV 13). In this account, which according to Herodotus is based on a poem by Aristeas from Proconnesus, it is said that the Cimmerians were driven out of Europe (and into the Near East) by the Scythians. In their turn the Scythians had been pushed out by the Issedones, while initially the Issedones had been pressed from their homeland by the Arimaspians.
33 Herodotus IV 71ff.
34 See Boyce and Grenet 1991.
35 See the priest depicted on a gold plague from the so-called Oxus Treasure (Dalton 1905: Pl. XIII, 48). Compare Boyce 1982:20–1.
36 Compare Boyce and Grenet 1991:163.

Archaeological Materials

Archaeologically, the period of Scythian immigration into Afghanistan and neighbouring lands belongs to the Iron Age, roughly to the Yaz II–III Periods. Various East Iranian sites from the early first millennium have yielded arrowheads with three wings. These so-called trilobal points are often associated with the Scythians from the north.[37] Of great interest is the site of Erk Kala, a settlement near Marw that later became the citadel of the Alexandrian city of *Alexandria in Margiana* (Gjaur Kala). Erk Kala has yielded large amounts of trilobal arrowheads and Yaz II and III pottery. The interesting point is its almost circular shape, measuring some 400/500 metres in diameter. A comparable, almost circular fortress is that of Balkh, ancient Bactra, but the exact history of this site is still unknown.[38] Another circular town in the oasis of Bactra is that of Altin Dilyar.[39] This place has a diameter of 1,000 metres and is dominated by a citadel in the centre that rises to a height of about 28 metres. The citadel is rectangular with circular towers at its corners.

Circular settlements are purpose-built. The round shape recalls the camp of nomads on the move. It is the circle of wagons protecting the people and herds in the middle. From the early first millennium BC, there are a number of other circular sites in the northeast of the Iranian Plateau.[40] They are sometimes associated with high citadels in the centre. Similar citadels are also found in South Afghanistan, as for instance at Old Qandahar, but the date of these structures remains problematic. The site of Old Qandahar, which will be discussed in the next chapter, dates back to the early or mid-first millennium BC, from the time of the Early Achaemenids or slightly before. Whatever the exact date, the building of high citadels in the middle of a circular or rectangular fortress is not a tradition that is evidently West Iranian. It is far more a local, East Iranian development, related to the platforms erected in the same area in the Yaz-I period of the late second millennium BC. That this local tradition further developed under the influence of powerful Scythian 'masters', is a distinct possibility.

---

37   Vogelsang 1992b:298–300.
38   Leriche 1999.
39   Ball 1982:38.
40   Compare Francfort 1979:17.

7

Opening Up to the West

By the mid-first millennium BC, local rulers of Scythian descent were established along the northern belt of the Iranian Plateau. They constituted the ruling class, in the same way as much later the Turks would come to dominate the same area. Other groups of Scythians roamed the countryside, continuing the traditions of their ancestors in Central Asia. In what is now Afghanistan, the north was thoroughly Scythianized and local levies in the Persian Achaemenid army were dressed in the Scythian fashion. In the south however, although by now largely controlled by Scythians, most of the local population still followed their own customs. In this way they were linked to other Iranian groups in the southern belt of the Iranian Plateau, including the Persians. A glimpse of this gap between north and south, and especially between North and South Afghanistan, can be obtained in the early history of the Persian Achaemenids.

In 550 BC, a Persian prince, who in the Classical world came to be known as Cyrus, defeated his overlord, the Median king Astyages.[1] Herodotus describes Cyrus as Astyages's grandson.[2] Whether this was the case or not, the prince from *Pârsa* (the Persia of the Greeks), in Southwest Iran, became the successor of the Median king. Consequently he was the lord of a huge extent of land stretching from the borders with Lydia (Western Turkey) to Eastern Iran, and from the Armenian mountains in the north to the coasts of the Persian Gulf in the south. Whether Cyrus conquered the lands of Afghanistan or simply inherited them from the Medes, or both, remains a moot point, but it is evident from the sources that at the time of his death in 530 BC all of modern Afghanistan, and adjoining lands, was incorporated into the Persian Achaemenid Empire.

1 For the Persian Achaemenid Empire, the most up-to-date and extensive account is by Briant 1996.
2 Herodotus, *Hist.* I 75.

The names of all the well-known Classical districts of Afghanistan are listed in the so-called Behistun text. This trilingual document (engraved in Elamite, Akkadian and Old Persian) was carved in the rocks near modern Hamadan, West Iran, on the orders of Darius shortly after his accession to power in 522 BC. The districts include, in the Old Persian version of the text, *Bâxtrish* (Bactria); *Haraiva* (Areia); *Zra^nka* (Zrangiana or Drangiana, modern Sistan);[3] *Harauvatish* (Arachosia); *Thatagush* (Sattagydia),[4] and *Ga^ndâra* (Gandhara).[5] Since there is no evidence that Cambyses, Cyrus's son and successor (*r.* 530–522 BC), ever campaigned in the east, these lands were probably added to the Empire in the time of Cyrus or before. In fact, there are many stories about Cyrus's exploits in the eastern parts of the Plateau. He is said to have destroyed the fortress and town of *Capisa*, just north of Kabul.[6] He is also said to have been in or near Sistan in connection with the people of the Ariaspians.[7] He furthermore is alleged to have established a fortress on the banks of the Syr Darya, not far from modern Khodzhent (former Leninabad).[8] He also died in this part of the world, in 530 BC, probably in or near the wastes of the Qara Qum (Turk. 'Black Sand') desert north of modern Iran.[9] He was eventually buried in his palace park of Pasargadae, north of Persepolis, where his tomb can still be seen today.

The Struggle for the Persian Achaemenid Throne

The opposition on the Iranian Plateau in the mid-sixth century BC between the Scythianized north and non-Scythianized south is reflected in the events that surrounded the rise to power of Darius in 522 BC.[10] In that year Cambyses died. He had been Cyrus's son and successor, and at the time of his death he and his army were on their way home from Egypt to Persia in order to deal with a revolt by

---

3   The difference between these two renderings, Drangiana and Zrangiana, is related to the typical Old Persian development of the original palatal 'j', via 'z' to 'd'. See Vogelsang 1992b:45, n. 34.

4   Ibid.

5   In the Behistun text, the Elamite and Akkadian versions provide the name of the Paropanisadae, instead of Gandhara (see Vogelsang 1992b:51–2). For this name, see also Sims-Williams 1997:24.

6   Pliny, *NH* VI 92 (*Capisene habuit Capisam urbem quam diruit Cyrus*). The site may be identical with the ruins of Begram, north of Kabul (Ball 1982: No. 122).

7   Vogelsang 1992b:228.

8   Called Cyra or Cyropolis; Arrian, *Anab. Alex.* IV 2.2; Strabo XI 11.4.

9   Vogelsang 1992b:187–9.

10   For the following account, compare Vogelsang 1998.

someone who either was, or claimed to be Bardiya, Cambyses's brother. Herodotus called this man Smerdis. When Cambyses suddenly died, Bardiya was subsequently crowned king, which took place on 1 July 522. However, barely three months later, on 29 September, a young man of the Achaemenid clan murdered Bardiya in Media. The murderer was Darius, who would be king of the Empire until 486 BC. In his famous Behistun inscription he openly declared that Bardiya had been an impostor and that the real Bardiya had been killed years before by Cambyses. The impostor, Darius says, was in fact a Median priest, or *magus*, called Gaumata. Darius furthermore tells that after 29 September, a series of revolts against his rule broke out all over the empire, but Darius and his generals, according to the text, crushed these revolts within one year.

In the Behistun text, which Darius had engraved soon after his ascent to power, he uses the word 'truth' so many times that the modern reader cannot help but feel somewhat sceptical. 'Stretching the truth' is not an unknown phenomenon, especially among politicians. There are doubts about the identity of the 'impostor', but also about the nature of the revolts. Did Darius kill an impostor, or did he murder the real brother of Cambyses? What was the character of the revolts that broke out, according to Darius, when he acceded to the throne, and how did Darius manage to defeat his opponents? The events of 522/521 BC are often described as part of the continuing opposition between the Medes and their erstwhile Persian vassals. Herodotus correspondingly says that Darius saved the Persians from again becoming subordinate to the Medes.[11] However, it is evident that the situation was far more complex than that. The complicating fact is that Darius, according to the sources, commanded both Persian and Median troops and generals, and that one of his main opponents was a Persian. A clear-cut opposition between Medes and Persians, as so often surmised, therefore seems unlikely. So what happened?

One of the revolts described by Darius occurred in Margiana, around modern Marw, in the northeast of the Empire, and it was led by someone called Frada. In the relief which accompanies the text, this 'rebel' is shown wearing Persian clothes, very different from the (Scythian) riding costume that the Margians, who lived along the northern belt of the Iranian Plateau, were normally wearing. Frada therefore was apparently a Persian, perhaps the Persian governor. Darius tells that Frada's rebellion broke out while he was in Mesopotamia, where he had gone after 29 September in order to sup-

---

11 Compare Herodotus, *Hist.* III 65.

press a Babylonian revolt.[12] Darius later informs his readers that his satrap (governor) in Bactria, called Dadarshish, crushed the revolt in Margiana on 10 December of the same year,[13] thereby killing more than 50,000 Margianians.

The time span between the supposed start of the rebellion (sometime after 29 September, when Bardiya/Gaumata was killed) and the date of its cruel suppression (10 December) is extremely tight. The seat of Dadarshish (Bactra, modern Balkh in North Afghanistan) lies some 600 km from Margiana, along a circuitous route that avoids the desert that lies between the two places. Since there is no reason to doubt the date of the battle against the Margianians, the conclusion is that the rebellion must have started, or was at least plotted, before 29 September and that Darius purposely postponed the actual date of the revolt. This means that Frada, apparently the Persian governor in Margiana, rebelled against Bardiya, and not against Darius.

Around the same time, a revolt broke out in Persis, in the homeland of the Persian Achaemenids. According to Darius in his Behistun text, this revolt also started when he was in Mesopotamia (after 29 September), and it was led by a Persian by name of Vahyazdata. The 'rebel' called himself Bardiya, thus claiming to be the son of Cyrus and the brother of Cambyses. Vahyazdata in this way also implied, like Darius, that King Bardiya was an impostor.

According to Darius, this Vahyazdata/Bardiya sent an army to Arachosia in the east. The next we hear is that Vahyazdata's troops were defeated on 29 December, 522 BC, at a site called Kapishakanish (north of modern Kabul; the Capisa of Pliny), more than 2,000 km northeast of Persis. Vahyazdata's troops were beaten, according to Darius, by a general called Vivana, whom Darius calls his servant and satrap in Arachosia. On 21 February, a second battle took place, much further to the south, in which Vivana again vanquished Vahyazdata's forces. Sometime later a third battle followed, in which Vivana completely crushed his opponents, who subsequently fled back to Persis. From the course of events it can be deduced that Vivana pursued Vahyazdata's troops from north of modern Kabul southwestwards along the road to Persis. Since the first battle was fought at the southern side of the Hindu Kush, it is equally evident that Vivana came from north of the mountains, from Bactria.

---

12   The Babylonian revolt certainly started before 29 September, in spite of Darius's claims to the contrary. See Vogelsang 1998:200.
13   For this date, see Vogelsang 1986.

Considering the dates it is unlikely that Vahyazdata started his rebellion after 29 September. There simply was not enough time for him to plan his insurrection, gather an army and send troops all the way as far as the Hindu Kush mountains. Hence it is clear that the people of the southern belt, including Persis and ancient Arachosia in South Afghanistan, started their 'rebellion' before 29 September against King Bardiya, and not against Darius.

North against South

The revolts of Frada and Vahyazdata indicate that Darius in his Behistun text was fairly liberal with the truth. He was one of the rebels against King Bardiya. He certainly was not, as he claimed to be, the only one. The important difference is that he was the one to kill the king. Being an Achaemenid by birth and having murdered the king in or near one of the Achaemenid capitals, he could relatively easily take charge of the royal palace and other symbols of royal authority. He was therefore well positioned to claim overall control. This he did successfully. His first problem were his 'fellow-rebels'. None of these voluntarily submitted to the young upstart (Darius was some 25 years old when Cambyses died). They had risen against the same authority as that which had led to Darius's palace coup. If they were 'rebels', so was Darius. In order to portray them as 'liars', Darius was thus forced to proclaim that he, and he alone, was the legitimate king and that the 'rebels' revolted against him. In his Behistun text, Darius therefore stresses the fact that he was a descendant of Achaemenes, the eponymous ancestor of the Achaemenids. He also tells the world that it was he alone who knew that Bardiya was an impostor, and that he was the one to initiate the conspiracy that led to Bardiya's death. Darius also frequently invokes the name of Ahuramazda, by whose favour he did what he had to do.

In spite of Darius's lengthy statement, it is clear that Darius's coup was not a freak occurrence and that he was not the only one to think that Bardiya was an impostor. In various parts of the Empire, Persian leaders revolted against their king. Bardiya had obviously lost the loyalty of many of his Persian subjects. He was accused of being a *magus*, one of the priests who are depicted on various reliefs and objects as wearing Scythian trousers, tunic and *bashlyq*. There may well be a grain of truth in this accusation. While his brother Cambyses was king, Bardiya, as known from written sciences, was governor in the Scythian dominated north. When he revolted against his brother, and later when he was crowned king, he probably felt that he could only hold his position against the leading Persians who had accompanied Cambyses to Egypt by trying to create another power base to prop up his regime. This he found among the leading Medes and others from the north where he used to be governor. The opposition on the Plateau between the Scythianized north and non-Scythianized south was thus exploited by leading Persians, including Darius and Bardiya, to pursue their own goals.

It is intriguing to compare this situation with what occurred more than two thousand years later in Afghanistan. Ahmad Shah Durrani, a Pashtun leader and founder of the Kingdom of Afghanistan, was in 1773 succeeded by his son, Timur Shah, who in previous years had been the governor of (Iranian) Herat. The new king tried to uphold and expand his authority at the cost of the traditional Pashtun leaders, and he did so with the help of Iranian troops and administrators. He was subsequently accused of being 'Persian' rather than Pashtun. Rumour spread that he hardly spoke any Pashto and his fellow Pashtuns simply did no longer accept him. Within a few years he was forced to move his court from Qandahar, in the middle of Pashtun country, to Kabul, outside *Pashtunistân*.

The dynastic conflict, which started with Bardiya's revolt against his brother, subsequently led to a much larger struggle that engulfed much of the Iranian Plateau and the rest of the Persian Achaemenid Empire. A number of leading Persians, at various places, revolted against Bardiya. Bardiya went to Media for help. The Persians accused him of being an impostor and a *magus*, a Scythianized priest. Frada in Margiana and Vahyazdata in Persis revolted against Bardiya. Both of them were Persian. Vahyazdata soon controlled much of the southern belt of the Iranian Plateau, from Persis in the west to Arachosia and the Kabul valley in the east. Support for Bardiya came from officials in Bactria, the most important Achaemenid centre in the northeast and thoroughly Scythianized in preceding centuries. Dadarshish moved west, towards Margiana, and Vivana moved south, across the Hindu Kush, towards Kapishakanish and Arachosia. Both men succeeded, but they could not prevent their king, Bardiya, from being murdered in faraway Media by the young Achaemenid prince, Darius.

Dadarshish and Vivana evidently supported Bardiya, and later, after subduing the rebels in Margiana and Arachosia and after hearing about Bardiya's death, realized that they had no choice but to take Darius's side. The new king calls them his servants and his satraps in Bactria and Arachosia respectively. He also expressly states that both men were 'Persian'. Are these terms merely honorifics? Elsewhere in the Behistun text another general is mentioned, also named Dadarshish. He is called an Armenian and sent by Darius to crush a revolt in the northwest of the Iranian Plateau. Was he the same person as the Dadarshish from Bactria? We will never know, but it is more than likely. In fact, Dadarshish and Vivana are the only two satraps mentioned in the Behistun text. Their position in the east must have been very powerful, and one may only wonder how much control Darius could exercise over his 'servants'. It may have been Darius's prime concern to get rid of them as soon as possible. Sending one of them to Armenia may have been an option. Whatever the case, Arachosia and Bactria were apparently the two main provinces of the Achaemenids in the east. Balkh had proved to be, around 522 BC, the bulwark of the northern, Scythian party within the Empire, while Arachosia was the coveted centre of the Empire in the southeast.

And what was Darius's role in all this? He opposed both Persian and non-Persian rebels. His army included Persians and Medes, and apparently also an Armenian general. The answer may lie, as so often, in Persepolis. The reliefs show how an usher leads all the delegates before the king. These ushers are depicted alternately in Persian or in Scythian/Median costume. Darius thus favoured both the Persians and the Scythianized Medes. He furthermore placated the Persians by building a new capital at Persepolis, in the centre of Persis, and by depicting himself in Persian royal garb. At the same time he ingratiated himself with the Medes by appointing some of their leaders in important positions,[14] and Ecbatana remained one of the capitals of the Empire.

Herodotus tells that during the famous Battle of Salamis, in 480 BC, when the Greeks defeated the Persians, the Persian ships were manned by trusted soldiers, either Persians, Medes or Scythians.[15] Darius had successfully bridged the gap between the north and south, and in truth he became the founding father of the Persian Empire.

The Lands of Afghanistan in the Achaemenid Period

Our knowledge of the lands of Afghanistan during the Persian Achaemenid period, between *c.*550 and 330 BC, is limited. There are some written sources, mainly Achaemenid and Greek, and there is some archaeological evidence. Excavations have brought to light extensive urban establishments, villages, irrigation works and other traces. They show that especially the north of Afghanistan was made into a highly productive area, with canals spreading out deep into the countryside. At the same time, we know that the ruling class of much

14   Darius appointed Datis, a Mede, as one of the commanders against the Greeks in Eritrea and Athens (*Hist.* VI 94).
15   *Hist.* VII 184.

Figure 2   *Delegation of Scythian subjects of the Persian Achaemenid kings,
as taken from the Persepolis Apadana.*

of Eastern Iran, and especially in the Northeast, consisted of descendants of the Scythian invaders from the early first millennium. They controlled the countryside, while acknowledging their King of Kings in faraway Persepolis as their overlord.[16]

Of great interest is the army roster of the Persian Achaemenid army that marched against the Greeks in 481/0 BC.[17] Herodotus, no doubt on the basis of Persian sources, tells that the army was divided into various contingents, some of which can be identified with districts in what is now Afghanistan. One of these contingents consisted of the Bactrians and the Amyrgaean Sakas, who were headed by Hystaspes, the son of Darius (Fig. 2). The inclusion of the Sakas is of great interest. The name of the Sakas in Persian Achaemenid sources refers to the Scythians as known to the Greeks. In fact, the name is the same, and Herodotus already commented upon the fact that the Persians called all Scythians by the name of Sakas.[18] The fact that Herodotus here uses the name of the Sakas, rather than the Greek rendering 'Scythians', would indicate that it is a direct borrowing from Persian sources and they can be identified with the *Sakâ Haumavargâ*, the '*Haoma*-using (?) Sakas' of the Persian Achaemenid sources. The army of the Persians also included separate contingents of the (Scythianized) Sogdians, the Parthians and the Choresmians, all living north and west of Bactria. The Amyrgaean Sakas can consequently be located directly northeast and east of Bactria, in the valleys and mountains across the Amu Darya and in modern Badakhshan.

The presence in this area of a clearly recognizable group of people, related to the Scythians from the deserts and steppes to the north and northwest, would explain an otherwise enigmatic statement in Clas-

16   For Bactria during the Achaemenid period, compare Briant 1984.
17   Herodotus, *Hist.* VII 61ff.
18   Herodotus, *Hist.* VII 64.

sical sources. This passage describes a Gandharan town called Kaspapyros as an *akte* (promontory, shore) of the Scythians.[19] This statement would mean that the town of Kaspapyros, which is probably
identical to Classical Capisa and the Achaemenid settlement of
Kapisha-kanish (as mentioned in the Behistun inscription), was
located close to land occupied by Scythians. Since Classical Capisa
lay north of modern Kabul at the (southern) foot of the Hindu Kush
mountains and can be identified with present-day Begram,[20] it may
be deduced that the Hindu Kush mountains were indeed occupied
by nomadic or semi-nomadic Scythians. This would also explain
Herodotus's statement that the people of Kaspatyros (Kaspapyros)
resembled the Bactrians in their way of life.[21] Considering what was
said earlier, and bearing in mind the information that in the early
Achaemenid period the people from Gandhara used to carry Bac-
trian/Scythian weaponry, the presence of Scythians in the Hindu Kush
is not surprising. Their kinsmen dominated much of the rest of North
Afghanistan and beyond. The point is that the Bactrian Scythians
were called Bactrians, after their land and capital. As the *de facto*
rulers of the land, they had no doubt adopted many aspects of the
settled existence of the equally Iranian local population, including
their Zoroastrian religion. The other Scythians, northeast and east of
Bactria, were still called by their own ethnic name. They would still
conduct a life of (semi) pastoralism. Many of them would migrate
each spring into the mountains and return in the autumn. The name
of the *Sakâ Haumavargâ*, incidentally, may still live on in that of the
valley of Munjan in the centre of Badakhshan.[22]

The habitat of the Amyrgaean Sakas would also indicate that they,
and their Bactrian kinsmen, should not directly be linked with the
Scythians and others who roamed the steppes of South Central Asia.
The latter no doubt reflected a more recent arrival in this area, much
later than the original infiltration of Scythian/Saka nomads in the
early first millennium. This point is also illustrated by the one characteristic of the Badakhshani Scythians that, to the Persians, clearly
differentiated them from the other Scythians, namely their apparent
use of *Haoma*. The use of *Haoma* was particular to the Indo-
Iranians who migrated to the Iranian Plateau in the second millennium BC. There is no evidence that *Haoma* was still being used by

19 Hekataios, *Periegesis*, Fragm. *FgrHist*. 1 F295. Compare also the Kaspatyros of
Herodotus (*Hist*. III 102; IV 44). Herodotus tells that this place lay in Paktya. See
also Vogelsang 1992a.
20 Ball 1982: No. 122. The site lies some 80 km north of Kabul.
21 Herodotus, *Hist*. III 102.
22 Bailey 1958:132.

the Scythians in Central Asia by the mid-first millennium BC. This would underline the assumption that the Amyrgaean Sakas belonged to an earlier wave of Scythian migrants. They adopted the use of *Haoma*, and with it perhaps also the religion of Zarathustra, from the local, equally Iranian inhabitants of the region. In other words, they retained many of their Scythian aspects, probably including their nomadic or semi-nomadic existence in the Badakhshan mountains. At the same time, however, they adopted, in imitation of their kinsmen who settled in the Bactrian plains, a number of hallmarks of the local Iranian community, including the use of the sacred drink.

Another point of interest is the name of the commander of the Bactrians and Amyrgaean Sakas, namely Hystaspes, the son of Darius. Hystaspes is the Greek rendering of the name of Vishtaspa as mentioned in the Old Persian texts. He probably was the satrap (governor) of Bactria at that time. He was thus also the grandson of another Vishtaspa, the father of Darius, who according to the Behistun text, held a position in the northeast of the Empire around 522 BC. It is also the name of the patron of Zarathustra, as known from the Avesta. Furthermore, it was the name of a grandson of Darius and the son of Darius's successor, Xerxes (and also satrap of Bactria). In all cases, there is a clear link between the name, which is not 'purely' Old Persian but Avestan, and the province of Bactria. It may have been a satrapal name or title, which linked the official to Zarathustra's faith.

The Achaemenid governor of Bactria must have been an important official. Apparently many of them were the sons of the reigning king and they bore a title that linked them to the ancient history and the prevalent religion of the area. The governor was called *Vishtâspa*, the viceroy, and his power was based both on secular strength and religious authority. Secular strength may have counted for little among the unruly pastoralists of the Achaemenid Northeast, but religious authority may well have been very important indeed, especially among the *Haoma*-using Sakas of Badakhshan.

Another interesting contingent in Xerxes's army against Greece included the Gandarians and Dadicae. They lived in the valley of the Kabul River and beyond, in the Classical province of Gandhara. They were commanded by Artyphius, who according to Herodotus was the brother of the commander of the Caspians, another contingent of Xerxes's army. The latter should probably be related to the town of Capisa, north of modern Kabul, and that of Kaspapyros or Kaspatyros mentioned above.[23] Herodotus tells that in Xerxes's army the

23 Compare Vogelsang 1992b:195–6.

Caspians were armed with Persian (read: Median) swords. These must have been the Scythian short swords, the *akinakes*.[24]

Some of the Achaemenid provinces in modern Afghanistan are again mentioned in another Persian Achaemenid text, namely the Foundation Charter of Darius's palace at Susa.[25] Here are listed the materials and their places of origin that were used for the construction of the royal buildings. *Bâxtrish* (Old Persian) is listed as one of the places (together with Lydia in modern western Turkey) that provided gold. *Ga^ndâra* is mentioned as the origin of the *yakâ*-wood.[26] *Harauvatish* (Arachosia), together with *Hi^ndush* (South Pakistan) and *Kusha* (southern Egypt/Sudan), is referred to as the origin of ivory. The gold from Bactria probably refers to the gold that can still be found in the rivers of Badakhshan and in the extreme north of modern Pakistan. Elsewhere in his *Historiae*, Herodotus tells that the Indians contributed huge amounts of gold to the Achaemenid Treasury. He also tells how this gold was won, namely with the help of gold-digging ants. All this refers to the gold from northern Pakistan, but until recently gold was also found nearby, along the northern slopes of the Hindu Kush.[27] The ivory from Arachosia reflects the trade in ivory from India.[28] The shortest route from India to Persepolis leads via Qandahar in ancient Arachosia.

Indians and Iranians

The Persepolis texts and reliefs indicate that Indians and Iranians lived side by side along the eastern borders of the Plateau.[29] There are four delegations depicted at the Apadana and elsewhere at Persepolis that are obviously Indian (Fig. 3). They are depicted wearing loincloths, bare-chested and with bare feet or sandals. They derive from *Ga^ndâra*, *Thatagush*, *Hi^ndush* and *Maka*. The location of *Ga^ndâra* is clear. It comprised in the main the valley of Peshawar in present-day northern Pakistan. In the Elamite and Akkadian versions of the Behistun text this district is called Paruparaesanna, comparable to the Classical name for the Kabul valley, the Paropanisadae.

Hi^ndush and *Maka* covered the lower Indus Valley (modern Sind Province) and the coastal stretch of Baluchistan along the Indian

24 Herodotus, *Hist.* VII 67.
25 For this text, see Vogelsang 1992b:132–4.
26 For this wood, see Eilers 1983:116–18; Gershevitch 1957, 1958; Maxwell-Hyslop 1983.
27 Vogelsang 1989.
28 Vogelsang 1985.
29 For this section, see Vogelsang 1985 and 1988a.

Figure 3   *Delegation of Indian subjects of the Persian Achaemenid kings, as taken from the Persepolis Apadana.*

Ocean, the Makran coast. The district that is of great interest to us here is *Thatagush*. In various Achaemenid texts, the district of *Thatagush* is linked to that of *Harauvatish*, the area around modern Qandahar in South Afghanistan. Herodotus mentions the same district.[30] He calls it Sattagydia and combines it with the Gandharans and two other groups into one tax-paying *nomós*. The location of Sattagydia remains a moot point. Yet, the Achaemenid texts seem to be clear about the juxtaposition of Arachosia and Sattagydia and the land should therefore be located somewhere east or northeast of modern Qandahar. Whatever the exact location, it does mean that ancient Arachosia was a borderland and marked the eastern extension of the Iranian world.

Another Indian/Iranian frontier town was Kaspapyros. Earlier I identified this place with the Capisa of Pliny, the fortress of Kapisha-kanish of the Behistun text, and with the modern site of Begram north of Kabul. It lies at the southern entrance to the Salang Pass and two other major routes across the Hindu Kush, namely along the Ghorband river towards Bamiyan, and along the Panjshir river towards the Khawak Pass. According to Herodotus and other Classical writers, Scythian influence had spread across the mountains and into the plain. At the same time we know from Achaemenid and Classical sources that the people living here and further east were at least partly Indian. The name of Kaspa-pyros probably reflects the Indian element in this area, namely by the suffix *-puros*, which may be derived from the Indian word for town or fortress (Sanskrit *pur* or *pura-*), very much like the suffix *-kanish* in the Persian equivalent Kapisha-kanish.[31] Indian presence in the plains and valleys south of

30 Herodotus, *Historiae* III 91.
31 The suffic -kanish is probably derived from the same Iranian root (*kan-*; Skt. *khan-*) that underlies the word *kant* or *kot* still widely used in this part of the world for 'town' (compare Samarqand; Tashkent, etc.).

the Hindu Kush continues to the present day. The Dardic (Indo-Aryan) speaking Pasha'i or Kohistanis live in a wide belt along the northern fringes of the Kabul valley.[32] As for further Iranian and Scythian influence in this region, the name of the Paropanisadae ('the land which lies beyond the mountains called the *upa'risaêna*') is obviously an Iranian/Scythian name given to the Kabul valley by people coming from north of the mountains.

Art and Culture

Excavations in Eastern Iran have shown that Persian Achaemenid domination of the region did not lead to a drastic change in material culture. Yet certain shifts did occur. From the fifth century BC onwards, the Aramaic script and language were used throughout the Persian Achaemenid Empire. This led to Aramaic script being adopted by various peoples in the east to write down their language.[33] In the years after the fall of the Achaemenid Empire, Aramaic was used to write Parthian, Sogdian and Choresmian.[34] It also was used in the northwest of the Indian subcontinent to write the Prakrit (Middle Indian) languages. Here it developed into the Kharoshti-script, which for many centuries continued to be used throughout Northwest India, Central Asia, and western China.

The official currency used in the east during the Achaemenid period was the silver *siglos* and the golden *dareios*. However, from the various hoards and deposits found in Afghanistan it is clear that uncoined silver, including old Greek coins, were also widely used. The hoards include the famous Oxus Treasure (with some 1,500 coins),[35] from between the early fifth and the late third century BC. Another find was the Balkh hoard, discovered in 1966, with some 150 Greek coins dating to a period before *c*.380 BC.[36] There is also the Chaman-i Hauzuri hoard, found in Kabul in 1933, of which some 150 coins were saved.[37] South and east of the Hindu Kush, in ancient Gandhara, the normal currency in the fourth century BC were the so-

---

32 See Chapter 2.

33 Compare the Aramaic inscription from Taxila, which mentions Ashoka as governor under his father (Marshall 1951:164–166).

34 And perhaps also Bactrian. Compare an ostracon from Ay Khanum in Aramaic script, but apparently in an Iranian (Bactrian?) language (Bernard 1972:631–2).

35 Recently more coins have been found in the Panjshir valley. Allegedly they once formed part of the Oxus Treasure (see Pichikyan 1997).

36 Troxell and Spengler 1969:1–19.

37 Other minor hoards from the Achaemenid period are listed in Macdowall and Taddei 1978:203.

called Punch Marked Silver coins. According to the numismatist, Joe Cribb, these were used across most of northern and northwestern India from the fourth century BC onwards, and were inspired by Iranian and Greek examples from the west.[38]

The Oxus Treasure, mentioned above, contained a large number of other objects. The Treasure was discovered in 1877 somewhere north of the Amu Darya, in ancient (North) Bactria. Many of the objects were since lost in Afghanistan and only a small part of the Treasure ended up in the British Museum.[39] The objects are mostly imperial Achaemenid in character, but there are also objects that reflect local traditions and influences from the nomadic north. Until recently, however, their origin remained obscure. Since 1977 excavations were carried out at the site of Takht-i Sangin, at the confluence of the Wakhsh and the Panj (Amu Darya) rivers and just north of the border with Afghanistan. This is the land of the above-mentioned *Sakâ Haumavargâ*. The excavations brought to light an extraordinarily well-preserved Zoroastrian temple, which dates to the turn of the fourth and the third centuries BC, but which contained many objects that date to the fifth and fourth centuries and clearly recall the objects of the Oxus Treasure.[40] It is very well possible that the Oxus Treasure in the British Museum originates from this site.

However, this is not the end of the story. In 1993, local farmers along the upper course of the Panjshir river (northeast of Kabul) discovered a hoard of objects that they claimed to form part of the Oxus Treasure.[41] The objects from the Panjshir do indeed recall the items of the (earlier) Oxus Treasure, and they may well form part of the original hoard.[42]

Of great interest to the study of Afghanistan are the many gold plaques of the Oxus Treasure with depictions of priests carrying bundles of twigs, the *barᵊsman* or *barsom* of the Zoroastrians.[43] The priests are dressed in trousers, tunics, a *bashlyq* and they each carry an *akinakes* along their right side. These plaques constitute the bulk of the objects, both from the Oxus Treasure in the British Museum and from the hoard discovered in the early 1990s. Priests holding the

38 Compare Mac Dowall and Taddei 1978:201ff. and Cribb 1985. See also Vogelsang 1988b.
39 Some 200 items, plus about 500 coins. For this Treasure, see Barnett 1968; Dalton 1905; Pichikyan 1997.
40 Compare Litvinsky and Pichikjan 1995.
41 Pichikyan 1997. This hoard from the Panjshir valley is now, together with many other recently looted objects from Iran and Afghanistan, proudly housed in the Miho Museum, Japan.
42 Always presuming the newly discovered objects are not fakes.
43 See Boyce 1975:167.

barsom twigs are also sculptured in the round, in gold or silver. Interest lies in the dress of the people depicted. They are clearly wearing the Scythian outfit, as could be expected from a site in this part of the Iranian world. They are also likely to have been involved in Zoroastrian rituals. If so, it would make the link between Zoroastrianism, the Scythian Bactrians, the Amyrgaean Sakas, and the use of the name of Vishtaspa for the Persian Achaemenid governor in Bactria, even stronger. It is not surprising that in later years Bactria became known as the birthplace of Zarathustra and the heartland of Zoroastrianism.

Achaemenid Period Settlements

Archaeology has revealed a large number of Achaemenid period sites in Afghanistan, especially in the north of the country. This imbalance in the distribution of Achaemenid sites may be based on the spread of archaeological work in the country, but it may also indicate a much higher level of economic development in ancient Bactria. It is highly speculative to pursue this line of reasoning, but it is important to note that after the fall of the Persian Achaemenids, ancient Bactria soon became the centre of a large and highly successful colony of Greeks and Macedonians. Their accumulated wealth enabled them in later years to expand their influence over much of Eastern Iran and the northwest of the Indian subcontinent.

In the centre of ancient Arachosia, some 3.5 km west of Qandahar City, lie the ruins of Old Qandahar (*Shahr-i Kuhna* or *Zur Shahr*) (Ill. 4). Excavations at this site between 1974 and 1978 revealed that the settlement dates back to the Achaemenid Period or earlier.[44] The site encompasses an area of about 1,100 × 600 metres and is surrounded by massive ramparts. In the centre rises a citadel of 200 × 100 metres (originally twice as large), still rising to a height of some 30 metres, with circular towers at the corners. At the foot of the citadel, archaeologists found two fragments of Elamite Achaemenid tablets, which are comparable to finds made at the Persian Achaemenid capital of Persepolis where they are dated to the late sixth and early fifth centuries BC.[45] There can hardly be any doubt that this was the capital of Achaemenid Arachosia, which, according to Pliny, bore the same name as the nearby river and the surrounding district.[46]

---

44   Ball 1982: No. 522. MacNicoll and Ball 1996; Helms 1982; 1997.
45   Helms 1982:11ff.; 1997:101.
46   Pliny, *NH* VI 61.

Illustration 4　*The citadel of Achaemenid Qandahar (photograph: author, autumn 1978).*

An interesting feature of Old Qandahar is its origin. The earliest levels yielded pottery that is identical to that found in Periods VI and VII at nearby Mundigak. Moreover, the architecture of the earliest ramparts and citadel of Old Qandahar show characteristics that link up strongly with other sites in the eastern parts of the Iranian Plateau, rather than in West Iran. The citadel in particular, with its circular towers, shows an Eastern Iranian tradition. A comparable citadel, some 36 metres high, was found at Nad-i Ali, at the hill of Sorkh Dagh, in Afghan Sistan.[47] This site dates roughly to the same period as the earliest levels of Old Qandahar, as can be deduced from the ceramic finds. Furthermore, it should be realized that the pottery from Sorkh Dagh and the lower levels at Old Qandahar, and the pottery from Mundigak VI and VII, do not contain any wares that link up with West Iranian traditions. Instead, there are some ceramic types that show analogies to wares from the lands in the north, as for instance the cylindrical-conical bowls.

The Persian Achaemenid occupation of Afghanistan did of course not necessarily lead to an immediate and drastic change in pottery traditions and architecture, and both Old Qandahar and Nad-i Ali

47　Ball 1982: No. 752. The hill measures 200 × 50 metres. A comparable mound (Sefid Dagh) lies some 400 metres to the south. The whole plan of the site is roughly comparable to that of Old Qandahar.

Illustration 5   *The citadel of ancient Balkh (photograph: author, January 1979).*

may still well belong to the Early Achaemenid period. However, there are a number of sites in this part of the world that are clearly Achaemenid in character, although they are probably of somewhat later date than the 'East Iranian' style structures. One of these is Dahana-i Ghulaman in Iranian Sistan.[48] Between 1962 and 1965 Italian excavators unearthed here, not far southeast of the regional capital of Zabol, a number of mud-brick structures, the architecture of which is clearly Persian Achaemenid in character. Typical is Building No. 3, which measures 53.2 × 54.3 metres. It consists of a courtyard surrounded by four pillared porticos. In the corners there are closed rooms and stairways, and the entrance to the building is along the south side. The walls are made of pressed earth on stone foundations.[49] The pottery from this site shows a number of wares that are related to West Iranian types.

Similar structures as at Dahana-i Ghulaman have been unearthed in North Afghanistan, at Altin-10 near Balkh.[50] The remains consist of two buildings: the 'summer palace' (80 × 55 metres) with a pillared portico on all four sides; and a square building (36 × 36 metres) consisting of a series of rooms with a courtyard in the middle. Both sites would indicate that during the Persian Achaemenid period, both

48   Compare Vogelsang 1992b:260ff.
49   Of great interest are the remains of altar-like structures in some of the buildings (Vogelsang 1992b:261ff.).
50   Ball 1982: No. 37.

a native 'eastern' and an intrusive 'western' tradition in architecture and ceramics were active.

Apart from Altin-10, there are many other archaeological sites in North Afghanistan that should be dated to the Achaemenid period. A site that was certainly occupied in the mid-first millennium was Balkh (Ill. 5).[51] However, archaeological research has revealed very little of its earlier history. In the Achaemenid Period it probably comprised a roughly circular fortress of 1,000/1,200 metre in diameter with a citadel in the southeast. Much further to the east, along the foothills of Badakhshan, extensive irrigation networks have been found that indicate a dense population in the Achaemenid Period and before.[52]

The sites from the mid-first millennium BC in the northeast of the Persian Achaemenid Empire are easily recognizable by their pottery, which includes a high percentage of wheelmade, cylindrical-conical vessels.[53] These vessels have a long history in this part of the world, dating back to the late second and early first millennia BC, when they started to replace the painted handmade pottery of the Yaz-I Period. Cylindrical-conical vessels have also been found, although in smaller numbers, at Sorkh Dagh and Dahana-i Ghulaman and at Mundigak. They are not found west of the Iranian deserts.

51 Ball 1982, no. 99.
52 Gardin and Gentelle 1976.
53 Compare Cattenat and Gardin 1977.

8

The Greeks

Until the time of the Persian Achaemenids, the people living in the valleys and plains of Afghanistan remained relatively untouched by what went on in Western Iran and the Near East. Outside influences mainly originated from the north. Even during the Persian period, the eastern provinces remained very much aloof from cultural developments in the west. Of course there were changes, but one may wonder whether people in the countryside were aware of the existence of a Great King in faraway Persia. People continued to build according to their own traditions and they went on using their cylindrical-conical vessels. Even local administration may not have been very different from how it was before. Persian Achaemenid rule was based on delegation of power. Local rulers, often themselves of northern, Scythian descent, continued to control the lands for generations while acknowledging the Achaemenids as their distant overlords. In all, life went on as it had done for centuries.

This all changed in the late fourth century BC, with the start of an era in which Greeks and Greek culture spread to the east. The new rulers were strangers, without any knowledge or understanding of Iranian culture. They were Greeks, and all others were mere barbarians. The Greeks were soon to dominate the settled communities of the Iranian Plateau, thus rapidly widening the gap between sedentary and nomadic life. Excavations show a sharp change in pottery traditions and the introduction of many types that derive from the west. The expansion of Hellenism started with the rise to power of a young prince in faraway Macedonia.

In the spring of 334 BC, the 22-year old Macedonian king, Alexander, crossed the Hellespont with an army of some 20,000 men and set off on what would become one of the most daring and successful campaigns ever undertaken in military history.[1] In the years

1   The literature about Alexander of Macedonia is enormous. The best accounts, in my opinion, are those by Bosworth 1988 and Robin Lane Fox 1973. Another impor-

to follow, he defeated the Persian Achaemenid armies headed by their King of Kings, Darius III Codomannus. After burning down the palaces of Persepolis and finding the murdered body of Darius III somewhere east of modern Tehran, he finally reached present-day Afghanistan in the autumn of 330 BC. Marching through the west, south and southeast of the country, he arrived in the Kabul valley in the winter of 330/329 BC. He crossed the Hindu Kush mountains in the following spring and completely unexpected by his adversaries quickly made himself master of the Bactrian north. For two consecutive years, the town of Bactra was his base for operations in the lands across the Amu Darya, in modern Turkmenistan, Uzbekistan and Tajikistan. His main opponent was the local Scythian leader Spitamenes, who had his base in the plains of the Qara Qum. This man was eventually defeated, but his important position in the Northeast of the former Achaemenid Empire, even after his death, may be gauged from the fact that his daughter Apama in later years was married to Alexander's general, Seleucus.[2]

Alexander went as far as the banks of the Syr Darya, where he founded a town called Alexandria Eschata, not far from modern Khodzhent, and not far either from the Cyropolis founded some two hundred years earlier by his predecesssor, the Achaemenid Cyrus the Great. Here both Cyrus the Great and Alexander the Great established the most northeastern limits of their empires.[3]

Finally, in the summer of 327 BC, Alexander again crossed the Hindu Kush mountains, this time from north to south. Once in the Kabul valley, he continued his conquests by moving east, along the Kabul river, towards the Indus valley and beyond. He only stopped when his soldiers simply refused to go on. The Hyphasis (Beas) river in the eastern Panjab marked the farthest extent of Alexander's conquests and in late 326 BC the Greek/Macedonian army turned around and started the long march back home. In the spring of 324 BC Alexander finally returned to Persepolis, which he had left six years earlier. He died in Babylon in 323 BC.

For the purpose of this book the campaigns of Alexander are of great importance. Alexander's army was accompanied by a wide

tant work is the edition and annotated translation of Arrian's *Anabasis Alexandri* and his *Indica*, by Wirth and Von Hinüber 1985. See also Holt 1988 and, recently, Wood 1997.

2   For the name of Spitamenes, see Mayrhofer 1979: I/77. The name of Spitama may also have been that of the eponymous ancestor of Zarathustra's family.

3   The importance of these fortresses lay in the fact that they protected the northern access to the passes of Ushrusana, that lead to the valley of the Zarafshan river with the town of Samarqand (ancient Marakanda) as its main centre. From the Zarafshan valley, which covers the ancient province of Sogdia, the rest of South Central Asia and the Iranian Plateau are within easy reach.

array of geographers, botanists, historians, biographers and others. They collected a wealth of information about the campaign itself and about the terrain and the people that the Macedonians encountered. In this way, a considerable amount of information was provided about the lands and peoples of what is now Afghanistan.

The Persian Achaemenid Army

The final and decisive battle between the Macedonians and the Persians took place in northern Mesopotamia, at Gaugamela, on 1 November 331 BC.[4] The battle order of the Persian army, as passed down by Classical writers, indicates that the eastern provinces of the Empire, plus the other 'Scythian' lands such as Cappadocia and Armenia, provided the bulk of the cavalry forces placed on the flanks of the army.[5] The biographers make special mention of the Bactrians, Arachosians, Sakas and Scythians (!). Dressed in trousers and tunics and with a *bashlyq* covering their heads, and armed with their compound bows, short swords, and battle axes, they formed an enormous and intimidating threat to the Macedonian army.

Apart from this, the biographers of Alexander the Great also describe the composition of the contingents from Afghanistan. Arrian, one of Alexander's biographers, tells that the Achaemenid satrap of Bactria, called Bessus, was in charge of the Bactrians, the Sogdians and the Indians 'bordering on the Bactrians'. He also informs us that 'Sakas' led by someone called Mauaces had joined Bessus's contingent. Another group, in which troops from present-day Afghanistan were included, was that of Barsaentes, the satrap of Arachosia and Drangiana. He led, according to Arrian, the Arachosians and the 'Indian hillmen'. Since Barsaentes, following Arrian, was also in control of Drangiana, we may safely assume that troops from modern Sistan also joined his standard. Finally, we read about the satrap Satibarzanes, who was in command of the troops from his province, Areia, around modern Herat.

In this way it is made clear that in the late fourth century BC there were three top Achaemenid officials in modern-day Afghanistan, namely the governors (or 'satraps') of Bactria, Ara-chosia/Drangiana and Areia. Their centres correspond to the districts around modern Balkh in North Afghanistan, the Qandahar district in South Afghanistan and the surroundings of Herat in West Afghanistan. This situation thus hardly differs from that in the late

4   Arrian, *Anab. Alex*. III 8.3ff.; III 11.3–7. See also Brunt 1976:509–14, and Wirth, in Wirth and Von Hinüber 1985:860–1.
5   Arrian, *Anab. Alex*. III 11.3–7; Curtius IV 12.5ff.

sixth century BC, when the satraps of Bactria and Arachosia are listed in the Behistun inscription as the two main Persian Achaemenid officials in this part of the world.

Bessus, the Last Achaemenid Satrap of Bactria

The composition of the three contingents offers an interesting piece of information that sheds more light on our knowledge gleaned from the earlier, Achaemenid-period sources. The most important contingent from Afghanistan was undoubtedly that of Bessus from Bactria. He commanded his own Bactrians, the troops from Sogdia (along the Zarafshan river north of Bactria) and the 'Indians bordering on the Bactrians'. The latter included, as is clear from these and other sources, the Indians who lived on the other side of the Hindu Kush, in or near the Kabul valley. They must be the same as the (Indian) Gandharians and Dadicae with Bactrian (Scythian) weaponry, listed by Herodotus as forming part of Xerxes's army against Greece in the early fifth century BC.

Bessus was obviously the most important 'Eastern' satrap. He was the one who, after the death of Darius III, proclaimed himself as successor and king. He called himself Artaxerxes (IV) and wore the upright tiara and royal garments of the Persian Achaemenid kings, thus stressing his ambitions.[6] Another Alexander biographer, Curtius, illustrates the wide array of support that Bessus could receive in his struggle against Alexander: the Sogdians, Dahae (a Scythian group from east of the Caspian Sea), Massagetae (Scythians from south of the Aral Sea), Sakas (Scythians, apparently from north and east of Bactria) and Indians.[7] It is clear that Bessus, after the death of Darius III, was regarded as the leader of the northeastern lands of the (former) Achaemenid Empire. In this way, the fortress of Bactra, modern Balkh, was obviously the main centre of Persian Achaemenid rule in the northeastern lands of the Persian Empire. His apparent control of the Indians living south of the Hindu Kush passes also meant that he dominated the strategic route from Iran, across the mountains to the Kabul valley and the Indus plains.

The Sakas of Badakhshan

The position of Mauaces and his Sakas is also very interesting. According to Arrian, these Sakas did not join Bessus as subjects of

6 Arrian, *Anab. Alex.* III 25.3.
7 Curtius VI 3.9.

the Bactrian satrap, but because they had direct obligations towards the Persian king.[8] It shows that these Sakas constituted a group relatively independent of local Persian administration. But who were they?

The Persian Achaemenids called all the Scythians Sakas, while the Greeks preferred in almost all cases the name of the Scythians. The exception are Herodotus's Amyrgaean Sakas, and the Sakas who are listed in the Alexander biographies. There can be no doubt that both Saka groups are identical, and that they are the *Sakâ Haumavargâ*, or 'Haoma-using Sakas' of the Achaemenid sources, whose distinctive, apparently Zoroastrian character was discussed above. According to the Alexander biographies, these Sakas included, apart from Mauaces, two other, very powerful leaders, Oxyartes and Sisimitres. They seem to have lived north of the Amu Darya along the modern borders between Uzbekistan and Tajikistan, northeast of Bactria and far away from the steppes and deserts east of the Caspian where the 'plains' Scythians were living. The Sakas put up a stiff resistance against the Macedonians. Oxyartes was later, after his surrender, installed as Alexander's satrap of the Paropanisadae, in the modern Kabul area. He received this post obviously because Alexander regarded him as a trustworthy man with the necessary contacts to guard this area; someone who would protect the Macedonian rear during the Indian campaign.[9] Alexander also married his daughter, Roxane, who would become the mother of Alexander's posthumously born son, who was also called Alexander.[10]

Achaemenid Arachosia and the Indians

The other important official was Barsaentes, the satrap of Arachosia and Drangiana. He not only commanded his own Arachosians and the troops from Drangiana, but also Indian hillmen. The identity of these Indians remains unclear. They probably lived east and northeast of ancient Arachosia, along the modern border between Afghanistan and Pakistan, probably in the land called Sattagydia by Herodotus and the Achaemenid sources. They may be identical with the 'Indians on this side of the Indus',[11] where Barsaentes sought refuge when his territory was invaded by Alexander.

8   Arrian, *Anab. Alex*. III 8.3.
9   Arrian, *Anab. Alex*. VI 15.3.
10 For this name, compare Avestan *raoxshnâ-*, 'light', 'brilliance'.
11 Arrian, *Anab. Alex*. III 25.

The proximity of 'Indian' people to Arachosia at the time of Alexander is also reflected by Arrian in his book, the *Anabasis Alexandri*. It tells how the Macedonian invaders, between Arachosia and the Kabul valley, came upon 'the Indians nearest the Arachosians'.[12] It is evident that people regarded as Indians lived very close to the heartland of ancient Arachosia. The near-Indian character of the Qandahar oasis, which was already discussed in the preceding chapter, is a detail to which we will return when in the third century BC this part of modern Afghanistan came to be part of the Indian realm of the Mauryas.

The jurisdiction of Barsaentes thus reached from the delta of the Hilmand in modern Sistan, to the Indian borderlands in the east, thus covering all of modern South Afghanistan. Besides, the Alexander biographers tell that two tribes in the southern part of the Panjab, in modern Pakistan, used to pay tribute to the Arachosians.[13] The exact mechanisms remain unclear, but it is very well possible that the leading (Scythian) Arachosians, or at least their Persian Achaemenid satrap, used to exercise some form of control over parts of the Middle Indus valley.

The Lands of Afghanistan in Alexander's Time

The biographers of Alexander give various details about the peoples and the country of modern Afghanistan. They indicate that the main military force of the people from Bactria and Arachosia consisted of cavalry troops. The biographers tell that Bessus, when resisting Alexander, was supported by 8,000 cavalry.[14] Cavalry also followed Satibarzanes, the satrap of Areia, when, after his initial surrender, he revolted against Alexander. Much later, in India, cavalrymen from Arachosia and the Paropanisadae strengthened Alexander's army.[15] Arrian furthermore tells that, while in India, the Companion cavalry of Alexander's army was augmented by cavalrymen from Bactria, Sogdia, Arachosia, Drangiana, Areia and Parthia.[16] Whether or not the Macedonians welcomed these Iranians as comrades or as hostages to guarantee the good behaviour of their people back home, may be a superfluous question.

The widespread use of the horse is reflected in the name of a people encountered by Alexander in the southwest of Afghanistan.

12 Arrian, *Anab. Alex.* III 28.1.
13 Curtius IX 7.14; compare Vogelsang 1992:239–41.
14 Curtius VII 4.20; 7,000 according to Arrian (*Anab. Alex.* III 28.8).
15 Arrian, *Anab. Alex.* V 11.3.
16 *Anab. Alex.* VII 6.3.

Here, Alexander and his Macedonians met a people whom the biographers call the Ariaspoi or Arimaspoi.[17] They were also called the *Euergetai*, the 'Benefactors'. Cyrus the Great, according to the biographers, conferred this title upon them when they rescued him during his 'Scythian' campaign. According to Arrian, they governed themselves in a manner that was completely different from the other peoples in the region. The specific nature of this group, combined with the fact that in the sources they are somehow related to a 'Scythian' campaign, is highly intriguing. It may indicate that they were descendants of the Scythians who in the early first millennium migrated to this area via the Herat corridor in the north, and for centuries retained their own character. If their name is passed down correctly, it includes the Iranian word *asp-* for 'horse', perhaps indicating the importance of the horse to the Ariaspians, and reflecting their Scythian origins.[18]

In the west and south of Afghanistan, Alexander passed through a number of urban settlements.[19] These included Artacoana, the capital of Areia (also named Alexandria in Areia);[20] Phra or Phrada, renamed (Alexandria) Prophthasia, the main centre of Drangiana (probably near modern Farah);[21] and (Alexandria in) Arachosia, the capital of the province bearing the same name (Old Qandahar).[22] From the records, it is clear that these places constituted the local centres of Persian Achaemenid power.

Alexander does not seem to have had many problems in occupying Southeast Afghanistan. Diodorus, one of the biographers of Alexander, tells that it took Alexander only a few days to establish his control there.[23] The Macedonians did not stay long in Arachosia, but they left behind a Greek official named Menon with a strong garrison of 4,000 infantry and 600 cavalry troops.[24] The strength of the

17   Arrian, *Anab. Alex.* III 27.4–5. For the Arimaspoi, see Curtius VII 3.1 and Diodorus XVII 81.1–2. See also Pliny, *NH* VI 94 and Strabo XV 2.10. Compare Gnoli 1967:47–51, and 1980:143, n. 116; and Vogelsang 1992b:228.
18   Compare the name of Zariaspa ('with yellow horses') for Bactra (Strabo XI 8.9).
19   For this subject, compare Fraser 1996.
20   Arrian, *Anab. Alex*, III 25.5–6. See also Curtius VI 6.33 (Artacana); Diodorus XVII 78.1 (Chortacana); Pliny, *NH* VI 61, 93; Strabo XI 10.1 (Artacaena). In the early nineteenth century a cuneiform cylinder seal was found in or near Herat. Compare Ball 1982: No. 428.
21   Arrian, *Anab. Alex*, 25.8. See also Curtius VI 36; VII 1; Diodorus 78.4. Plutarch *Mor.* 328F. Steph. Byz. *s.v.* Phrada. The site may be identical with the Farah Bala Hisar. See Ball 1982: No. 318.
22   Pliny *NH* VI 61 simply calls it the *Oppidum Arachosiorum*. Strabo refers to Arakhotoi. See Vogelsang 1992b:48–9.
23   Diodorus XVII 81.3.
24   Curtius VII 3.5.

garrison was no doubt instigated by the strategic importance of the Qandahar oasis. How important exactly was made clear some years later, when a large part of the Macedonian army, with their elephants, marched from the Middle Indus valley via Arachosia back to Persia, led by Alexander's trusted general, Craterus.[25] Alexander himself, followed by some of his troops, took the much more difficult southern route, through the Baluchistan desert.

Long before that, in the autumn of 330 BC, Alexander had marched northeast from Qandahar to the Kabul valley, along the same route that in the summer of 1880 General Roberts would take from Kabul in order to relieve Qandahar. The biographers describe the hardships that Alexander's troops had to endure on their 500 km march. The troops finally settled along the southern flanks of the Hindu Kush (which they called the Caucasus). Here, at the confluence of the Panjshir and Ghorband rivers, near modern Charikar, Alexander refounded the centre of Capisa (Alexandria ad Caucasum or Alexandria sub Caucaso), the old Kapisha-kanish of the Achaemenids.[26]

In the spring of 329 BC Alexander and his army descended down the northern slopes of the Hindu Kush mountains into the plains of ancient Bactria. His opponent, Bessus, left the country and fled to the north,[27] upon which Alexander occupied the land. The Alexander biographers mention the presence of three main towns: Drapsaka, Aornos and Bactra. The location of Bactra is of course clear, but the identification of the first two is still unknown.[28] In Bactria itself hardly any resistance to Alexander was put up. As in other parts of modern Afghanistan, the defeat of the Persian Achaemenid satrap meant the end of Persian rule. There was no local form of government that remained loyal to the Persians. The local rulers of Bactria, called the 'hyparchs', were called together by Alexander for a *syllogos*.[29] There is no evidence that these hyparchs were at all adverse to their new rulers. They no doubt hoped that their situation would not change, and that they merely would have to send their tokens of submission to another (distant) monarch.

The situation in the 'settled' lands of North Afghanistan was completely different from what happened in the lands north of the

25 Arrian, *Anab. Alex.* VI 17.3.
26 Arrian, *Anab. Alex.* IV 22.4; Curtius VII 3.23; Diodorus XVII 83.1; Strabo XV 2.10.
27 For Alexander and Bactria, see Holt 1988.
28 The name of Warnu is mentioned in recently discovered Bactrian documents from the first millennium AD. See Sims-Williams 1997b:16–17. For Aornos, see Bernard 1996.
29 Arrian, *Anab. Alex.* IV 1.5; Curtius VII 6.15. See also Briant 1984:82–4.

Amu Darya, where Alexander for two years waged a devastating war against local rulers and Scythian marauders from the deserts along the Caspian. The Macedonians terrorized the local people. The fierceness of these struggles was instigated by the completely different political organization of these peripheral lands. In the plains of modern North Afghanistan, local rulers who based their wealth on agricultural produce controlled the people. Peace and tranquillity were to everyone's advantage, and the hyparchs had grown accustomed to the distant control of the Achaemenid king and his representatives. North of the Amu Darya, the people were far less dependent on agriculture. Animal husbandry was far more important, and many people moved every season with their flocks from the plains into the mountains. They lived in close proximity to the nomadic Scythians, probably their kinsmen, who roamed the Qara Qum ('Black Sand') and Qyzyl Qum ('Red Sand') deserts. These Scythians had for two centuries maintained a careful balance in their relationship with the Persian Achaemenids. They recognized the Persian king as their sovereign, but for the rest they were left in relative peace. The fall of the Persian Achaemenids and the arrival of Alexander changed all this. Alexander did not plan to leave the Iranians and Scythians north of the Amu Darya in peace. He was obviously not content with a mere acknowledgement of his suzerainty. A cruel war was the result.

The Succession of Alexander

At the death of Alexander the Great in Babylon, in June 323 BC, a series of wars broke out between the *diadochoi*: the generals and other high officials of Alexander's army who vied for Alexander's heritage.[30] These struggles seriously undermined the strength of the Macedonian empire. It should not be forgotten, however, that even before Alexander's death, Macedonian presence in the Indian provinces had been reduced and almost annihilated, and in Eastern Iran, Greek and Macedonian settlers had revolted and started to return home.[31] In fact, most of Eastern Iran was in a state of turmoil by the time of Alexander's death. It was an uncertain legacy that Alexander left to his successors.[32]

---

30 This left Roxane and her son, Alexander IV, as pawns in the hands of the generals. Both of them were eventually killed by Cassander in 311/310 BC, in Macedonia.
31 Curtius IX 7.1–11; Diodorus XVIII 7. Compare Holt 1988:87–91.
32 For Eastern Iran after Alexander's death, see in particular Holt 1999, Kuhrt and Sherwin-White 1987 and Sherwin-White and Kuhrt 1993.

The numbers of settlers in the east were large: in Bactria alone, Alexander had stationed some 13,500 Greek and Macedonian soldiers. In Arachosia, there were 4,600 men, excluding camp followers and others.[33] It is clear from the sources that most of them simply wanted to go home. They did not like living in the vast expanses of Eastern Iran and South Central Asia, amidst all those 'barbarians' who could not even speak Greek. Classical sources tell that upon Alexander's death the rebellious Greek/Macedonian settlers in Bactria and neighbouring districts gathered an army of some 23,000 men. Such a large army was a serious threat to the Macedonian leaders in Mesopotamia and it also meant that most of the Greek/Macedonian settlers in the East were planning to march home. A large part of Alexander's conquests was about to be evacuated. Immediate action was warranted, and Perdiccas, who acted as regent for Alexander's heirs, ordered another general called Pithon to march east with some 20,000 men. Pithon succeeded and eventually defeated the rebellious settlers in the East. The rebels were forced to stay, although it was clear that most of them did not give up their dreams of ever returning home.

In spite of these events, the Greek/Macedonian satraps in Eastern Iran remained a powerful force in the continuing power struggle. In 317 BC they fielded an army of 6,500 men and defeated their colleague Pithon, by that time the governor in Media.[34] A year later the Eastern satraps again fought a battle, this time with the Greek Eumenes against the Macedonian Antigonus; at the Battle of Paraetacene (West Iran), the satraps of Arachosia, Areia and Drangiana, Bactria and the Kabul valley all united in order to protect their own position.[35] But apparently the colonists were far from united, and there were troops from Parthia and from other parts of the Northeast that joined Antigonus. When the eastern satraps were defeated and Antigonus emerged as victor, the latter claimed overall sovereignty and appointed a number of new satraps in the East. However, he could not replace Oxyartes, the satrap of the Paropanisadae (the Kabul valley), the father of Roxane and the grandfather of Alexander's infant son. Although Oxyartes had supported Eumenes against Antigonus, his position was too strong for anyone to try to remove him. He was firmly entrenched amidst and behind the mountains of the Hindu Kush. The political situation thus remained very unstable. What followed was a time of growing autonomy of the Greek/Macedonian and local governors in the East. Central power

---

33 For Bactria, see Arrian, *Anab. Alex.* IV 22; for Arachosia, Curtius VII 3–4.
34 Diodorus XIX 13.7 and 14.
35 Diodorus XIX 14.6–8.

was absent, and many settlers returned home. Scythians from the north, Indians from the east, and local Iranians reclaimed their lost positions. Alexander's legacy in the east was about to disappear.

It was in the end one of Alexander's officers, Seleucus, who gained the upper hand on the Iranian Plateau after defeating his main Greek/Macedonian opponents. He victoriously entered Babylon in 312/311 BC. Seleucus was married to Apama, the daughter of Spitamenes who for so long had fought Alexander in the North. In this way Seleucus (styled Seleucus *Nikator*, 'The Victorious') and his son Antiochus (styled *Sôter*, 'Saviour') were by kinship particularly involved in the affairs of Eastern Iran. Although the Classical sources are not always clear, it may fairly be surmised that Seleucus campaigned in the East after his occupation of Babylon. He reorganized the political structure of the eastern satrapies, appointed satraps and reinvigorated Alexander's policy of settling Greeks and Macedonians and others in Greek-style cities.[36]

However, Seleucus's position was seriously threatened from the west, by his former colleague Ptolemaeus who had gained control of Egypt, and by his old adversary, Antigonus, the ruler of Anatolia. Before Seleucus could complete his work in the East, he therefore had to return west. He was consequently forced to conclude a treaty with the Indians, who after centuries of Iranian expansion were finally reasserting themselves along the eastern borders of Seleucus's realm.

The Mauryas

The rising star in India at that time was Chandragupta Maurya. He was the founder of the Mauryan dynasty that in the late fourth and third centuries BC ruled much of northern and central India. The Greeks knew him as Sandra Kottos. In *c.*303 BC, before he left the eastern provinces to move west, Seleucus signed an agreement with Chandragupta Maurya. It stipulated, according to the sources, that the lands of Gandhara, the Paropanisadae (Kabul valley), Arachosia and Gedrosia were ceded to the Mauryas, in return for 500 elephants.[37]

The French historian, Paul Bernard, argues that the treaty marked a *fait accompli* and that the Indians already occupied large parts of

36 For the organization of the Seleucid empire, see the classic study by Bikerman, 1938.
37 See *Pliny* VI 23, 69; Strabo XV 1.10; 2.9. In some sources Areia is also mentioned, but it is hardly likely that the Herat area was also ceded (see however MacDowall 1979:46).

Eastern Iran.[38] Whether this is true or not, the situation may have been more complicated than that. The areas ceded to the Mauryas were located at the extreme eastern edge of the Iranian Plateau and south and east of the Hindu Kush mountains. They apparently included the valley of the Kabul river, the valley of the Arghandab (ancient Arachosia), and the lands of eastern Baluchistan. They were in the main, perhaps apart from the Arghandab valley, populated by people who were regarded as Indian, although for centuries most of these lands had been under control of an Iranian (or Iranian/Scythian) upper class. Furthermore, during the fourth century the main type of coin used in the lands south of the Hindu Kush was the silver Punch Marked coin, which was of 'Indian' origin, thus indicating the extent of cultural influence from the Indian subcontinent upon the eastern parts of the Achaemenid empire.[39] The increase of Mauryan control as far northwest as the foothills of the Hindu Kush may thus reflect more than merely the expansion of Mauryan political authority. It may indicate the conscious inclusion by the Mauryas of lands that they regarded as being Indian and being populated by Indians.

At first sight this may seem a rather modern, nationalistic principle. Of great interest in this respect, however, is Kautilya's *Arthashâstra*, a Sanskrit work dating back to the early centuries of the modern era but reflecting information from the time of the Mauryas. In this book the idea is put forward that the dominion of a true *chakravartin* (ruler) would extend from the Himalayas in the north to the seas in the south.[40] Similar references, sometimes referring to the Wakhshu (Amu Darya) as the northernmost border of *Bhârata-varsha* or *Jambu-dvipa* (India), are found in later Indian texts. Mauryan domination of Arachosia and the Kabul valley may thus be more than mere imperialistic expansion and reflect an existing idea as to which lands were regarded as being 'Indian'.

The fascinating point is that the oasis of Qandahar (Arachosia) was apparently included into these 'Indian' lands. In earlier pages I have drawn attention to Achaemenid and Classical references that testify to the close proximity of 'Indians' in the Qandahar oasis. It may not be fortuitous that in later centuries Arachosia was known as 'White India'.[41] Whatever the case, by the third century BC, the hilly lands east of Arachosia, now the habitat of (Iranian) Pashtun tribes, were obviously still 'Indian', and the Qandahar oasis itself also passed under Indian rule.

38   Dani and Bernard 1994:89–90.
39   See also Vogelsang 1988b, in which I describe Indian influence on the ceramic repertoire of Gandhara in the mid-first millennium BC.
40   Sircar 1971:5.
41   Isidore of Charax, *Parthian Stations* paragraph 19.

Chandragupta Maurya was succeeded in *c*.298 BC by Bindusara, known to the Greeks as Amitrokhates.[42] He in turn was followed in *c*.273 BC by his famous son, commonly known as Ashoka (*c*.273–232 BC). This king is known for numerous edicts and inscriptions that were engraved on pillars and rock faces throughout the Mauryan empire.[43] The texts were written in the local language and script.

Since the early 1930s a number of such texts have been found in Afghanistan, although placed and executed in a less 'grand' style than in the subcontinent.[44] The first of these was a Prakrit (Middle Indian) text in Aramaic script and with Aramaic paraphrases. It was placed on a stone tablet that was found near Pul-i Darunta (near Jalalabad) in 1932.[45] More Ashokan texts, this time in Aramaic script and language, were discovered in 1969 and in 1973 on a rock surface in the Laghman valley some ten km northwest of its confluence with the Kabul River. A bilingual Greek-Aramaic inscription (Qandahar I) was found in 1958 on a large boulder just north of Old Qandahar in South Afghanistan (Ill. 6).[46] Another Mauryan text, this time only in Greek and inscribed on a stone slab, was also found in Qandahar, in 1963.[47] The slab probably formed part of a much larger monument perhaps containing all the fourteen major rock edicts of Ashoka. Another text, written in Aramaic script but Aramaic-Prakrit in content was found in Qandahar in the same year.[48] In the valley of the Kabul river, the Mauryas thus used Aramaic script and language, plus the Prakrit language. In Arachosia they used Greek script and language, Aramaic script and language, and mixed Aramaic-Prakrit language. In other words, Greek was only used in Arachosia, while Aramaic and Prakrit were used in both places.

In the texts, there are frequent references to the peoples of the northwest of the Mauryan empire, including the Yavanas (Greeks) and the Kambojas.[49] The name of the Yavanas, a word ultimately derived from the name of Ionia along the eastern coast of the

42 Compare Sanskrit *Amitraghâta*, 'killer of enemies'. According to Athenaeus XIV 652–3, Bindusara politely asked Antiochus I for wine, figs and a philosopher.
43 This does not mean that it was Ashoka himself who ordered these inscriptions to be made (pers. comm. Dr H. Tieken, Leiden). For the inscriptions as found in Afghanistan, see MacDowall and Allchin 1978:192–8. For a survey of all inscriptions, see Allchin and Norman 1985. For the Greek texts, compare Christol 1983.
44 For this supposed 'missionary' activity of the Indians, see D. A. Scott 1985.
45 According to Allchin and Norman (1985:46), it contains apparently quotations from Ashokan edicts.
46 This bilingual text seems to contain Minor Rock Edict I.
47 This text contains parts of Rock Edicts XII and XIII.
48 This text contains parts of Pillar Edict VII.
49 Compare Töttösy 1956 for the Indian name of the Greeks.

Illustration 6   *The bilingual Greek/Aramaic Ashoka inscription of Old Qandahar (photograph: author, autumn 1978).*

Aegaean, clearly refers to the Greek population of Eastern Iran; the Old Persian inscriptions of the Achaemenids refer in this case to *Yauna*. The Greek presence in Arachosia in the third centrury BC, albeit apparently under overall Mauryan control, is further illustrated by the find at Old Qandahar in 1978 of a Greek inscription, dating to *c.*280 BC.[50] As for the Kambojas, this name was commonly used in Indian sources to indicate the Iranian population of the borderlands.[51]

50   See Fraser 1979.
51   For the Kambojas, see Sircar 1971:195–200.

This is the time that tradesmen, diplomats and others frequently passed through what is now Afghanistan.[52] One of the Greek diplomats travelling to India was Megasthenes. He apparently spent a long time at the court of the Mauryas at Pataliputra, in northeast India. His *Indica*, although not fully extant, is still known from many fragments. He is said to have stayed frequently with Sibyrtius, the Greek governor in Arachosia in the last decades of the fourth century.[53] In the Ashokan inscriptions (Edict XIII) it is furthermore stated that the Indian king sent messengers to the west, 'where reigns the Greek King named Amtiyoga (perhaps Antiochus II, *r.* 261–246 BC) and beyond the realm of that Amtiyoga in the lands of the four kings Tulamaya (Ptolemaeus II Philadelphus? *r.* 285–247 BC), Antekina (Antigonus Gonatus? *r.* 276–239 BC), Maka (Magas of Cyrene? who died in 258 BC) and Alikyashudala (Alexander of Ephirus or Alexander of Corinth?).[54]

Indian presence in Arachosia and the rest of the borderlands is also indicated by the find during excavations at Old Qandahar of pottery of clearly Indian origin.[55] Furthermore, Mauryan coins have been found in eastern Afghanistan, including Qandahar. These included silver Punch Marked coins, which was the silver currency of the Mauryan empire, and square copper coins, which are known from Begram, Ay Khanum and the Mir Zakah hoard.[56] The latter is one of the most spectacular finds from the country. In early 1947 reports reached Kabul that huge amounts of coins were being found in a well near the village of Mir Zakah, about 50 km northeast of Gardiz. Scientists from Kabul subsequently visited the place and recovered some 5,500 Indian coins of the Mauryan period. The same hoard also included about 2,500 Indo-Greek issues (mainly second century BC) and approximately 3,500 Indo-Scythian (first century BC) and other coins from the post-Mauryan period.[57] The well probably served a religious function that continued for many centuries.

The Later Seleucids

After the Battle of Ipsus in 301 BC and the defeat of Antigonus, Seleucus I Nicator soon returned his attention to the East and started to further promote the Greek/Macedonian colonization of the East. Classical sources indicate that many Greeks and others now moved

52   For the interaction between Indian and Mediterranean cultures, see Sedlar 1980.
53   Arrian, *Anab. Alex.* V 6.2.
54   Trans. by Thapar 1961.
55   Vogelsang 1985:64–5.
56   Ball 1982: No. 728.
57   N. H. Dupree et al. 1974:110.

east, from the Mediterranean to the expanses of South Central Asia. The Seleucid focal point in the East was Bactria and the cities located along the routes leading there from Mesopotamia. Seleucus founded Greek *poleis* and in general created the conditions that were conducive to Greek colonization. He well understood the economic wealth of the area, its rich potentials and its strategic location.[58] During the latter part of his reign his son, Antiochus (*r.* 281–261), acted as viceroy in the East. We may safely assume that Antiochus resided in Bactra, just like the Persian Achaemenid prince/governors of the East before him.

Growing Greek involvement in the East led to opposition from the side of the Scythians living along the fringes of the settled areas. Bactria was rapidly being Hellenized and the Greeks had little understanding of 'barbarian' culture. The age-old symbiosis between the settled and the nomadic (Scythian) people of South Central Asia was being disturbed. There were new rulers, with a new culture, and there was no place for the nomads from the north. Around 290 BC, the latter established their own form of contact. According to the sources, Scythian groups from the north destroyed towns in Margiana and Areia.[59] The incursions were repulsed, but the threat was clear. The Greeks subsequently built enormous walls around the major agricultural districts, as for instance that of the Marw oasis.[60] The walls around the Balkh oasis, described by the Arab geographers as extending for 65 km, may also date back to the Hellenistic period.

All the while, the Seleucids continued to found or re-found towns. These places were given the name of Alexandria, Seleucia, Apamaea, or Antiochia.[61] The capital of Margiana is a huge refoundation. The Achaemenid centre of this region, the ancient site of Erk Kala, was made into the citadel of a much larger city, called Alexandria in Margiana, measuring some 1,500 metres along its four sides. The town of Bactra was also more than doubled in extent, to the south of the Achaemenid settlement (Ill. 7).

Another city, which may have been founded by Alexander himself, was the famous settlement of Ay Khanum, at the confluence of the Kokcha and Amu Darya rivers, in Badakhshan.[62] It is illustrative of Afghan archaeology that explorers visited the site from the early nine-

---

58 Its close location to India assured a ready supply of elephants. Compare the cuneiform tablet from Babylon dated to 276–274 BC that refers to elephants sent to the king (Antiochus I) by the Bactrian satrap (Holt 1999:174–5).

59 Pliny, *NH* VI 47.

60 Strabo tells that the oasis was protected against the northern nomads by a wall of some 1,500 stadia in length (*c.*250 km). Remains of this rampart have been discovered in the north of the oasis.

61 Compare Fraser 1996.

62 Ball 1982: No. 18.

Illustration 7   *The southern walls of Classical and Islamic Balkh (photograph: author, January 1979).*

teenth century onwards, but its importance was never fully realized.[63] It was 'rediscovered' in the early 1960s by French archaeologists following a chance find of some Classical objects by a hunting party of the Afghan king.[64]

Ay Khanum is the most 'Greek' of all the excavated Hellenistic sites in the east. Its ramparts enclose an area of some 1,800 × 1,500 metres. It boasts an acropolis, a gymnasium, temples, a theatre (seating about 6,000 people), a stone fountain, and so forth. The architecture of the town shows predominantly Greek features, like the rectangular towers along its ramparts. The palace, however, was constructed mainly according to Persian-Achaemenid models, with clusters of rooms being surrounded by corridors. In turn these clusters were placed along a series of courtyards. The complex spread over an area of some 350 × 250 metres. The main courtyard was located in the northeast. It measured 137 × 108 metres and it was surrounded on all four sides by pillared porticos.

The importance of Ay Khanum was based on the agricultural produce of the surrounding countryside, which was irrigated on a grand scale. Its significance was also enhanced by the nearby mines of stones in the mountains of Badakhshan. The Treasury adjoining

63   Wood 1872:259–60 tells about his visit to the site in about 1840.
64   Compare Levi 1984 (1972):134, and 228, n. 22.

the Palace contained debris of various kinds of stones, including agate, beryl, carnelian, garnet, lapis lazuli, onyx, pearl, ruby and turquoise.

The French archaeologists discovered some Greek inscriptions, including one in the *temenos* of Kineas (apparently the founder of the city). It is dated to *c.*275 BC and tells how someone called Clearchus of Soli copied a maxim from Delphi: 'In childhood, learn good manners; in youth, control your passions; in middle age, practise justice; in old age, be of good council; in death, have no regrets.' Other Greek texts were inscribed on papyrus, parchment and ostraca. One of these texts contained a passage from the work of Aristotle. In truth, Greek culture had penetrated deeply into the heartland of Iranian and Zoroastrian civilization.

The Graeco-Bactrians

The apotheosis of Greek rule in Eastern Iran came in the third century BC. Probably during the reign of the Seleucid ruler Antiochus II Theos (*r.* 261–246 BC), or shortly after, the Bactrian Greeks under their leader, Diodotus, openly revolted against their Seleucid king.[65] The transition from Seleucid to Graeco-Bactrian rule is reflected in the variety of coins found with the Oxus Treasure. It includes coins of Alexander the Great, Seleucus I, Antiochus I, Antiochus II, and also of this Diodotus. The Diodotus coins, however, for a time still carry the name of Antiochus, but the Seleucid reverse symbol of the seated Apollo is replaced by that of a naked Zeus about to throw his thunderbolt. In fact, numismatics constitute an enormously important tool for the study of these so-called Graeco-Bactrians; without its help many kings would simply be unknown, and others would remain ephemeral figures from a distant past and distant lands.[66]

Sometime around 230 BC, the house of Diodotus was overthrown by Euthydemus.[67] His silver and bronze issues are widely found in Bactria, especially at Ay Khanum.[68] The rule of Euthydemus was the period of greatest prosperity for the Graeco-Bactrians. According to Apollodorus of Artemita, it was the fertility of Bactria that gave the Graeco-Bactrians the wealth that eventually led them to India.[69]

---

65 For the Graeco-Bactrians, see Tarn 1951; Narain 1957; Kuhrt and Sherwin-White 1987; Sherwin-White and Kuhrt 1993; Holt 1999, and many others.
66 See Bopearachchi 1991 and Holt 1999.
67 Polybius XI 34.
68 Bernard 1994:100.
69 Strabo XI 11.1.

Surveys and excavations have indeed shown that by this time irrigation networks covered much of the land.

Around 208 BC the Graeco-Bactrians were, at least officially, brought back under Seleucid control when Antiochus III the Great (*r.* 223–187 BC) invaded their land and defeated Euthydemus along the Hari Rud river.[70] A subsequent two-year long siege of the town of Bactra was only lifted when the Graeco-Bactrians pointed out to their opponents that they should unite against the northern barbarians. According to Polybius, writing in the first century BC, Euthydemus told Antiochus III: 'If Antiochus does not accept my request, the situation of both parties will suffer. Huge hordes of nomads are massed along the border, posing a threat to both of us, and if the barbarians cross the border they will certainly conquer the land.'[71]

Antiochus III could not take Bactra and he had no choice but to accept Euthydemus's offer of nominal sovereignty. He returned to the west in 206–205 BC, via the Hindu Kush passes and Arachosia, along the way concluding a treaty with a local Indian ruler, Sophagasenos, who must have been a successor of Ashoka or another Indian princeling controlling parts of the Indo-Iranian borderlands.[72] As soon as Antiochus left northern Afghanistan, the Graeco-Bactrians under Euthydemus again issued their own coins, thus demonstrating their independence.

The Rise of the Parthians

Euthydemus's threat that northern nomads would overrun the Graeco-Bactrian and Seleucid dominions in Iran was certainly not groundless.[73] The Greeks were very well aware that north of the Iranian Plateau there was an enormous reservoir of restless tribes keen on profiting from the rich and fertile oases and plains that for centuries had prospered under the aegis of the Persians and Macedonians. By the early third century BC nomads had already destroyed a number of places on the Plateau. By the mid-third century BC, another of these restless groups had moved into the province of Parthia and established a dynasty. Originating in the barren plains of the Qara Qum desert, they came to be known as the Parthians, after the first 'civilized' province that they conquered. Their kings were called the Arsacids, after the name of their eponymous

---

70   Polybius X 49.
71   Polybius XI 34.5.
72   Polybius XI 34.11.
73   For Parthian history, see the many studies by Wolski, esp. 1993.

ancestor, Arsaces. One of their first main urban centres was Nisa, just northwest of modern Ashkhabad. The real founder of the Parthian Empire was Mithradates I (who reigned between *c.*171–138 BC). When he died, his armies had taken Media and Babylonia and had brought the Seleucids to their knees. His empire stretched from the Mesopotamian plains in the west to the borders of the Graeco-Bactrian domains in the east.

The Indo-Greeks

In the early second century BC, while the Parthians were extending their domain in the west, the Graeco-Bactrians extended their control to the south and southeast. This push across the Hindu Kush seems to have been instigated by Demetrius, the son of Euthydemus. His involvement in the conquest of the southern lands can be deduced from the name of the town of Demetrias in Arachosia, as known from later sources.[74] This is also the period that the power of the Mauryas had collapsed, and the local Indian successors were no match for the Greeks.

However, while the Greeks extended their domains south of the Hindu Kush, in Bactria itself dynastic changes took place. In about 170 BC, the house of Eucratides replaced that of Euthydemus and Demetrius.[75] Eucratides has been described as one of the great military leaders of his age. His rule is marked by many innovations, expressed in his coinage.[76] However, south of the Hindu Kush, a number of Indo-Greek kings from the house of Euthydemus continued to rule. Two of the famous names in this respect are Apollodotus I and Menander, and their silver drachms are known from Qandahar.[77] Menander can probably be identified with the main character from a Buddhist work, written in Pali (Middle Indian), called the *Milindapañha*.[78] Menander's name is also found in an inscription that was found in Bajaur, northwest of Peshawar. It is a Prakrit text in Kharoshthi script on a steatite casket.[79]

The dynastic vicissitudes of the Graeco-Bactrians and Indo-Greeks from the early second century onwards are far from clear, and various princelings may well have reigned simultaneously. An interesting

74   Isidore of Charax, *Parthian Stations*, 19.
75   Compare Justin XLI 6.
76   Bernard 1994:101.
77   MacDowall 1985:67.
78   Bernard 1994:117 refers to Buddhist influence on the Indo-Greeks. For Menander, see especially Fussman 1993.
79   Compare Majumdar 1937.

feature is the fact that they used two different standards for their coins. North of the Hindu Kush they minted coins struck according to the Attic standard of weight, and solely with Greek legends, while south of the mountains they issued coins according to the Indian standard of weight, with Greek and Prakrit legends, the latter in Kharoshthi script.[80] The copper coins struck south of the mountains at first also imitated the square or rectangular form of the Maurya copper coins. The silver coins were circular, apart from one type struck by Apollodotus I, which was square.[81]

Religious life in Eastern Iran after the arrival of the Greeks was characterized, as so much else, by Greek and local beliefs, and a synchretism of these two traditions. Next to the names of the main Greek gods, such as Apollo, Artemis, Athena, Dionysos, Helios, Heracles, Zeus and so forth, mentioned on coins and in inscriptions, attempts were being made to identify these Greek gods with local, Iranian deities. In this way, Iranian Ahura Mazda became linked to Zeus; Verethraghna was identified with Heracles; Mithra was compared to Helios and Apollo; Nana was likened to Artemis.

Increased contacts with the Indian subcontinent also brought about the inclusion of Indian elements. Buddhism was apparently spreading: there is a stupa (Buddhist burial mound containing a relic) depicted on the coins of the Indo-Greek ruler Agathocles from the second century BC. Furthermore, Hindu deities also make their appearance. One of the coins issued by Agathocles contains the image of Vasudeva Krishna (Vishnu).[82]

Local deities continued to be worshipped in local temples. One of these has recently been excavated at Takht-i Sangin, along the northern banks of the Panj river in modern Tajikistan.[83] Here, among other finds, a votive altar was found with a Greek inscription, stating that this was an offering to the Iranian god Wakhshu (Oxus). The worshipper's Iranian name is Atrosauka, and the relief is that of the Greek god Marsyas playing a double flute. Local city-deities were also worshipped. Eucratides issued coins with the image of Capisa, the goddess of the city with the same name (modern Begram). She is depicted in a way comparable to Zeus sitting on a throne, but the addition of an elephant and a *chaitya* (Indian shrine) adds a distinctly Indian atmosphere.

By the middle of the second century BC, much of what is now Afghanistan had thus become a melting pot of Greek, Indian and

80 Two kings also issued coins in the Prakrit language, but in Brahmi script. These were Pantaleon and Agathocles.
81 MacDowall 1984:71.
82 MacDowall 1978:209.
83 Compare Harmatta 1994:314.

Iranian influences. Greek Zeus is found next to Iranian Ahura Mazda and Indian Vishnu. Local Iranian religions, including Zoroastrianism, vie with Buddhism for the favour of the local rulers. The autochthonous, Iranian population is dominated by Greek/Macedonian princelings, who also came to dominate the principally Indian lands south of the Hindu Kush. In the west looms the rapidly expanding realm of the Parthians. But in the north appears a far more dangerous enemy.

9

Northern Rulers

In the mid-second century BC, new migrants from South Central Asia moved into the northern parts of Afghanistan. They followed in the footsteps of the Scythian nomads who migrated onto the Plateau in the early first millennium BC and in those of their Indo-Iranian kinsmen of the second millennium. Some information on this momentous occurrence is contained in Strabo's *Geographika*. This Greek geographer lived around the beginning of the modern era, but he based his information on older sources. He tells that the invaders included the Asioi, the Pasianoi, the Sakarauloi and the Tokharoi. Much has been written on the identity of these groups.[1] The most attractive explanation is by (Sir) Harold Bailey, who linked the name of the Asioi to the modern Caucasian Ossetes, who still speak an Eastern Iranian language and who are generally regarded as being the descendants of a Central Asian group of Scythians. As for the Pasianoi, Bailey suggested a link with the modern Pashtuns.[2] The latter hypothesis, from an historical point of view, is very interesting, since it would support the suggestion that Pashto should be classed as a Northeast Iranian language and it would give an approximate date as to the introduction of Pashto in Eastern Iran. As to the Sakarauloi, or Sakaraukoi according to other sources, their identity is still disputed, but their name would indicate their affiliation to the Sakas or Scythians. The identity of the Tokharoi is equally unknown.[3] Their name was much later used by Western scholars to describe an Indo-European (but not Iranian) language that was used in the extreme western parts of China, sometime during the second half of

1 Strabo XI 8.2 (on the authority of Apollodorus of Artemita). Justin XLII (from Pompeius Trogus) mentions the Sa(ca)raucae and the Asiani. For these names, compare Frye 1984:191–2.
2 Bailey 1993.
3 But see Bailey 1978:4, who translates the name with 'Great Mountain [People]', from Chinese *Ta* for 'great', and an Iranian word for mountain (Avestan *gari-*).

the first millennium AD. There is, however, no evidence whatsoever to link the Classical Tokharoi with the people speaking the 'Tokharan' language.

Whether Bailey's suggestions are correct or not, we may safely assume that many of the newcomers spoke an Iranian language and were related to the Scythian tribes that for hundreds of years had dominated the vast expanse of Central Asia. In this context the name of the 'Saka'-rauk(l)oi is of course significant. We may also safely assume that the vanguard of the invasion was made up of the 'plains' Scythians from the steppes and semi-deserts east of the Caspian and Aral Sea, and perhaps also by the Sakas from Badakhshan and the lands along the northern banks of the Amu Darya. Both groups, it should be noted, had been in contact with the sedentary world of the Plateau for hundreds of years.

The invaders started their great trek to the south under pressure of other groups, ultimately as a result of events that occurred along the northern and northwestern frontiers of China. The snowball effect cannot have been very very different from what is told by Herodotus when he talks about the origins of the Scythians and Cimmerians hundreds of years earlier.

One of the factors behind the process of migrations of the second century BC was China's unification under the Qin dynasty in 221 BC and its replacement by the powerful Han dynasty some decades later. Following the internal reorganization of the Chinese empire, Chinese troops soon started to put pressure on the nomadic tribes living along the borders.[4] As part of the ongoing struggle and in order to win information about the nomads, the Han emperor Wu (c.140–87 BC) sent an ambassador, called Zhang Qian, to the west.[5] When he returned in the mid-twenties of the second century BC, after travelling for many years, he reported that the so-called Yuezhi who used to live along the northwestern borders of China, had been pushed from their homelands by the Xiongnu. Eventually, after much wandering, the Yuezhi had settled north of the Amu Darya. On the way, according to the Chinese sources, they also defeated the Saiwang, a tribe whose name reflects that of the Sakas, who were pushed on in front of them towards the south.[6]

The ethnic origin of the Yuezhi is unknown, and there is even no firm evidence as to their relationship with the various ethnic groups

4 Compare Barfield 1989.
5 His journal is included in the *Shih-chi* (chapter 123) of Sima Qian (c.90 BC); in the *Han shu* of Pan Ku (c.AD 92; see also Pulleyblank 1970), and in the *Hou Han shu* of Fan Yen. Compare Hulsewé and Loewe 1979.
6 Literally: Sai-king. Suggestions have been made as to the identification of the Sakaraukoi with the Saiwang (Bailey 1979:27–8; Harmatta 1994b:409).

mentioned by Classical sources.[7] We are neither certain about the exact routes followed by the Yuezhi. What is clear, however, is that the trek of the Yuezhi from Inner Central Asia to the banks of the Amu Darya brought about an avalanche of other migrating tribes. Waves of migrants penetrated from the north down onto the plains of Bactria.[8] Most of them, including the Sakaraukoi and the Saiwang, were descendants of the Scythians and Iranians who had remained in Central Asia while their kinsmen moved south centuries earlier. Others, including the Yuezhi, may have belonged to other ethnic groups. We simply do not know.

From Chinese and Classical sources it is clear that the nomads soon overran Bactria. The Bactrian-Greek rulers north of the Hindu Kush were deposed. Coin finds show that for some time Greek princes continued to control certain lands south of the mountains, but in all Greek military rule in this part of the world was drawing to an end. Some of the Scythians from the north soon pushed on towards the heights of Badakhshan and the Hindu Kush. From this period dates the Early Islamic name of the western foothills of Badakhshan. This area, around modern Qunduz in northern Afghanistan, came to be called Tukharistan, named after the Tokharoi of Classical sources.

Other groups of invaders moved south and west, through the Herat corridor onto the Iranian Plateau. They subsequently came into contact with the young empire of the Parthians, in present-day Iran. For years to follow the newcomers and the Parthians waged a merciless war. Within a decade, between 130 and 120 BC, the immigrants killed two Parthian kings (Phraates II and Artabanus II) and almost managed to completely defeat their opponents. If the newcomers had succeeded, they would soon have appeared in West and Northwest Iran and perhaps even further west, just like their ancestors so many years before and just like Turkic tribes a thousand years later. However, history never repeats itself exactly, and the Parthians were eventually saved by the military genius of Mithradates II (*r.* 123–88 BC),[9] who rallied the Parthian forces and warded off the enormous threat that had suddenly appeared along the northeastern and eastern frontiers.

Thwarted from moving west by the Parthians, large groups of newcomers moved to Southwest and South Afghanistan, in what came to be called *Saka-stâna*, 'land of the Sakas', modern Sistan.[10] Although defeated by the Parthians, they subsequently continued to play an

7   Compare Enoki, Koshelenko and Haydary 1994, who suggest a Scythian origin.
8   Whether or not the invaders were responsible for the fall of Ay Khanum remains unclear. The town was deserted by the Greeks shortly after 147 BC.
9   Compare Justin XLII 2.
10   See Daffinà 1967 and, recently, Ball 1997.

important role in the East. According to Classical authors, for instance, they acted as kingmakers when in *c.*78 BC they put the Parthian prince Sinatruces on the throne.[11] In later centuries, the Sakas of South Afghanistan remained equally influential, as will be discussed later in this book. Eventually the Sakas of South Afghanistan were regarded as the 'Iranians' *par excellence*, and their name features prominently in Firdawsi's *Shâhnâme*.

Some of the Sakas moved on, past Arachosia and across the borderlands into the lower Indus valley. Here, by the second century AD (but reflecting earlier sources), the Classical geographer Ptolemy located the land of Indo-Scythia.[12] Later some of the Sakas migrated even further southeast, towards Gujarat in modern India, where they established the kingdom of the so-called Western Satraps that would last until the late fourth century. The Central Asian Sakas thus established a political and cultural horizon that extended from South Afghanistan all the way east, across the Indo-Iranian borderlands and the future home of the Pashtuns, to the lower Indus valley and the lands further southeast, into Gujarat and beyond.

Saka Principalities

The Sakas not only occupied much of Eastern Iran and South Afghanistan, some of them also moved into the middle Indus valley. This is the Classical province of Gandhara with its ancient capital of Taxila, in modern northern Pakistan.[13] The first known king of apparently Saka descent in this part of the world was called Maues.[14] He ruled in Gandhara and beyond, sometime during the early first century BC. He is probably identical with the 'Great King, King Moga', mentioned in the famous Taxila Copper Plate.[15] His silver and copper coins imitated those of his Indo-Greek predecessors and were struck according to the 'Indian' weight standard. They also still showed a Greek legend on the obverse and a Kharoshthi text on the reverse. The coins are sometimes overstruck by an Indo-Greek king called Apollodotus, or *vice versa*. This would indicate that by Maues's time, there were still Greek princelings ruling parts of the Indo-Iranian borderlands. Maues calls himself 'King Maues'. On other

11 Lucianus, *Makrobioi* 15.
12 Ptolemy VII 1.55.
13 For this period in the history of the borderlands see also, still useful, Lohuizen-de Leeuw 1949.
14 Called Moa in Kharoshthi script, and possibly Moga. The name may be related to Khotanese Saka *mauya*, *muyi*, 'tiger'; compare Harmatta 1994a:410.
15 For this and further information, see Puri 1994a:193–4.

issues, perhaps struck at a later date, he is styled 'The Great King of Kings Maues'.

Maues's rule was followed by that of others, including Azes I, Azilises, and Azes II. Their names, like that of Maues, have been given a Saka etymology.[16] Azes I, like his predecessor, seems to have ruled a large part of the borderlands, still with ancient Gandhara as the centre, but excluding the Kabul valley and South Afghanistan.[17] He and his successors issued silver drachms and tetradrachms that were used all over their domains, while different series of copper coins were used for specific regions. They stopped with the old Greek tradition of showing the bust of the king on the obverse of the coins. Instead their silver coins included the motif of the king on horseback, holding a lance or a whip. Coins of Azes I are known from Mir Zakah (near Gardiz) and from Chaman,[18] east of Qandahar. Azes II also issued special coppers that were used in his western lands, along the modern Afghanistan/Pakistan border. They show an Indian humped bull (perhaps representing the bull of the Indian god Shiva) and the name and titulature of Azes in Greek on the obverse, and a lion and the name of Azes in Kharoshthi script on the reverse. His coins were found at Mir Zakah; in a hoard discovered near Khost, in Paktya, and in a hoard from Gardiz. In addition, they are known from the Peshawar area.[19]

The origins of Maues and his Sakas remain unclear. Their dynasty (or dynasties, since we do not know whether Maues and Azes I were kinsmen) seems to have focused on the Peshawar and Taxila regions in northern Pakistan. The Kabul valley and (apparently) South Afghanistan remained outside their influence. It is very well possible that they migrated into Gandhara directly from north of the Hindu Kush, rather than via Sistan.[20] Scythians had lived north of the mountains from the early first millennium onwards. They had moved south by Achaemenid times or earlier, although apparently in small numbers. Large waves may have followed around 100 BC, being pushed on by kindred immigrants from further north and northwest.

Perhaps the name of Maues sheds some light on this problem. The Alexander biographers refer to the Sakas (the *Sakâ Haumavargâ* of the Achaemenid sources) who joined the Bactrian satrap, Bessus,

16   Harmatta 1994a:409.
17   MacDowall 1985a.
18   Ball 1982: no. 1106 (Spin Baldak).
19   MacDowall 1985b:51–5.
20   A similar suggestion was made by Narain 1957. Puri (1994a) suggests a route along the modern Karakorum Highway. In spite of the find of many petroglyphs in this area, such a route for what must have been a fairly sizeable group seems difficult to accept.

against Alexander at the Battle of Gaugamela in 331 BC. They were led by a princeling called Mauaces. The name of Mauaces is probably related to that of the Maues or Moga of Gandhara at the beginning of the first century BC. If the name also reflects ethnic affiliation, the Sakas who ended up in Gandhara under Maues would be different from the 'plains' Scythians who, so we would assume, penetrated around that time into West and South Afghanistan. This difference seems further indicated by linguistic evidence, which points out that both groups had a different vocabulary.[21] If all this is correct, the Saka conquest of Gandhara in the early first century BC under Maues did not directly reflect the arrival of newcomers from faraway Central Asia. It would rather illustrate the rise to power of an ethnic group of Scythian descent that for centuries had lived in close proximity to the Persian Achaemenid and Macedonian/Greek rulers in the Bactrian plains.[22] The transition from Indo-Greek to Saka rule in the Kabul valley may therefore have been fairly smooth, at least culturally, allowing for an uninterrupted transition from Hellenistic to Hellenized Indian art in the Gandhara tradition, as will be discussed below.

In the meantime, in what by then was being called Sakastan, another dynasty of local princelings assumed power and issued their own coins. These rulers included kings called Spalahora and Spalagadama.[23] Both of them struck silver and copper coins according to the Indian standard and with Greek and Kharoshthi legends. Both of them also listed the name of Vonones on the obverse of their coins. Vonones happens to be the name of a Parthian king (*r*. AD 10–12), but of course the two need not be identical. He may have been another Parthian overlord, or a Saka who had adopted a name that was also common among the Parthians. Another princeling of the same dynasty was Spalirises, who issued coins together with Azes (I or II).[24] It is clear that the political situation in South Afghanistan around this time is hard to reconstruct. Sakas certainly dominated the countryside, but the Parthians may well have exercised some influence as well.

Some light on the situation in South Afghanistan around the turn of the millennium is shed by an ancient document, namely the *Parthian Stations* by Isidore of Charax.[25] This 'road atlas' provides

21   Compare Harmatta 1994a:409–16.
22   The Jandial temple at Taxila may illustrate the amalgamation of Saka (fire-worship) and Greek (architecture) influences.
23   For the etymology of these names, see Harmatta 1994a:410.
24   Compare MacDowall and Taddei 1978:190, but see also Puri 1994a:194. The succession of the various kings of this dynasty is still unclear.
25   Edited and translated by Schoff 1914. See also Walser 1985.

information on the route between the Mediterranean and Arachosia, via northern Iran, Classical Areia and Sakastan (Sistan). Isidore, who probably wrote in the time of the Roman emperor Augustus (*r.* 27 BC–AD 14), informs his readers that Sakastan was located along the lower Hilmand, beyond a district called Zrangiana. He adds that a city called Sigal was the royal residence of the Sakas. Further east, at the farthest extreme of Parthian rule, lay Arachosia, which according to Isidore was also called 'White India'. One of its towns was called Biyt, a name that most probably reflects the ancient town of Bust (or Bist) at the confluence of the Hilmand and Arghandab rivers.[26] The capital of Arachosia, according to the *Parthian Stations*, was the 'Greek polis' of Alexandropolis, located along the Arakhotos river. This place must have been the site of modern Old Qandahar, the old Achaemenid and Mauryan capital of the region.

All this would mean that Isidore's information was collected at a time that Scythians had settled along the lower Hilmand river, and that Parthian rule, however nominal, extended as far east as Arachosia. Such a situation would eminently suit the political context of the first century BC. It also underlines the political separation of South Afghanistan, dominated by Scythian newcomers, from the Kabul valley and ancient Gandhara, controlled by other Scythian groups and/or Indo-Greek princelings. This does not mean that South Afghanistan was culturally isolated from the other lands; quite the contrary. Politically, however, this was a very confused period in which various groups moved from one place to another, and in which the suzerainty of a faraway king meant very little. This situation changed in the early years of the first century AD.

Around AD 25 a new dynasty emerged in South Afghanistan and beyond, namely that of Gondophares[27] and his nephew and successor, Abdagases. These kings, commonly called the Indo-Parthians, replaced the dynasty of Spalirises in the south and of Azes in Gandhara and in this way they ruled all of the borderlands, from Sistan to Taxila. Gondophares's coins include copper tetradrachms with Victory (*Nike*) holding a wreath on the reverse, and a bust of the king on the obverse, and these issues were imitated by his successors. Under Abdagases, silver coins were struck much in line with Parthian issues. They include the figure of a seated archer, copied from the

26   Compare the *Bestia Desoluta* of the *Tabula Peutingeriana* (Fischer 1967:193–4).
27   His name reflects Old Iranian *Vindafarna*, 'the winner of glory'. Gondophares may be the Gundaphar mentioned in the *Apocryphal Acts of Thomas*. It tells that St Thomas was forced to stay at the court of King Gundaphar and his brother, Gad (see James 1924:373–5).

Parthian drachm. The successors of Abdagases continued to rule in Sistan and neighbouring lands for a long time, apparently deep into the second century AD or later. Their names are known from their Nike copper coins: Orthagnes, Pacores, Gondophares (II), Sarpedanes and Satavastra.[28] The Kabul valley and the Indus plains, however, soon fell to the new superpower, namely that of the Kushans. For some two centuries, South Afghanistan would again politically be separated from the north and northeast.

The Tilla Tepe Hoard

In the late 1970s, a sensational discovery was made in Northwest Afghanistan. It was a cemetery with graves containing thousands of gold objects from around the beginning of the modern era. The excavators were V. Sarianidi and Z. Tarzi, and the site is called Tilla tepe, near Shibarghan.[29] Six unmarked graves were excavated, five of which contained the bones of women. The garments in which the corpses were buried had been embellished with countless metal objects, mostly made of gold. In total some 20,000 metal items were recovered, which show a variety of artistic traditions. The majority is clearly local and belongs to the realm of the Scythians and other groups. Some of the objects belong to the ancient artistic tradition of Bactrian goldsmiths. Others show clear influences from the Scythian north, the Hellenistic west or the Indian east.[30]

There are also some Roman, Indian and Parthian coins, Roman glass items, an ivory comb of apparently Indian character and a Chinese silver mirror. These are all imported objects. The Roman gold coins include issues of Emperor Tiberius (*r.* AD 14–37), thus giving a *datum postquem* for the graves. There are no coins that were issued by the Kushan rulers of later years. All the objects were buried at a time that the Scythians from north of the Amu Darya had established themselves firmly in what is now Afghanistan, south of the river. They settled in lands that for centuries had acquired riches through agriculture and trade. They also settled in lands and among people that for a long time had been influenced by Hellenism. The

28 Simonetta 1958, MacDowall 1978 and Puri 1994b:198.
29 Sarianidi 1985.
30 The present whereabouts of the collection are unknown. They seem to have survived the destruction and looting of the Kabul Museum since 1993. The latest news is that they are still packed into crates and stored in various administrative buildings in Kabul (Luke Harding, the *Guardian*, 17 November 2000). The wave of Taliban vandalism in February–March 2001 may of course have changed all this.

synchretism that followed reached its apogee in the time of the Kushans.

The Rise of the Kushans

In the first century of the modern era, a new powerful dynasty rose in North Afghanistan and Gandhara. These were the Kushans. Their origins lie among the waves of migrants, most of them of Scythian origin, that in preceding years had penetrated onto the Plateau. Most of the newcomers had settled in the plains and along the foothills of Bactria, north and south of the Amu Darya, and here also lay the original centre of Kushan power.[31] It subsequently spread from Bactria, across the Hindu Kush, towards the Kabul valley and Gandhara. Eventually, the Kushans also dominated the greater part of northern India as well as large parts of South Central Asia. Yet their name is hardly ever mentioned in Classical sources. Instead they are sometimes referred to as the Bactrians, thus recalling the works of Herodotus and Ctesias who also at times used the name of the Bactrians to indicate the much earlier waves of Scythians.

One of the most renowned Kushan kings was Kanishka, who reigned in the second century AD and has become known in Buddhist sources as a great propagator of the Buddhist faith. Whether this renown is based on reality or not remains an open question; what is clear is that during the Kushan period, roughly from the late first to the early third centuries AD, Buddhism spread from Northwest India, via Afghanistan, deep into Central Asia. With the Kushans, Afghanistan truly became the crossroads of Asia.

Kushan domination followed in the footsteps of the Scythian and Scythian related immigrants that in the preceding years had spread from the steppes of Central Asia onto the eastern parts of the Iranian Plateau and down into the plains of northern India. In this way the establishment of Kushan authority may be compared to the history of the Scythians of the early first millennium and the succeeding empires of the Medes and Persians. The main difference is the fact that the first wave of Scythians moved west, while the second wave was impeded from doing so by the Parthians and mainly moved east, towards the Indian subcontinent. In both cases, the lands of what is now Afghanistan played, literally, a pivotal role.

---

31 One of their early capitals may have been the site of Dalver'zin tepe, along the upper Surkhan Darya, in modern Uzbekistan. This place, measuring about 500/400 × 600 metres, was defended by walls with rectangular towers and a citadel in the southeast. Coins were almost exclusively of Kushan date (Pougachenkova 1999).

The story of the Kushan rise to power is told in various Chinese sources. They inform their readers that the Kushans formed one of the five sub-groups of the Yuezhi in ancient Bactria.[32] In the *Hou Han shu* (Later Han Annals), the story is told as follows:[33]

> Formerly, when the Yüeh-chih had been routed by the Hsiung-nu, they moved to Ta-hsia (Bactria?) and divided the country into five *hsi hou* (*yabghu*): Hsin-mi, Shuang-mi, Kuei-shuang, His (or Pa)-tun, and Tu-mi (Termez/Tirmidh?). More than a hundred years passed, the yabghu of Kuei-shuang, (called) Ch'iu-chiu-ch'üeh, attacked and destroyed (the other) four yabghu, set himself up as king. The kingdom was called Kuei-shuang. The king invaded An-hsi (Parthia), took the country of Kao-fu (Kabul?). He also destroyed P'u-ta and Chi-pin, and completely subjugated them. Ch'iu-chiu-ch'üeh died at the age of more than eighty. Yen-kao-chen succeeded him as king. He in turn destroyed T'ien-chu (northern India) and placed a general to supervise and govern there. Since that time the Yüeh-chih have become most rich and prosperous. (People of) many countries speak of the king of Kuei-shuang, but in China they are called Ta Yüeh-chih, according to their old name.

The story of the Han Annals is supported by numismatic and other evidence. The earliest copper coins referring to a leader of the Kushans are apparently those by the enigmatic Heraus or Heraeus, although his identity remains a problem.[34] His coins were replaced by those of Kujula Kadphises, who is apparently the Ch'iu-chiu-ch'üeh (Qiujiuque) of the Chinese sources. He was a close contemporary of Gondophares, since his coins are often overstrikes of those of the Indo-Parthian king from south of the Hindu Kush. This information, plus the Chinese annals, suggest that Kujula Kadphises took the Kabul valley from the Indo-Parthians under Gondophares and his successor, Abdagases, whose coins are also widely found in this part of the world. The Kushan ruler probably also took the heartland of Gandhara further to the east from the last Indo-Parthian ruler there, Sasan.[35] In this way, Kujula Kadphises became the first ruler north and south of the Hindu Kush passes after the fall of the Graeco-Bactrians.

32 For the Yuezhi and the Kushans, see Zürcher 1968 and Hulsewé and Loewe 1979. For Bactria in the first century BC, compare Posch 1995.
33 Zürcher 1968:367. The spelling of the Chinese names is not according to the Pinyin-system.
34 According to Cribb 1993, the enigmatic Heraus is no other than Kujula Kadphises.
35 The identity of this Sasan is also a moot point. Was he another son of Gondophares?

According to the *Hou Han shu*, and if our identifications are correct, Kujula Kadphises was succeeded by Yangaozhen (Yen-kao-chen), who extended the Kushan empire to the east, deep into the Indian subcontinent. The problem is that none of the names of Kushan kings known from coins and other sources corresponds to Yangaozhen. Numismatic evidence indicates that Kujula was succeeded by a king who on his coins calls himself 'Soter Megas', the Great Saviour. The copper coins of this 'nameless king' are known from a wide area stretching from Bactria in the northwest to Mathura in northern India, and he actually was the Kushan ruler who introduced a uniform coinage system all over the empire. Before that, Kujula Kadphises had simply copied the various types of coins used by his predecessors in the various lands that he had subjugated. The new 'imperial' copper coins of Soter Megas show the rayed head of (supposedly) Mithra on the obverse and a man on horseback on the reverse (thus continuing the earlier tradition started by the Saka rulers Azes and Azilises). There are some varieties, but the reverse of all coins carries the Greek legend 'King of Kings, Great Saviour' (*Soter Megas*). The Indo-Parthian ruler of South Afghanistan, Pacores, overstruck this type, thereby indicating the independence of South Afghanistan and the relative chronology of the two rulers.

The identity of Soter Megas has probably finally been established with the discovery, in March 1993, of a monumental inscription that was found near the village of Rabatak, some 40 km east of Samangan (Haybak),[36] in northern Afghanistan.[37] The text dates to the time of King Kanishka, the most famous Kushan king of the second century AD. The text, although its reading is not without problems, refers to Kanishka's great-grandfather, named Kujula Kadphises, to his grandfather, who is called Vima Tak[to], and his father, Vima Kadphises.[38] If the reading is correct, it would identify Soter Megas with Vima Tak[to]. Whether he should also be identified with the Yangaozhen of the *Hou Han shu* remains a moot point. It is very well possible that the name in the Chinese sources is simply incorrectly transmitted. It is also possible that the Chinese name represents a title or another name carried by the king.

---

36 Samangan is the modern (and ancient) name for the town that until 1964 was called Haybak.

37 The site lies 25 km north of Pul-i Khumri; it is named Rabatak Kafir Qal'a in Ball 1982: No. 944. See Sims-Williams and Cribb 1996; Sims-Williams 1997a:336–8, and 1998. The inscription has since been taken to the Kabul Museum and exhibited when it reopened in August 2000. Its present condition is unknown.

38 Sims-Williams's reading is not in all cases accepted by Fussman (1998).

The Great Kushans

Soter Megas, or Vima Tak[to], was succeeded by Vima (II) Kadphises and the so-called Great Kushans: Kanishka, Huvishka and Vasudeva. Vima (II) Kadphises was the first to issue, apart from coppers, also gold coins. In doing so he consciously copied the Roman *aureus*. As with all other Kushans, he did not issue silver coins, as had been the custom of the Graeco-Bactrians, Indo-Greeks and Parthians. The gold issues are characterized by the representation of the Indian god Shiva (called Oeso[39]) on the reverse. The obverse shows a sitting or riding figure, with a heavy coat and boots, before an altar, apparently representing the king. Gold coins of Vima Kadphises, together with those of his son Kanishka, were, among other places, found at the Buddhist sanctuary of Shiwaki, 11 km south of Kabul.[40] Together with these coins, which were recovered in a steatite vase inside the remains of a stupa, was a gold coin of the Roman emperor Trajan (AD 98–117), which means that the deposit with Vima Kadphises's coins was made after AD 98.

The gold coins of his succesor, Kanishka, show on the obverse the standing king in Central Asian garb. On the reverse they depict various Indian, Greek or Iranian gods. Iranian deities, however, predominate, and this is especially the case with Kanishka's copper coins. They include, in Bactrian, *Mioro* (Mithra), *Moa* (the Moon), *Athsho* (Fire) and *Oado* (the Wind). Indian Shiva and originally Mesopotamian Nana are also sometimes depicted. The legends of Kanishka's early coins are in Greek script and language, but on his later coins, the Greek script is used to write Bactrian.[41] These and other coins illustrate the highly diverse nature of religious beliefs in the Kushan empire, and at the same time it undermines the traditional fame of Kanishka as the great propagator of the Buddhist faith. It seems more likely that he, as so many politicians before and after him, was merely opportunistic and seeking a situation that would best support his power base.

Under Kanishka's successor, Huvishka, the gold coins of Kanishka remained in production, but his copper coins are different. They show three variations on the obverse: the king on an elephant; the king seated cross-legged; and the king reclining on a couch. Coins of

39   Oeso; compare Prakrit: *Vesa*; Sanskrit *Vrisha*, 'bull', an appellation of Shiva. It may also reflect Sanskrit *Bhavesha*, 'Lord of Life', Shiva.
40   Ball 1982: No. 1087.
41   The decision to use Bactrian instead of Greek may date to the early years of Kanishka's reign, see Sims-Williams 1997a:4.

Huvishka, together with those of Vima II Kadphises and Kanishka, were found in the Ahin Posh Tope (stupa), some two km south of Jalalabad.[42] Together with these Kushan coins, a number of Roman *aurei* were recovered, including those of the emperors Domitian (AD 81–96), Trajan (AD 98–117), and of Sabina, wife of Hadrian (AD 117–38), thus giving a *datum postquem* for the deposit of AD 117.

Huvishka was succeeded by Vasudeva, traditionally the last of the so-called Great Kushans. His name (Sanskrit *Vâsudeva*) is identical to that of the Hindu god Krishna (son of *Vasudeva*), a reincarnation of Vishnu. He issued mainly two types of gold coins. The first shows Shiva and a bull on the reverse and the king standing at an altar on the obverse, a type of coin that would remain popular in the western lands also after the fall of the Kushans. The other type shows an enthroned (Bactrian) *Ardochsho* (Verethraghna) on the reverse and carries a Brahmi legend. The latter coins were copied later by Indian kings, including those of the powerful Gupta dynasty of northern India. The copper coins of Vasudeva and his successors show a great variety and include coins with Shiva and the bull and coins with Ardochsho.

The extent of Kushan control in modern Afghanistan is still unknown. There is no doubt that the north of the country (ancient Bactria) and the Kabul valley fell under Kushan sway for most of the time, but whether the south and west were ever under Kushan domination remains uncertain. The south probably remained at least nominally autonomous. Here the Indo-Parthian kings continued to rule what was called Sakastan. In this way, the Kushan kingdom centred on the mountain passes across the Hindu Kush, and the Kabul area was therefore of extreme importance. It constituted the axis of the Empire, connecting the fertile Bactrian plains in the north-west with the plains of India in the southeast. The lands of modern South Afghanistan seem to have been left to the Sakas and their Parthian overlords.

Kushan Monuments

One of the most imposing Kushan monuments in Afghanistan is the majestic temple site of Surkh Kotal, north of the Hindu Kush passes and not far south of Rabatak.[43] Here, a monumental stairway of some 55 metres high leads in four flights to a sanctuary on top of a

---

42   Ball 1982: No. 17.
43   The name of the hill is modern. For Surkh Kotal, see Ball 1982: No. 1123; Schlumberger et al. 1983; and Fussman et al. 1990. For the inscription, see also Lazard, Grenet and de Lamberterie 1984, and Sims-Williams 1985.

Illustration 8 *The main altar on top of the Kushan sanctuary of Surkh Kotal (photograph: author, January 1979).*

hill overlooking the vast plains. At the foot of the stairway is a large well, which is approached via another long flight of stairs, built carefully in line with the rest of the complex. The sanctuary was built as a temple dedicated to the divine kingship of the Kushan rulers. As such, it may have been one of a series of temples that were built all over the Kushan empire. The main cella on top of the steps (Ill. 8) is often described as a fire temple, but there is no evidence to support this, and the fire in the cella may have been 'dynastic', rather than 'divine'.

The whole plan of the complex and its building techniques are described by its excavator, the French archaeologist D. Schlumberger, as being mainly Iranian in character, in spite of its (Greek-style) rectangular towers and other Hellenistic features. Other finds at the site, which was excavated between 1952 and 1963, also testify to its Iranian/Kushan character. In the sanctuary on top, the remains were found of three statues, probably representing Kushan rulers, who are shown in a frontal position. They wear trousers and a long mantle. As such, the statues are very unlike anything Greek or Roman. Parallels can be found further west, in the art of the Parthians who dominated the rest of the Iranian Plateau. The effigies from Surkh Kotal also very much resemble the famous Kanishka statue from Mathura, in northern India.[44] The inscription placed on the mantle of this effigy tells it all: 'The Great King, the King of Kings, His Majesty Kanishka'.

44   Compare the illustration in Rowland 1970:151.

The site has yielded a number of inscriptions, written in Greek script but in the (Iranian) Bactrian language, very similar to the above-described text from Rabatak. One of these texts, the so-called Great Inscription, mentions *Kanishka Oanindo*, 'Kanishka the Victorious'. It was placed at the main entrance to the staircase. The text tells that the temple was originally built on the orders of Kanishka and was restored by a local overseer called Nukunzuk after a period of decline when the water supply to the temple had dried up. Earlier versions of the text were found scattered among the walls of the well at the foot of the monumental staircase.

Another Kushan text, in various versions, was discovered in 1967 near the Dasht-i Nawar plain, about 50 km west of Ghazni and south of the Hindu Kush watershed.[45] The group of inscriptions, five in total, was placed at a height of more than 4,000 metres. Unfortunately the reading of the texts is still problematic and it is not even known whether all five inscriptions, in different scripts and languages, contain the same message. One version is written in the same Greek script and Bactrian language as were used at Surkh Kotal and at Rabatak. Next to it is an apparently identical text in Middle Indian and with Kharoshthi script. The same text is also written in a hitherto unknown language (perhaps Saka), apparently in Kharoshthi script. The two other inscriptions are in Greek and Kharoshthi script respectively, but impossible to read. The Bactrian and Middle Indian texts refer to Vima, but whether this is Vima Kadphises or his predecessor, Vima Tak[to], is still unclear. The location of these inscriptions is of great interest. Nowadays this part of Afghanistan is only thinly populated, but in Kushan times the situation may have been very different. Archaeological exploration in this part of Afghanistan may one day elucidate this problem. One of the most fascinating sites that await controlled archaeological excavations is that of Wardak, some 30 km northwest of Ghazni.[46] Surveys have shown that the site reflects a large fortified urban settlement with a regular street plan. Outside the ramparts there are the remains of other structures, including a number of stupas and what appears to be a monastic complex. From one of the stupas an inscribed relic casket was obtained that is now in the British Museum.

Excavations at Begram, north of Kabul, have shown the extent of Kushan contacts with the outside world. Begram, ancient Capisa, was located at a place that was of great strategic importance to the Kushans. It dominated the life-line between their Bactrian possessions

---

45   For the inscriptions of the Dasht-i Nawar, see Ball 1982: No. 265; MacDowall and Taddei 1978:238–40. See also Harmatta 1994b:422ff. and Fussman 1998.
46   Ball 1982: No. 1229; see also Upasak 1990:182.

and those in the Indian subcontinent. The importance of Capisa was of course not merely strategic, but also economic. During the Kushan period, Afghanistan was linked up to the famous Silk Road between the Near East and China. The Silk Road itself passed north of modern Afghanistan, via ancient Sogdia where now lie the cities of Bukhara and Samarqand. A branch of the Silk Road, however, led across Afghanistan to the Indian subcontinent. Some of the merchandise from China was thus carried across modern Afghanistan to the Indus valley and vice versa: western goods, brought to the Indian coast by sea, together with Indian goods were transported up north to South Central Asia and hence to China.[47] In times of war between the Roman empire and the Parthians, the southern route via the Indian possessions of the Kushans formed an attractive alternative, the more so since the goods could be transferred by boat to and from India via the Egyptian Red Sea coast.[48]

The large site of Begram lies about 50 km north of Kabul and some eight km east of modern Charikar, near the confluence of the Panjshir and Ghorband rivers.[49] The site was partly excavated by French archaeologists between 1936 and 1946.[50] It covers an area of about 800 metres from north to south and about 450 metres from east to west. In the northwest lies the citadel, the Burj-i Abdullah, which may date back to the Achaemenid period. In the south there was a large building, apparently a palace. The ramparts of the settlement were built of square sun-dried bricks on a stone foundation, very much following building traditions introduced by the Greeks. The walls were strengthened by square towers, again according to western traditions.

The most fascinating finds from the site include a large collection of art objects, including a bronze statue of Serapis/Heracles and one of Harpocrates, Indian ivories, Chinese lacquer ware and western glass. The latter group included an 18 cm high transparent glass vase with carved decorations. It depicted the Pharos lighthouse of Alexandria, one of the seven wonders of the world. The date of all these finds is difficult to establish. In general the objects should be placed in a period between the first century BC and the early third century AD. The present whereabouts of these objects are unknown; they were housed in the Kabul Museum that was looted in the early 1990s.[51]

---

47 For trade between India and China, see Xinru Liu 1994.
48 For this subject, see the *Periplus Maris Erythraei*.
49 Ball 1982: No. 122.
50 In 1974 the Indians signed an agreement with the Afghan government to restart excavations. These never materialized.
51 The Kabul Museum was reopened (if only for a few days) in August 2000, but the few remaining objects were apparently destroyed by Taliban militia in

Gandhara Art

The above finds indicate that the Kushan empire remained in close contact with developments in the West. This is made very clear by the so-called Gandhara art that flourished in ancient Gandhara and beyond in the early centuries of the first millennium and later.[52] Gandhara art is mainly characterized by the amalgamation of Graeco-Roman and Indian traditions. The indigenous curved gable was used next to the Classical triangular pediment. The round pilasters with a bell-shaped capital of Indian tradition remained in use, but the Classical flat pilaster with a Corinthian capital was also very popular, and so were Classical motifs including atlantes, tritons and putti with garlands. This eclectic art style was developed in ancient Gandhara, hence its name, but it soon spread to lands far beyond. It is found along the trade routes between Northwest India, via Afghanistan and Central Asia, towards China.

In the first centuries of the first millennium, Gandhara art was time and again fed by artists and artistic impressions from the Roman world, and it is evident that the Kushans kept in close touch with developments in the Mediterranean.[53] I referred to this point before when discussing the introduction by the Kushan kings of golden coins that so clearly imitate Roman issues. In time, however, western influence was replaced by more pronounced Iranian, Indian and Central Asian aspects. The influence from India became stronger, and the refinement and elegance of the Gupta art of northern India, which flourished between the early fourth and late sixth centuries AD, is found with many artistic products from Afghanistan. In secluded valleys in modern Afghanistan, as at Funduqistan along the Ghorband river, Buddhist statues and paintings were made as late as the seventh century AD that are almost completely 'Indian'.

Gandhara art is in the main Buddhist art. Statues of Buddha abound, together with reliefs depicting episodes from his life and pre-

February–March 2001. The story of the lost treasures from the Kabul Museum is still not fully known. Most of the objects seeem to have been taken across the borders with Pakistan. Some of the Indian ivories were sold by a Pakistani businessman to a London-based arts dealer and subsequently donated to the Musée Guimet in Paris. A former Pakistani Minister of the Interior has admitted buying one of the ivories for $100,000.

52   There is a huge library of books and articles on Gandhara art. Compare Rowland 1967 (1953) and Rosenfield 1967. For a recent study, see Errington and Cribb (eds) 1992, and R. Allchin et al. (eds) 1997.

53   The famous reliquary of King Kanishka, found in 1908 at the site of Shah-ji-ki-Dheri in Peshawar, bears the (Greek) name of its manufacturer, Agesilas (Rowland 1967:135).

vious incarnations. Its popularity indicates the strength of the Buddhist faith in this part of the world in the early centuries of the first millennium. At first, Buddha was mostly indicated by symbols, such as his throne or his footsteps. The idea of depicting Buddha as a person, which developed almost simultaneously in Gandhara and in the Ganges valley (the so-called Mathura Art), was related to a growing movement in the early centuries of the modern era towards personal devotion. This movement would later lead, throughout the first millennium, to the replacement of the *Hinayâna* (a derogatory term meaning 'Little Vehicle') branch of Buddhism, which places emphasis on doctrine, by the *Mahâyâna* ('Great Vehicle') branch. The latter is more concerned with personal adoration of the Buddha and his emissaries. In this way, in early Gandhara art the statues mostly depict Buddha himself (*Buddha Sâkyâmuni*) or the Buddha of the Future (*Maitreya*). Later, there are statues of the so-called Bodhisattvas, as for instance Avalokiteshvara, who is usually depicted with a lotus in his left hand. The Bodhisattvas are mythical beings who renounced their place in heaven and reincarnated in order to help all creatures on earth. In Gandhara art, the Bodhisattvas are often depicted as the princes of their time, dressed in kilts, turbans and with considerable amounts of jewellery. Their appearance may well represent that of the patrons who provided the means to erect the statue.

Initially the Gandharan artists used stone for their products, and especially the blue schist and green phyllite from the region. This material, however, is difficult to use and in later years the craftsmen almost exclusively used stucco and lime plaster. This development is often described as reflecting western (Iranian) influence. This may well be the case, for the use of stucco was at that time very popular in Iran. Furthermore, it should be realized that the artistic products of the Gandharan craftsmen and architects were brightly coloured. At Tepe Maranjan, just east of Kabul, the remains have been found of stucco still covered with plaster that was coloured pink, red, brown and blue.[54]

Chinese visitors to the region in the first millennium AD describe the many monuments that they found. Many of these monuments, although in ruins, can still be seen today. The *stupas* and *vihâras* or *sanghârâmas* (monasteries) testify to the prosperity of the Buddhist community. One of these complexes is located just southeast of Kabul, at Guldarra (Ill. 9).[55] It includes two stupas and a fortified monastery and is generally dated to the third and fourth centuries

54   Ball 1982: No. 1173.
55   Ball 1982: No. 389; Rao, Pinder-Wilson and Ball 1985.

Illustration 9   *The Buddhist stupa and monastery of Guldarra, south of Kabul (photograph: author, summer 1978).*

AD. Nearby, close to the village of Shiwaki, lie the ruins of another stupa and monastery.[56] Highly interesting and spectacular was the Minar-i Chakri, a 19 metre high pillar crowned by a lotus motif, and originally perhaps also by the Buddhist symbol of the wheel (Sanskrit *Chakra*).[57] It stood some 15 km southeast of Kabul on top of a pass looking across the Kabul valley. The tower collapsed in March 1998. Another conspicuous column nearby was that of Surkh Minar, which collapsed in 1964.[58]

In Kabul itself, a Buddhist monastery and stupa were found in 1930 on a spur of the Kuh-i Shir Darwaza (the mountain which borders Kabul to the south).[59] Incidentally it would indicate that the city of Kabul, or at least a settlement at this place, would date back to at least the pre-Islamic period.[60] Another famous Buddhist monastery was that of Shotorak, some 65 km northeast of Kabul and about four km north of Begram/Capisa.[61] The ruins are located along the Panjshir river and were excavated by French archaeologists in

56   Ball 1982: No. 1087.
57   Ball 1982: No. 718.
58   Ball 1982: No. 1124.
59   Ball 1982: No. 1168.
60   The settlement of Kabul is also mentioned by the Greek geographer Ptolemy (second century AD). He lists the name of a town called *Kaboura*.
61   Ball 1982: No. 1088.

Illustration 10   *Bamiyan valley (photograph: author, summer 1978).*

1936/7. It included the monastery proper and some ten stupas. The buildings were decorated with schist bas reliefs depicting the life of the Buddha.

A very important Buddhist centre was Hadda, located in a flat plain some eight km south of modern Jalalabad.[62] It is the Nagarahara of Indian and Chinese writers. It was a sacred place for the Buddhists and attracted large numbers of pilgrims. It was perhaps the most important settlement in the Jalalabad area during the first half of the first millennium, and its ruins cover an area of some 15 square km. All over the place are the ruins of stupas (more than one thousand), monasteries and other buildings. Excavations since 1923 have yielded large numbers of stucco sculpture, reliquaries, coins and inscriptions.

Another major centre of Buddhist art is the famous valley of Bamiyan (Ill. 10).[63] This valley lies some 240 km west of Kabul, at an altitude of about 2,500 metres above sea level, in the middle of the Afghan Mountains. The valley itself stretches for about 4.5 km from east to west, and approximately 3.5 km from north to south. Nearby are other valleys, with similar Buddhist monuments, as for instance those of Fuladi[64] and Kakrak.[65] The Bamiyan valley lies

62   Ball 1982: No. 404.
63   Ball 1982: No. 100. See also Baker and Allchin 1991.
64   Ball 1982: No. 330.
65   Ball 1982: No. 508.

Illustration 11   *The large Buddha statue of Bamiyan (photograph: author, summer 1978).*

along one of the major thoroughfares across the Hindu Kush and was used as a staging post ever since at least the time of the Graeco-Bactrians, since some of their coins have been found in the valley. The northern rock face of the Bamiyan valley is honeycombed by artificial caves that served as living quarters, meeting places and sanctuaries for the Buddhists living there. Most conspicuous, although their present state is unknown, are the two huge Buddha statues.[66] The one

66   According to the latest reports, both Buddha statues were virtually destroyed by the Taliban in February–March 2001.

to the east is 55 metres high and it is probably the largest statue in the world (Ill. 11). Some 1,500 metres to the west is another statue, which is 38 metres high. The two statues are of great interest, but not only because of their height. Originally, both statues must have been brilliantly coloured. The walls of the caves in which the statues are placed are decorated with paintings; those in the cave of the small Buddha recall Sasanian art from Iran, especially from the sixth and seventh centuries. The paintings along the large Buddha are Indian in style. Of course the Buddha statues need not, and cannot be dated to the time of the paintings. All we know for certain is that when the Chinese pilgrim Xuanzang visited the valley in about AD 632, the two Buddha statues were there. What is important is the eclectic nature of much of the artwork at Bamiyan. This is of course not surprising, considering the character of the site and its location between Central Asia, Iran and India.

Bamiyan is not the only place in Afghanistan where caves were hewn out of the rock and inhabited by Buddhists. Unfortunately, the date of these various sites is often difficult to establish. One of the most spectacular sites is that of Takht-i Rustam, near Samangan (Haybak), north of the Hindu Kush passes.[67] It includes a complex of a stupa with monastery, hewn out of the rock. Other caves have been found near Jalalabad and at the site of Humay Qal'a, southwest of Ghazni.[68]

Buddhism and Gandhara art, however evolved, long outlasted the reign of its ertswhile patrons, the Kushan kings, that came to an end in the third century AD. Serious decline, and the destruction of many Buddhist buildings, only started in or around the sixth century AD when Turkic newcomers from Central Asia overran the land. Yet, in many places Buddhism and developed forms of Gandhara art, however 'Indianized', lived on. The stupa that overlooks the present ruins of Old Qandahar in ancient Arachosia was still in use after *c.*650.[69] The Buddhist sanctuary at Funduqistan near Bamiyan may likewise date to the late seventh or early eighth century, as shown by the many Arabo-Sasanian coins that were found there.[70]

67   Ball 1982: No. 1135.
68   MacDowall and Taddei 1978:278; Ball 1982: No. 434.
69   Compare Baker and Allchin 1991:9.
70   Ball 1982: No. 332.

10

The Reassertion of
the Iranian West

While Gandhara art continued to develop in the Indo-Iranian borderlands and Buddhism was still spreading, the political power of their main patrons, the Kushan rulers, slowly diminished. The decline of Kushan rule in Afghanistan in the third century AD coincided with the fall of the Parthians and the rise of a revived Iran under the leadership of a new dynasty, that of the Sasanians.[1] For the next four hundred years, until the advent of Islam in the mid-seventh century, the Sasanians would be the dominant power on the Iranian Plateau. During all these years, however, Sasanian hold on the Hindu Kush passes and the lands immediately to the north and south would be continuously challenged by wave after wave of yet more groups of Central Asian migrants.

The early Sasanians set out to restore the ancient glory of the Persian Achaemenids.[2] Their origins and political centre were located in ancient Fars, close to the homeland of the Achaemenids. The first Sasanian kings had themselves portrayed in the same rockface of Naqsh-i Rustam, near Persepolis, that contain the tombs of some of the most illustrious Persian Achaemenid kings. Their main political objective was to bring all the lands formerly under 'Persian' control back into an Iranian empire. The new rulers were also keenly aware of the potential power of an imperial religion. They thus elevated the ancient Iranian creed of Zarathustra to the status of a state religion.[3] In doing so they followed the example of King Darius, who in his Behistun text repeatedly invoked the name of Ahuramazda as the god of all the Iranians.

1 For the Sasanians, compare Christensen 1944; Dani and Litvinsky 1996; Gyselen 1989; Lukonin 1983; Mukherjee 1976; Schippmann 1990.
2 Compare Classical references: Cassius Dio LXXX 4 and Herodian VI 2.2. For the Classical sources, and their editions, see Christensen 1944:74–7.
3 Ably supported, or instigated, by the priest Kartir (Kirder), who left various inscriptions in ancient Persis, including a famous text at the site of Naqsh-i Rustam.

During the Sasanian period, the sacred texts of Zarathustra and his followers were collected and codified. Zoroastrianism became organized in the same, strongly centralized and hierarchical manner as the secular state. Fire temples were built all over the Iranian Plateau. The high status of Zoroastrianism led to a renewed interest into the affairs of Eastern Iran, the cradle of Zarathustra's religion, and many of the later Sasanian kings carried names that were taken from the ancient legendary past of the Eastern Iranians.[4] Sasanian secular and Zoroastrian religious authority thus clashed with the rising tide of Buddhism, which during the Kushan period had penetrated deeply onto the eastern parts of the Iranian Plateau and which would continue to spread in the centuries to follow.[5] Yet, Buddhism and Zoroastrianism were not the only religions being practised in the East.[6] By the early seventh century, when Islam was introduced to the Plateau, there were adherents of a number of other creeds, including Judaism, Hinduism, Manichaeism[7] and (Nestorian) Christianity.[8]

Sasanian Domination

The beginning of Sasanian rule is usually dated to around AD 224. In that year a local leader from Southwest Iran, called Ardashir, defeated his Parthian overlord, Artabanus V. Ardashir, whose name reflects that of the Achaemenid Artaxerxes, claimed descent from Sasan. This man probably was the priest of a local temple at Istakhr, a town just north of ancient Persepolis.[9] After defeating the Parthian king, Ardashir set off on a series of military campaigns against the Romans in the west and the Kushans and others in the east. Accord-

4   Compare the name of Khusraw, from (Kavi) Haosravah, the eighth king of the great Kayanian dynasty (compare Boyce 1975/1989:105).
5   For Buddhism in Eastern Iran, see Melikian-Chirvani 1974 and Tardieu 1988.
6   For all these religions I refer the reader to two articles on the subject in the *History of Civilizations of Central Asia*, Vol. III, Paris 1996, by Ph. Gignoux and B. A. Litvinsky and by B. A. Litvinsky and M. I. Vorobyova-Desyatovskaya respectively.
7   A syncretic religion, strictly separating good from evil, established by Mani in the third century AD. From the late third century onwards, Marw and Balkh were important centres of Manichaeism in the East. It eventually spread along the Silk Road to China.
8   A Christian community in Herat is attested by AD 430 (compare Litvinsky and Vorobyova-Desyatovskaya 1996:421). The Nestorian church was named after Nestorius, the main apologist of the Dyophysites, who split from the other section of the Church in the fifth century.
9   Whether or not Sasan was the grandfather of Ardashir is unknown. Compare Schippmann 1990:10ff.

ing to the Arab historian, al-Tabari (AD 839–923), Ardashir conquered large parts of Eastern Iran, including Sakastan (Sistan) and Bactria.[10] Subsequently, according to the same writer, envoys from the Kushans, from Turan and from Makran, arrived at Ardashir's court to offer their submission.

Makran was, and still is, the coastal area of Baluchistan along the Indian Ocean. Turan was located south of modern Quetta in eastern Baluchistan, Pakistan. Its capital in the Early Islamic period was Khuzdar, which still exists under the same name.[11] The name of Turan itself is very interesting. In later Iranian legends the name is normally used to describe the non-Iranian peoples living to the north of Iran. The name is probably linked to that of the Turks.[12] Whatever the case, the name was generally used to describe the opponents of the Iranians. It is hardly likely that in the third century AD there were already Turks residing in Baluchistan. It is more likely that the name was used to describe the (Dravidian-speaking) Brahuis, who still live in this part of the world. Whether this identification is correct is unknown, but Ardashir's realm apparently included, in some form or other, all of the southeastern parts of the Iranian Plateau as far as the lower Indus valley.

Al-Tabari's account is supported by near-contemporary information. In AD 262, Ardashir's son and successor, Shapur I (r. AD 241–71), ordered a trilingual (Persian, Parthian and Greek) inscription to be engraved at the old burial site of the Persian Achaemenid kings at Naqsh-i Rustam, not far from Istakhr.[13] In this text the king tells that at the time of his father, there were three subject kings in the East, namely those of Marw, Kirman and of the Sakas. All three were called Ardashir. This, it should be noted, would indicate that the three kings were royal Sasanian princes, appointed by their sovereign, perhaps their father, brother or uncle.[14] These three kingdoms were thus firmly incorporated into the Sasanian realm. The text also mentions the Kushans 'as far as *Pshkbwr*', as subjects of the Sasanians. *Pshkbwr* has often been identified with (Sanskrit) *Púrushapura*, modern Peshawar in North Pakistan. This would suggest that the Sasanians dominated, at least nominally, the heartland of the Kushans. However, the identification is merely a conjecture.[15] Even

10   See al-Tabari, edited by Nöldeke 1879 (1973), pp. 17–18.
11   The ruler of Turan is reported to have been converted to Manichaeism by Mani himself in the third century AD (Sundermann 1971:375–6).
12   Compare Boyce 1975/1989:65, 104–7, 250.
13   For this inscription, see Back 1978. Very important are earlier studies, including Honigmann and Maricq 1953 and Maricq 1958.
14   Al-Tabari (Nöldeke 1879/1973:10) correspondingly tells that Ardashir appointed one of his sons, also called Ardashir, as king of Kirman.
15   Compare Honigmann and Maricq 1953:101–5; Humbach 1968:45–8; Frye 1996:147–8.

if correct, it does not mean that the Sasanians actively controlled all of the Kushan lands. Whatever the case, among the various governor-kings subject to the 'King of Kings' and mentioned in the inscription at Naqsh-i Rustam, there is no Sasanian subject king in *Kushânshahr* (the land of the Kushans) or in the northern parts of modern Afghanistan. This would mean that in the mid-third century AD the Kushan lands were probably still governed by local, Kushan princes, although perhaps owing allegiance to the Sasanian ruler. Or in other words, the Sasanians did not (yet) dominate the Hindu Kush passes between Bactria and the Kabul valley.

Sakastan

While Sasanian control in ancient Bactria and in the Kabul valley in the third century AD is still difficult to ascertain, Persian domination of South Afghanistan at that time is evident. In the realm of the (Sasanian) Saka King, a series of copper coins was struck according to the 'Indian' standard, following in the tradition of the Indo-Parthian issues struck by Gondophares and his successors. The coins have Pahlavi legends and show a Sasanian fire altar from the time of Ardashir. The issue of these coins accentuates the special position of Sakastan in the Sasanian empire.[16]

From the Naqsh-i Rustam inscription we know that Ardashir, King of the Sakas, was succeeded during the reign of Shapur I by a prince called Narseh.[17] He was called the 'Zoroastrian Aryan, *sk'n MLK*' ('King of the Sakas'). Narseh was a son of Shapur I and perhaps identical with the later King of Kings with the same name (*r.* AD 293–302). According to the inscription at Naqsh-i Rustam, Narseh's realm as King of the Sakas included not only the land of the Sakas, but also that of Hindustan and Turan. It thus stretched from the delta of the Hilmand to the land of the Indians. This, it should be remembered, was also the land administered almost six hundred years earlier by the Persian Achaemenid governor of Arachosia and Drangiana. More directly, it is also the land that was occupied by Sakas in the late second and first centuries BC.

It is safe to assume that the title King of the Sakas was not newly invented with the advent of the Sasanians, but that the function and the extent of its authority dated back to pre-Sasanian times. It is furthermore clear that the land of the Sakas must have been the land of the so-called Indo-Parthian kings, including Gondophares, who issued their own coins in South Afghanistan before the time of the Sasani-

16   MacDowall and Taddei 1978:214.
17   SKZ inscription. Back 1978:334–5.

ans. For all these years, the Land of the Sakas apparently retained its own character and its own ruling class of Sakas. The heartland of this entity cannot be identified, but it was probably located at least for some time in modern Southwest Afghanistan. In the early first century AD, Isidore of Charax in his *Parthian Stations* identified here, between Zrangiana and Arachosia, a land called Sakastan.[18]

Looking at the map, it is evident that the King of the Sakas was one of the Wardens of the Marches of the Sasanian Empire. He controlled the southeastern parts of the realm. His importance is illustrated by later developments. The Greek historian Agathias, who lived in the sixth century AD, tells that King Bahram II (*r.* 276–93) waged war against the people of Sakastan.[19] This must be the Saka revolt led by the King's brother (or his cousin), called Hormizd, which is mentioned in other sources.[20] Claudius Mamertinus, another Classical historian, accordingly tells that this rebel brother received the support of the 'Gils, Bactrians and Sakas'.[21]

From the second year of Shapur II (*r.* AD 309–79) there is an inscription at Persepolis of another Shapur who is called, 'King of the Sakas, King of Hindustan, Saka-land and Turan as far as the Sea'.[22] He calls himself son of the King of Kings, Hormizd (II). He tells that he travelled from Istakhr to Sakastan, and stopped at Persepolis to eat. He was in the company of the satrap of Zarangia (Drangiana), and 'other Persian and Saka noblemen'. The King of the Sakas was apparently a brother or half-brother of Shapur II. The text again underlines the importance of the position of the King of the Sakas. It also differentiates between Persian and Saka noblemen and it refers to Zarangia, the ancient *Zra"ka* or *Dra"ka* of the Achaemenid texts, and the Zaranj of later, Islamic sources.[23]

The Kushano-Sasanian Governor-kings

By the fourth century, Sasanian control in North Afghanistan and in the Kabul valley and beyond, was considerably strengthened. Hormizd II (*r.* 303–9) is reported to have established a marriage alliance with the (Kushan) king of Kabul.[24] There is also numismatic

18   *Parthian Stations* (trans. Schoff): paragraph 18.
19   Agathias IV 24.8.
20   Claudius Mamertinus, *Panegyr.* III 17.
21   As for the Gils, their name lives on in that of the Iranian district of Gilan, along the Caspian Sea.
22   This is the SPs-I inscription, see Back 1978:492–4.
23   To be identified with the ruins of Nad-i Ali in Afghan Seistan. Ball 1982: No. 752.
24   Compare Schippmann 1990:31.

evidence to indicate growing Sasanian influence in the east. Sasanian silver drachms of Shapur II and his successors have been found at many sites in modern Afghanistan. These include places in Sistan, at Herat, at Maymana, near Tashqurkhan, at Begram, and at various stupas at Hadda near Jalalabad.[25] An important hoard with Sasanian coins was found at Tepe Maranjan, near Kabul.[26] It contained silver drachms of Shapur II (r. AD 309–79), Ardashir II (r. AD 379–83) and Shapur III (r. AD 383–8).

In the centre of their empire, the Sasanians had adopted the Parthian numismatic system, which in its turn was based on the tradition of the Attic standard of silver drachms. Gold was only used for special issues, and there were no copper coins. In other lands, however, the Sasanians tended to adopt the numismatic traditions of their local predecessors, as for instance the coppers from Sakastan, discussed earlier, which were struck according to the 'Indian' standard. In their northeastern lands, the Sasanians accordingly adopted the coinage system of the Kushans. The coins were struck by the so-called Kushano-Sasanian governor kings and were used next to the 'real' Sasanian issues.

The various governors that issued these coins included, in chronological order, Ardashir I, Ardashir II, Firuz I, Hormizd I, Firuz II, Hormizd II, Bahram I and Bahram II.[27] They called themselves 'King of the Kushans' or even 'King of the Kings of the Kushans', thus indicating that they regarded themselves as successors to the (real) Kushan kings. The issues include gold and copper coins that imitate those originally struck by the Kushan king, Vasudeva. Among these are the famous Kushano-Sasanian gold scyphate (saucer-shaped) coins. They show Shiva and his bull (Nandi) on the reverse, with a Bactrian legend in cursive Greek script that reads *borzaoando iazado* ('the exalted god').[28] On the obverse there is an effigy of the standing governor-king with his individual crown and his name and title. The gold coins were found at various places in modern Afghanistan. The corresponding copper coins were widely found at Balkh and some of the coins even bear the legend of *Bahlo* on the obverse.

Apart from Kushan type coins, there are also Sasanian type coins in gold and copper struck, presumably, in Marw and Herat. They

25   MacDowall and Taddei 1978:251.
26   Ball 1982: No. 1173.
27   I follow Dani and Litvinsky 1996:105–8. Literature on the Kushano-Sasanian coins is extensive. See Bivar 1979; Cribb 1981, 1990; Curiel and Schlumberger 1953; Herzfeld 1930; Lukonin 1967.
28   Shiva often has a nimbus around his head. It may be that he was associated with Mithra.

show a fire altar on the reverse and on the obverse the portrait of the king with his individual crown. The type of crown and the name of the governor are often identical to those on the 'Kushan' type Kushano-Sasanian coins. They carry texts in Middle Persian and in Pahlavi script. These issues would indicate the control by the Kushano-Sasanian governors of lands that had formerly not belonged to the Kushan empire, contrary to the lands of North and East Afghanistan, where the Shiva and Nandi coins were struck.

Finally, there are rather thick copper coins, somewhat similar to the preceding group, which also bear the image of a fire altar on the reverse. These coins are known in particular from the Indus valley, but also from the Jalalabad area and Begram, and north of the Hindu Kush. Their legends are in Middle Persian, in Pahlavi or Bactrian (Greek) script. These coins are based on issues of Shapur II.

The date of the Kushano-Sasanian coins remains a problem. The *communis opinio*, supported by written evidence, would suggest that the coins were for the greater part issued during the late third and fourth centuries AD.[29] Hormizd I or II may be the man who rebelled against King Bahram II in the late third century AD. The names of the governors mentioned on the coins include those carried by the Sasanian kings, but the people were probably not identical. It seems that the governors belonged to the royal family and they carried or adopted names befitting their status. Something like this occurred with the Persian Achaemenid governors of Bactria who often carried the name of Vishtaspa. It is evident, and this should be clearly understood, that the Kushano-Sasanian governors occupied an important position. This is not only indicated by their coins and their (throne-) names, but also by the fact that they all had their own individual style of crown. This feature is also known from the portraits of the Sasanian kings themselves as depicted on the Sasanian silver coins and in reliefs.

Thus, in the late third and fourth centuries AD, much of the former lands of the Kushans were governed by a mighty representative of the Sasanian monarch, who issued his own coins with his own portrait. Moreover, he issued gold coins, in line with the Kushan tradition, but quite contrary to Sasanian practice. It is also evident that the governor resided in the northeast of the Plateau, and the city of Balkh may have been one of his capitals. The role of the (Sasanian) Kushan Shah was comparable to that of his colleague in the southeast, the King of the Sakas. Both of them were important Sasanian officials; both of them were often princes of the royal court.

Little is known of daily life in Bactria in the time of the Kushano-Sasanian governors. In recent years, however, a large number of texts

29 Compare Frye 1984:345 and 1996:148–9. See also Cribb 1990.

written in Bactrian have been brought to light north of the Hindu Kush.[30] These texts were mostly written on leather, on both sides, and in cursive Bactrian script. More than one hundred of these new documents have been recovered to date. According to their editor, the British scholar Nicholas Sims-Williams, they all appear to derive from the same source, but they do not date to the same period. Most of the documents should be placed between the early fourth and late eighth centuries. Many of the texts are letters, some of them still sealed when first discovered. The documents were probably written in a district just north of the Hindu Kush passes, in the early Islamic period known as the Kingdom of Rob. One of these documents mentions a Kushan Shah called Warahran. This was probably the Bahram who is known as one of the last Kushano-Sasanian governor-kings, or Kushan Shahs, of the area.

The Chionites

Sasanian supremacy in the East did not last long, and soon its position was challenged. As usual in the history of this part of the world, the threat originated in the north. Sometime in the middle or second half of the fourth century AD, people from the north invaded the northeastern lands of the Iranian Plateau. This invasion was different from the preceding incursions in one important aspect. It reflected an important change occurring in the steppes of Central Asia, namely the advent of Altaic speaking peoples from Mongolia and their pushing aside of the Iranian speaking groups that hitherto had dominated the Central Asian plains.

The Altaic language family is named after the Altai mountains in Central Asia, along the Siberian/Chinese border. The Altaic tongues are generally grouped into three main branches, namely the Turkic, Mongol and Manchu-Tunguz languages. Korean and Japanese are also sometimes included. The origins of these languages should clearly be sought in the Mongolian steppes along the northern borders of China. With the great migrations that started in the late first millennium BC many Altaic speaking people were pushed to the west, thus starting a movement that some thousand years later would lead to their presence across a large part of Central Asia and the Near East.

The first of the invaders in North Afghanistan by the mid-fourth century were the Chionites.[31] Their name recalls their Hunnish char-

---

30 Sims-Williams 1997a.
31 For the Chionites and Hephthalites, compare Ghirshman 1948, Göbl 1967, Zeimal 1996.

acter and that is how they, and the Hephthalites that succeeded them, became known to the outside world. Their exact ethnic and linguistic affiliations are still unknown, but it is generally accepted that they belonged to Altaic-speaking peoples and some scholars assume that they were related to the Turkic branch. The migrations that brought the Chionites and subsequently the Hephthalites to Afghanistan and northwestern India coincided with other large-scale movements. These brought other Hunnish tribes towards the Ukraine and Central Europe as far west as modern France. Under Attila they almost succeeded in occupying all of the West Roman Empire, before they were narrowly defeated at Chalôns in AD 451.

The Chionites are first mentioned by Ammianus Marcellinus, the Roman historiographer from the fourth century AD. He tells about the campaigns of the Sasanian king, Shapur II (AD 309–79), against the Euseni (Cuseni, Kushans?) and the Chionitae in AD 356.[32] Soon after, according to the same source, the Sasanian king concluded an alliance with the Chionites, the Gils and the Sakas.[33] The alliance, which in fact may have marked the defeat of the Chionites, probably included the incorporation of Chionite troops in Shapur's armies that were used against the (East) Roman empire. In AD 360, Shapur laid siege to the town of Amida (Diyarbakr), in modern eastern Turkey, apparently supported by Chionite troops. During the siege, the son of Grumbates,[34] the Chionite king, was killed. According to the sources, his body was cremated and his bones were deposited into an urn.[35]

By the late fourth century AD the Chionites were united under the dynasty of the Kidarites.[36] The name of this dynasty is derived from that of the king, Kidara, who is known from coins that were found, among other places, at Tepe Maranjan, Kabul, in association with Sasanian issues. He struck scyphate gold coins in the Kushano-Sasanian style, with the title of Kushan Shah (in Bactrian: *Bago Kidara Vazurka Košano Shao*). He also struck silver drachms that copied those of the Sasanian kings (Shapur II and III).

The presence of the Chionites in North Afghanistan probably did not lead to a permanent demise of Sasanian control. While the Chionites dominated eastern Bactria, Sasanian troops probably still held much of Northwest Afghanistan and the important centre of Herat.

---

32   Ammianus Marcellinus XIV 3.1; XVI 9.3–4; XVIII 6. See also Zonaras II 15.
33   Ammianus Marcellinus XVII 5.1.
34   For this name, which may be read in one of the Bactrian documents from the old Kingdom of Rob just north of the Hindu Kush passes, see Sims-Williams 1997:13. It was dated to the late fifth century AD.
35   Ammianus Marcellinus XIX 1.7–11;2.1.
36   See Zeimal 1996.

This may be deduced from the fact that the Chionites did not seem to have advanced further south through the Herat corridor, but to the contrary they eventually, according to Chinese sources, moved southeast across the Hindu Kush down into the Kabul valley. South of the mountains, the Chionites under Kidara and his successors subsequently created a powerful kingdom that features prominently in Indian history.[37] The same Chinese sources refer to the Chionite capital south of the Hindu Kush, and its name probably refers to modern Peshawar.

The arrival of the Chionites in Gandhara does not seem to have immediately disrupted cultural life in the region. Of great importance in this context is the travelogue of a Chinese Buddhist pilgrim, called Faxian, who visited the district of Jalalabad around AD 400.[38] His description of Gandhara and the Kabul valley clearly illustrates the wealth and prosperity of the Buddhist community in his time. When he arrived from China in the extreme north of modern Pakistan, Faxian found a flourishing Buddhist community of the Little Vehicle (*Hinayâna*) branch. Via the district of Swat, he subsequently arrived in Gandhara. According to the pilgrim, most of the people here also adhered to *Hinayâna* Buddhism. Later he went to the city of Peshawar. Here he visited the huge stupa built, according to the pilgrim, by the Kushan king Kanishka,[39] and he also mentions the famous alms bowl of Buddha.[40] Faxian subsequently travelled west to Nagarahara (the Jalalabad district), to the city of modern Hadda (*Xiluo*), where there was the famous *vihâra* with Buddha's skull-bone. Faxian describes a large number of Buddhist sanctuaries in this area. From here, he travelled south across the 'Little Snowy Mountains' (Safed Kuh?), back towards the Indus.

The Hephthalites

Meanwhile, along the western borders of the Kidarite kingdom, the Sasanians tried hard to regain lost territory. This was the time of the kings Bahram V and Yazdajird II, who ruled between AD 420 and

37 Compare Biswas 1973.
38 Translated by Samuel Beal 1884.
39 This must be the famous Shah-ji-ki-dheri Buddhist sanctuary where the reliquary of King Kanishka was found in 1908 (see Rowland 1970:122).
40 This is the alms bowl that according to legend subsequently found its way to Qandahar (Ferrier 1857:318) and that was rediscovered in 1925 at the shrine of Mir Ways near Qandahar. It was subsequently exhibited in the Kabul Museum (N. Dupree 1974:11–12, and photograph no. 48). The Qandahar bowl dates to about the fifteenth century.

457. However, new waves of northern invaders soon posed an even greater threat to the Sasanians. The new migrants are generally called the Hephthalites.[41] They were probably ethnically related to the Chionites who moved before them. The Hephthalites are known from Arabic sources as the *Haytal* or (plur.) *Hayâtila.*[42] The Byzantines called them the (Red or White) Huns, or the Abdelai/Ephthalitai.[43] The Chinese knew them as the *Yida,* while they called their king *Yandaiyilituo.* The coin legends, but also texts engraved on gems, would suggest that the Hephthalites, or at least their leaders, spoke an Eastern Iranian language. The names of the Hephthalite kings as given by al-Tabari are also Iranian. However, it is more than likely that the Hephthalites originally spoke an Altaic language and that they, or at least the upper classes among them, adopted the language of Bactria when they occupied these lands.[44]

Contemporary information about the Hephthalites is scarce. In the sixth century, Procopius of Caesarea described the Hephthalites as follows:[45]

> though they are of the stock of the Huns in fact as well as in name . . . they do not mingle with any of the Huns known to us . . . They are not nomads like the other Hunnic peoples . . . they are the only ones among the Huns who have white bodies and countenances which are not ugly. It is also true that their manner of living is unlike that of their kinsmen, nor do they lead a savage life as they do; but they are ruled by one king, and . . . possess a lawful constitution.

The early history of the Hephthalites in northeastern Iran is still very vague, since the sources do not always distinguish between the Chionites, Kidarites and Hephthalites. Al-Tabari tells how by *c.*AD 457 the Sasanian pretender Firuz sollicited Hephthalite help against his brother, King of Kings Hormizd III.[46] According to al-Tabari the Hephthalites had shortly before conquered Tukharistan, a name that since the late first millennium BC had come to be used for ancient Bactria and the mountainous lands to the east. Hephthalite assistance subsequently helped Firuz to conquer the Sasanian throne (*r.* AD 459–84). Soon after, however, war started again along the eastern

---

41 For the Hephthalites, see Litvinsky 1996.
42 Probably to be read *Habtal* and *Habâtila* (Tomaschek 1888).
43 Indian sources refer to the *Śveta-hûnas,* or White Huns, and to the *Hâra-hûnas* (Red Huns ?). See Bailey 1954:12–16.
44 For their ethnic origins, see also Enoki 1959.
45 *Hist.* I 3; trans. Loeb.
46 al-Tabari (Nöldeke 1879/1973:114–16).

frontier. In the 460s and 470s, Firuz conducted at least three wars in the East, at one time leaving his son Kubadh as hostage among his opponents. When his son was returned against the payment of a huge ransom, the war continued. The result was that Firuz eventually lost his life and left his empire at the mercy of the enemy. For many years to come the Sasanians were tributary to the Hephthalites and lived in perpetual fear of these northern warriors.

Eventually the Hephthalites established a large realm on both sides of the Hindu Kush, stretching as far as the banks of the Indus river, thus pushing aside their predecessors, the Chionites and Kidarites. The lands north of the Hindu Kush, however, remained the centre of Hephthalite power. The Early Islamic writer al-Biruni tells that the old capital of the Hephthalites was called Warwaliz and was located in Tukharistan.[47] This place remained known until Saljuk times, in the early second millennium. It probably lay at, or near the modern town of Qunduz north of the Salang tunnel.

From later sources it is clear that the Hephthalite realm was relatively loosely organized, with fairly autonomous districts headed by hereditary leaders. The initial impact of the Hephthalites on cultural life in the conquered areas seems to have been limited. The Chinese pilgrim Songyun, who travelled through what is now modern Afghanistan and ancient Gandhara around AD 520, tells that the Buddhist community was flourishing and that the Buddhist monuments were still standing.[48] On the other hand, he informs his readers that 'foreign gods' and 'demons' were also being worshipped.

The Bactrian documents recently brought to light in North Afghanistan and which derive from the Kingdom of Rob also include references to the Hephthalites. A letter that according to Sims-Williams may date to the late fifth century refers to the Hephthalite ruler of the area.[49] Another text, which Sims-Williams interprets as a contract dating to AD 527, refers to 'Hephthalite tax'.[50]

Hephthalite coins are known from various places in Afghanistan. They are based on the silver drachms of the Sasanians and include the depiction of a fire altar on the reverse. On the obverse, the coins show the bust of the king and a legend in Bactrian. At the site of Hadda (Tope 10), near Jalalabad, Hephthalite coins were found in association with gold coins of Theodosius, Marcianus and Leo (AD 457–74).[51]

47   Compare Enoki 1977:88.
48   Trans. Samuel Beal 1884.
49   Sims-Williams 1997:16.
50   Sims-Williams 1997:14.
51   MacDowall and Taddei 1978:251.

The Turks

But also the power of the Hephthalites came under attack, also from the north. In the mid-sixth century AD, Turkic tribes assembled along the northern borders of modern Afghanistan. Their presence in the area formed part of the same upsurge of Altaic speaking peoples that brough the Huns to the Iranian Plateau and to Europe. The Turks were united in the so-called Khaqanate of the Western Turks.[52] In AD 559/560, their *yabghu*, Istämi (also called Sinjibu) and the Sasanian king, Khusraw I Anushirwan (r. AD 531–79), attacked the Hephthalites from the north and south respectively and defeated their opponents.[53] On paper this marked the end of Hephthalite power. However, direct Turkic or Sasanian influence in the lands of modern North Afghanistan remained at first marginal and Hephthalite principalities continued to exist. They fought at times with the Turks against the Sasanians, and at other times with the Sasanians against the Turks.

The Chinese *Bei Shu* accordingly tells that in the early 580s the Hephthalites and Sasanians together fought against the Turks.[54] At first they did so without much success, since Tardu, Istämi's successor, apparently succeeded to move as far south as Herat. In AD 588/9, however, the famous Sasanian general Bahram Chubin (the later King of Kings, Bahram VI), defeated a Turkic army and captured Balkh, that apparently earlier had been taken by the Turks.[55] Struggles continued. During the reign of the Sasanian king Khusraw II (r. AD 590–628), the Turks assisted the Hephthalites, defeated the Iranians, and advanced as far as Rayy (near Tehran) and Isfahan.[56] The Turks were later defeated, but they retained their influence in the former Hephthalite lands. By AD 630, when Eastern Iran was visited by the Chinese pilgrim Xuanzang, much of modern North Afghanistan was governed by Turks and they were rapidly extending their influence south of the mountains. It is clear that a new era had started, in which the Iranians on the Plateau would make place for new Turkic immigrants and rulers.

---

52 For the history of the early Turks, see Scharlipp 1992:18–29.
53 Compare Widengren 1952, and al-Tabari (Nöldeke 1879/1973:156–7).
54 *Bei Shu* XLIV, p. 4 (Chavannes 1903:50).
55 Bahram VI was later forced to flee to the Turks, who killed him (al-Tabari, Nöldeke 1879/1973:271).
56 According to Armenian sources; see Harmatta and Litvinsky 1996:369.

Xuanzang

The travelogue of Xuanzang is one of the most fascinating accounts of ancient travelling. In the *Xiyou ji* ('Records of the Western World'), which contains his travelogue, a tantalizing view is given of the lands of modern Afghanistan and the Indian subcontinent. The same story, although slightly different in detail, is told in Hui Li's *The Life of Xuanzang*.[57] Xuanzang started his journeys in Chang'an in the west of China, around AD 629. In search of wisdom and in order to see the holy Buddhist places and to collect manuscripts, he travelled by way of the Turfan oasis and Samarqand towards the north of modern Afghanistan, and hence to the Indian subcontinent. He returned to China in AD 645.

In his report he describes the country of Tukharistan. He tells that it covered all the lands between the Hindu Kush to the south and the Hisar range north of the Amu Darya. It thus roughly corresponded to Classical Bactria and the mountainous lands to the east. Xuanzang adds that the land had been split up into 27 districts, after the demise of the royal clan, and as a group was now dependent on Turkic tribes. Xuanzang furthermore tells that the people were mean and cowardly. They read from left to right and they used gold and silver coins. Most of the people wore cotton clothing, others used wool. The Chinese pilgrim, apparently rather disappointed, adds that the people's knowledge of the Faith (Buddhism) was limited.

Xuanzang in particular refers to the district of *Buhe*, which must be identical to Bactra. We read that there were many monks (some three thousand) in and outside the main town, all adhering to the Little Vehicle (*Hinayâna*) branch of Buddhism. In *The Life of Xuanzang*, it is added that there were some one hundred monasteries. Xuanzang also describes the stupas here and in nearby places. Modern archaeological work has brought to light the remains of Buddhist sanctuaries near ancient Bactra, including the extant ruins of a large stupa just south of the town, now called Tepe Rustam. These ruins lie close to the ruins of Takht-i Rustam, which probably is identical with the ancient monastery of Naw Bahar (compare Sanskrit *vihâra*, 'monastery').[58]

---

57 The *Records of the Western World* were translated by Samuel Beal, London 1884 (reprint New Delhi 1983). The *Life of Xuanzang* has also been translated by Beal (1911).
58 Bailey 1943. For the ruins, see Ball 1982: No. 99. The Arab geographers from the tenth century AD tell that the ruins belonged to people who adhered to the same faith as the Chinese emperor and the King of Kabul (Barthold 1984:14).

The pilgrim subsequently tells about the land of *Fanyanna*. This is modern Bamiyan in the middle of the Hindu Kush, the Snowy Mountains of the Chinese. According to Xuanzang, the valley of Bamiyan lay outside of Tukharistan, although the writing, customs and money system were identical. Also the personal appearance of its population was very much the same, but the language was a little different. The people wore clothes made out of wool or skin. The people of Bamiyan are described as very religious (Buddhist), mainly adherents of the Little Vehicle and Lokottaravadins (a Buddhist sect intermediate between *Hinayâna* and *Mahâyâna*). Xuanzang also describes the two huge standing images of the Buddha:[59]

> To the northeast of the royal city there is a mountain, on the declivity of which is placed a stone figure of Buddha, erect, in height 140 or 150 feet. Its golden hues sparkle on every side, and its precious ornaments dazzle the eyes by their brightness. To the east of this spot there is a convent, which was built by a former king of the country. To the east of the convent there is a standing figure of Sakya Buddha, made of metallic stone, in height 100 feet. It has been cast in different parts and joined together, and thus placed in a completed form as it stands.[60]

Beyond Bamiyan, Xuanzang crossed the 'Black Ridge' and arrived in the district of *Jiabishi*, which is no other than Classical Capisa, modern Begram north of Kabul. The people here clearly did not find favour with the Chinese. He describes them as 'cruel and fierce; their language is coarse and rude; their marriage rites a mere intermingling of the sexes'. Xuanzang adds that their language and customs were somewhat different from those of the people in Tukharistan. The clothing of the people was of wool, with fur trimmings. The king of the city, a pious Buddhist, is said by the Chinese to have conquered some ten neighbouring states. Here the monks mainly followed the Great Vehicle (*Mahâyâna*) branch of Buddhism, although the Little Vehicle was also still popular.

East of Capisa, the Chinese pilgrim, according to his report, passed the border with India and passed through the districts of Laghman (*Lanbo*), Nagarahara (*Najieluohe*) and Gandhara (*Jiantuoluo*). According to Xuanzang, Laghman was dependent on Capisa.[61] Again the Chinese pilgrim is little impressed by the local people. He describes them as untrustworthy and thievish. He tells that they mostly wore white linen garments. The Buddhists in the region

---

59   Since destroyed by the Taliban, in February–March 2001.
60   Trans. Beal 1884/1983:50–1.
61   From *The Life of Xuangzang*, it appears that his rule extended as far as the banks of the Indus river.

mainly followed the *Mahâyâna* branch, but the pilgrim adds that there were also many temples dedicated to the worship of Hindu gods.

Nagarahara, around modern Jalalabad, was also dependent on Capisa, but the people obviously found more favour with the Chinese. They are described as simple and honest, and with an ardent and courageous disposition. Most of the people were Buddhists. The pilgrim regretfully notices that the stupas were deserted and in ruins. There were also some temples of non-Buddhists (Hindus). Southwest of the capital of the district, Xuanzang visited the site of *Xiluo* (modern Hadda) and the famous stupa that contained the skull-bone of Buddha. Continuing east from Nagarahara, the Chinese arrived in Gandhara and its capital Peshawar (*Bulushabuluo*). This district was at that time ruled by a governor sent from Capisa. Xuanzang indicates that town and district were deserted, and the stupas and monasteries were in ruins.

Years later, on his way back to China, Xuanzang again passed through the Indo-Iranian borderlands. He mentions the land of *Falana*, which was subject to Capisa.[62] According to *The Life*, this district lay far to the south of Peshawar and the Kabul valley, somewhere in the centre of the modern Northwest Frontier Province of Pakistan. It is described as being populated by an uncivilized population. Some of them were Buddhist (*Mahâyâna*); others worshiped the Hindu gods. To the west lay the land of *Jijiangna*. Here the people were organized in clans, living amid high mountains, and their land was famous for its sheep and large horses.[63] Beyond, travelling northwest, Xuanzang reached the borders of India.

Out of India, the Chinese pilgrim entered the land of *Caojutuo*, with its two capitals of *Hexina* and *Hesaluo*. While the first is perhaps identical with Ghazni, the second place is still unknown.[64] If the first identification is correct, the land of *Caojutuo* refers to the land of Zabulistan, the district between Qandahar and Kabul as known from Early Islamic sources. This identification is supported by the name of one of the rivers of the land, namely the *Luomayindu*, which could be linked to that of the Hilmand river, the Classical Etymandros. According to the Chinese there were many Buddhist monasteries, all *Mahâyâna*, in this area, and also the king was a fervent Buddhist. The identification of this district with Zabulistan is of great interest, especially as the Chinese pilgrim tells us that many people here

62 Perhaps identical with Avestan *Varᵊna*, and perhaps the *Varnu* of the Indian grammarian Panini (IV 2.103; 3.93).
63 Likely to be identified with Early Islamic Kizkanan or Qiqan, a district located in the borderlands.
64 Cunningham refers to Ozola, listed by Ptolemy.

worshipped a deity called *Chu* or *Chuna*.[65] His sanctuary, which is obviously non-Buddhist, lay in the south of the country, on a mountain top. The pilgrim adds that the god was introduced here from the north, from *Jiabishi*, and people of all ranks and sometimes from far away assembled once a year and came to the mountain top to offer gold, silver and other precious objects, and also sheep, horses and other animals.

From *Caojutuo* the Chinese travelled north and arrived in the district of *Folishisatangna* with the capital called *Hubina*. The identity and location of this land remain unknown.[66] The Chinese pilgrim informs us that a Turkic king, who was a fervent Buddhist, governed this district. The people were very akin to those of *Caojutuo*, although they spoke a different language. The district should perhaps be located not far to the north of the Ghazni area; the modern province of Wardak with its many Buddhist remains seems a logical possibility. From here the Chinese travelled northeast, passing through or skirting the Kabul area. They traversed the *Poluoxina*[67] pass across the Hindu Kush and descended into the district of *Antaluofo*, what is now called Andarab, on the northern side of the Khawak Pass. Xuanzang describes it as part of Tukharistan. In his time, the district was dependent on a Turkic ruler. Hence the pilgrim passed through Badakhshan (*Boduochuangna*) and returned back to China.

Xuanzang thus indicates that in his time, around AD 630, the north of modern Afghanistan was split up into various principalities, all owing allegiance to the Turks, while the Kabul valley as far east as Gandhara was dominated by the Buddhist ruler of Capisa. It is very well possible that in preceding years the Turks had carried out raids upon the lands south of the Hindu Kush and into Gandhara. At least one district south of the Hindu Kush was ruled by a Turkic prince (*Folishisatangna*). By Xuanzang's time, the Kabul valley had thus become an ethnic cauldron. New Turkic rulers were expending their power, at the cost of the descendants of the Chionites and Hephthalites, who in their turn had taken the place of the Kushans and other Scythian groups of the late first millennium BC. They all ultimately derived from Central Asia, and they all settled in lands that during the second millennium had been infiltrated by the Indo-Aryans, who also derived from Central Asia.

65   For Zabul and the god of the region, see also Marquart and de Groot 1915, and Sims-Williams 1997:19, for references.
66   The name may reflect that of the Parsuetai of Ptolemy, or the Pasha'i of modern date. *Hubina* is often held to be identical with Opian, north of Charikar. Xuanzang seems to have travelled back through the Panjshir valley.
67   Compare the *Upa'risaêna* of the Iranian tradition.

Buddhism had obviously passed through a difficult time and many monasteries and stupas had fallen into decay or had been destroyed. From the other Chinese accounts it appears that this had occurred relatively shortly before Xuanzang's visit, although he does not refer to any knowledge about such events. It is very well possible that the Chionites and Hephthalites, and their descendants, caused these destructions. Indian and Chinese sources refer in this context to two *Huna* kings, namely Toramana and Mihirakula, who reigned in North and Northwest India from the late fifth to the middle of the sixth centuries AD and were known for their destruction of Buddhist sanctuaries.

Although Xuanzang does not refer to the Sasanians, it may be safely assumed that by the time that he visited what is now modern Afghanistan, much of the south and west of the country was still held by Sasanian governors.[68] It is fascinating to think that some of these same officials would soon, within a few years, be confronted with the advance of Arab armies and succumb to a completely new political and religious order.

---

68   The so-called *Šahrestânihâ-yi Erân*, a Pahlavi text of the Muslim era but probably dating back to the early seventh century, provides a list of the provincial capitals of the Sasanian empire (Markwart 1931). It includes some well-known names, including *Kâbul*, *Rakhvad* (Arachosia), *Bast* (Qal'a-i Bust), *Frâx* (Farah), *Zâvalistân* (Zabulistan), *Zarang* (Zaranj) and *Hariy* (Herat).

11

The Advent of Islam

In the early seventh century, while Xuanzang and his followers passed through the Afghan mountains, the Sasanians were engaged in constant competition with the Hephthalites and Turks for the domination of the northeastern reaches of the Iranian Plateau. One of the main prizes was the control of the profitable trade in silk between China and the West, along the famous Silk Road. By the middle of that momentous century, three new forces entered the arena. These were the Chinese, the Tibetans and, most important of all, the Arabs. For the next two hundred years, between the mid-seventh and the mid-ninth centuries AD, modern North and Northeast Afghanistan would constitute the battleground for the ultimate control of the passes between East and West.

Arab Expansion

In AD 636, some four years after Muhammad's death, Arab armies defeated the Sasanians at al-Qadisiyya, in Mesopotamia. In AD 642 they won a second victory at Nihawand, southwest of modern Hamadan, in West Iran.[1] Soon they moved on, from Southwest Iran towards the east. In AD 650, the Arab governor of Basra in modern southern Iraq, named 'Abd Allah bin Amir, sent an army towards Sistan. At the same time another army was despatched towards Khurasan, which was by then the common name for the northeastern parts of the Iranian Plateau. These troops went in pursuit of the Sasanian king, Yazdajird III, who after the battle of Nihawand had fled eastwards, just like his predecessor Darius III had done more than nine hundred years earlier at the advance of Alexander of

---

1 The date of the battle is uncertain. For the Arab conquests in Central Asia, compare Gibb 1923.

Macedon. The Arabs marched straight through the Central Iranian deserts and after a long siege they took Nishapur, west of modern Mashhad and at that time one of the main cities of Khurasan. After that the Arabs moved on towards the Sasanian headquarters in the Northeast, the city of Marw. Around this time, somewhere along the Murghab river, Yazdajird III was assassinated.[2] Thereupon Sasanian imperial resistance collapsed completely and the Arabs occupied the plains of West and North Afghanistan, including the towns of Bactra and Herat. All this happened just a few years after the Buddhist monk Xuanzang had travelled through Afghanistan on his way back to China.

The Arab conquest of North and West Afghanistan did not mean that all resistance was over. Alexander the Great and his Macedonians had already found out that it was one thing to defeat and occupy the plains of the Iranian Plateau, but that it was something completely different to fully pacify the people in the countryside and along the Plateau's fringes. This situation applied especially to the hardy mountaineers and pastoralists along the eastern and northern rims. Furthermore, many of the local rulers in the Northeast were of Hunnish or Turkic origin and closely related to their kinsmen in the lands beyond the Amu Darya. The Arab position was made even more precarious when two other formidable forces moved in, namely the Chinese from the northeast and the Tibetans from the east.

Under the newly established Tang dynasty (AD 618–907), the Chinese had moved into the Tarim basin on the eastern side of the Pamir mountains. One of their main objectives was to further control the trade in silk. In doing so, they were soon confronted with the rising power of the Tibetans, who in the early seventh century had established an empire that for many years would compete with the Chinese for the control of the Silk Road. At first, however, the Chinese proved the strongest.

The first contacts between the new Arab rulers of Eastern Iran and the Chinese occurred when the son of Yazdajird III, Firuz, fled to China and asked for support against the Arabs. The Chinese agreed and Firuz returned to Eastern Iran, where he may even have been temporarily set up as ruler during the politically chaotic caliphate of Muhammad's cousin and son-in-law, 'Ali bin Abi Talib (AD 656–61).[3] At that time the Arab world was in great turmoil and the Chinese formally incorporated much of Eastern Iran into their empire.

2   There are tales that his body was recovered by the Christian bishop of Marw (Labourt 1904:326).
3   See Beckwith 1987:38–9 and Harmatta and Litvinsky 1996:372.

However, Chinese success did not last long. The Turks of Central Asia rose against them and forced the Chinese to withdraw across the mountains back to China. After the death of 'Ali bin Abi Talib and the accession to power of the Umayyad caliphs in AD 661, the Arabs reoccupied many of the cities of present-day Afghanistan, including Herat and Balkh. By the early 670s they felt confident in expanding their influence into the mountains of Afghanistan and across the Amu Darya towards Bukhara and Samarqand, into what they called *Mâ Warâ 'al-Nahr* (Arabic, 'the land that lies beyond the river'). In the meantime, however, the Tibetans had occupied many of the passes across the Pamir and thus could directly influence the course of affairs in Tukharistan.[4]

Another period of decline of Arab control started after *c*.AD 683, when the various leaders and tribes of the Arabs started to fight among themselves. It was only by AD 691/2, under Caliph 'Abd al-Malik (AD 685–705), that Umayyad rule in the East was somehow restored, but for many years North Afghanistan remained a frontier area. In AD 704, the Turks and Tibetans even attacked the town of Termez, along the northern banks of the Amu Darya. Soon after, however, the Arabs gained some considerable successes. In AD 705, Abu Hafs Qutayba bin Muslim was appointed governor of Khurasan. First he defeated a Hephthalite ruler, Tarkhan Nizak, who from his centre in Badghis west of Balkh had built up a coalition of anti-Arab forces in the area. In the following years, the Arabs under Qutayba occupied much of the South Central Asia, including Bukhara, Samar-qand and Choresmia south of the Aral Sea, and they marched as far as the rich plains of Farghana, east of Tashkent. When in AD 715, however, a new caliph came to the throne in Damascus, who was opposed to Qutayba, the successful general was forced into open rebellion and subsequently killed by his own troops. Soon after, the Chinese reoccupied Farghana and the position of the Arabs in the northeast of the Plateau, including North Afghanistan, was again threatened. Embassies from many independent principalities in Eastern Iran visited the Chinese court, asking for help against the Arabs.[5] They came from Tukharistan, from the Kabul valley, from Wakhan in modern Northeast Afghanistan, from Chitral in North Pakistan, and even from Zabulistan, between Kabul and Qandahar. The Chinese now not only threatened the Arab position, but also that of the Tibetans who still occupied the Pamir passes. Yet, the Chinese

4 Beckwith 1987:30.
5 The embassy was apparently led by a Manichaean high priest (Gignoux and Litvinsky 1996:418–19).

refrained from asserting themselves in Eastern Iran, thus giving the Arabs and Tibetans the time to reorganize.

North and south of the Amu Darya, the Turks and Tibetans, sometimes with the help of local princelings and sometimes with the backing of the Chinese, continued to harass the Arabs. In AD 737 the Turks attacked Khulm (Tashqurghan)[6] in North Afghanistan and subsequently occupied the capital of Jawzjan province, west of Balkh. Partly because of these ongoing struggles, the city of Balkh gained more and more importance as the Arab headquarters of the area, at the expense of Marw, the former capital of Khurasan in the years of the Sasanian empire. Balkh, which was first captured by the Arabs in AD 653, officially became the Arab capital of this part of the Iranian Plateau in AD 736.

In AD 747, the Chinese for the last time moved to the west. Under their famous general, the Korean Gao Xianzi, they occupied much of the Wakhan valley and the Baroghil Pass, thus cutting off Tibetan access to the west. The still independent rulers of Tukharistan again sent envoys to the Chinese court, offering their submission. However, four years later, in AD 751, the Chinese were decisively defeated by the Arabs along the Talas river, northeast of Tashkent. A few years later, China was plunged into political chaos when one of their generals rebelled against the emperor. The Tang dynasty could only be saved with the help of the (Turkic) Uyghurs, who by the mid-eighth century had established an empire along China's northern borders. As a result of all these developments, the Chinese no longer played a role of any significance in South Central Asia. This left the way for the Tibetans to reassert their position in and around the mountains of Central Asia. In AD 756, envoys from various principalities visited the Tibetan court, including those from Wakhan.[7]

In the early ninth century, Tibetan troops participated in the revolt of the Sogdian capital of Samarqand. The caliph in Baghdad, Harun al-Rashid, personally moved to the east, but he died near Tus in AD 809. His younger son, al-Ma'mun, became governor of the East and was confronted with widespread unrest, also from the side of the Buddhist king of Kabul. However, al-Ma'mun could not use his troops until he defeated his brother and became caliph himself. He then turned his troops against those who had long resisted Arab rule, often with the help of the Tibetans. The King of Kabul was one of them. In the end, however, Arab success was limited and the various

6 Modern Tashqurghan, founded in the eighteenth century, lies south of ancient Khulm (destroyed by Ahmad Shah Durrani in the mid-eighteenth century).
7 Beckwith 1987:144–5.

Hindu and Buddhist principalities in the valleys of the Hindu Kush and south of the mountains continued to defy the Arab rulers from the north and west. Yet, their days were numbered. By the mid-ninth century, the empire of the Tibetans crumbled under internecine strife and attacks from the side of the Chinese and from other peoples. This also meant the end of Tibetan influence in Afghanistan. The road was open for Muslim rulers to occupy all of the country.

The Wars in the South

While the Arabs were engaged in continuous warfare in the Northeast, a similar situation of ongoing fighting took place south of the mountains. The Arabs occupied Sistan (or Sijistan) and its capital, Zaranj, in the mid-seventh century AD. Soon they were thrown out, however, and replaced by local rulers, until under the first of the Umayyad caliphs, Mu'awiya (r. AD 661–80), the Arabs again occupied the area. They subsequently raided on the ancient settlement of Bust, at the confluence of the Hilmand and the Arghandab rivers.[8] Headed by the Arab commander, 'Abd al-Rahman bin Samura, they pushed on and for a brief time occupied Kabul much further up north.[9] However, Arab successes were ephemeral and for a long time they failed to permanently establish their power in Southeast and East Afghanistan. Sistan remained a frontier area where the so-called *ghâzi*[10] assembled to fight the non-Muslim peoples living to the northeast and east. At the same time Sistan became a bulwark of the heterodox Kharijite movement, which had been pushed towards this outpost of the Islam world.[11] Orthodox Muslim rule in Sistan was only firmly established with the rise of the local Saffarid dynasty in the mid-ninth century. And only by the end of the tenth century did Islamic forces permanently occupy the borderlands further to the east. From that moment the road to the Indian subcontinent lay open.

8 For its present ruins, see Ball 1982:149.
9 In doing so they may have captured the grandfather of Abu Hanifa, the founder of the Hanafite *madhhab* (school) of Islamic jurisprudence (see Adamec 1997:13 and J. Schacht in the *Enc. Isl*). It is also reported (see H. A. R. Gibb in the *Enc. Isl*) that captives from Kabul built him a mosque in Basra.
10 *Ghâzi* is an Arabic word that means 'fighter for the faith'.
11 The Kharijites ('Seceders') were thus named after their refusal to accept Caliph 'Ali's decision to submit to arbitration in his struggle with the Syrian governor, Mu'awiya. According to the Kharijites, only God could act as arbitrator, through the voice of all the people. They held the view that anyone could be elected Caliph if agreed upon by the whole community.

Zabulistan

In the intervening years, the borderlands were dominated by local rulers of Iranian, Hunnish/Turkic and Indian stock. One of these border districts was called Zabulistan.[12] It was located, roughly speaking, between Bust and the southern borders of the Kabul valley and thus covered much of what is now called Hazarajat and the southeastern foothills of the Afghan mountains. The Early Islamic geographers were inclined to regard this district as part of *Hind* (India). Incidentally, the Indian character of the area was underlined by the many elephants that were used by its king.[13] Zabulistan included, apart from the Ghazni highlands south of Kabul, two other important districts, namely that of *Zamin Dâwar* (or *Bilâd al-Dâwar*) and *Al-Rukhkhaj*. The first was located along the Hilmand river north of Bust and modern Girishk; the second is no other than Classical Arachosia, the oasis around ancient and modern Qandahar. The Arab geographers also mention two towns in this district: Panjway and Tiginabad.[14] Panjway still exists and lies west of modern Qandahar; Tiginabad is more difficult to locate. Its name, with various variants, consists of the word *Tigin* (*takin* or *tegin*), an ancient Turkic title for 'prince', and the Arab suffic -*âbâd* for 'town'. The name of the town would thus be 'town of the prince', 'residential palace', which would indicate that it was the descriptive name of the capital of the area. It therefore likely represents the site of Old Qandahar.[15]

Xuanzang, as discussed earlier, tells about the worship in a district called *Caojutuo* of the god *Chu* or *Chuna*. The district may well represent that of Zabulistan; Xuanzang's itinerary does indeed seem to place this area in Southeast Afghanistan.[16] The identity of the deity remains problematic. We do know that Buddhism was still thriving in this part of the world by the mid-eighth century, although Hinduism was becoming very popular. At the same time, the new Turkic

12 Compare Marquart and De Groot 1915; C. E. Bosworth 1963, 1968, 1994; Daffinà 1962; Forstner 1970. Compare also the many studies on this subject by G. Scarcia.
13 According to various sources, the ruler of Zabulistan carried the title of *zibil* (or *zunbil* or *rutbil*).
14 For Panjway, see Ball 1982: No. 798.
15 The earliest clear reference to the name of Qandahar is recorded from the late ninth century (compare Fischer 1967:192–3), and the name is again found from the thirteenth century onwards.
16 Some more information on this deity may be provided by the Bactrian documents from the Kingdom of Rob. One of the princes of the area in the late seventh century was called *Zhunlad*, 'given by Zhun'. Compare Sims-Williams 1997:19–20.

rulers of the area may have brought with them their own religion. Xuanzang's story that the god *Chu* first wanted to settle on a mountain near *Jiabishi* (Capisa north of Kabul), but later was forced to move to Zabulistan would indicate a northern origin. A northern origin of the main god of the region may also reflect a northern, Hunnish or Turkic origin of the royal dynasty.[17] Xuanzang's account of the general southward push of the Huns and Turks would support this hypothesis. This would mean that by the seventh century a large part of Southeast and East Afghanistan was ruled by a group of people of allegedly Hunnish or Turkic, or at least non-Iranian origin. The name of Tigin-abad for their capital would furthermore underline this possibility.

Zabulistan remained independent for a long time, although occasionally the Arabs from Sistan invaded it, as for instance in AD 710–11 when Qutayba b. Muslim invaded the land. Only in the late eighth century, when the Muslims again invaded Zabulistan, did Kabul and Zabulistan nominally recognize the Arab caliph al-Mahdi as their overlord. Much later followed the real conquest of the region.

Turkic and Hindu Rulers of East Afghanistan

The main centre of resistance against the rising tide of Islam in Eastern Afghanistan was the Kabul valley. Located along one of the few direct links between the Iranian Plateau and Central Asia on the one hand, and the Indian subcontinent on the other, it occupies a very strategic position. Ancient and modern cities in this area, as discussed earlier, include Begram (Capisa) at the southern end of the Hindu Kush passes; the ancient and modern town of Kabul; ancient Hadda and nearby modern Jalalabad; and Peshawar, at the eastern end of the Khaybar Pass and other thoroughfares.

Chinese sources (the *Tang Shu*) provide the name of the ruler of Capisa and Gandhara around AD 658, and this name (*Hexiezhi*) is generally regarded to be of Turkic origin.[18] It is very well possible that the Buddhist ruler of Capisa who was met by Xuanzang some years earlier, was also of Hunnish or Turkic origin. A Korean pilgrim, called Huichao, who traversed this part of the world around AD 727, correspondingly tells that in his days all the lands of modern East Afghanistan were under Turkic control, although the rulers had become Buddhists.[19] It is clear that the political constellation as

17   Harmatta and Litvinsky 1996:375.
18   Harmatta and Litvinsky 1996:373.
19   Fuchs 1938:444, 447–8.

sketched by Xuanzang, whereby in the early seventh century the lands north of the Hindu Kush were all under control of Turkic rulers, had firmly spread across the mountains into the Kabul valley and beyond, possibly also reaching Zabulistan.

The Kabul rulers are probably identical with the so-called Turki Shahi kings, who are known from other sources, as for instance from the work of the early Islamic geographer, Abu Rayhan al-Biruni.[20] This famous encyclopaedist from Choresmia lived from AD 973 to about AD 1050 and worked at the court of the later Islamic ruler of East Afghanistan, Mahmud of Ghazni. In his large work on India (*Ta'rikh al-Hind*), al-Biruni tells that the Turkic kings of Kabul and Gandhara claimed descent from King Kanishka, while at the same time they boasted of their Tibetan origins.[21] They reigned, according to al-Biruni, for sixty generations.

The fragmentary and legendary information of al-Biruni can be compared with other sources. From the seventh century, a series of silver and copper coins has been found at various sites in eastern Afghanistan (including Begram) and adjoining lands in Pakistan, which mention King Nizak,[22] a title which in the past was usually read as Napki Malik. The appellation probably refers to a dynastic name (perhaps also found in the name of the early eighth century Hephthalite ruler of Badghis, Tarkhan Nizak) and may have been carried by a series of monarchs.[23] The coins still have the Sasanian fire altar on the reverse and the busts of the king face right, as do the busts of the kings on the Sasanian coins. There are many minor varieties, and they carry different types of scripts.

The interesting point is that some of the silver King Nizak coins are overstruck by a ruler called Vrahitigin, who is perhaps identical with someone called Barhatigin who is mentioned by al-Biruni as the first of the Turki Shahi kings. Vrahitigin's coins bear legends in Bactrian, Pahlavi (Middle Persian) and (proto-) Sharada script, the latter being of Indian origin. The use of these three scripts again clearly illustrates the position of the Kabul valley in between the realms of Iran, South Central Asia and the Indian subcontinent. The obverse of his coins shows the bust of the king, wearing a crown in the form of a wolf's head (a Turkic symbol). On the reverse there is a divinity with flames, with a Pahlavi inscription, copied after the coins of the Sasanian king, Khusraw II (*r.* AD 591–628).

---

20 For the origins of the Turki Shahi dynasty, see also Stein 1893.
21 See the translation by E. C. Sachau (1888/1910, esp. Vol. II, pp. 10–14).
22 The reading of Nizak is supported by Chinese sources (Harmatta and Litvinsky 1996:374).
23 Harmatta and Litvinsky 1996:373ff.

According to al-Biruni, the last of the Turki Shahi kings of the Kabul valley was replaced by his Brahman minister, called Kallar. This development, which probably took place sometime in the ninth century, seems to symbolize the 'Hinduization' of the Turks south of the Hindu Kush. Kallar founded the so-called Hindu Shahi dynasty.[24] His reign may be linked to the introduction, sometime in the ninth century, of a new series of silver (billion) and copper coins, mostly showing a recumbent humped bull on one side and a horseman on the other. The legend is in (Indian) Sharada script. Some of the coins repeat the legend on the obverse, but this time in cursive Bactrian.

Artistic Products

In East Afghanistan, the period between c.AD 600 and 900 is often regarded as almost devoid of any artistic production. In a sense this is correct, but the blame should be attributed to the lack of controlled archaeological work, rather than on an actual lack of craftsmanship. Sporadic finds have been made that show the spread of Hindu influence, at the cost of Buddhism. This development is also reflected in the succession of Turki Shahi and Hindu Shahi kings. Furthermore, it should not be forgotten that in the Hindu Kush, Buddhism for a time continued to flourish and that some of the paintings and sculptures at Bamiyan and other places may well date to as late as the seventh century or the beginning of the eighth century AD. Yet, it is evident that Buddhist art was at its end. In the north and west of Afghanistan, Islam had become the prevalent religion, while in the east, Hinduism was in the ascendancy. Hinduism for a while replaced Buddhism, as it also did in much of the Indian subcontinent where Buddhism almost completely disappeared.

The latter development shows in the finds from the region. These include two marble statues of Surya, the Hindu god of the sun, which were found in the ruins of a Hindu temple at Khair Khana, near Kabul.[25] Another example are two statues of *Durgâ Mahishâsura-mardinî* from Gardiz.[26] They show, as the Sanskrit name says, the Indian goddess Durga, the consort of Shiva, slaying the buffalo demon. Equally interesting are the remains of what may have been a Hindu temple at Chaghan Saray, in the Kunar valley, in the extreme east of Afghanistan.[27] These remains, incorporated into a Muslim

24   For the Hindu Shahis, see Stein 1893.
25   Ball 1982: No. 546.
26   One of them was exhibited in the Kabul Museum. See N. H. Dupree et al. 1974:96–7.
27   Ball 1982: No. 154.

cemetery, indicate a style of architecture that is said to be reminiscent of similar buildings from the northwest of the Indian subcontinent, and dated to the late first millennium AD.

In addition, reference should be made to the Japanese excavations at the site of Tepe Skandar, 31 km north of Kabul.[28] Here the remains were found of a settlement dating to the second half of the first millennium AD. Finds included a marble statue of the Hindu god Shiva and his wife (*Umâ Maheshvara*). Another important site is that of Tepe Sardar (better to be known as *Tepe-yi Nagârâ*, 'Tepe of the Kettledrum') near Ghazni, which was occupied until perhaps the eighth century AD. From this period dates a huge statue of the *Parinirvâna Buddha* (Buddha lying down at the end of his cycle of rebirths) of unbaked clay. A very similar statue has been found just north of Afghanistan, at the site of Adzhina tepe in Tajikistan.[29] Yet, what is most interesting, was the find at the same site of a statue of the Hindu deity *Durgâ Mahishâsura-mardinî*.

Scripts

For some time, the Bactrian language written in cursive Greek script remained in use, also south of the Hindu Kush. At Bad-i Asya, some 20 km northwest of Ghazni, a number of Bactrian inscriptions were discovered, roughly dating to the Turki Shahi period.[30] Much further to the south, in Uruzgan, other Bactrian inscriptions have been found.[31] The last use of Bactrian, as far as is known to date, is in the inscriptions from the Tochi valley just across the border in Pakistan.[32] This group of inscriptions includes two bilinguals. The first is in Sanskrit and Arabic and dates to the mid-ninth century. The second is in Sanskrit and Bactrian. If all the texts from the Tochi valley roughly date to the same period, it illustrates the penetration of Arabic as one of the *lingua franca* of the region.

In the following years, Bactrian in Greek script was replaced in East Afghanistan by Middle Indian languages written in Sharada script, which developed from the Indian Brahmi and Gupti writings. Sharada texts have been widely found in Afghanistan, and one of them was engraved on a marble statue of the Indian elephant god Ganesha that was found near Gardiz. Another was inscribed on the large *Umâ Maheshvara* from Tepe Skandar, north of Kabul. The

28   Ball 1982: No. 1185.
29   MacDowall and Taddei 1978:293–5.
30   Ball 1982: No. 71.
31   Ball 1982: No. 1221.
32   Humbach 1966:105–17; 1971 and 1994.

Sharada inscriptions all seem to date to the eighth century AD and reflect the growing importance of Indian culture in the lands of East Afghanistan.

The Khalaj

Xuanzang in the early seventh century already referred to the extent of Turkic control south of the Hindu Kush. Later Chinese pilgrims indicate that after Xuanzang the Turks further extended their control of East Afghanistan. The ruling dynasties in Kabul and Zabulistan were probably of Hunnish or Turkic, or at least non-Iranian origin. In time the newcomers were apparently assimilated and they adopted Buddhism or Hinduism as their religion. In this way, various Turkic nomadic groups, following in the footsteps of the Chionites and Hephthalites before them, eventually crossed the Hindu Kush and settled in what are now South and East Afghanistan and neighbouring Pakistan among the autochthonous, Indian and Iranian population. One of these groups was called the Khalaj.[33] Their name seems to appear in the recently discovered Bactrian documents from the Kingdom of Rob, north of the Hindu Kush.[34] A text from the late seventh century refers to a *Khalas* slave boy. Another document, from the early eighth century, refers to a *Khalas* princess. According to Early Islamic writers, including the tenth-century geographers al-Istakhri and Ibn Hawqal, the Khalaj lived in Zamin Dawar, in South Afghanistan, but also further north in the Ghazni area. In the *Hudud al-'Âlam*, an anonymous work from the late tenth century, the Khalaj are described in this way:[35]

> In Ghazni and in the limits of the boroughs which we have enumerated, live the Khalaj Turks who possess many sheep. They wander along climates, grazing grounds and pasturelands. These Khalaj Turks [are] also numerous in the provinces of Balkh, Tukharistan, Bust and Guzganan.

Al-Khwarazmi, writing his *Mafâtih al-'Ulum* ('Keys of the Sciences') in the late tenth century AD, regarded them as descendants of the Hephthalites.[36] Al-Istakhri, writing at about the same time, tells that the Khalaj were Turks who long before had come to the land between India and Sistan; they were cattle-breeders and of Turkic appearance,

33 For the Khalaj, see Doerfer 1987. See also Barthold (Bosworth) 1984:72.
34 Sims-Williams 1997:20.
35 Trans. Minorsky 1970, p. 111. See Dani, Litvinsky and Zamir Safi 1996:180.
36 Bosworth and Clauson 1965:6.

also in dress and language.[37] Whether this was the case or not, they were generally regarded as Turks, and they were widespread south of the Hindu Kush. Many writers have commented upon the possibility that these Khalaj are related to the Ghaljis or Ghilzay, one of the most important Pashtun tribes from east of Ghazni.[38] C. E. Bosworth refers to a report on a campaign by Sultan Mas'ud (AD 1031–41), the successor of Mahmud of Ghazni, against some insurgents. One of the reports, written by al-Gardizi, refers to the rebels as 'Afghans', while another account, by al-Bayhaqi (tenth century AD), mentions the 'Khalaj'.[39] This of course does not prove that the Khalaj should directly be identified with the modern Ghaljis, but it does indicate that the term Afghan, at least in the eleventh century AD, was not exclusively used for Pashto-speaking groups, who by that date were still apparently unknown. Yet, the tradition that says that the Ghaljis descended from a Pashtun mother and a 'foreign' father would strengthen the possibility that the names of the Khalaj and Ghaljis are somehow related. In the course of time, groups of Khalaj may have adopted 'Pashtunhood' while retaining their original name, or groups of Pashto-speakers adopted the name and perhaps the leadership of some Khalaj. All this would mean that there are no compelling reasons to identify all of the Afghans mentioned by Early Islamic geographers and writers as Pashto-speakers.

37 Caroe 1958:89.
38 Bosworth and Doerfer 1978; Minorsky 1940.
39 C. E. Bosworth 1977:13–14.

12

The Iranian Dynasties

During the eighth and ninth centuries AD the eastern parts of modern Afghanistan were still in the hands of non-Muslim rulers. The Muslims tended to regard them as Indians, although many of the local rulers were apparently of Hunnish or Turkic descent. Yet, the Muslims were right in so far as the non-Muslim population of Eastern Afghanistan was, culturally, strongly linked to the Indian subcontinent. Most of them were either Buddhists or they worshipped Hindu deities. Others, perhaps those who had relatively recently arrived from north of the Hindu Kush, worshipped their own gods, as perhaps the god *Chu* or *Chuna* mentioned by Xuanzang.

At the same time the more western areas went through a period of rapid Islamization. Local people, either Zoroastrians, Buddhists, Christians, Manichaeans or adherents of other faiths, embraced the new religion brought by the Arab conquerers. A good example of Eastern Iranians who converted to Islam are the so-called Barmakids, or *al-Barâmika*s. In the late eighth and early ninth centuries they played an important role in Baghdad in the administration of the caliphate. Before that time, however, their ancestors appear to have been in charge of the Buddhist community in Balkh, and perhaps of all of Balkh as well.[1]

The spread of Islam, however, did not coincide with an equally successful spread of Arabic language and culture, contrary to what occurred in most of the other countries conquered by the Arab armies. In Eastern Iran, local traditions and culture remained very much alive and from the early ninth century onwards, the lands of Eastern Iran went through a period of general revival, often called the Iranian renaissance.[2] It marked a time in which the Iranian languages, and in particular Persian (*Fârsi*), and Iranian culture in

1 Barthold/Sourdel in the *Enc. Isl.*
2 For this period, see especially Frye 1975.

general reasserted themselves at the cost of Arabic influence. It has often been surmized that the origin of this revival should be looked for among the local landowners (the *dihqân*), who were inclined to preserve the culture of their ancestors. However, it is perhaps more likely that the main driving force were the masses of non-Arab converts who felt treated as second-hand citizens by their Arab rulers. Whether this is true or not, Eastern Iran (including much of modern-day Afghanistan) became the cradle of a reborn Iran, with Islam as its main religion, but with its own language(s) and cultures preserved to the present day.

The Iranian revival, paradoxically, took place at a time of growing Turkic pressure from South Central Asia on the Iranian people of the Plateau. Many Turks and Turkic groups migrated, voluntarily or not, from the north to what are now Iran and Afghanistan. The Iranian languages and cultures were thus threatened from two sides: from the west by the Arabs and from the northeast by the Turks. In Iranian legends, as for instance in the *Shâhnâme*, it is the struggle against the Turks (the *Turân*) that is most pronounced. As to the spread of Arabic language and culture, Iranian resistance was more subtle, since it was the Arabs who had spread Islam and they could hardly be portrayed as evil marauders. In the end, the new Turkic groups on the Plateau adopted Islam and mixed with the local Iranian population. In many cases they also adopted Persian as their language and much of Iranian culture as their own. By the turn of the millennium, the great Mahmud of Ghazni, himself of Turkic descent and ruler of an empire that stretched from West Iran to beyond the Indus, sponsored the famous *Shâhnâme* of Firdawsi, the apogee of medieval Iranian literature. The major theme of this book is the epic struggle of the Iranians against Turan. Did Mahmud of Ghazni identify with Rustam, the Iranian hero, or with his adversary, the Turanian king Afrasyab?

The cultural renaissance coincided with growing political autonomy; local rulers dominated the land, either or not nominally recognizing the caliph in Baghdad or his governors. One of the early centres of this movement was the district of modern Sistan.

Nimruz

Sistan was in the Early Islamic period also known as Nimruz ('Half-Day', 'South'), apparently because it lay south of Khurasan.[3] Islamic

---

3 For the Early Islamic history of the area, compare the *Târikh-i Sistân* and the many publications on this subject by C. E. Bosworth. In 1968 the most southwestern province of Afghanistan was renamed Nimruz (formerly called Chakhansur).

geographers tell that it contained few cities, but many smaller estates. It was located around the fertile *Hâmun-i Hilmand* in Southwest Afghanistan. Nowadays most of the land of Sistan is deserted. The large number of ruins, however, tell of a far more glorious past. Agrarian production was high, thanks to an intricate network of canals that were cut through the countryside and led water from the various rivers to the surrounding fields. The capital of the province was called Zaranj, after the old name of the region, Drangiana or Zrangiana. Nowadays its ruins lie some six km north of modern Zaranj.[4] It is the same site as that of Nad-i Ali discussed earlier in connection with a citadel dating to the Achaemenid and pre-Achaemenid periods and it indicates the century-old location of the region's capital.

The period of Sistani political and cultural growth started in AD 861, when a new and powerful dynasty arose, namely that of the Saffarids. This dynasty was founded by Ya'qub bin al-Layth, nick-named *al-Saffâr*, the 'coppersmith'.[5] In his time, Sistan was still a frontier area and it constituted an outpost of Islam. To the east lay the lands of Zabulistan and Kabul, still ruled by non-Muslim rulers. Sistan consequently attracted many people of dubious origin. In fact, Ya'qub's background is equally dubious and he is sometimes described as a highwayman. His powerbase were the local groups of Sunnites that fought against Kharijite heretics. Whatever he did in his youth, his humble origins are evident. He apparently did not understand Arabic and he probably simply did not like the aristocratic Arab rulers in Baghdad and their equally aristocratic governors in Iran.

Ya'qub quickly expanded his control, at first towards the east. He defeated the ruler of Zabulistan in AD 865 and subsequently also took Kabul. Statues and elephants were sent to Baghdad. He also took the valley of Bamiyan and destroyed, according to the sources, a large Buddhist sanctuary and the idols from that temple were also sent to Baghdad.[6] He then turned his attention to the north and occupied Herat. In AD 873, he managed to defeat his direct overlords, the Tahirid governors of Nishapur in modern Northeast Iran. His conquests also included the northern parts of modern Afghanistan. Thus, after many centuries, the north and south of Afghanistan were united, albeit nominally, under one, virtually independent Iranian ruler. Soon Ya'qub and his professional army of mercenaries marched west, and they took Kirman, Fars and Khuzistan (Southwest Iran). Later on,

---

4   For extensive archaeological surveys in Sistan, see Fischer et al. 1974/1976.
5   For his career, see especially Bosworth in the *Enc. Isl.*
6   *Enc. Isl.*; Marquart 1901:292.

Ya'qub even marched upon Baghdad. This turned out to be too much of an undertaking, and close to Baghdad he was defeated and subsequently he died (AD 879). His tomb can still be seen close to Ahwaz, in Southwest Iran.

Ya'qub was succeeded by his brother, 'Amr bin al-Layth (*r.* AD 879–901), who tried to extend his powers further to the west and north. At first he met with great success. The Caliph in Baghdad was consequently forced to officially appoint him as governor of Sistan, Khurasan and Fars. However, he was in the end, in AD 900, defeated near Balkh by the rising power of another Iranian dynasty, this time from north of the Amu Darya, namely that of the Samanids under Isma'il bin Ahmad (*r.* AD 892–907). 'Amr was sent as prisoner to Baghdad, where he was executed two years later. Zaranj was subsequently taken by the Samanids, in AD 911. Sistan passed at least nominally under their control. Until the early eleventh century, however, descendants of the Saffarids continued to rule the district, and their name remained popular among the local rulers to the end of the fifteenth century.

The *Noh Gonbad* in Balkh

The late ninth century AD, during the years that the Saffarids from Sistan dominated what is now Afghanistan, is roughly the time of one of the earliest Islamic religious buildings known to date in Afghanistan.[7] It is a nine-domed mosque that was excavated in Balkh. The type of building has been linked to comparable structures nearby, such as the mosques that were found in the Marw oasis, at Termez along the Amu Darya, and at the village of Hazara near Bukhara.[8] The building consists of a square of 20 metres, with four large baked-brick pillars in the centre and three walls to the southwest (the *qiblah*), northwest and southeast. Two other baked-brick pillars mark the open portico of the entrance in the northeast. Brick arches rising from the pillars and the columns attached to the mudbrick walls apparently supported the roof. The end-result was a series of nine domed niches, hence the name of the monument, *Noh Gonbad* ('nine vaults').

The decoration consists of stucco carvings, mainly with floral motifs, including palmettes, grape-leaves, fir-cones and vine-scrolls. Narrow lines, deeply cut into the surface separate the motifs. The

7   See the description in Levi 1984 (1972): 127–8.
8   See Golombek 1969 for parallels in the West; for more nearby buildings, see Ettinghausen and Graber 1987 (1994):214; Keruvan 1999.

style of decoration has been compared to that found in Samarra, in southern Mesopotamia, and in Na'in (Central Iran), and the mosque of Ibn Tulun, Cairo, all dating to the late ninth century AD, but also to remains found at nearby Nishapur and Samarqand.

The Samanids

The Samanids ruled much of Eastern Iran from AD 900, when they defeated the Saffarids, to the end of the tenth century when they were vanquished by Turkic incursors from the north (the Qarakhanids). Their nucleus of power was the valley of the Zarafshan river, ancient Sogdia, north of Afghanistan. They claimed descent from the Sasanian general and ruler, Bahram Chubin, thus indicating their regard for the pre-Islamic, Iranian past. The dynasty was founded by a rich landowner, apparently from the Balkh district, called Saman-Khuda and his son, Asad. The four sons of Asad served the Caliph al-Ma'mun (AD 813–33) to the latter's great satisfaction, and all four were given governorships in Khurasan, including Ilyas, who was appointed governor of Herat. The three other brothers received Farghana, Shash (Tashkent) and Samarqand, respectively. Most of the Samanid family subsequently sided with the Tahirid governors of Nishapur and were defeated in the struggle against the Saffarids.

In AD 875, the Samanid Nasr bin Ahmad, a descendant of the Samanid governor of Farghana, received the governorship of all of Transoxiana from the Caliph, al-Mu'tamid. The Caliph no doubt hoped that he would form a counterweight against the rising power of the Saffarids. Nasr did not succeed, but his brother Isma'il did. He ruled from AD 893 to 907 and was the one who founded the Samanid realm. In AD 900 he defeated the Saffarids near Balkh and was subsequently rewarded by the Caliph with the appointment as governor of Khurasan. He thereby became the *de facto* ruler of the northeastern part of the Islamic world. The following century would mark a period of peace and prosperity in much of the Iranian East. The Samanids were known and praised for the quality of their administration. The productivity of the land was increased and trade flourished.[9]

The Samanids always called themselves Amir ('commander'), thus underlining their subordinate position as towards the caliph in Baghdad. Their centres were in the north, in the cities of Bukhara and Samarqand, but their rule included much of modern-day

---

9   The Samanids produced enormous quantities of silver coins, some of which found their way to Medieval Europe.

Afghanistan as well. These lands, along the extreme northeastern frontier of the Iranian Plateau, had long profited from trade with China and Central Asia. One of the most important products were Turkic slaves. Huge numbers were imported into the Muslim world. The Samanids, like so many other dynasties, consequently depended heavily on Turkic slaves and mercenaries (called *ghulâm* in Iran), very much like the caliphs of Baghdad themselves, who from the ninth century onwards were surrounded by Turks. One of the consequences of this development, especially in Eastern Iran and Afghanistan, was a growing separation between rulers and ruled. The rulers and their Turkic soldiers became separated from the predominantly Iranian population of the cities and countryside.

The process of Turkicization was slow but steady. The Samanids themselves, although strongly supported by Turkic *ghulâm*, were Iranians. They were, even more so than the Saffarids, concerned with the revival of Iranian culture and Persian (*Fârsi*) as the language of the realm. Whether this was instigated by chauvinistic pride or political acumen is difficult to tell. It probably was a combination of both. The Samanids needed a language to communicate with all their subjects, and Arabic had not made the strong foothold in the East as it had done in Western Iran. Furthermore, they must have been aware of the use they could make of developing and propagating the arts of their lands. In this way they could enhance their own prestige and position, and they could distinguish themselves from other rulers and other lands. Furthermore, it helped to promote the unique identity of their realm and the self-awareness of its population. In this way, Persian soon became the *lingua franca* of the Eastern Iranian world, and Persian was being used for prose and poetry.

The Ghaznawids

The Samanids relied heavily on Turkic slaves from the north to protect their empire. However, as elsewhere in the Islamic world, the slaves did not remain slaves forever, and some of them founded their own dynasty. This happened in Egypt, where Ahmad ibn Tulun (*r.* AD 868–884), whose father had been sent as tribute from Bukhara to Baghdad, founded the dynasty of the Tulunids.[10] It also happened in Afghanistan.

In AD 961/2, Alptigin, a Turkic slave who had been the Samanid army commander of Khurasan, was ousted from his post by his Samanid superiors when he unsuccessfully meddled in dynastic

10   He built the famous Ibn Tulun mosque in Cairo.

affairs. He subsequently made for the east. On the way he defeated the ruler of Bamiyan and the Hindu Shahi king of Kabul, before he removed the local ruler of Ghazna, modern Ghazni, in East Afghanistan. He did not last long (he died in AD 963) and a period of anarchy followed, but in AD 977 the Turks firmly re-established themselves. This time they were led by a slave of Alptigin, whose family derived from South Siberia. His name was Sebüktigin (r. AD 977–97) and he founded the so-called Ghaznawid dynasty (AD 977–1186).[11] Sebüktigin, although virtually independent, regarded himself as the governor of Ghazna and adjacent lands, subordinate to the Samanid Amir. He fought a long war with the Hindu Shahi rulers of Kabul and Gandhara. The Turks were successful, and Jaypal, the last Hindu Shahi king of the Kabul area, was forced to seek refuge in the plains to the east.

Ghazna, as it was then called, never was a place of exceptional natural importance.[12] Located on the high plains of Eastern Afghanistan and some 145 km southwest of the modern capital of the country, it could never compete with the strategic location and the fertile surroundings of Qandahar and Kabul.[13] Yet, in the Early Islamic period it gained prominence as an entrepot for trade between the Iranian Plateau and India. For some time it also marked the most eastern outpost of Islam against the Hindu kings of the Kabul valley and ancient Gandhara. It thus gained some importance as rallying point for adventurers and others who wanted to fight the infidels.

Sebüktigin was, after a one-year interval,[14] succeeded by his son, Mahmud. As Mahmud of Ghazni he would become one of the most powerful monarchs of the Islamic world.[15] Until AD 999, he still ruled the area nominally as governor of the Samanids. In that year the Samanids were defeated by the Qarakhanids (or Ilek Khans, as they are also known), another group of Turkic invaders from the north.[16] Now independent, Mahmud continued to expand his power. He

11   For the Ghaznawids, see in particular the publications by C. E. Bosworth 1963, 1977, 1998.

12   Ghazni was originally called Ghaznin and also known as Ghazna. The name is probably related to Persian *Ganj*, for 'Treasury'. Ptolemy in the second century AD lists a town called Ganzaka located in the Paropanisadae. See also the *Hexina* of Xuanzang.

13   As also clearly expressed by Babur (*Baburnâme*, trans. Beveridge, p. 219). For Ghazni itself, see Bombaci 1957.

14   Sebüktigin had appointed his son Isma'il, the half-brother of Mahmud, as his successor, probably because Isma'il's mother was the daughter of Alptigin.

15   For Mahmud of Ghazni, compare Nazim 1931.

16   For this group, see Bosworth's article in the *Enc. Isl.* on the Ilek-Khans.

defeated the Hindu Shahi kings in a series of campaigns. Jaypal was decisively defeated in AD 1000 and sold as a slave in Khurasan. His successor Anandpal, together with his allies, was beaten in AD 1008.

Under his reign (AD 998–1030) and that of his son Mas'ud (r. AD 1031–41), the borderlands between the Iranian Plateau and the Indian subcontinent were definitively incorporated into the world of Islam, and Islamic forces subsequently finally managed to gain a permanent foothold in northern India. Once the frontier region was under control, Mahmud undertook a long series of military campaigns to the east. Almost each winter he marched down to the Indian plains and collected huge amounts of booty.[17] The most notorious event was the sack of Somnath (Sumanat), in modern Gujarat, in AD 1015/1016. Here Mahmud pillaged the town's famous and incredibly rich temple. Pieces of the main statue of the temple were sent to Mecca and Medina to be walked over by the Muslims. The doors of the temple were allegedly taken to Ghazni, to become the object of great political uproar in the nineteenth century when the British invaded the country. Plunder was undoubtedly the main motive of Mahmud, but he also professed to fight the 'infidels', including all those who did not recognize the caliph in Baghdad. The latter accordingly offered Mahmud various honorifics.

Along the periphery of his empire, Mahmud installed puppet kings who owed alligiance to him, but were for the rest very much left in peace. It was their task to protect the centre of the empire against attacks from the outside. Some of these vassal kingdoms were located in the north, along both banks of the Amu Darya, where they formed a buffer against the Qarakhanid confederation of tribes that dominated the ancient centre of the Samanid empire around Bukhara and Samarqand. The Qarakhanids constituted a formidable threat, which became all the more evident in AD 1006 when they invaded the lands south of the Amu Darya while Mahmud was in India. Mahmud had to rush back and after heavy fighting managed to defeat them somewhere near Balkh, upon which the Qarakhanids withdrew north of the river.

In spite of Qarakhanid power, however, Mahmud also annexed Khwarazm south of the Aral Sea (AD 1017). In Iran itself, he supported the (Sunnite) Caliphs against the Shi'ite Buyid dynasty of northern Iran. Near the end of his life, in AD 1029, Mahmud succeeded in taking Hamadan and Rayy from the Buyids. After his death

17 Perhaps including a statue of Brahma, the Hindu deity, which was found in Ghazni (N. H. Dupree 1974:79).

in AD 1030 he was buried in Ghazni, and his tomb can still be found in the nearby modern village of Rawza-yi Sultan. The monument itself is modern, but it houses a beautiful marble grave cover.[18]

After his death, Turkic pressure in the north increased. The Qarakhanids disappeared as a major force, but new Turkic groups, generally known as the Ghuzz, took their place.[19] By AD 1040 the Ghaznawids under Mas'ud (r. AD 1031–41) were defeated at Dandanqan, near Marw, by one of these groups, the Saljuks. The same year the Saljuks took the former Ghaznawid capital in Khurasan, Nishapur. Eventually both parties concluded a peace treaty, and the northern and western parts of modern Afghanistan were left to the Saljuks, while the Ghaznawids would continue to control the lands south and east of the Hindu Kush.

These events marked a turning point in the history of Iran and, partly, also of Afghanistan. With the rise of the Saljuks the Iranian Plateau was laid wide open to further Turkic penetration from the north, thus changing the ethnic and linguistic pattern of the Plateau until the present day. Parallels with the Indo-Iranian and Scythian invasions in the second and first millennia are obvious. In both cases the newcomers from the Central Asian north soon moved on, towards the west. In AD 1055, the Saljuks occupied Baghdad. The Saljuks were Sunnites and they regarded themselves as the restorers of Sunnite orthodoxy, against the Shi'ite Buyids from West Iran who for some time before had controlled Baghdad. The 'Abbasid Caliph, however, soon realized that the arrival of the Saljuks was a mixed blessing. They made him into a mere puppet, without any secular power. Real power lay in the hands of the Saljuk Sultan. In spite of these misgivings, Saljuk advances continued. By AD 1071 the Saljuks were in Anatolia, at Malazgird, where their Sultan Alp Arslan (r. AD 1063–73) defeated the Byzantine emperor, Romanus Diogenes. Large numbers of Türkmen now poured into Anatolia, soon giving their name to the country. Thus, as in the case of the Scythians more than 1500 years before, the various Turkic tribes found themselves the rulers of a huge extent of land, stretching from Afghanistan in the east to half-way modern Turkey in the west.

---

18   Ball 1982: No. 358.
19   In fact, the Saljuks also belonged to the Ghuzz. The name of the Ghuzz or Oghuz derives from the Turkish appellation *Toquz Oghuz*, 'Nine Clans', and refers to a Turkish confederation of tribes in Central Asia from the seventh century AD onwards. Some of them moved south towards the Iranian Plateau in the early eleventh century, under the clan of the Saljuks. The Türkmen or Turcoman, who are mentioned from the late tenth century onwards, also formed part of this group. Groups of Ghuzz eventually settled in modern Azarbayjan, in northwest Iran, and hence, under their kinsmen the Saljuks, in what after them came to be called Turkey.

With the Saljuks focussing their attention on the west, the Ghaznawid sultans Ibrahim (*r.* AD 1059–99) and Mas'ud III (*r.* AD 1099–1115) concentrated their efforts on the further conquest of northern India. For almost a century, the Ghaznawid empire continued to thrive, although much reduced in extent since the days of Mahmud, but perhaps stronger as a result of it. No longer did the Ghaznawid rulers from southeast of the Afghan mountains aspire to control the lands of Khurasan on the other side of the divide. In fact, the lands of modern Afghanistan had been split in half. This situation did not really change until the time of the last Ghaznawid ruler, Bahram Shah (*r.* AD 1118–1152), when Ghazni was several times occupied by the Saljuks under their last great ruler, Sultan Sanjar (*r.* AD 1118–1157), and finally taken by the Ghurids from the mountains of Central Afghanistan.

Ghaznawid Art and Culture

Under Mahmud and his son Mas'ud, Ghazni became the political and cultural centre for much of the Iranian Plateau and northern India. This manifests itself in the many ruins of large and impressive buildings that are still scattered in the Ghazni countryside.[20] Early Islamic authors from the time of the Ghaznawids describe the many gardens, mosques, minarets, madrasas and palaces of Ghazni. Not much has survived the ravages of time, but two minarets are still standing.[21] One of these was built by Mas'ud III. The other, nearby, was constructed by Bahram Shah. Both minarets were built of baked brick and on the plan of an eight-sided star. Both buildings have lost their upper storeys, but sketches and photographs from the nineteenth century show that at that time the minarets still rose to a great height, up to some 60 metres, with cylindrical shafts on the star-patterned basement.[22]

Near Mas'ud's minaret archaeologists have unearthed a palace complex, which probably dates back to the reign of the same king. The building is planned around a courtyard of 50 × 31 metres, with four *aywân*s (ivan: monumental arched doorway) along its four sides. The open court is paved with marble. The northern ivan acted as entrance to the courtyard, while the southern ivan included the throne hall. The walls of the courtyard were embellished with sculp-

---

20 Apart from the monuments listed below, Fischer (1978:315ff) also refers to some other, minor Ghaznawid monuments in Afghanistan.
21 For the archaeological finds at Ghazni, see Ball 1982: No. 358.
22 Compare Trousdale 1984:6 and note 34 on p. 149; Hill and Grabar 1967, Pl. 145.

Illustration 12   *Inside the ruined Ghaznawid palaces of Lashkar-i Bazar (photograph: author, autumn 1978).*

tured stucco and terracotta, painted in various colours. Wall paintings adorned various parts of the palace and these may well have included illustrations taken from the history of the Sasanians (as indicated by contemporaries).

The complex is especially marked by its abundant use of marble and by a text in Persian (*Fârsi*) carved into the marble that lined the lower part of the walls around the courtyard of the palace. The text extends for a total of 250 metres. The grouping of the four ivans along the sides of the courtyard seems to be a Ghaznawid innovation and it later became the characteristic feature of Iranian architecture (for mosques, madrasas and caravanserais).

Another large complex of Ghaznawid palaces can still be found at Lashkari Bazar, along the banks of the Hilmand river, between Bust and Lashkargah (Ill. 12).[23] This place was excavated by French archaeologists between 1949 and 1952. The various palaces, as at Ghazni, are marked by courtyards with ivans, and sculptured stucco and wall paintings adorn the walls. Again, as in Ghazni, the main building material was brick, and the bricks were used to provide a strikingly decorative effect. The largest, and southernmost of the three palaces forms a rectangle of about 100×250 metres. The rooms of the palace are grouped around a rectangular courtyard, which is flanked on all four sides by an ivan placed in the middle of each side. Distemper paintings on the walls and pillars show guardsmen, fully armed, against a background of flowers, animals and other motifs. Walls with semi-circular towers surround almost the whole complex.

The *Shâhnâme*

One of the main attractions of medieval Ghazni was its library. This and the newly acquired wealth of its rulers attracted artists, historians and other scholars. Abu Rayhan al-Biruni, the encyclopaedist from Choresmia, worked here. Another famous author from the Ghaznawid period was Abu 'l Fazl al-Bayhaqi, the secretary and historian of the Ghaznawid court, who wrote a Persian-language history of the reign of Mas'ud.

Perhaps the most famous and lasting monument of the Ghaznawid era is Firdawsi's *Shâhnâme* ('Book of Kings'). This book includes myths and legends from Iran's pre-Islamic past. Written in *Fârsi*, it contains some 60,000 verses. It was completed in AD 1010 and dedicated to Mahmud of Ghazni. Abu 'l Qasim Firdawsi lived at Mahmud's court, but he was born in Tus, near Mashhad, where he was also buried. The *Shâhnâme* has become the symbol of Iran's glorious past and it still very much forms part of Iranian culture. To this day, stories from the *Shâhnâme* are still being told and recited all over Iran. Firdawsi consciously tried to avoid using Arabic words, and this feature, plus its contents, have made the *Shâhnâme* into the symbol of Iranian revival. The main theme of all the stories is the battle between Iran and Turan, between the Iranians and those who live beyond its northeastern borders. The location of many of the legends from the *Shâhnâme* consequently lies in Eastern Iran and

23   For these monuments, see the bibliography contained in Ball 1982: No. 685.

Afghanistan.[24] In fact, Sistan and the Sakas feature prominently in this book.

The main story line of the *Shâhnâme* is that of the family of Rustam. He is the son of Zal and the grandson of Sam. They are described as the kings of Sistan, and Rustam is correspondingly often called a Saka. Rustam's father, Zal, was brought up by a bird, called the Simurgh.[25] Zal's wife, and the mother of Rustam, was Rudaba, the daughter of the king of Kabul. Rustam himself married Tahmineh, the daughter of the king of Samangan. In the *Shâhnâme*, Samangan is located in the land of the Turanians. If Firdawsi regarded this Samangan identical with the Samangan that nowadays lies north of the Hindu Kush, it would put the struggle between Rustam and his family from Sistan against the Turanians in modern North Afghanistan and beyond.

Firdawsi did not write his *Shâhnâme* out of nothing. He tells in the introduction to his work that he used orally transmitted stories and written accounts. During the tenth century, a series of *Shâhnâme* had been composed. These collections reflected the revival of Iranian culture and self-esteem. Two of these works were written by people with clear links to modern Afghanistan: Abu 'l-Mu'ayyad al-Balkhi and Abu 'Ali Muhammad bin Ahmad al-Balkhi. Another *Shâhnâme* was composed in the mid-tenth century near Tus itself, the birthplace of Firdawsi. This work was composed by Abu Mansur Muhammad al-Ma'mari. Finally there was a *Shâhnâme*, never finished, by a converted Zoroastrian called Abu Mansur Daqiqi, and part of his *Shâhnâme* was incorporated into Firdawsi's work. All these *Shâhnâme* versions recorded ancient stories of the Iranian kings, and were perhaps ultimately inspired by a Middle Persian (Pahlavi) book, now lost, called the *Khwatây-nâmak* ('Book of Rulers').

The Ghurids and Khwarazm-Shahs

Ghaznawid power was eventually brought to an end by the Ghurids. This dynasty originated in the mountainous lands east of Herat, commonly known to the Early Islamic geographers as the district of Ghur. The people living in this secluded area apparently remained unaffected by Islam until well into the eleventh century.[26] At that time, the Ghaznawids raided the mountainous lands of Ghur and made the

24 For the topography of the *Shâhnâme*, see especially Davoud Monchi-Zadeh 1975.
25 The name of this bird is the same as that of the *Saêna $M^\partial r^\partial gha$*, or Saena bird from the Avesta.
26 For the early history of Ghur, see Barthold 1984:51–2, with references.

local family of the Shansabanis (descendants of Shansab/Shanasb), with their stronghold at Ahangaran,[27] into their vassals and representatives. The Ghaznawid advance was led by Mas'ud, the son of Mahmud and at that time governor of Herat. With the demise of Ghaznawid power and the rise of that of the Saljuks, 'Izz al-Din Husayn (*r*. AD 1100–46), of the Shansabani family, openly acknowledged the Saljuks as his overlords and paid tribute to the Saljuk ruler, Sultan Sanjar. The Ghurids at the same time took possession of Bamiyan and made it into the capital of a vassal kingdom that included much of modern Northeast Afghanistan.

By AD 1141 another group of Turkic newcomers from the far north, the Qarakhitay, defeated Sultan Sanjar and his Qarakhanid allies. Although Sanjar eventually escaped from captivity and the Qarakhitay did not push on to south of the Amu Darya, the authority and strength of the Saljuks had suffered seriously. Consequently, other principalities saw a chance of extending their influence, including the Ghurids. Around AD 1150, under 'Ala' al-Din Husayn, one of the many sons of 'Izz al-Din Husayn, they emerged from the mountains of Central Afghanistan and set off on a expedition that led them to East and South Afghanistan. In AD 1150/1 the Ghurid king sacked Ghazni, a memorable feat that earned him his name of *Jahân-suz*, 'world-burner'. Afterwards he moved with his army to the south and pillaged Lashkari Bazar. However, his successes did not last, and the first Ghurid bid for supremacy was cut short by Sultan Sanjar. He defeated the Ghurids in AD 1152 and captured their *Sultân*. 'Ala' al-Din Husayn, however, was shortly afterwards released and in the remaining years of his life managed to expend his realm to the north. He died in AD 1161. In the meantime, in AD 1153, the Saljuks under Sultan Sanjar were again defeated, this time by other groups from among the Ghuzz.[28] It meant that the road was open for the Ghurids to try again.

While the Turks north of the Amu Darya continued to fight each other, the Ghurids recovered. They were led by two brothers and nephews of 'Ala' al-Din Husayn, namely Shams al-Din (Ghiyas al-din) Muhammad (*r*. AD 1163–1202/3) and Shihab al-Din (Mu'izz al-Din) Muhammad (until AD 1206). Together they expanded the Ghurid empire. The Ghurids entered Ghazni in AD 1173/4, after it had been occupied by a group of Ghuzz for some twelve years. They also took Herat and Balkh. Ultimately they defeated the last of the Ghaznawids at Lahore in the Panjab in AD 1186. Ghiyas al-Din had his centre at Firuzkuh, in Ghur itself, while Mu'izz al-Din resided

---

27   Ball 1982: No. 15.
28   Sultan Sanjar eventually died in AD 1057. His tomb in Marw is still extant.

mainly in Ghazni. While the first defended and enlarged the empire in the west, his brother continued Ghaznawid policies and extended Turkic/Iranian authority in the Indian subcontinent. The empire of the Ghurids soon stretched from near the Caspian to deep into northern India.

Ghurid power on the Plateau, however, did not last long. It flourished during much of the lifetime of the two brothers, but when they grew old the weaknesses of the Ghurid empire became clear. The Ghurids had hopelessly overstretched their resources. The government was divided among rivalling clan members and the Ghurid armies simply could not cope with the growing pressure from the north. In AD 1204 the Ghurids under Mu'izz al-Din, who after the death of his brother had become the sole leader of the Ghurids, were defeated by the joint forces of the king of Choresmia (the Khwarazm-Shah) and the Qarakhitay. In AD 1215 the Khwarazm-Shah finally deposed the last of the Ghurid Sultans, thus bringing to an end a most remarkable episode in the history of Afghanistan.

The demise of the Ghurid empire, however, was not really the end of the story. In India the place of the Ghurids was taken by the so-called Slave Dynasty, which was founded by a slave of the former Ghurid king. He was called Sultan Qutb al-Din Aybak. He was the one who ordered the construction of the famous Qutb Minar, the huge tower of red sandstone that still rises to a height of some 80 metres above the outskirts of Delhi. The basement of this minaret shows an alteration of eight rounded and eight angular buttresses. Incidentally, the stylistic origins of this monument are sought in Afghanistan, and an early example of this tradition can be found in Sistan. In this ancient district, at the site of Khwaja Syah Push, there are the remains of a twelfth-century, baked brick minaret.[29] It rises above a massive medieval settlement of about one square km and it shows the same ground plan as the Qutb Minar in New Delhi.

In Afghanistan, the place of the Ghurids was taken by the rulers of ancient Choresmia (medieval Khwarazm). The most important Khwarazm ruler was 'Ala' al-Din Muhammad (*r.* AD 1200–20), who in AD 1215–16 occupied both Ghur and Ghazni. His ancestors descended from a Turkic slave of the Saljuks, who rose to power in their secluded homeland south of the Aral Sea. For much of the second half of the twelfth century they remained vassals of the Qarakhitay. In AD 1194, under 'Ala' al-Din Tekish (*r.* AD 1172–1200) they defeated the last of the Saljuks. After defeating the Ghurids they subsequently freed themselves from the yoke of the Qarakhitay, and in the early thirteenth century, just before the advent of the Mongols,

29 Ball 1982: No. 607.

the Khwarazm-Shah was the ruler of a large empire that stretched from West Iran to eastern Afghanistan.

Ghurid Remains

The capital of the Ghurids was located, according to early historical accounts, at Firuzkuh.[30] This place has since tentatively been identified with the district around the famous minaret of Jam, in Central Afghanistan, some 220 km east of Herat.[31] It is located along the south bank of the Hari Rud, near its confluence with a southern tributary, the Jam Rud. An inscription on the first shaft of the Jam minaret relates to the Ghurid ruler, Ghiyas al-Din Muhammad (r. AD 1163–1202/3). The tower rises to a height of 65 metres, and it consists of an octagonal base that is nine metres wide, and four tapering cylindrical shafts on top. There is a double staircase inside the base and the first shaft. The whole tower, which is made of baked brick, is covered on the outside by decorative brickwork, including patterns that form inscriptions, including the 19th Sura of the Qur'an (the Sura of Mary). In the neighbourhood of Jam, a large number of fortifications and towers have been discovered. They may well have formed part of the defensive works protecting the heartland of the Ghurid empire.

Of Ghurid origin is a large part of the great Friday mosque of Herat.[32] It contains the tomb of Ghiyas al-Din Muhammad Ghuri, who died in Herat in AD 1202/3. Another important monument is the *madrasa* (school) of Shah-i Mashhad, northeast of Herat, along the left bank of the Murghab river.[33] Ghurid remains, or at least buildings dated to the time of the Ghurids, have also been identified in Bamiyan (Shahr-i Zohak and Shahr-i Gholghola), and at Chisht west of Herat.[34] A famous minaret from this time is that of Daulatabad, just north of Balkh.[35] It was built in the early twelfth century. Finally, the famous arch of Bust may also belong to the Ghurid period. This edifice rises at the foot of the Bust citadel and may have served as the entrance to a great mosque, or to the citadel. The decoration of this arch has been compared to that of the minaret of Daulatabad.

30 For Ghurid architecture, compare Sourdel-Thomine 1960.
31 Ball 1982: No. 468.
32 Ball 1982:428. For the Friday mosque, see Melikian-Chirvani 1970.
33 Casimir and Glatzer 1971. See also Ball 1982: No. 1023.
34 Ball 1982: No. 212.
35 Also referred to as the minaret of Zadiyan. See Ball 1982: No. 1245.

13

The Mongols

By the early thirteenth century, the king of Khwarazm ruled most of Eastern Iran. From south of the Aral Sea he controlled all the trade going on between the Middle East, the Indian subcontinent and Central Asia and China. However, his realm would only last for a few years, for while the Khwarazm-Shah was still establishing his realm, another storm was building up along the northeastern borders of the Iranian world. This time it was not going to be another passing-by of plunderers or the establishment of yet another dynasty that would quickly adopt the local language and culture. This time the invasion would shake the Muslim civilization of Iran and Afghanistan to its very core. The threat was that of the Mongols from East Central Asia.

In spite of attempts by many modern historians to soften judgement on the Mongols,[1] their presence on the Plateau brought about the death of hundreds of thousands of people, the destruction of most of the cities, and the general devastation of the irrigation works so much needed for agriculture. The Mongols were led by Chingiz-Khan. Originally called Temüchin ('blacksmith', so named after a Tatar hostage held by his father), he became the supreme chief of all the Mongols in AD 1206 and soon after he set out to subdue neighbouring peoples and civilizations, including China. In AD 1215 he occupied and sacked Beijing. The Mongols then turned west, towards the rich lands of South Central Asia and the Iranian Plateau. In AD 1218, a Mongol force crossed the Pamirs and penetrated into Badakhshan. However, this was only a minor invasion. The main push came two years later, when the Mongols defeated the armies of the Khwarazm-Shah. The next year Chingiz-Khan reached

---

1 Compare P. Christensen 1993. It is clear however, that much of eastern Iran had suffered heavily from the continuous warfare between Ghaznawids, Ghurids, Qarakhanids, the Choresmians and others, since at least the mid-twelfth century.

Afghanistan. Bactra was taken in February 1221 and destroyed. Marw was taken in the following month, and so was the valley of Bamiyan. Here one of Chingiz-Khan's grandsons was killed, and the Mongol reply was the massacre of all living creatures in the valley. Legend says that afterwards even the birds were gone. The fortress of present-day Shahr-i Gholghola, just south of the cliffs, still testifies to this calamity. Settled life in Khurasan was almost brought to a standstill, and accounts by travellers in the years following the Mongol advances speak of complete destruction.

The Choresmian king, who had fled his capital, died in AD 1220/1221 on the island of Abasgun, in the southeastern corner of the Caspian, but his son, Jalal al-Din, fought the Mongols in eastern Afghanistan. In Parwan, close to Kabul, he defeated a Mongol advance garde in October 1221.[2] It was led by Tolui, the youngest son of Chingiz-Khan. Herat, which had voluntarily surrendered before, subsequently revolted, and it took the Mongols seven months to recapture the town. The punishment was draconian: Islamic sources provide numbers of 1,600,000 or 2,400,000 people being killed. The fall of nearby Nishapur led to the death, according to reports, of 1,747,000 people. The numbers may be exaggerated, but they do indicate the scale of destruction and slaughter. The destruction of the irrigation networks in the countryside, and the fact that there were hardly any people left to maintain them, also led to a deep decline of economic life.

After forcing Jalal al-Din across the Indus, Chingiz-Khan returned in slow marches to the north and he died in Mongolia in AD 1227. The lands conquered by Chingiz-Khan were divided among his sons with his favourite wife, Bortei. Jochi, the eldest, had died just before his father, but his son Batu received large extents of land in the west of the empire, in western Siberia and Russia. Transoxiana, north of modern Afghanistan, was given to another son of Chingiz-Khan, called Chaghatai. Ögedei, Chingiz-Khan's third son, was elected to succeed his father as Great Khan (r. AD 1229–41). The youngest son, Tolui, inherited the centre of the Mongol empire, Mongolia.

Under Ögedei and his two successors as Great Khan (Güyük and Möngke), in the period between AD 1229 and 1259, the Mongol empire passed through a period of relative stability, although much of the Iranian land had to be reconquered after Chingiz-Khan's death. In the east, a local ruler called Sayf al-Din Hasan Karlugh seems to have held for some time much of the Indo-Iranian borderlands, but

2 Jalal al-Din subsequently escaped across the Indus. After less than two years in India he went to Iraq via Baluchistan and southern Iran. He was assassinated in AD 1231.

the area was probably soon reoccupied by the Mongols. Pressure was built up along the frontiers with India, and the Kabul and Ghazni area received strong Mongol detachments. Some of the towns on the Iranian Plateau were rebuilt. In AD 1244, the control of Herat was granted to the local ruler of a nearby settlement. He was called Shams al-Din Muhammad Kart, who became the founder of the so-called Kart dynasty that would rule the town and a large part of modern Afghanistan until the late fourteenth entury, although for most of the time under nominal tutelage of the Mongols.

The situation changed after the death of Möngke in AD 1259 when two of his brothers, namely Qubilai and Ariq-Böqe, competed for the Mongol throne. Although Qubilai eventually installed himself as Great Khan, his position was not widely recognized and he was not in the position to enforce his rule over all Mongol lands. Qubilai's centre of control lay in China and the steppes to the north. He was, however, recognized by his brother Hülegü, who had been appointed as the representative of the Great Khan in Iran by Möngke and who arrived in Iran in AD 1256. Hülegü was the founder of the Il-Khanid dynasty of Iran. One of his first military feats was the defeat of the Assassins of northern Iran and the destruction of their fortress of Alamut, just west of modern Tehran. Two years later, in February 1258, he took Baghdad, the ancient seat of the Muslim caliphs. Mongol successes in the Near East, however, did not last, and after the death of Hülegü the realm of his successors was restricted to basically what is now modern Iran. Their main competitors in the east were the successors of Chaghatai. Soon the land of modern Afghanistan was turned into a transitional area contested by the Chagatayids and the Il-Khanids.

The position of Afghanistan at this time is well illustrated by Marco Polo, who allegedly passed through this part of the world in the 1270s when he travelled from the Mediterranean to the court of Qubilai Khan in modern China. About Balkh he tells the following:[3]

> Balkh is a splendid city of great size. It used to be much greater and more splendid; but the Tartars [Mongols] and other invaders have sacked and ravaged it. For I can tell you that there used to be many fine palaces and mansions of marble, which are still to be seen, but shattered now and in ruins. It was in this city, according to local report, that Alexander took to wife the daughter of Darius. The inhabitants worship Mahomet. And you should know that this city, which marks the limit of Tartar lordship of the Levant [the Il-Khanids], stands on the east-north-easterly frontier of Persia.

3 Marco Polo, trans. by Latham 1958:74.

In the late thirteenth century, the Mongol princelings gradually shed their native background and adopted local languages and cultures. In Iran, the Il-Khans slowly embraced the customs of their autochthonous Iranian subjects. In AD 1295 the Il-Khan Ghazan converted to Islam and in the ensuing years many Christian churches, Jewish mosques and Buddhist shrines were destroyed.[4] Especially the opposition to Buddhism is important, since some of the successors of Hülegü seem to have been Buddhists themselves, albeit strongly affected by Tibetan Lamism.[5] Economic life on the Plateau slowly revived, although a series of crises and a large degree of maladministration characterize the whole period. The introduction of paper money at the end of the thirteenth century was a huge fiasco. The accession of Ghazan, however, and especially the coming to power of his minister, the Persian aristocrat Rashid al-Din, brought about a further resurgence of economic activity.

Among the Chaghatayids, the process of Islamization proceeded somewhat slower, but eventually, under Tarmashirin Khan (r. AD 1326–34)[6], they also converted to Islam.[7] One constant feature, however, was their enmity as towards the Il-Khanids of Iran. In the late thirteenth and early fourteenth centuries AD, the Chaghatayid rulers of Transoxiana managed to extend their control to the south, across the Amu Darya, and at the cost of the rulers of Iran. This process was especially promoted by Kebeg Khan, who ruled between AD 1318 and 1326. He is credited with the rebuilding of Balkh, which was destroyed by his ancestor, Chingiz-Khan. Before long, almost the whole of modern Afghanistan fell under Chaghatayid control, including Qunduz, Baghlan and Badakhshan in the northeast, and Kabul, Ghazni and Qandahar in the east and southeast. Ibn Battuta, passing through East Afghanistan in AD 1333, mentions the presence of Chaghatayid governors all over the area. An exception was the Herat district controlled by the Karts, and the Sistan area, which remained under control of local rulers. Both districts acted more or less as a buffer between the two Mongol realms.

The Chaghatayid ulus

The direct line of Chaghatayid princes stopped when Tarmashirin Khan was deposed by his own followers from East Turkestan, in AD

4 For a Christian (Nestorian) church outside of Herat, see Szuppe 1992:64.
5 Compare Morgan 1986:158.
6 His name may reflect Sanskrit *Dharmaśila*, 'pious', a Buddhist name.
7 Although Mubarak-Shah in AD 1266 also adopted Islam. He, however, reigned very briefly.

1334. About the same time, the Il-Khanid dynasty of Iran came to an end. While Iran was split up between various local and Turco-Mongolian dynasties, the former lands of the Chaghatayid princes remained within a common political and cultural tradition, commonly described as the Chaghatayid *ulus*.[8] The *ulus* was formed by a confederation of Turco-Mongolian tribes and other groups, whose leaders vied for political control. Some of these tribes and other groups lived in modern Afghanistan. They included the Suldus, with their basis in North Afghanistan (Balkh area) and adjacent tracks north of the Amu Darya;[9] the Arlat, from modern Northwest Afghanistan;[10] the Apardi, from Shibarghan[11] and the Qarawnas, from the Qunduz/Baghlan area and across the Hindu Kush to Ghazni.[12] Also listed are the Negüderi troops, from the Qandahar area, who were often regarded as identical to, or as a section of the Qarawnas.[13] The tribes were thus centred in North Afghanistan, and across the Hindu Kush passes and the Kabul valley in the southeast of the country. The west of modern Afghanistan was dominated in the main by native rulers and ethnic groups, who used to receive support from the Il-Khanids and other Iranian potentates.

The various constituent parts of the Chaghatayid *ulus* were held together by a common, basically Mongol tradition and ideology. Politically, the *ulus* expressed itself in a continuous struggle for overall control and command of the tribes and other groups belonging to the *ulus*. For administrative tasks the leaders of the various tribes made use of local Iranian officials. The Mongols themselves tended to focus on military duties. They formed the ruling class, and the various Turco-Mongolian tribes that settled in this part of the

8 For this subject, compare the excellent study by Manz 1989.

9 Probably named after the commander of a thousand troops given by Chingiz-Khan to his second son, Chaghatai.

10 The Arlat are mentioned from the time of the Mongol conquest.

11 The Apardi may originally have been a regiment named after their Mongolian leader. They seem to have been closely related to the Qarawnas. Apart from modern Northwest Afghanistan, they also had a centre north of the Amu Darya, in Khuttalan. Both groups of Apardi had their own leaders.

12 The origin and history of the Qarawnas is extremely complex (see esp. Aubin 1969 and Shimo 1977). They apparently derived from 'imperial' garrison troops established in modern East Afghanistan in the early thirteenth century to protect the eastern frontiers of the Mongol empire. Compare Marco Polo's account, who describes them as a band of marauders in eastern Iran (ed. Latham 1958:64–5).

13 The Negüderi were troops stationed along the Indian borders. They consisted in the main of troops provided by the Jochid princes, and they were originally led by Negüder. Hence their name. After AD 1261–6, when Hülegü tried to wipe out Jochid influence in his realm and many Jochi troops fled east, the Negüderis became even more a force to be reckoned with. Marco Polo (trans. Latham 1958:65) tells that the Qarawnas were led by Nigudar, thus underlining the close link between both groups.

world provided the Mongol rulers with soldiers for their armies. A nomadic life remained the ideal, and it has often been surmized that the Turco-Mongolian love of garden residences should be seen in this light.

What is important to realize for the history of Afghanistan is that with the advent of the Mongols the powerbase shifted from the cities to the countryside. Wealth and political power were no longer restricted to towns such as Ghazni, Herat and Balkh. These places only slowly recovered from the devastations wrought upon the country by Chingiz-Khan, if they ever did. Instead, Turco-Mongolian tribes constituted the focus of political strength.

For some time in the fourteenth century, and preceding the rise to power of Timur, the power base of the *ulus* lay in the south, mainly among the Qarawnas and their supporters, who lived north and south of the Hindu Kush passes. In AD 1346/47, Qazaghan, leader of the Qarawnas, deposed the (nominal) Chaghatayid Khan, Qazan, and replaced him by another Khan. Qazaghan called himself *beg* and *Amir*. He remained in power until his death in AD 1357/58. When his son tried to succeed his father as leader of the *ulus*, he was deposed and killed. As leader of the Qarawnas he was succeeded by his nephew, Amir Husayn, who soon became the opponent of the rising star from among the Turco-Mongolian Barlas tribe, Timur bin Taraghay Barlas. In AD 1369, Timur defeated Amir Husayn near Balkh, who soon after was murdered. On 9 April 1370 Timur officially proclaimed himself as the new Amir.

Timur

In AD 1369 the lands of the Chaghatayids effectively passed under the control of Timur, or Timur-i Lang, 'Timur the Lame', as he was called in *Fârsi*.[14] He belonged to the Turco-Mongolian tribe of the Barlas (the Mongolian Barulas), which since the thirteenth century had settled in Transoxiana, in the lands along the Kashka Darya and around the cities of Shahrisabz (medieval Kish) and Karshi (medieval Nasaf/Nakhshab). Timur was born, according to some sources, in AD 1336, at Kish. Timur soon embarked on a long career of conquest and plunder. He carved out a vast empire that by the end of the fourteenth century stretched from northern India to modern Turkey. He captured Herat in April 1381, when the Kart ruler, Malik Ghiyas al-Din, refused to answer Timur's call to present himself to a *kuriltay*. Zaranj, the capital of Sistan, followed in AD 1384. Kabul,

14   For Timur, see especially Hookham 1962 and Manz 1989.

Qandahar and Ghazni were also taken. In AD 1398, he ordered Pir Muhammad, his grandson and governor of Qunduz, Kabul, Ghazni and Qandahar, to march upon India. According to the *Zafar Nâme*, Pir Muhammad plundered the land of the Afghans, who lived along the Sulayman Kuh, and proceeded into the Indus valley towards Multan. When he heard that his grandson met much resistance in India, Timur himself led an army into the Indian subcontinent and after a successful campaign he took and pillaged Delhi. Four years later, Timur was in Anatolia where he defeated the Ottoman Turks near Ankara. Timur died on 18 February 1405 near Utrar, along the Syr Darya, while leading his army against China. He was eventually buried in Samarqand, in the *Gur-i Amir*. He was succeeded, after initial dynastic quarrels, by his fourth son, Shah Rukh (r. AD 1409–47), who in AD 1397 had been appointed by his father as governor of Khurasan, Sistan and Mazanderan (south of the Caspian).

Timur's Successors

Shah Rukh took Samarqand in AD 1409 and thereby established his claim to the realm of his father. He, however, did not stay there, but appointed his son Ulugh Beg as governor and returned to his own capital, Herat. Under his rule and that of his successors, this place became one of the most outstanding cultural centres in the Middle East. Official contacts were established with China, Northern India and other countries. Nominally he was still, at least for some years, the suzerain of the Ottoman rulers of Turkey and the Indian kings in Delhi! The town attracted poets and philosophers, painters, illuminators and calligraphers, architects and other gifted men. It was a time in which trade flourished again and some of the urban centres regained their former glory. At the same time, the Persian-speaking inhabitants of the cities once again came to the fore. On the other hand, the rule of Timur and the upheavals following his death, combined with the revitalization of some of the Iranian cities, led to some decline in the power of the Turco-Mongolian tribes that before Timur's time had dominated the field.

Shah Rukh ordered the reconstruction of Herat's defences and the layout of Timurid Herat has been preserved to the present day. The ramparts, which existed until the 1940s, enclosed a town of about 1,450 × 1,350 metres. The town was divided into four quarters by two thoroughfares leading from the four gates. They met in the middle of town, at the *Chahâr-Suq* ('four markets'). The citadel, constructed by the Karts, lies in the northwest and the famous

Friday mosque lies in the east. The Timurids also established a series of large gardens outside the city. These *bâgh*s, as for instance the *Bâgh-i Morâd* (or *Bâgh-i Jahân ârâ*)[15] constituted the real centres of power, since it was here that the king or governor resided for most of the time.

Shah Rukh reigned for an exceptionally long period: 42 years. After his death, in March 1447, he was succeeded by his son Ulugh Beg (*r*. AD 1447–9), who had been governor of Transoxiana and during his brief reign remained in Samarqand. He was assassinated on the orders of his son, 'Abd al-Latif, who subsequently occupied the throne, but again for a very short time (AD 1449–50).[16] After some years of dynastic confusion in which the former empire of Timur fell apart, a great-grandson of his, called Abu Sa'id, took Herat in AD 1455. He, however, was killed fighting in Northwest Iran in AD 1469. His place in Herat was then taken by Sultan Husayn ibn Bayqara (AD 1469–1506), who re-established order in Herat and built new splendours.[17]

The fifteenth century was the period of greatest prosperity in Herat.[18] One of the patrons was Gawharshad Begum, the wife of Shah Rukh. Her name is linked to some of the most beautiful Islamic monuments in Afghanistan and Iran. In Herat, she commissioned the building of the so-called Musalla Complex, which was started in AD 1417. It included a *madrasa* (school) and a *musallâ* (place of worship), and was completed in AD 1432. Also part of the complex was the mausoleum of Gawharshad herself, built by Shah Rukh,[19] and a *madrasa* later built by Husayn Bayqara. The mausoleum, also known as the *gonbad-i sabz* ('green tomb') is crowned by a ribbed dome, similar in appearance to that of the *Gur-i Mir*, the tomb of Timur, in Samarqand. Most of the buildings have since been torn down.[20] Only the mausoleum and six minarets are still standing, or were so by the early 1990s.

One of the sons of Shah Rukh was Ghiyas al-Din Baysonghor, a patron of calligraphers and other artists.[21] He built an atelier-library

---

15   Located close to the Gazirgah.

16   'Abd al-Latif himself was murdered by a servant of Ulugh Beg.

17   Described by Babur in his autobiography (trans. Beveridge 1922:304ff.).

18   For Timurid architecture in and around Herat, see Allen 1983 and O'Kane 1987.

19   Gawharshad was murdered in AD 1457; whether she was buried here, or elsewhere, as for instance in the octagonal mausoleum at Kuhsan (about 111 km west of Herat; Ball 1982: No. 634), remains unknown (compare Levi 1984 [1972]:94).

20   Most of these Timurid buildings were destroyed in AD 1885 when the British feared for a Russian attack upon the city.

21   He died young (aged 37) in AD 1433, probably due to excessive drinking. He was buried in Gawharshad's mausoleum.

in Herat, which was completed in AD 1420 (the *ketâbkhâne*). Here craftsmen were engaged in copying manuscripts, including one of Firdawsi's *Shâhnâme* that is now in the Gulistan palace in Tehran.

Sultan Husayn Bayqara ordered the restoration of the famous Friday mosque of Herat, the origins of which date back to the tenth century or earlier. Destroyed by Chingiz-Khan, and again restored by the Karts,[22] it was finally repaired under the auspices of Husayn Bayqara's minister and poet, Mir 'Ali Shir (with the *nom de plume* of Nawa'i), who lived between AD 1441 and 1501. The latter was also a close friend of another famous Herati writer and poet, Mawlana Nur al-Din 'Abd al-Rahman Jami.

A famous building in Herat, some five km east of the centre, is the Gazirgah.[23] It is a shrine on a low hill north of Herat with the same name, and was built for Khwaja 'Abd Allah Ansari, a Sufi poet and philosopher who was born in Herat in AD 1006. His tomb was restored in AD 1428.

In later years, another famous artist lived and worked in Herat. This was Ustad Kamal al-Din Bihzad (*c.*AD 1460–1535).[24] Bihzad is one of the most famous calligraphers and miniaturists of the Iranian world. For a long time he lived and worked in Herat, until the town was taken in AD 1510 by Shah Isma'il of the newly established Iranian Safawid dynasty. Bihzad was invited to the Safawid capital, Tabriz, where he became director of the library.

The reign of Husayn Bayqara also marked the restoration of the shrine of Hazrat 'Ali in Mazar-i Sharif.[25] The tomb of 'Ali, nephew and son-in-law of Muhammad, was 'discovered' in the early twelfth century. The first shrine to cover the tomb was built by the Saljuk Sultan Sanjar, but destroyed by the Mongols. The tomb made Mazar into a wealthy place, which eventually replaced nearby Balkh.

22　The immense bronze cauldron that could be found in the southeast part of the courtyard of the Friday mosque, bears an inscription which dates it to AD 1375. The cauldron is 4.8 metres in diameter, and 4.5 metres deep. It also bears a Persian inscription from Sa'di.

23　*Gazir-gâh*, apparently from *Kârzâr-gâh*, 'place of the battle' (Barthold/Bosworth 1984:57). See in particular the study by Golombek 1969.

24　For Bihzad, see Bahari 1996.

25　The other reputed burial place of 'Ali is at Najaf, in modern Iraq. The story goes that the body of the Caliph was put on a white camel and that the body would be buried on the spot where the camel would stop.

14

Towards the Kingdom of Afghanistan

The history of Afghanistan during the sixteenth and seventeenth centuries is narrowly linked to a series of momentous events and developments that around AD 1500 occurred within and beyond its present borders. This was the time that the Turco-Mongolian prince Babur moved with a few men from South Central Asia, via Kabul, to the Indian subcontinent where he established the Mughal empire that would last until the mid-nineteenth century. In the west, the Türkmen leader Isma'il Shah and his Qizilbash ('red head') followers founded the Safawid dynasty (or the 'Sophies' as they used to be called in the West), which led Iran towards a period of great prosperity and cultural development. And in the north, in Transoxiana, there was the settlement and rise to power of the Özbeks under the dynasty of the Shibanids. The Safawids stopped the Özbek advance to Iran in AD 1510, but the newcomers from the north occupied all of Transoxiana and much of northern Afghanistan, and continue to dominate most of this area to the present day.

In addition, another development took place that in the end would alter the whole constellation of the Middle East and South Asia: the emergence of the West European sea-borne empires. At first, the influence of the Europeans was minimal. Gradually however, trade routes shifted from overland tracks to transport by sea, and the ancient Middle Eastern cities suffered accordingly.

Finally, Pashto-speaking groups from the Sulayman Mountains along the modern border between Afghanistan and Pakistan started to expand their habitat. They went westward towards South Afghanistan, and northward towards the Kabul valley and hence to the east towards the plains of Peshawar. The reasons behind these massive migrations are still difficult to fathom, but they moved into a vacuum that had been created by the demise of the Turco-Mongolian tribes in the fifteenth century and the virtual withdrawal of Timurid control from the borderlands.

For the meantime, Afghanistan became a buffer area between the empires of the Safawids, Özbeks and Mughals, and coveted by all three. Balkh, Herat, Qandahar and Kabul were the four cities that by the early sixteenth century still controlled the trade routes between Iran, Central Asia and the Indian subcontinent. Their occupation was a prize worth fighting for, although the actual importance of at least some of these cities may have been more imaginary than real. The imperial rulers in India and Iran knew very well that Qandahar ('the mound of dust') produced very little, and its occupation actually cost them money.[1] Prestige may have been a prime motivator.

While military strife in the borderlands led to destruction and death, it also led to an influx of money and prestige goods, since all three contestants invested in the setting up of local middlemen to raise taxes and control the local population. In this way the people of modern Afghanistan, and especially the Pashtuns or Pakhtuns who around this time came to live along the major highways passing through the land, were strongly influenced by outside developments.

The Özbeks

The Özbeks are relative newcomers in Afghanistan. Sometime in the fifteenth century they migrated from the steppes of Central Asia to the oases of the south. They were named after a Mongol leader called Özbek, who was Khan of the Golden Horde in the early fourteenth century. Among these Özbeks the descendants of Shiban, a grandson of Chingiz-Khan, played a prominent role. In AD 1430/1 one of these men, the Shibanid Abu 'l-Khayr, took Choresmia south of the Aral Sea and in the years to follow he and his Özbeks carried out raids into the Timurid lands to the south. In AD 1499/1500 his grandson Muhammad Shaybani Khan (also called Shahi Beg) took Transoxiana and in AD 1504 the Özbeks also conquered Farghana further to the east. Soon afterwards they moved south again and crossed the Amu Darya onto the Iranian Plateau. One of the first important cities to fall to the Özbeks was Herat, which was occupied in AD 1507.

History seemed to repeat itself, with another Central Asian group invading the Plateau. The Özbeks may well have succeeded. It is clear from what happened in Herat that they were not like the Mongols or the armies of Timur. Their treatment of Herat was, in the terms of those days, moderate, and they reinstated most of the Herati officials into their former positions. In fact, life soon continued its

---

1 Compare 'Qandahâr' in the *Enc. Isl.*

normal course. In doing so, the Özbeks showed that they were aware of the importance of the Iranian cities and their administrators for running the country and, of course, for collecting taxes. By their moderate behaviour they may also have convinced other Iranian cities to follow Herat's example, and open up their gates for them. In this way, an Özbek empire of Iran may well have been a success.

However, Özbek advance was stopped short in AD 1510 when Shah Isma'il, the founder of the Safawid empire of Iran, defeated Shaybani in a battle near Marw and pushed the Özbeks back to Transoxiana. In AD 1511 the Safawids and Özbeks concluded a treaty in which the Amu Darya was established as the border between the two empires. This did not stop warfare continuing, but the situation never drastically changed. The Shibanid dynasty continued to rule Bukhara and the rest of Transoxiana until AD 1599, when it was replaced by another Özbek family, namely that of the Tuqay Timurids (AD 1599–1785). These were in turn replaced by the Özbek Mangits (AD 1785–1920). Other Özbek khanates were eventually established in Khiva and Khokand.

After the defeat of the Özbeks, the Persians occupied Herat and, for a brief period, also Balkh, and throughout the sixteenth and seventeenth centuries Herat remained in Safawid hands, although it was frequently subject to Özbek raids and brief periods of Özbek occupation. The local population, at first Sunnite, slowly embraced the Shi'ite belief.[2] The north of Afghanistan, however, was gradually occupied by Özbek nomads. Their leaders, the *Amir*s or *beg*s, became the rulers of the various oases. By the end of the sixteenth century these included Andkhuy, Balkh, Qunduz and Badakhshan. Of these, Balkh was undoubtedly the most important. Together with Bukhara, Samarqand and Tashkent, it formed one of the four major 'sub-states' of the Shibanid and Tuqay-Timurid realm.

Babur

Babur ('Tiger') was the nickname of Zahir al-Din Muhammad, who was born in AD 1483 as the eldest son of 'Umar Shaykh Mirza, the Timurid ruler of Farghana.[3] He was a direct descendant of Timur and through his mother he could also boast of Chingiz-Khan as one of his ancestors. When still very young he was driven from Transox-

---

2 For Herat in the early sixteenth century, see Szuppe 1992.

3 For Babur, see his autobiography, written in the *Chaghatây* language (trans. Beveridge 1922; Bacqué-Grammont 1980; Thackston 1996); see also the *Târikh-i Râshidi* by Muhammad Haydar Mirza Kurkan.

iana by the Özbeks. He eventually found his way south across the Hindu Kush towards Kabul, where his uncle (Ulugh Mirza) used to rule until he died in AD 1501/2.[4] Babur claimed the Kabuli throne and in AD 1504 he managed to oust Ulugh's successor, who belonged to the Arghun family from Qandahar.[5]

Babur and the Arghuns subsequently fought a long war for the control of East and Southeast Afghanistan. In AD 1507 Babur managed to take Qandahar, and he left his brother Nasir Mirza in control and returned to Kabul. At that moment Babur decided that he should be called Supreme Lord (*Pâdshâh*), rather than the more humble *Mirzâ*. In this way Babur claimed supremacy over all Timurid princes. Soon he received the news, however, that the Özbeks under Shaybani Beg after taking Herat had laid siege to Qandahar. The Özbeks eventually took the city and gave it back to the Arghuns. The war in the borderlands continued, and only in May 1522 did Babur manage to definitively throw the Arghuns out of Qandahar.[6] To commemorate this event, Babur ordered the inscription of a text in a niche, high up along the northern edge of the Qaytul Ridge, which bounds the old town of Qandahar to the west. This monument, now know as the *Chehel Zina* (forty steps),[7] lies very close to another monument, erected on behalf of another prince more than seventeen hundred years earlier, namely the Greek/Aramaic rock inscription of King Ashoka, from the third century BC.

With his rear defences secured, Babur started preparations for the invasion of India. In AD 1526, Babur and his followers defeated Ibrahim Lodi, the (Pashtun) Ghalji ruler of Delhi, and founded the Mughal empire. Fighting did not stop, however, and opposition against Babur, also from the side of the Pashtun leaders in North India, continued. Babur did not long enjoy his new conquests. After many years of almost continuous fighting he died at Agra, aged 48, on 26 December 1530. His body was first buried at Agra, but some ten years later it was taken to Babur's beloved Kabul. He lies buried in the *Bâgh-i Bâbur*, along the western slopes of the Kuh-i Shir Darwaza.[8]

---

4 Upon the death of Ulugh Mirza, his son 'Abd al-Razzak took the throne, but he was soon replaced by Muqim of the Arghun family. Ulugh Mirza is the man accused by the Yusufzay Pashtuns of having killed their leaders when they passed through the area in the late fifteenth century.
5 In the late fifteenth century Zu 'l-Nun Beg Arghun built up a large realm that covered most of South Afghanistan and the neighbouring parts of Pakistan. His capital was Qandahar.
6 The Arghuns subsequently settled in Shal, modern Quetta.
7 Babur's descendant Akbar added his own lines to the text.
8 In AD 1646, his descendant, the Mughal emperor Shah Jahan ordered a small mosque to be built nearby, in order to commemorate his occupation of Balkh in North

Between Mughals and Safawids

Babur had established the idea of an Indian Mughal empire. When he died opposition in India against the newcomers from South Central Asia, however, was still very strong. The real establishment of the Mughal empire had to wait for his descendants.

Babur was succeeded by Humayun, his son by his principal wife, Mahim Begim. He was born in Kabul in AD 1506 and when his father died he was only 24 years old. For a number of years, Humayun managed to retain the conquests of his father, although his three brothers, Kamran, ʿAskari and Hindal, who had been given important governorships, did all they could to promote their own interests. In this way, Humayun could not stop the Safawid Iranians from briefly occupying Qandahar in AD 1537/38, although it was soon recovered. Internally, Humayun's position was opposed by the old Pashtun rulers of India. Their influence was still very strong, and in AD 1540 Humayun was forced to leave India. His place was taken by the (Pashtun) Sur dynasty.

Humayun fled to the west, through Sind and Baluchistan to Qandahar. His position seemed hopeless, even more so when in AD 1543 he was refused entry to Qandahar by his own brother and governor of the city, ʿAskari. Humayun then sought refuge with the Safawid king, Shah Tahmasp, who received Humayun cordially. No doubt he was pleased to show hospitality to a descendant of the Timurid princes with their illustrious past and their long opposition against the Özbeks. With Iranian help, Humayun subsequently planned his return to India. First, however, he had to defeat his brothers who controlled much of modern Afghanistan.

With Tahmasp's active assistance, Humayun gathered his forces and in September 1545 he marched against Qandahar, still held by his brother, ʿAskari. The Safawids clearly intended to take Qandahar and keep it for themselves, but in the end the forces of Humayun managed to occupy the strategic town and keep the Iranians out. The next year Humayun took Kabul from Kamran,[9] and finally on 23 July 1553 he took Delhi. However, like his father before him he did not enjoy his success for long, for he died within five months, on 26 January 1556, having fallen down the steps of his library.

Afghanistan. Babur's tomb was embellished by Amir ʿAbd al-Rahman Khan. For this garden, see Parpagliolo 1972.

9   He lost the town again that same winter when Kamran took it in a surprise attack, but in AD 1547 Humayun reoccupied it. Two years later the story repeated itself. This threat to Humayun disappeared when in AD 1553 Kamran was captured and blinded.

He was succeeded by his son, Jalal al-Din Muhammad Akbar (*r.* AD 1556–1605), aged thirteen. History somehow repeated itself. The young king in India was confronted with a hostile brother in Kabul. This time it was Akbar's half-brother, Muhammad Hakim Mirza, who officially acted as governor of Kabul.[10] Akbar, young and cut off from his Afghan possessions, therefore could do nothing to prevent Qandahar from falling into the hands of the Safawids under Shah Tahmasp, who occupied the town in AD 1558.

The Safawids would continue to control Qandahar and Southeast Afghanistan for many years, until AD 1595. During this period, the Iranians appointed headmen (*kalântars*), as representatives of the tribes. One of these local chiefs was Sado, who belonged to the Popalzay tribe of the Abdali confederacy in South Afghanistan. Sado was entrusted by Shah ʿAbbas (*r.* AD 1587–1629) to guard the road between Herat and Qandahar. Sado also was granted the title of *Mir-i afâghina*. Eventually, in AD 1597/8, he received from Shah ʿAbbas almost exclusive control over the Abdalis. He became the ancestor of the Sadozay clan of the Abdalis, later called the Durranis, who would rule Afghanistan for more than fifty years in the late eighteenth and early nineteenth centuries.

In the early years of Akbar's rule, the weakening of Mughal power allowed for the Özbek chief, ʿAbd Allah bin Iskandar, to occupy North Afghanistan and Badakhshan. He took Balkh in AD 1568, and in AD 1588 the Özbek ruler even managed to take Herat from the Safawids. Özbek power, which was almost completely based on cavalry, seemed unstoppable. However, with the death of his half-brother Hakim Mirza in AD 1585 Akbar gained more grip on events in the northwest of his empire. In AD 1588, when the Özbeks took Herat, Akbar concluded a treaty with the Özbek leaders that stipulated that the Özbeks would retain the north, but would refrain from attacking the south. In this way, the Mughals gave up all claims on their ancestral lands in North Afghanistan and Transoxiana, but protected their lands south of the Hindu Kush. This in fact separated North Afghanistan from the south and east.

The treaty freed Akbar's hands to deal with some of the Pashtun tribes in the Indo-Iranian borderlands, which had risen against Mughal rule as followers of the so-called Rawshaniyya sect.[11] The rebelling Pashtuns had settled along the main highway between Kabul and Peshawar. Control of this thoroughfare was absolutely essential for the Mughals in order to defend Kabul, the place where their

10   The town of Jalalabad was founded during Akbar's reign.
11   For the Rawshaniyya movement, see Caroe 1958:193–204 and the article on Bayazid Ansari in the *Enc. Isl.* by M. Shafi. See also Arlinghaus 1988.

ancestor Babur was buried. Fighting was heavy, and the Pashtuns proved more than a match to the Mughal forces, but slowly Akbar managed to gain control again and to restore Mughal supremacy in the borderlands. This was also the time that the famous Khaybar Pass between Peshawar and Jalalabad was first made suitable for wheeled transport. Akbar in the end managed to 'pacify' the Pashtuns, although at great cost.

Akbar's successes continued. A crowning victory was achieved in AD 1595, when the Safawid governor of Qandahar surrendered the town to the Mughals. The year before, Akbar had gained control of Baluchistan, including the Makran coast. The Özbek threat to the Mughals was finally averted with the death in AD 1598 of the feared Özbek chief, 'Abd Allah.[12] By about AD 1600, Mughal control in the borderlands was thus firmly re-established.

Akbar died in AD 1605. He was succeeded by his son Salim, who took the title of Jahangir (*r.* AD 1605–27).[13] During his reign, in AD 1622, the Mughals again lost Qandahar to the Iranians under Shah 'Abbas.[14] In the ensuing years, the Abdali Pashtuns from the Qandahar region, with Safawid blessing, continued their migration to the west and northwest, towards Herat. This meant that by the late seventeenth century the equally Pashtun Ghaljis were the only powerful Pashtun group that remained in the Qandahar area. At the same time, the Abdalis became all-powerful in the Herat district, at the cost of the local population. All the while, Pashtun nomads migrated anually into the western mountains of modern Afghanistan, which hitherto had been dominated by Turco-Mongolian groups. This process, which is attested in historical records, was probably a mere repetition of what happened some years earlier in East and Southeast Afghanistan, when the Pashto-speakers moved into this area and pushed the Hazaras into the mountains.

In the meantime, much of northern Afghanistan remained in the hands of the Özbeks, who sometimes also raided across the Hindu Kush. In AD 1629 they even captured Bamiyan. But times were changing, and Mughal power soon reasserted itself, also in Southeast Afghanistan. In AD 1637 the Safawid governor of Qandahar, 'Ali Mardan Khan, handed the city over to the Mughals, who subsequently also occupied Girishk along the Hilmand and the district of

---

12   The Safawid ruler, Shah 'Abbas, reacted immediately and took Nishapur, Mashhad and Herat.

13   Jahangir's famous wife, Nur Jahan, was born in Qandahar in AD 1577 when her father moved from Persia to India.

14   The man appointed as governor of Qandahar was Ganj 'Ali Khan, the former ruler of Kirman. He is known for various public buildings, including the Ganj 'Ali Khan bathhouse, in the centre of Kirman.

Zamin Dawar.[15] In the north, in AD 1646, a Mughal army defeated the Özbeks near Shibarghan and occupied Balkh and Termez. The Mughals were led by Prince Awrangzib, the third son of Shah Jahan (r. AD 1628–57) and the future Mughal emperor. Although the Özbeks were beaten, they still managed to fight a successful guerrilla war and eventually forced the Mughals to evacuate North Afghanistan. This marked another turning-point in the history of the borderlands, and the first of a series of Mughal set-backs. In February 1649, the Safawid Shah ʿAbbas II (r. AD 1642–66) managed to occupy Qandahar again. In the same year he even laid siege to Ghazni, but failed to take it. Three times, between AD 1649 and 1653, the Mughals tried to recapture Qandahar. The first attempts were made by Awrangzib, and the third time the Mughal army was led by his eldest brother Dara Shikuh. In all three cases the Mughals failed.

Awrangzib (r. AD 1659–1707) was formally acknowledged as the Mughal emperor in AD 1659, after he had defeated his three brothers and imprisoned his father.[16] As regards Afghanistan, his reign was marked by a series of military campaigns against the Pashtun tribes. In AD 1667 he crushed an uprising of the Yusufzay in the lands north of Peshawar. An uprising of the Afridis, southwest of the town, followed in AD 1672. The tribesmen inflicted heavy losses on a Mughal army near the Khaybar Pass. In the next year, they again defeated a Mughal force, this time in the Karappa Pass nearby. The Pashtuns could only be pacified following Awrangzib's personal presence in the region.[17]

Throughout Awrangzib's reign Qandahar remained in Safawid hands. The border between the Safawid and Mughal empires lay somewhere near Muqqur, between Qandahar and Ghazni. Still in the mid-nineteenth century, the Afghans distinguished here the borderline between Khurasan and Hindustan, according to the French traveller Ferrier.[18]

Awrangzib died in AD 1707. His son Muhammad Muʿazzam (also called Shah ʿAlam), with the regnal title of Bahadur Shah, succeeded him on the Mughal throne. He was already well in his sixties. He died five years later, in AD 1712. Muhammad Shah, who would reign

15   The Safawid governor feared, probably correctly, that he was in line of being executed when he was summoned to return to Isfahan by the new Shah, Shah Safi, who had succeeded ʿAbbas in AD 1629.

16   Shah Jahan died in AD 1666.

17   This is the time of one of the great Pashtun poet-warriors, Khushhal Khan Khatak (AD 1613–89). He belonged to the Khatak tribe that lives southeast of Peshawar, and therefore outside modern Afghanistan. His name and fame among the modern Pashtuns is still widespread (compare Caroe 1958:221–46).

18   Ferrier 1857:322.

until AD 1748, succeeded him in 1719, after much dynastic upheaval. The Mughal dynasty was clearly in decline.

The Rise of the Afghan Kingdom

In the seventeenth century, the Ghaljis of Eastern Afghanistan were generally inclined to support the Safawids, who at that time and in that region were the traditional enemies of the Mughals. They did so especially in AD 1653 when the Mughals for the last time tried to secure Qandahar. The situation changed during the time of the last Safawid king, Shah Husayn (r. AD 1694–1722) (Ill. 13). His governor in Qandahar, in the early years of the eighteenth century, was ʿAbd Allah Khan, apparently a Georgian. Being dissatisfied with the Safawid king, he opened negotations with the Mughal prince-governor in Kabul, Shah ʿAlam (the future emperor), with the intention of handing the city over to the Mughals. Most of the Ghaljis were opposed to these plans, but before ʿAbd Allah Khan's plans could be carried out he was defeated by a Baluchi force from the south.

Relations between the Safawids and their erstwhile protegees, the Ghaljis, did not improve. One of the factors that contributed to this development was the Safawid pressure upon the Sunnite Pashtuns to convert to Shiʿism.[19] The next Safawid governor, another Georgian called Gurgin Khan (or Giorgi XI), soon came into conflict with the very wealthy Ghalji leader of Qandahar, Mir Ways (Amir Khan), of the Hotak tribe. Mir Ways led a subsequent Ghalji rebellion, but was defeated and sent into exile to Isfahan, the Safawid capital. There he led a comfortable life, flattering and bribing his way into the highest Isfahani circles. According to Pashtun folklore he consequently learned about the weaknesses of the Safawids. He even received permission to perform the *hajj* to Mecca, where he managed to obtain a *fatwâ* permitting him to start a revolt against the heretic Shiʿites. Via Isfahan he returned to Qandahar, and in AD 1709 he managed to defeat and kill Gurgin Khan and to become the *vakil* of the Ghaljis in Qandahar, thus establishing the so-called Hotaki dynasty. To gain further support, Mir Ways turned to the Mughal emperor of India, and the latter recognized Mir Ways as his governor of Qandahar.

Mir Ways was soon confronted with an attack on his position from the side of the Safawids. They sent against him their general, Kay Khusraw,[20] together with Georgian and Qizilbash troops. Kay

19 Compare Sayyid Amir Arjomand 1984:191.
20 A nephew of Giorgi XI.

Illustration 13   *Shah Husayn, the ill-fated Safawid king of Persia, defeated by the Afghans (from Cornelis de Bruijn,* Reizen over Moskovië, . . . *Amsterdam, 1711).*

Khusraw was also supported by a Pashtun Abdali chief, namely ʿAbd Allah Khan Sadozay, a descendant of Sado. After initial successes, the Safawid army was defeated in AD 1711 and Mir Ways Khan Hotaki became the undisputed leader of Qandahar. He called himself the *Vakil*, or Regent of Qandahar. Soon after, in AD 1715, he died and he was buried just outside of Qandahar.[21] He was at first succeeded by his brother, ʿAbd al-ʿAziz, but the new *vakil* showed sympathies for the Safawids and was soon, in AD 1717, murdered and replaced by his nephew and son of Mir Ways, Mir Mahmud.

At about the same time, in AD 1716, the Abdalis around Herat also proclaimed their independence from the Safawids. They were led by the same ʿAbd Allah Khan Sadozay who had earlier supported the Safawids against Mir Ways.[22] The Abdalis took Herat and

---

21   His tomb lies some ten km west of modern Qandahar along the main road to Herat. It is a modern twentieth century copy of Ahmad Shah Durrani's mausoleum in Qandahar. Lockhart (1958:92) gives a reference to Mir Ways by Voltaire (*Deuxième Discours de la Liberté*):

> L'oppresseur insolent, l'usurpateur avare
> Cartouche, Miriwits, ou tel autre barbare

22   This man is reported to have derived from Multan in the Panjab, where in the seventeenth century many Abdalis had been settled by the Mughals after the latter, although assisted by the Abdalis, failed to take Qandahar in AD 1653.

defended their newly acquired possessions against a series of Persian counter-attacks. When finally the Persians stopped trying to retake Herat, the Abdalis clashed with the Ghaljis. ʿAbd Allah's son, ʿAsad Allah, the governor of Farah in Sistan, subsequently marched against the Ghaljis of Qandahar. He was, however, defeated in AD 1719/1720 by Mir Mahmud near the settlement of Dilaram, about half-way between Herat and Qandahar. ʿAsad Allah was killed and his head was sent to the Safawid king, Shah Husayn, in Isfahan. ʿAbd Allah Khan Sadozay of Herat was deposed and killed by a kinsman, Muhammad Zaman Khan Sadozay, the ancestor of the future Afghan kings.[23]

The Pashtuns Defeat the Safawids

In AD 1720, having secured his position among the Ghalji Pashtuns, Mir Mahmud gave up all pretenses as to his loyalty to the Safawid court and led his Ghalji troops against the 'infidel' Shiʿites and the equally 'infidel' Zoroastrians of Iran. They took the ancient town of Kirman and killed most of the Zoroastrian community. The Afghans subsequently returned to Qandahar because of the continued resistance put up by the Safawid commander of Kirman, Lutf ʿAli Khan, but also because Mahmud had to crush a rebellion that had broken out in Qandahar. It was clear, however, that Safawid power in the East was crumbling. Around that time the Abdalis in Herat also took their chances and defeated a Safawid army: under the aforementioned Muhammad Zaman Khan they won a victory near Islam Qalʿa, west of Herat. The Ghaljis and the Abdalis were now both, independent of each other, in revolt against their Safawid king. Neither the Mughals nor the Safawids themselves seemed capable of doing anything about it.

In AD 1721 Mir Mahmud again marched upon Kirman. He took the town, but again failed to take the citadel. He thereupon moved further northwest, to the town of Yazd, where he again was repulsed. He did not return, nor did he wait for the city to fall. He simply moved his army further northwest, towards Isfahan, the Safawid capital, and on 8 March 1722 at the battlefield of Gulnabad (some 20 km from the town) the Ghaljis, with an army of some 20,000 men, defeated the Safawid army with double the number. Subsequently, after a long siege in which thousands of Isfahanis died, the Ghaljis took Isfahan.

---

23 He was the son of Dawlat Khan. Whether Zaman Khan poisoned his rival, as widely believed, remains unknown. Zaman Khan was later buried just south of Herat in the Rawza-yi Bagh.

Mir Mahmud made a pompous entry on 25 October and to mark his new role as King of Iran he married Shah Husayn's daughter. Only one of the sons of Shah Husayn had managed to escape, Tahmasp (II), who on 10 November in the town of Qazvin declared himself the new Shah.

Contrary to the Ghaljis, the Abdalis never really managed to extend their realm. One of the reasons for the relative lack of success may be the fact that there was not one singular family that was generally recognized as the leaders of the confederacy. Their erstwhile leader, Muhammad Zaman Khan Sadozay, was pushed aside by Muhammad Khan Afghan Sadozay. In AD 1722 they took the town of Mashhad, but they were driven out four years later, upon which Muhammad Khan Afghan was deposed and replaced by Muhammad Zaman Khan's son, called Zu 'l-Fiqar Khan.

In the meantime, in Isfahan, Mahmud proved to be a bloody tyrant. One of his atrocities was the murder of most of the high ranking Persians in Isfahan, including almost all the sons of Shah Husayn. Mahmud was eventually killed by his own men in April 1725 and the next day Ashraf, the son of the murdered ʿAbd al-ʿAziz Hotaki, was proclaimed king. Mir Mahmud's brother, Husayn Sultan, remained in control of Qandahar and refused to recognize his cousin as supreme leader. The Ghaljis in Iran were thus cut off from their homeland.

Ashraf's position was threatened on many sides, especially since the Russians and Turks had agreed to carve up the Persian empire. From AD 1725, the Turks occupied the western part of the country, including Tabriz, Hamadan and Qazvin. However, in AD 1727, they were decisively defeated by the Ghaljis. The Pashtuns clearly still formed a formidable force, and the Ghalji cavalry from all accounts was a devastating weapon. The Turks subsequently recognized Ashraf as the *Shâh* of Persia, while the Ghaljis recognized the Turkish Sultan as the head of the Muslim world. The Ghaljis also fought a war against the Russians (AD 1727–9). This struggle did not lead to the same successes as against the Turks; Ghalji forces were seriously weakened and their prestige and fame of invincibility had gone. It would not be long before the Afghans were thrown out of Iran.

Nadir Shah

During this time, rivalry had grown in the camp of Tahmasp II, the son of Shah Husayn. Tahmasp was supported by three important, local Iranian leaders, but their help was not based on loyalty towards their king, but on the promotion of their own and their clan's interests. The three contestors were Fath 'Ali Khan Qajar, the leader of the Qajar Turks and governor of Astarabad southeast of the Caspian, modern Gurgan City; Nadir Quli Beg (Khan), a chief from among the Afshar Turks in northeast Iran; and Malik Mahmud, the ruler of Mashhad. Strife among these three local leaders led to much bloodshed and a further weakening of Tahmasp's position. Eventually Fath 'Ali Khan Qajar, ancestor of the future Qajar dynasty of Iran (AD 1779–1925) was beheaded on the orders of Tahmasp, while Malik Mahmud was defeated when Nadir Khan as the king's supreme commander took Mashhad in November 1726.

Two years later, most of southern and western Iran was still occupied by the Ghaljis, while the Abdali Pashtuns continued to dominate the west of modern Afghanistan and constituted a constant threat to the position of Tahmasp and his followers in the north and northeast of Iran. While in Mashhad, Nadir Khan decided first to deal with the nearby Abdalis, thus trying to eliminate the most direct threat to his and Tahmasp's position. By that time the Abdalis were, almost traditionally, led by two rivals, namely Allah Yar Khan, who was the brother of Muhammad Khan Afghan, and the aforementioned Zu 'l-Fiqar Khan. The first had become the ruler of Herat. The second, the son of Muhammad Zaman Khan, was the governor of Farah. The Iranian attack on the Abdalis was successful and Nadir Khan defeated them in AD 1729. At that time the major battle with the Ghaljis still had to be fought, and Nadir Khan decided to try to reconcile the traditional enemies of the Ghaljis, the Abdalis, and to win them for his cause, namely the defeat of the Galjis. He therefore re-appointed Allah Yar Khan as the Safawid governor of Herat. In the end, Nadir Khan did not need the support of the Abdalis, although they would much later, and after various insurrections against his rule, join him in the siege of Qandahar.

In AD 1729, after his first victory over the Abdalis, Nadir Khan fought a number of battles against Ashraf and his Ghaljis. Each time Nadir proved to be the better general, and finally, at Murchakhur, north of Isfahan, Ashraf was decisively defeated. He fled with his troops towards Shiraz and eventually towards Qandahar, where he was soon killed, apparently on the orders of Husayn Sultan, his uncle and the ruler of Qandahar. The Iranian empire of the Pashtuns had come to an end. After the defeat of the Ghaljis, still in AD 1729, Tahmasp was again crowned king in Isfahan. His rule, it may be clear, was completely dependent on Nadir Khan's support. It ended three years later when he was replaced by his infant son, Shah 'Abbas III (r. AD 1731–6), with Nadir Khan as regent.

The next year, in AD 1730, Zu 'l-Fiqar Khan, the erstwhile Abdali ruler of Farah, allied himself with his erstwhile enemy, the Ghalji chief

Husayn Sultan of Qandahar. They occupied Herat and replaced Allah Yar Khan. Together they advanced against Mashhad while Nadir Khan was still campaigning in the west. The Pashtun forces, however, were soon repulsed. Nadir subsequently moved east and defeated the Abdalis various times, each time reappointing the Abdali governors in their positions. Finally, in February 1732 after a siege of some ten months, Zu 'l-Fiqar Khan was driven from Herat and the Ghaljis withdrew to Qandahar and imprisoned Zu 'l-Fiqar and his younger brother, Ahmad. Herat was henceforth governed by a Persian, and many Abdalis were forced to migrate to the west. The power of the Abdalis, which had never reached great heights anyhow, seemed broken, while that of their kinsmen, the Ghaljis, was restricted to Qandahar and its environs.

The Fall of Qandahar

In AD 1736, Nadir Khan finally deposed the young Safawid king and declared himself Shah (*r.* AD 1736–47). He subsequently went east with an army of some 80,000 men, and assisted by many Abdalis, he moved against Qandahar. The siege of this city, at that time also called Husaynabad after its ruler, started in April 1737. Nadir Shah realized he would not be able to take the city by direct assault, so he built a ring of forts around the town and garrisoned his own troops in a walled fortification (Nadirabad), a place which can still be visited south of modern Qandahar City.[24] At the same time a Persian force marched east from Bandar 'Abbas, along the Persian Gulf and the Makran coast and forced the ruler of Kalat in Baluchistan to submit to Nadir Shah.

The siege of Qandahar lingered on for almost a year. The modern visitor to what is now called Old Qandahar is still impressed with the fortifications of the place and its location along the eastern flanks of the Qaytul Ridge. Not much has changed since the days of the Early Achaemenid satraps. The ramparts still follow the same contours, and in the middle of the town rises the same citadel. However, the fortifications of this stronghold did not stop the Persians, and in the end, Nadir Shah managed to take the town on 12 March 1738. The surrender of Qandahar marked the end of Ghalji power in Southeast Afghanistan. Many Hotaki Ghaljis from the Qandahar area were deported to Khurasan, taking the place of the Abdalis who were allowed to settle in the Qandahar area. Husayn was also sent in exile

24 Compare especially Fischer 1967.

to Mazandaran, and so were the Abdali chief Zu 'l-Fiqar and his 15-year-old brother, Ahmad.

Nadir Khan subsequently moved against the Mughal empire. In the early summer of 1738, he crossed the border, which in those days was located just south of Ghazni. Near Jalalabad he was joined by his son, Reza Quli Mirza, who just before had occupied North Afghanistan and even had crossed the Amu Darya in pursuit of Özbek forces. The main force of the Persian army subsequently proceeded across the Khaybar Pass, while Nadir and a small group of men took a more southern route and attacked the Indians defending the eastern entrance to the Khaybar in the back. Early 1739 he occupied the Panjab and continued his march further east, until on 24 February 1739 he defeated the Mughal army near Panipat, close to Delhi. Delhi itself was occupied and plundered. By mid-May 1739 Nadir left Delhi again, laden with spoils, including the Peacock Throne of Shah Jahan and the famous Kuh-i Nur diamond. Nadir Shah then turned his attention to the lands north of the Amu Darya, and between 1740 and 1741 he conquered much of Transoxiana, including Samarqand, Bukhara and Khiva. He returned to his capital, Mashhad, in AD 1741. The latter years of Nadir's life, one of the greatest generals of his time, were dominated by his growing suspicions of anyone near him. He was a Sunnite, and never really accepted by his predominantly Shi'ite Iranian subjects. He even had his own son blinded. Whether he was going mad or not is unclear, but his position became impossible. In June 1747, Nadir Shah was killed by his own troops when he was camped near Quchan, south of Ashkhabad.[25]

25 The Teppeh-yi Nadir where Nadir Shah was murdered lies just northwest of the modern town of Quchan.

15

The Sadozay Dynasty

The death of Nadir Shah caused great turmoil in the Persian camp. Nadir Shah had ruled Iran and his troops with an iron fist, and when he died there was no generally accepted heir. Into this vacuum stepped a 25-year-old Abdali Pashtun officer in Nadir Shah's army, called Ahmad Khan. He was a son of Muhammad Zaman Khan, the former ruler of Herat, and a brother of Zu 'l-Fiqar Khan. Born in Herat in 1722, he belonged to the Sadozay branch of the Popalzay tribe of the Abdali confederacy.[1] He thus belonged to one of the leading families of the Abdalis of southern and southwestern Afghanistan. After the capture of Qandahar, Nadir Shah had sent him to Mazandaran where the young Pashtun became governor. At the time of Nadir's death, he commanded a contingent of Abdali Pashtuns. Realizing that his life was in jeopardy if he stayed among the Persians who had murdered Nadir Shah, he decided to leave the Persian camp, and with his 4,000 troops he proceeded to Qandahar. Along the way and by sheer luck, they managed to capture a caravan with booty from India. He and his troops were rich; moreover, they were experienced fighters. In short, they formed a formidable force of young Pashtun soldiers who were loyal to their high-ranking leader.

The death of Nadir Shah meant that the Abdalis and Ghaljis had another opportunity of breaking away from Persian control. This time the Abdalis played the leading role; the power of the Ghaljis had been crushed after the fall of Qandahar, the more so because many of them, including their leaders, had been deported to Khurasan. One of the key players was of course Ahmad Khan, backed by his troops and his ancestry. The decision as to who would lead the Pashtuns was

---

1 For Ahmad Shah Durrani and his life, see also Abdurrahman 1900 and Ganda Singh 1959; see also Ahmad's biography, the *Târikh-i Ahmad*, by ʿAbd al-Karim ʿAlawi (Lucknow 1266). Also important are Dorn 1836, Elphinstone 1815:541–58, and Gankovsky 1958.

taken in October 1747, at the tomb of Shaykh Surkh at Kushk-i Nakhud, west of Qandahar, at a meeting of all the leading Abdali Pashtuns from the Qandahar area. After nine days, Ahmad Khan was elected as leader.[2] He was proclaimed *pâdshâh durr-i dawrân* ('King, pearl of the age'). He called himself Ahmad Shah and subsequently coins were struck in his name, thus showing the independence of the Abdalis.[3]

From the start, there was rivalry between the Sadozay, who belonged to the Popalzay tribe, and another important Abdali tribe, namely the Barakzay. This rivalry would much later lead to the fall of the Sadozay dynasty and the rise of the Barakzay. For the time being, the leader of the Muhammadzay clan of the Barakzay, Hajji Jamal Khan (1719–70/71), was appointed vizier.

The reasons for Ahmad's election were manifold. He was a young charismatic leader with obvious military and administrative qualities. He also was the leader of the influential Sadozay clan of the Popalzay tribe. He commanded a 4,000 men cavalry force. He was a descendant of Sado, the Abdali protégé of Shah ʿAbbas. Besides, he was a man with luck, since he had got hold of the treasures that a caravan was taking from the east to Persia. Another point was the support he received in the *Jirga* from the side of a local religious leader, although it is difficult to assess what really went on. The tribal leaders at the gathering probably hoped that this young man would be an excellent general without the influence to meddle too much in the internal affairs of the tribes. In other words, he would help them in gaining more wealth without affecting their own power.

Ahmad Shah Durrani: His Career

The new king knew what was expected of him. Almost immediately upon becoming King in 1747, as *Pâdshâh*, *Durr-i Dawrân*, or later *Durr-i Durrân* ('Pearl of Pearls'), he embarked upon a campaign to the Indian subcontinent, no doubt in imitation of his erstwhile chief, Nadir Shah of Persia. He probably regarded himself as Nadir Shah's successor and the legitimate heir to the latter's Indian possessions. Leaving Qandahar in December 1747, he took Ghazni, Kabul and Peshawar, and soon, with an army that had increased to some 30,000 horse, entered the city of Lahore, the capital of the Panjab. From Lahore they moved on Delhi. Here the Pashtuns ran out of luck. On

2   Compare Ferrier 1857:316.
3   Ahmad Shah later apparently changed his name to *Durr-i Durrân*, 'Pearl of Pearls' (see Adamec 1997:7 and Noelle 1997:230–1).

11 March 1748, at the battlefield of Manupur near Delhi, a Mughal army defeated them. This weakened Ahmad Shah's position, the more so since a revolt had broken out in Qandahar. He did not hesitate, and he immediately returned to his capital where he decisively suppressed all opposition. The rebel leaders, including his nephew, were executed.

Soon, Ahmad Shah Durrani planned new campaigns in India. Around that time, in late 1748, a Mughal namesake of Ahmad Shah had become the new emperor in India (Ahmad Shah, *r.* 1748–54) after the death of his father, the hapless Muhammad Shah. The Pashtuns saw new chances and hurried back to India. In the second half of 1749 Ahmad Shah Durrani was back in Lahore, but this time he refrained from marching further east, deciding first to secure his rear. On his way home, Ahmad Shah Durrani forced the Pashtun leaders of Dera Isma'il Khan and Dera Ghazi Khan, two important towns along the right bank of the Indus, to recognize his sovereignty, and the same happened to the Brahui Khan of Kalat, in Baluchistan. He now controlled all the borderlands and was free to penetrate deeper into the subcontinent. However, he decided first to extend his realm to the west, albeit after first subduing another insurrection in Qandahar.[4]

In 1750 Ahmad Shah led his troops to Herat, which he took after a long siege. He then marched to Mashhad, the capital of Mirza Shah Rukh, grandson of Nadir Shah, who up till then controlled Khurasan. Mashhad was taken, but soon afterwards the Afghans were defeated when they tried to take nearby Nishapur. A year later, in 1751, they tried again, and now they succeeded. Shah Rukh, who remained governor of Khurasan, recognized Ahmad Shah as his sovereign and handed him the famous Kuh-i Nur diamond. An Afghan army was subsequently sent up north to subdue other peoples, including Türkmen, Özbeks and Tajiks. In this way, the northern Afghan towns of Maymana, Balkh, Qunduz and the district of Badakhshan were added to Ahmad Shah's possessions. Also the Hazaras of Bamiyan were forced to recognize Ahmad Shah. Ahmad himself in the meantime had marched even further towards the west, but the Iranians defeated him near Gurgan City, ancient Astarabad, just southeast of the Caspian Sea. Any dreams of Ahmad Shah to emulate the successes of his Ghalji predecessors, and to effectuate his claims as successor of Nadir Shah, were given up. For the next twenty years, he would focus on India as his main source of income.

In December 1751 Ahmad Shah again invaded India. The Indian governor of the Afghan possessions in the Panjab had rebelled and

4 Led by Nur Muhammad 'Alizay, a former commander in Nadir Khan's army.

had joined the Mughal emperor. The Pashtuns defeated him, and reinstated him as governor for the Afghans, while the Mughal emperor recognized Afghan control of the Panjab, including Multan. Shortly after, still in 1752, an Afghan army also conquered Kashmir. After these successes, Ahmad Shah returned to Afghanistan, but his Indian possessions proved difficult to control without the presence of the main Pashtun army. In late 1756, after the Mughals had occupied part of the Panjab, Ahmad Shah Durrani again had to move down into the Indian subcontinent. In December he took Lahore. This time he felt confident enough to march further east, towards Delhi, and he took the town in January 1757. This time Delhi was plundered, and the same happened to Agra and Mathura. Ahmad's son, Timur, pillaged Amritsar. The Mughals were forced to recognize Afghan control over the Panjab, Kashmir and Sind, and Timur was given a daughter of the new Mughal emperor ('Alamgir II, *r.* 1754–9) as bride, while Ahmad Shah married a daughter of the late Mughal emperor, Muhammad Shah.

The Afghan successes on the battlefield, however, again did not lead to a permanent and enduring Afghan control of northern India. After Ahmad Shah had withdrawn from India, revolts started all over the lands controlled by the Afghans. Timur, the Afghan governor (*nizâm*) of the Panjab and Ahmad's son, could not do much to stop the tide, because new forces had emerged in the Indian continent, namely the Sikhs and the Marathas. The Sikhs from the Panjab constituted, as they still do, a religious-political group that adhered to the teachings of a fifteenth century leader, Guru Nanak (1469–1538), who combined Hindu and Islamic beliefs. In the late eighteenth and early nineteenth centuries they proved a formidable opponent to the Afghans and, after them, to the British. Their allies in the struggle against the Afghans were the Marathas. Their realm was founded in the late seventeenth century in Central India and they soon formed a major threat to the Mughals. They were staunch Hindus and opposed to the Islamic empires of the Mughals and Afghans. In 1758 the Marathas and Sikhs combined forces and drove the Afghans from Lahore. The Marathas even managed to take Peshawar, although only for a few months.

Pashtun rule in the Indian subcontinent seemed at an end. Even the Brahui leader in Kalat, Nasir Khan, revolted. He was only pacified when a matrimonial alliance was concluded with Ahmad Shah. Nasir Khan was allowed to remain in power, promising not to harbour any enemies of Ahmad Shah.

Ahmad Shah had to move fast in order to save his position. In 1759 he moved down into the Indian subcontinent. This was his fourth invasion since he took power in 1747. It also proved the most important and longest campaign. He retook Lahore and on 14 January 1761, after months of manoeuvring, the Afghans defeated the Marathas at Panipat, near Delhi. This was the momentous event that stopped the rising tide of the Marathas, although it did not lead to permanent Afghan control in India. Ahmad Shah soon left the country again to return to his beloved Qandahar.

The rise of Sikh power in the Panjab, however, at the cost of the Pashtuns, could no longer be stopped. Between 1762 and 1767, Ahmad Shah invaded India three more times. In 1762 he recaptured Lahore, defeated the Sikhs and destroyed much of Amritsar. In 1764 he again returned to India, to take Lahore, but the Sikhs were not really defeated. In 1766–7 the Afghans again captured Lahore, but again, it was a Pyrrhic victory. In the summer of 1767 Ahmad Shah returned to Qandahar, for the last time. Afghan control in the Panjab was still strong, but it was clear that their rule would not last.

At that time, a large-scale rising against the Pashtuns took place in Khurasan, and a desperate battle was fought outside Mashhad that was in the end won by Timur, the Afghan commander. Subsequently the Afghans laid siege to Mashhad and took the city after a number of months. Meanwhile, some Afghan troops marched southwest and took the town of Tabas, deep within Central Iran. To seal the surrender of the Persians of Khurasan, Shah Rukh gave one of his daughters in marriage to Timur, Ahmad Shah's son.

There were also problems with the Emirate of Bukhara, which claimed districts in the north. The Pashtuns, however, were still strong enough to withstand the Özbeks, and in the end a treaty was concluded that established the Amu Darya as the border between the two countries. To seal the agreement the Bukharan Amir presented Ahmad Shah with the *khirqa-yi mubâraka*, a fragment of the holy mantle of the Prophet.[5] The relic was taken to Qandahar and is to the present day kept in a specially built mosque, next to Ahmad Shah's mausoleum.

In June 1773 Ahmad Shah Durrani, or Ahmad Shah *Bâbâ* ('Father') as he came to be called, died at Murgha, in the Achakzay Toba hills east of Qandahar.[6] He was only about 50 years old. Sir Percy Sykes, one of the 'old hands' of the borderlands, described him with the following words: [7]

> a monarch whose high descent and warlike qualities made him peculiarly acceptable to his aristocratic and virile chiefs, as well as to his

5 However, there are other traditions as to its origin. See esp. McChesney 1991:222–7.
6 Elphinstone 1815:557.
7 Sykes 1940, I:367.

warlike subjects in general. In short, he possessed all the qualities that enabled him successfully to found the kingdom of Afghanistan.

Ahmad Shah lies buried at Qandahar in an octagonal mausoleum opposite the citadel, in the north of the town. It stands next to the small mosque that houses the *khirqa-yi mubâraka*.[8]

Ahmad Shah and His Kingdom

Political cohesion among the peoples of Afghanistan is, to say the least, a rare achievement. The rise to power of Ahmad Shah Durrani, who in the end controlled an area which stretched from east of the Indus to west of Mashhad, and from the Amu Darya in the north to the Indian Ocean in the south, therefore can be regarded as a minor miracle. How did this happen?

There can be no doubt that Ahmad was a charismatic person who could rally the unruly Pashtun groups behind his standard. It is also clear that he could make use of the decline of his two powerful neighbours, India and Iran. And thirdly, it is also evident that the Pashtuns were great warriors. They had proven so during their occupation of Iran in the 1720s. Another factor that contributed to the Durrani rise was the shift in economic power from the cities to the countryside, as discussed earlier.[9] Power was no longer the prerogative of the cities; the tribesmen roaming the countryside dominated the political arena. But was all this enough to create an empire that would endure, although less powerful and covering a smaller extent of land, to the present day?

To answer this question, it is necessary to study the structure of the Durrani empire. When doing so, it becomes obvious that its build-up was based on the structure of Pashtun society and geared towards conquest and the collection of booty and tribute. Ahmad Shah Durrani was first of all the leader of his own tribal confederacy, the Abdalis or, as they came to be called after their leader, the Durranis. He gave most of the important offices to his own tribesmen. To further win their support, he granted them special favours. He provided his kinsmen with land in the Qandahar region in return for the provision of armed horsemen for his army. The Qandahar area thus became thoroughly 'Durranized', the native people of other ethnic stock being forced to move. In the mid-eighteenth century there were, according to estimates, some 100,000 Durrani families, and they pro-

---

8   The mausoleum also contains, at least by 1979, the sceptre and helmet of the king.
9   Compare Olesen 1995:43.

vided some 6,000 horsemen.[10] For these men, they received their lands rent-free. He also instituted an advisory council of nine tribal leaders (seven of whom were Durrani and two Ghalji), which he consulted before any major decisions. He also refounded the city of Qandahar, in the centre of Pashtun land.[11] The new city of Qandahar was built some five km east of Old Qandahar and just north of the former Persian army camp. To enhance its prestige, the Cloak of the Prophet Muhammad was housed here, in a new mosque.

Yet all this would not ensure the survival of his rule, and vocal support from the side of the Durrani chiefs did not provide him with the means to extend his power. There was no way in which Ahmad Shah could force the Afghan tribes to pay taxes. To the contrary, he needed funds to 'buy' the allegiance of the chiefs. Ahmad Shah was therefore more or less forced to acquire wealth from beyond the Pashtun lands. According to Elphinstone, Ahmad Shah 'had the penetration to discover that it would require a less exertion to conquer all the neighbouring kingdoms, than to subdue his own countrymen'.[12] The largest part of the Durrani income consequently came from the Indian provinces along the Indus river, and from Kashmir. Ahmad Shah himself seems to have said that the west of his empire gave him his warriors, and the east gave him money.[13]

But even in the conquered lands, Ahmad Shah generally refrained from administering the lands directly. This was probably a conscious decision, namely not to attempt to administrate and directly control the conquered areas. Instead he forced the local rulers to collect taxes and wealth and to hand the treasures over to the Afghans. Thus, local potentates were mostly left in place. As described above, local princes were time and again reinstated as local governors after they had revolted. In this way, the Afghans did not need to administrate large extents of land. They solely used the force of their arms to compel others to pay tribute. The Afghans had clearly learnt from their disastrous attempt to rule Iran. Shah Rukh was kept in place in Mashhad; Indian governors continued to administrate Lahore.

The whole structure of Ahmad Shah's empire was therefore rather flimsy. It was built on military force that was needed to acquire the money to pay for it. Such a situation simply could not last. Without central authority that had the means to extend its power among its major constituent parts, namely the Pashtun tribes, the empire was doomed to fail. This is the main reason of the eventual decline of

---

10   See Adamec 1997:89–90. Elphinstone 1815 refers to 12,000 men.
11   The city was therefore also called *Ahmad Shâhi.*
12   Elphinstone 1815/1972, I:233.
13   Gankovsky 1981:86.

Ahmad Shah's empire. Whatever his charisma and influence, Ahmad Shah could not infringe upon the traditional rights of the Afghans, and especially the Pashtun groups. They only followed him if he could provide them with booty. Within traditional Pashtun society, he was regarded as the leader of the army. He had no rights as to the control of the tribes themselves, apart from that of his own, Durrani group. Among the tribal leaders, or Khans, he was a *primus inter pares*. This situation would not change for more than a hundred years. Until the end of the nineteenth century, Afghanistan remained in essence an amalgamation of tribes and tribal states, headed by the Durranis. Only during the reign of Amir ʿAbd al-Rahman Khan in the late nineteenth century, with the large influx of subsidies from the side of the British and without the attraction of unprotected lands beyond Afghanistan's borders, central authority would drastically infringe upon the power of the local potentates.

The Decline of the Kingdom

Timur was the son of Ahmad Shah Durrani's favourite wife. He was born in 1746 at Mashhad, one year before his father became king.[14] During his father's reign, he was often stationed in the Panjab although at the end he was governor of Herat, in the west. Here he still resided when his father died. Timur was the appointed heir, but his absence from Qandahar did weaken his position and this led to his elder brother, Sulayman Mirza, to take his father's place, with the support of his father-in-law and vizier of Ahmad Shah, Shah Wali Khan. Timur had to move fast and he soon managed to drive his brother to India, while Shah Wali Khan was executed.

Timur realized very well the weakness of his position. He lacked the authority and prestige that his father had built up over the years, and he was consequently far too dependent on the goodwill of the tribal leaders. In order to free himself from the power of these chiefs, he moved the capital in 1775/6 from Qandahar to Kabul, outside of Pashtun country.[15] Kabul became his summer capital, while during the winter he preferred Peshawar.[16] At Kabul he laid out the royal gardens some five km north of the old city, now long gone. He also surrounded himself with Tajik administrators and established a personal bodyguard of (Shiʿite) Qizilbash. It is no wonder that the

14   According to Elphinstone (1815:322), Timur's mother was the daughter of a chief of the Arabs who had settled near Jalalabad.
15   In Kabul he erected the *Bâlâ Hisâr-i pâyin*, the lower citadel, as opposed to the older *Bâlâ Hisâr-i bâlâ* (see Burnes 1834: I, 155; Noelle 1997:23).
16   Kabul was visited in 1783/1784 by George Forster (Forster 1798).

Pashtuns tended to regard him as pro-Persian, instead of pro-Afghan.[17] He may even have been less than proficient in Pashto, preferring to speak Persian instead. Elphinstone in 1815 wrote about him:[18]

> His situation did not lead him to adopt the character and manners of his countrymen; and he never seems to have been perfectly familiar with their language. While he was yet a youth, he was stationed in the Punjaub, and afterwards was appointed governor of Heraut, where the bulk of the inhabitants are Persians.

His unpopularity among the Pashtuns led to a series of revolts all over the empire. While Timur was thus engaged in consolidating his position among his own Pashtuns, the Sikhs were extending their influence in the Panjab. In 1781 they took Multan. The Afghans retook the city during the same year, but their position remained under threat. In the north the Afghans were also under attack following the accession in 1785 of the Özbek leader, Amir Murad of Bukhara, the founder of the Mangit dynasty. The Özbeks invaded northern Afghanistan, but although they were soon forced to withdraw, northern Afghanistan became virtually independent of Kabul control. In the west, Timur's forces could claim some successes by propping up the governorship of the blind Shah Rukh, grandson of Nadir Shah, against the rising tide of the Qajars.

In 1791 a dangerous attack on his position by Mohmand and Afridi Pashtuns from near Peshawar drove Timur to execute two of the main opponents, in spite of solemn assurances to the contrary, which cost him even more credit from the side of the Pashtun tribes.[19] He fell ill in the spring of 1793, on his way from Peshawar to Kabul, and he died in Kabul on 20 May, amidst rumours that he had been poisoned. His mausoleum can still be seen in the centre of Kabul, south of the river. He left 23 sons and 13 daughters.

The Collapse of the Afghan State

When Timur Shah died, his eldest son, Humayun, was governor of Qandahar and absent from the capital. He was the son of a Sadozay

17   In all this, there is a strange parallel with the brother of Cambyses, Bardiya, who around 522 BC was accused by the Persians of being a Mede, although in fact he was the son of Cyrus the Great, the founder of the Persian Achaemenid empire.
18   Elphinstone 1815:558. See also Caroe 1958:260.
19   The tribesmen wanted to replace Timur by Iskandar Khan, a son of Sulayman Mirza, Timur's brother.

mother. Another son, Mahmud, was governor of Herat and also away from Kabul, together with his full brother Hajji Firuz al-Din. They were the sons of a Popalzay mother. ʿAbbas, the governor of Peshawar and the son of an Ishaqzay mother, was not there either. The prize thus fell to two brothers who were in Kabul at the time. They were Zaman and Shujaʿ al-Mulk, born to a Yusufzay mother who was the favourite wife of Timur.

Zaman Shah, the eldest of the two and governor of Kabul, was the one who consequently succeeded in obtaining the throne. He did so with the support of the Barakzay leader, Payinda Muhammad Khan Muhammadzay, the son of Ahmad Shah's erstwhile vizier, Hajji Jamal Khan. Many of the other royal princes who were in Kabul at the time were imprisoned in the Upper Bala Hisar. The same fate also befell Humayun, who was first blinded.[20]

For the first few years Zaman Shah managed to thwart all attempts to push him from the throne. He removed many people from their hereditary posts and many of his subjects were executed. His position gradually weakened, however, especially as he failed to win the leaders of his own Durrani clan for his cause. Instead he surrounded himself with Shiʿite Qizilbash, who formed his bodyguard. Unrest was growing, and overall Durrani control was in decline.

In the west a new dynasty had come to the throne in Iran, namely the Qajars. The founder of the dynasty, Agha Muhammad Shah, took the city of Mashhad in 1796 and captured the aged Shah Rukh, the grandson of Nadir Shah. The hatred of the Qajars for Nadir Shah, who had pushed aside their ancestor Fath Ali Khan, was still manifest. Shah Rukh was tortured and killed, and the bones of Nadir Shah were dug up from his grave in Mashhad and brought to Tehran, to be buried again under one of the floors of the Qajar palace.[21] The presence of the new Persian rulers in Mashhad caused great anxiety in Kabul, since the Afghans feared for a further Persian advance to the east, towards the strategic city of Herat.

Agha Muhammad Shah, however, soon managed to placate the Afghans and even politely asked Zaman Shah to cede Balkh, so the Persians could advance upon the Amir of Bukhara. The whole plan collapsed when the Russians attacked the Persians in the Northwest. In 1797 the Persians completely withdrew from Khurasan when the Shah was assassinated. Mashhad thereupon passed under the control of Nadir Mirza, the son of Shah Rukh, but the Persian threat

---

20 Some of Timur's sons, in wretched condition, were met by Alexander Burnes in Kabul in 1832 (Burnes 1834: I, 156).

21 The remains of Nadir Shah were returned to Mashhad after the fall of the Qajars in 1925, and buried in a mausoleum close to the centre (completed in 1959).

remained, especially since Zaman Shah's half-brother Mahmud was inclined to accept Persian assistance in winning the Kabul throne. Throughout his reign, however, Zaman Khan was preoccupied with the Indian subcontinent and he ignored the threat in the west.

Zaman Shah was the last Afghan king to occupy Lahore. Three times he invaded the Panjab to stop the rising tide of the Sikhs. While still in India after his third invasion, however, the news reached him that his half-brother Mahmud was advancing towards Kabul. Shah Zaman hurriedly evacuated Lahore in February 1799, leaving the Sikh chief Ranjit Singh as his (nominal) governor. Zaman Shah now realized that the threat posed by Mahmud was serious, the more so since his half-brother was supported by Fath Khan, the son of Payinda Khan Muhammadzay, whom Zaman Shah had executed shortly before for treachery. Mahmud could also count on Durrani support because his mother was a Durrani, while Zaman Shah's mother belonged to the Yuzufzay Pashtuns from north of the Peshawar valley. Fath Khan himself was also a Durrani, of the Barakzay tribe, which Elphinstone in 1815 described as the most powerful of the Afghan tribes. Therefore, when Mahmud and Fath Khan joined hands, they soon, with the help of many Durranis from in and around Qandahar, defeated Zaman Shah. This occurred in 1800. Zaman was blinded and ended his life in 1844 as a British pensioner in Ludhiana.[22]

Mahmud Shah remained on the throne for only three years. He was ably supported by Fath Khan and he handsomely rewarded all his adherents. Mahmud's son Kamran was made governor of Qandahar, and his brother, Hajji Firuz al-Din, was appointed governor of Herat. Mahmud initially met with considerable success. In 1802 he subdued a large-scale rising of the Ghaljis, who at some moment had occupied Qandahar but who failed to take the fortress of Ghazni. Mahmud also managed to defeat the Özbeks from Bukhara, who were forced to withdraw across the Amu Darya. Twice he and his troops also had to deal with a tribal army led by Shuja', the brother of Zaman Shah. In spite of all these successes, however, Mahmud soon lost the support of his subjects in and around Kabul. He simply did not succeed in winning the support of larger groups. In the words of Mountstuart Elphinstone: 'his reign more resembled the temporary success of a military adventurer than the establishment of a regular government.'[23] Fath ʿAli Shah of Persia (r. 1797–1834), the

---

22 In 1832, Alexander Burnes (Burnes 1834 I:127) was shown a group of trees where Shah Zaman had been blinded. That was some three miles from Jagdalak, along the road between Kabul and Jalalabad.
23 Elphinstone 1815:580.

Illustration 14 *View from the ancient walls above Kabul upon the Bala Hisar (photograph: author, summer 1978).*

successor and nephew of Agha Muhammad Shah Qajar, in the meantime completed the Persian conquest of Khurasan, and took Mashhad in 1802. Nadir Mirza, the great-grandson of Nadir Shah, was captured and with 38 other members of his family taken to Tehran. They were all, bar one, executed.

In late 1802 Fath Khan left Kabul for a long campaign along the Indus, while Shah Mahmud remained behind in the capital. During Fath Khan's absence unrest grew in Kabul, and by June 1803 Shah Shujaʿ could enter Kabul as the new king, and Mahmud was imprisoned in the Upper Bala Hisar (Ill. 14). Shah Shujaʿ ul-Mulk, the seventh son of Timur Shah, ascended the throne, but this could not stop the decline of central authority in Afghanistan. Shah Shujaʿs years, as those of his brothers and half-brothers, were marked by continuous fighting. One of his particular problems was that before coming to the throne he had made many promises to local leaders in lieu of their support, and now the time had come to pay. Consequently Shah Shujaʿ had little money left for his army and for the maintenance of the state administration.

Soon after occupying the Kabul throne Shah Shujaʿ captured Qandahar, after Fath Khan had persuaded Kamran, Mahmud's son, to evacuate the place and retire to Herat. Fath Khan himself retired to his family possessions nearby. Qaysar Mirza, a son of Zaman Shah and nephew of Shah Shujaʿ, was appointed governor of Qandahar, but he rebelled various times, each time being reinstated by his uncle. Problems also rose in Kabul, where at some moment another son of Timur Shah, ʿAbbas Khan, was made king. During the confusion, Mahmud Shah managed to escape from the Upper Bala Hisar, an event that would have dire consequences later on.[24] Shah Shujaʿ re-established his authority in the city, but later, in 1808, while he was in Sind trying to reclaim the arrears in taxes, his nephew Qaysar Mirza was proclaimed king in Kabul. He and his supporters even managed to occupy Peshawar, but in the end Shah Shujaʿ also managed to subdue this revolt.[25] By the end of the year he defeated, near Qandahar, an army led by Mahmud Shah and Fath Khan. In January 1809 he finally returned to Peshawar, the traditional winter capital of the Afghan kings. All seemed well.

In June 1809, while still in Peshawar, Shah Shujaʿ received the famous British embassy led by Mountstuart Elphinstone (1779–1859). The delegation, accompanied by some 300 military, had left Delhi in October 1808 on instruction of Lord Minto, the British Governor-General, and it marked Afghanistan's inclusion into western politics. While in Peshawar, Elphinstone and Shah Shujaʿ concluded a treaty of 'eternal friendship.' The treaty was directed against the French and Persians, as part of the grand British strategy to contain Napoleon.[26] With the Treaty, the Afghans committed themselves to help the British if the French and Iranians would attack the Indian subcontinent. Although in the end the Treaty came to nothing, Elphinstone's visit led to the first full western report of Afghan history and society, *An Account of the Kingdom of Caubul*, which was first published in 1815 and has retained its value to the present day.

Shah Shujaʿ's position, however, was far weaker than it appeared. When Elphinstone left Peshawar, Shah Shujaʿ was confronted by yet another revolt headed by his half-brother, Mahmud. In the same year, in 1809, near Nimla along the road between Jalalabad and Kabul and not far from the place where his brother Shah Zaman had been blinded in 1800, Shah Shujaʿ was subsequently forced to fight a battle against Mahmud and his supporter, Fath Khan. Shah Shujaʿ had an

---

24 Sykes 1940:386 tells that Mahmud was escorted to Girishk by Dust Muhammad Khan, the later Amir of Afghanistan.

25 Qaysar Mirza was eventually murdered by his nephew, Kamran, the son of Mahmud.

26 The Treaty of Tilsit of 1805 between Napoleon and Alexander II of Russia included a plan to organize a joint expedition through Persia to India. In 1807, Jaubert, Napoleon's envoy, visited the Iranian Qajar king, Fath ʿAli Shah. However, when the Persians were defeated by the Russians at Arpatch, the Persians turned to the British. In 1809, when Elphinstone visited Peshawar, all danger to the British, imagined or not, was already averted.

army of some 15,000 men, and his opponent only some 2,000.[27] Still, Mahmud won the day and subsequently entered Kabul on an elephant, as the new king. Shah Shujaʿ fled to Qandahar, where he was again defeated, and then was taken as prisoner all the way to Kashmir. He eventually escaped and moved to the court of the Sikh ruler, Ranjit Singh in Lahore, where in 1813 he was forced to hand over his Kuh-i Nur diamond, but gained little in return. In 1818 he joined his blind brother, Zaman Shah, as a British pensioner.[28]

For the second time Mahmud was king in Kabul. Yet, the decline of the Afghan empire could not be stopped. These were the years of rapid ascendancy of the Sikhs under Ranjit Sing, the erstwhile governor of Lahore. They took the famous fortress of Attock along the Indus in 1813 when the Afghan army under Fath Khan was defeated outside the fort.[29] Multan in the southern Panjab fell in 1818 and the rich province of Kashmir was taken in 1819.[30]

Kabul control in the north of the country also disappeared. The various Özbek principalities were virtually independent and continuously at strife with each other, using Tehran, Herat, Bukhara and Kabul as tools in their internecine wars. By the early nineteenth century, a prominent role was played by the ruler of Tashqurghan, Qilich ʿAli. When he died in 1817, the Amir of Bukhara occupied parts of the north. After his withdrawal, power passed to the Özbek ruler of Qunduz, Murad Beg (r. 1817–40?). For a time he controlled most of North and Northeast Afghanistan, and also lands further to the north, across the Amu Darya. After his death, power reverted to one of the sons of Qilich ʿAli, Mir Wali, who from Tashqurghan controlled much of the north until 1850 when the area was finally brought back under Kabul control.

In the meantime, in Kabul, political strife continued, this time between the Popalzay under Shah Mahmud and his son, Kamran (the governor of Qandahar) on the one hand, and their erstwhile supporters, the Muhammadzay clan of the Barakzay tribe under Fath Khan, on the other. Developments reached a climax when in 1818 Fath Khan, while in Herat, was blinded by the Popalzay, and some months later tortured and killed. This was in fact a great blow to the Afghan state, since Fath Khan had virtually ruled the land since 1809.

---

27 Burnes 1834: II, 300.
28 The story of the Kuh-i Nur diamond is well known. It fell into the hands of the British in 1849 after the defeat of the Sikhs, and was subsequently given to Queen Victoria. It weighed 191 carats, but was cut down in Europe to 108 carats.
29 One of the Afghans fighting in this battle was the younger brother of Fath Khan, Dust Muhammad Khan, the later Amir of Afghanistan.
30 Dera Ghazi Khan along the Indus fell in the same year, followed two years later by Dera Ismaʿil Khan.

Although he had lost much territory in the east to the Sikhs, he had brought the provinces of Sind and Baluchistan back under the aegis of the Afghans, thus providing the Afghan rulers with some much needed tribute. During these years his Barakzay brothers occupied most of the important posts in the country. The direct cause for his downfall was his occupation in 1816 of the town of Herat. He did so upon the request of its governor, Hajji Firuz al-Din, who feared an attack from the side of Fath ʿAli Shah of Persia. However, Fath Khan's brother Dust Muhammad Khan was soon afterwards accused of having violated the governor's harem, which included one of Mahmud's sisters. Dust Muhammad Khan himself escaped, but his elder brother could not avoid Mahmud's wrath.

The Barakzay

Fath Khan's murder led to the general rising of his many brothers, including the youngest, Dust Muhammad Khan.[31] Together they were far more powerful than Shah Mahmud, and the latter was soon removed from the Kabul throne. He fled to Herat, which had become the power base of his son Kamran, where he ruled until 1829.[32]

In the first few years after the fall of Shah Mahmud, the Barakzay brothers (some 20 in total) tried to install a puppet regime of a Sadozay prince. They invited Shah Shujaʿ, but soon withdrew their support when he refused to obey their orders. They also invited Ayyub Mirza, another son of Timur Shah, but again they eventually removed him. The end result was that the Barakzay brothers carved out their own domains and, individually or in ever-changing coalitions, fought for the control of Kabul. At the same time they were confronted with the growing power of the Sikhs, who in 1823 defeated and killed one of the Barakzay brothers, Muhammad Aʿzam Khan, at the Battle of Nowshera, which resulted in the loss of Peshawar. Some stability in Afghanistan was only reached in 1826, when Dust Muhammad Khan, the youngest of Fath Khan's brothers, managed to outwit his rivals and was generally recognized as the ruler of Kabul.

Dust Muhammad Khan was born in 1792 of a Qizilbash mother. In his struggle for power he was consequently strongly supported by this Shiʿite, Persian-speaking ethnic group. Not only his mother was

---

31   For this important figure in the history of the country, see Lal 1846 and Noelle 1997.

32   He was succeeded in 1829 by his son, who in turn left most of the work to his vizier, Yar Muhammad Khan. Kamran was eventually killed in 1842.

Qizilbash, he also married a Qizilbash woman. Since the Qizilbash constituted a powerful group in Kabul, independent of the Pashtun tribes, he could thus find support both among his own Barakzay tribe and among the urban Qizilbash. In this way the control of Afghanistan passed from the Sadozay/Popalzay branch of the Durranis to the Muhammadzay/Barakzay branch. His rule was however restricted to Kabul and its direct environment, since Qandahar remained in the hands of his half-brothers,[33] and so did Peshawar, although under the ultimate rule of the Sikhs.[34]

When Dust Muhammad Khan took control in Kabul, at that time a town of some 60,000 people, Afghanistan had changed dramatically since the glorious years of Ahmad Shah Durrani. Most of the provinces in the Indian subcontinent, including Kashmir, the Panjab and Sind, had been lost and consequently the stream of funds formerly used to subsidize the Pashtun tribes had dried up. The rise of the Sikhs in the Panjab also precluded the possibility of military raids. In addition, the fall of the Sadozay and the crumbling of central authority had given the Ghaljis and other Pashtun tribes along the important trade routes between Qandahar, Ghazni, Kabul, Jalalabad and Peshawar more power. They could, and they did, control these routes and impose transit dues. In fact, during the first few years of his reign Dust Muhammad Khan was no more than one of the local warlords.

Even in Kabul his position was threatened. This time the British were involved. They supported their ally, the Sikh leader Ranjit Singh, and they were favourably inclined towards Shah Shuja', who had long realized that he could only reclaim the Kabul throne with Sikh assistance. In the early 1830s, and with Sikh support, Shah Shuja' subsequently tried to take Kabul, this time by way of Qandahar. He did so with the tacit approval of Captain C. W. Wade, the British Political Agent at the court of Ranjit Singh. In lieu of Sikh assistance, Shuja' officially handed over the administration of Peshawar to Ranjit Singh. The city was subsequently occupied in 1834, and the Peshawar *sardârs* took refuge with their half-brother in Kabul. Shah Shuja' laid siege to Qandahar in 1834, while he established his camp among the ruins of Old Qandahar just west of the city. His army included some 22,000 men, which was a formidable number. In the summer of the

33 These included Purdil, Kohandil, Sherdil, Mehrdil and Rahmdil. They were sons of a (Hotaki) Ghalji mother.
34 The Peshawar *sardârs* included Yar Muhammad Khan (who died in 1828) and Sultan Muhammad Khan. Two other, younger brothers were Pir Muhammad Khan and Sa'id Muhammad Khan. They are the ancestors of the Musahiban family, the rulers of Afghanistan from 1929 until 1978, also called the Yahya Khel, after Yahya Khan, the son of Sultan Muhammad.

same year, however, Shuja' was defeated by the army of Amir Dust Muhammad. In this way, the position of Dust Muhammad Khan in Afghanistan was strengthened, although his real influence among the Pashtun tribes was still negligible.

In 1836, while planning a war against the Sikhs, Dust Muhammad Khan had himself declared *Amir al Mu'minin* ('Commander of the Believers'). By assuming this title, Dust Muhammad clearly stated his claims: to rule his Muslim subjects and to lead them in war. The coronation was modelled after that of Ahmad Shah Durrani, thus showing that the Sadozay prince who had established the kingdom of Afghanistan was the model for his own rule. It is important to note that he still did not claim to be king (*Shâh*), as the Sadozay leaders had done, but was content with the title of Amir.[35] With his new title, he did, however, claim religious legitimacy, which he had also done when in the early 1830s he had forbidden the use of alcohol, thus driving the many Armenians and Jews out of the city. Military success followed soon. In April 1837, his son, Muhammad Akbar Khan, crushingly defeated the Sikhs at Jamrud, at the eastern entrance to the Khaybar Pass and just a few kilometres from Peshawar. At that moment, however, the Afghans stopped. They were apparently unwilling to try to take Peshawar from the Sikhs for fear of confronting the British, the Sikhs' allies. Instead, Dust Muhammad Khan sought assistance from the British, in the person of the new Governor-General, George Eden, Lord Auckland (1836–42), to counter the power of the Sikhs.[36]

35   Noelle (1997:17) tells that Dust Muhammad Khan was regularly reminded of his humble origins by one of his wives, a granddaughter of Timur Shah, who called him her 'slave'.
36   His sister, Emily Eden, kept a diary (Eden 1866).

16

War with Britain

The British were not inclined to give up the Sikhs in favour of the Afghans. Besides, there was anxiety in England about growing Russian influence in Siberia, Central Asia and Iran, and the British feared that the Russians might try to occupy Afghanistan and in this way disrupt their comfortable position in the Indian subcontinent. Here lay the seeds of what later came to be called the Great Game.

In 1837, Lord Auckland sent a Scotsman called Captain Alexander Burnes to Kabul.[1] He was despatched officially to arrange economic ties, but in fact to negotiate in a settlement between the Afghans and the Sikhs. Burnes was an old hand in Central Asia, for in previous years he had made a famous journey through Afghanistan to Bukhara.[2] When he arrived in Kabul in September of the same year, the negotiations at first went well, but in the end the Afghans were not prepared to relinguish their claims on Peshawar, as demanded by Auckland. The situation became more complex when in November 1837 the new Persian king, Muhammad Shah Qajar (r. 1834–48),[3] laid siege to Herat with active support of the Russians. At that time Herat was still ruled by Kamran, the son of Shah Mahsud and an opponent of Dust Muhammad Khan in Kabul. Kamran may happily have handed Herat over to the Persians, were it not for a young British officer, Lt. Eldred Pottinger, who happened to be in Herat at the start of the siege and prompted the Heratis and their Pashtun rulers to resist the Persians.[4]

While Herat was under siege and the Persians and their Russian advisers were expected soon to take the town and march on to Qandahar, there arrived in Kabul, in December 1837, a Russian (or

---

1 Burnes 1842.
2 Burnes 1834.
3 He had succeeded his father, Fath ʿAli Shah, in 1834.
4 Pottinger 1983. See also the historical novels by Maud Diver.

better: a Polish) envoy called Captain Ivan Viktorovich Vitkevich. He
carried various official letters, including one from the Russian ambassador in Tehran, Count Simulch Simonich. Vitkevich had travelled
from Iran, via Herat and Qandahar. Kohandil Khan, who was one
of the (half-)brothers of Dust Muhammad Khan and de facto ruler
of Qandahar, had most cordially welcomed him in his city and had
agreed to assist the Persians in the siege of Herat.[5] In this way he in
fact handed himself and his city over to the Persians and their Russian
allies. The arrival in Kabul of Captain Vitkevich and the news and
letters he brought with him put Dust Muhammad Khan in an impossible situation. His first objective was the recovery of Peshawar, for
which he had to oust the Sikhs. To do so, he needed the consent and
perhaps the support of the British. Burnes, on the other hand, could
not give any guarantee as to British approval, since his superiors were
keen on supporting the Sikhs. To put some pressure on the British,
Dust Muhammad Khan could welcome Vitkevich and start further
negotiations. However, this was a dangerous gamble, since he realized that it could antagonize the British even further. At the same
time, negotiations with the Russians would strengthen the position
of the Persians. Their capture of Herat and Qandahar would give
them and their Russian allies a very strong position as regard Kabul,
and Dust Muhammad might lose not only any chance of ever regain-
ing Peshawar, but also of losing his throne altogether. The negotations in Kabul dragged on for months, both Burnes and Vitkevich
being in constant, but slow contact with their superiors. In the
end, the situation proved to be irresolvable, and in April 1838,
both Burnes and Vitkevich had to leave Kabul, without either of
them having reached a successful agreement with Dust Muhammad
Khan.

This left the British with the danger of Herat and Qandahar falling
into the hands of the Persians and Russians. Lord Auckland subsequently ordered the occupation of Kharq Island in the Persian Gulf,
in June 1838, in order to put pressure on the Persians. This proved
to be a successful strategy, and the Qajar king was forced to lift
the siege, which he did on 9 September 1838. At the same time,
Auckland decided that the situation in the Northwest had become
too volatile, and that the problem of Afghanistan should be solved.
He wanted an Afghanistan that was led by a king who was
favourably inclined towards the British and who would not antagonize the Sikhs, the British allies. He thus decided to put Shah Shujaʿ
back on the Kabul throne. Shujaʿ had been a British pensioner for a
long time, and some years before had openly renounced any claims

---

5   Thus repeating earlier promises (Pottinger 1983:47).

on the city of Peshawar. He was therefore, in the eyes of the British, the most attractive candidate for the Kabul throne.

This policy was actively supported, if not pushed, by the Ulsterman William Hay Macnaghten (1793–1841), at that time Chief Secretary to the (British) Indian Government. In the summer of 1838, Macnaghten visited Lahore and he prompted Ranjit Singh and Shah Shuja' to reiterate their earlier agreements. These referred to the relinguishing of all Afghan claims on the Sikh-controlled lands west of the Indus (including Peshawar), and to Sikh support for Shah Shuja' to reclaim the throne of Kabul. The British in fact guaranteed this agreement, and it subsequently came to be known as the Tripartite Treaty,[6] which would lay the ground for the First Anglo-Afghan War.[7]

The First Anglo-Afghan War

Upon the conclusion of the Tripartite Treaty, Lord Auckland decided upon prompt action, and on 1 October 1838 he issued the Simla Manifesto, which openly stated that Shah Shuja' was to reoccupy the Afghan throne with active British and Sikh support.[8] Preparations were made for a military campaign, and in November 1838 a large military force, the Army of the Indus, was assembled at Firuzpur, in the extreme northwest of British controlled India. As 'Envoy and Minister on the part of the Government of India at the court of Shah Soojahool-Moolk', the army was accompanied by William Macnaghten. Alexander Burnes, now nicknamed 'Bukhara Burnes', would also march with the army, officially appointed to act, under supervision of Macnaghten, as envoy to the state of Kalat, south of the Bolan Pass.

The Army of the Indus included some 20,000 troops and almost 40,000 camp followers and it was under overall command of General Sir John Keane. It was a huge caravan, with about 30,000 camels to carry all the food, ammunition and other necessaries, including bottles of wine and boxes of cigars. There was also a smaller and separate force that was led by Colonel Wade and Muhammad Timur, Shah Shuja''s son, which would march directly from Peshawar to Kabul, rather than taking the long route via Qandahar.

Both in England and in India there was strong opposition to the whole affair, right from the beginning. To many people it was evident

6 For the text of this Treaty (more accurately to be known as the Triplicate Treaty), see Kaye 1874, Vol. I, 332–5.
7 For the First Anglo-Afghan war, see Buist 1843, Kaye 1874, Stocqueler 1843, Yapp 1962, 1963, 1964, 1980.
8 For the text, see Sykes 1940, II:339–43.

that, in spite of assurances to the contrary, the Sikhs would not commit their troops to an invasion of Afghanistan. At the same time, it was felt that Shah Shuja', once in power, would retract his promises as to his claims on Peshawar. However, the die was cast and on 10 December 1838 the Army of the Indus left Firuzpur to reach Quetta, northwest of the Bolan Pass, on 26 March 1839. Exactly one month later, on 25 April, Shah Shuja' entered Qandahar, upon which the *sardârs*, Dust Muhammad Khan's half-brothers, fled to the west. The army stayed in Qandahar for some two months to recuperate from the exertions during the long march from India. On 27 June the British left Qandahar again and marched north towards Kabul. The first serious opposition was met near Ghazni, where the British defeated an Afghan army led by Ghulam Haydar Khan, one of the sons of Dust Muhammad Khan. A few days later, on 23 July, the British took Ghazni after a spectacular attack on the Kabul gate.[9] Finally, on 6 August, the British arrived near Kabul, and on the next day they entered the Afghan capital where Shah Shuja' was installed on the throne. Early September, the British position in Kabul was further strengthened with the arrival of the troops under Wade who had marched from Peshawar. Wade's position had been particularly difficult since the death on 29 June of Ranjit Singh, the Sikh leader. However, all seemed well, and in the autumn, Shah Shuja' and many British officials left Kabul for Jalalabad, to enjoy the warmer climate.

Dust Muhammad Khan had fled to the Özbeks in the north, to the court of Mir Wali of Tashqurghan. The Mir, however, refused him any help, whereupon the hapless Amir was forced to go further north to the court of the Amir of Bukhara, Nasr Allah (*r.* 1827–60). There he remained virtually a prisoner, together with two of his sons, Afzal and Akbar.

In the eyes of the British all seemed well in Kabul and many of their troops returned to India. Also General Keane left, and he was replaced by General Sir Willoughby Cotton. The British received further good news when the Russians failed to take Khiva in ancient Choresmia. The Great Game seemed won before anything dramatic had happened. To further secure their position, the British built a cantonment in Kabul and entrenched themselves at various other places in Afghanistan, including Bamiyan, Charikar, Qal'at-i Ghilzay, Qandahar and Jalalabad.

The following year, 1840, brought further successes to the British. Dust Muhammad Khan escaped from Bukhara in August and

---

9   General Keane was consequently named Lord Keane of Ghuznee. The fall of Ghazni was heralded as the first military success in the reign of the young Queen Victoria.

returned to Afghanistan. He joined forces with the Özbek Beg of Tashqurghan, Mir Wali, who this time was willing to help, but the Afghans were defeated on 18 September in Bamiyan. On 2 November, however, he gained a victory over the British at Parwan, close to Kabul, when he was supported by the Kohistanis from north of the city. Yet he realized that his position was hopeless, and on 4 November he rode into the British camp and surrendered. Some days later he was sent off to India to become a British pensioner. That winter, the court of Shah Shuja' and many British again resided in Jalalabad, enjoying the relative warmth of the place. Afghanistan seemed well on the way to being 'pacified'. That this was due mainly to British weapons and especially British gold remained a point not realized by those in charge.

Impending Doom

In 1841, the British position in Afghanistan deteriorated. British troops were increasingly being used in various campaigns against the Afghans, mostly in order to enforce taxation. Moreover, the British decided to cut the allowances to various groups, and even a smaller allowance was subject to inflation brought about by the presence of so many foreign troops in the country. The uprisings often broke out spontaneously, in different districts, without any coordination. The direct reasons for unrest, apart from taxation, were often internal. It could be a change in local leadership following the restoration of the Sadozay, or the change in stature of the local leaders because of reduced accessibility to the Kabul court, or even the reduced importance of tribal levies because of the presence of British troops.

There were other problems. Herat under Kamran and his vizier Yar Muhammad drew large amounts of British subsidies, but the Afghans continued to negotiate with the Persians and with disaffected Afghans.[10] The Herati rulers, in spite of the long siege of 1837–8, wanted Persian help in order to dislodge the British from Afghanistan in return for the surrender of Herat. The position of the British mission in Herat became impossible, and in the end, in 1841, the British representative, Major D'Arcy Todd, was recalled from Herat.

The British retreat from Herat was only a minor setback. A major problem were the British themselves. Early 1841, General Cotton was replaced as military commander by the nearly 60-year-old Major-General William Elphinstone (1782–1842), a cousin of the Mountstu-

---

10 This made Yar Muhammad into one of the most hated figures among the British (Pottinger 1983:29).

art Elphinstone who had visited Peshawar in 1809. He was far too old for the job; his last experience in active duty was as commander of the 33rd Foot at Waterloo. From all accounts it is evident that Elphinstone was not up to what was expected of him, and indecisiveness and physical ailments prevented him from taking necessary action. He has been described as 'the most incompetent soldier that was to be found among the officers of the requisite rank'.[11] In August 1841 he wisely asked his superiors in India to be relieved of his duties. This request was granted some months later, and from that date Elphinstone awaited a chance to depart for India.

Another problem for the British was the position of William Macnaghten. For long he had been hoping for promotion, and any unrest in Afghanistan, he felt, would jeopardize his chances, and his reports were therefore in general more positive than warranted. The next in line for political command, Alexander Burnes, for long felt unheeded by Macnaghten and refrained from taking any action. Eventually, in August 1841, the formal appointment of Macnaghten as Governor of Bengal was sent to Kabul. However, when he received the long-awaited letter the roads back to India were closed by the winter weather and by the growing number of Afghans blocking the Kabul–Peshawar highway. He would never take up his new post.

A further problem was the location of the British cantonment in Kabul. It measured some $1,000 \times 600$ metres and was built just north-east of the old town, in marshy area along the northern banks of the Kabul river.[12] It lay very close to the *Bâgh-i Shâh*, the Royal Garden, along the road from Kabul to Kohistan. It was overlooked from two sides by mountain ridges, and the British themselves regarded this position as absolutely indefensible. The location was even more precarious since the commissariat and ammunition stores were kept outside the ramparts, and the residence of Macnaghten and his staff also lay outside the cantonment, on the other side.

The End

One of the most important Afghan leaders was Muhammad Akbar Khan, the eldest son of Amir Dust Muhammad Khan. In the autumn of 1841 he fled from Bukhara, where he had taken refuge together with his father, and went to Kabul, passing through Afghanistan that

11   Compare Morris 1973:102.
12   Its exact location along the modern road from the city to the airport can still easily be established with the help of numerous drawings and paintings that were made at the time (compare Pottinger 1983). The canal that according to contemporary maps ran between the Kabul river and the cantonment is still there.

by the day was becoming more difficult to control by the British. He hoped to link up with the Pashtuns living east of Kabul, since he was married to the daughter of one of the local leaders in that area. Before Akbar Khan arrived in Kabul, however, on 2 November, an attack had been made on Alexander Burnes and his brother, Lt. Charles Burnes, and both were killed by an angry mob in their compound in the centre of the city.[13] Paradoxically, the attack seems to have been instigated by former supporters of Shah Shujaʿ who had become dissatisfied with their king.[14] The British who were entrenched in their cantonment just outside of Kabul did not react, and the Afghans in Kabul, surprised about the absence of any British reprisals, now felt that they were strong enough to push the foreigners out of their country.

Akbar Khan arrived in Kabul on 25 November. He soon established his position among the leaders of the opposition against the British. Contacts were also laid with the British themselves, who had come to the realization that their hold on Kabul had evaporated, and they were in fact under siege. On 11 December, the British consequently signed an agreement with the Afghans that stipulated their withdrawal east of the Indus. What happened during the following days is not clear. It seems that the British heard that the Afghans were not united, and that some of the Afghans, dependent on the king, realized that with the retreat of the British the position of Shah Shujaʿ would be hopeless. Not all of the Afghans were apparently eager to see the return of Dust Muhammad Khan and his sons and preferred to have a Sadozay prince on the throne. The British tried to make use of this split in the Afghan ranks. However, Muhammad Akbar Khan found out about the British plans, and at a meeting on 23 December between the Afghan leaders and the British, just outside the cantonment, Macnaghten and others were killed.

The position of the British was now completely hopeless. The 16,500 people in the cantonment were stranded, and a new agreement, underlining the stipulations of the 13 December treaty, was signed on 1 January 1842.[15] The famous Retreat from Kabul started a few days later, on 6 January 1842, when a total of some 16,500 military and camp followers left the cantonment.[16] The story of the 'Death March' has been told and retold.[17] The column was attacked from all sides, sometimes with the active support of the Afghan leaders who had shortly before guaranteed a safe passage to the

13 By that time Burnes had been appointed Resident in Kabul.
14 Noell 1997:49–56.
15 For the text of this Treaty, and various drafts, see Sykes 1940, II:344–51.
16 Including some 700 Europeans and almost 4,000 Indian soldiers.
17 Compare Dupree 1967 and Pottinger 1983.

British. It is unlikely that they fully controlled the Ghaljis along the route, but on the other hand, Akbar Khan and the other chiefs realized that the column, once it reached Jalalabad and its British garrison, would still form a dangerous threat. They also knew very well that their authority depended on the successes they could offer their Pashtun followers: defeating the British, driving those 'infidels' out of their land, and forcing them to leave behind all the food and other goods that they had, was truly a success!

Marching through the winter landscape east of Kabul, the British and their followers were under constant attack. Many British officers surrendered and were taken hostage.[18] On 12 January, the famous last stand was made near the village of Gandamak, some 45 km southwest of Jalalabad, where the remaining British were killed.[19] As tradition tells, the only survivor was Dr W. Brydon, who arrived in Jalalabad on 13 January. The news of the British disaster in Afghanistan hit hard, and one person who must have been pleased to leave India was Lord Auckland, who on 28 February 1842 was replaced as Governor-General by Lord Ellenborough.[20]

The struggle in Afghanistan continued. The Afghans took Ghazni from the British on 10 March. However, Qalʿat-i Ghilzay remained in British hands, and so did Qandahar under General Nott.[21] Meanwhile, in Kabul, the Afghan leaders forced Shah Shujaʿ to lead an Afghan force against the British at Jalalabad. However, on 5 April just outside the Kabul Bala Hisar he was killed when he rode out with his followers. Spring was now coming to the area, and with it the opening up of the mountain passes. At around that time, a British force from Peshawar, headed by Major-General Pollock, forced the Khaybar Pass and on 18 April reached Jalalabad. The unity of the Afghans, if there ever was one, was now crumbling. Many of the Ghaljis went back to their villages. Fighting among the Afghan leaders also did not help. Nominally the Afghans were led by Shujaʿ's son, Fath Jang, but he did not wield any real power. The Popalzay

18   Compare Eden 1866. The hostages included General Elphinstone, who died on 23 April and was eventually buried at Jalalabad.

19   In 1879, the bones of those who were killed at that place were still all lying scattered over the hilltop (or so it was assumed). They were collected and buried under a cairn, on top of the hill (the 'Forty-Fourth Hill'; Sykes 1940, II:36; Trousdale 1984:16).

20   Auckland continued his career as First Lord of the Admiralty. He died in 1848. Lord Ellenborough became President of the Board of Control of the East India Company after the 1841 elections, and had himself appointed to succeed Auckland as Governor-General in India.

21   General Nott was assisted by the Political Officer, Major Henry Creswicke Rawlinson, the same man who copied the famous Behistun text of the Achaemenid king, Darius, between 1836 and 1847.

Durranis supported him, but the more powerful Barakzay did not. The only Pashtun left with some authority was Muhammad Akbar Khan, who on 29 June was appointed vizier.[22]

In the summer, the British decided to take revenge and to capture, once again, the Afghan capital. Early August 1842 General Nott and his 6,000 men left Qandahar en route to Kabul.[23] Between 28–31 August 1842, they fought a series of battles against the Afghans near Muqqur and early September they retook Ghazni. Here they removed the gates of Mahmud of Ghazni's tomb, as instructed by Lord Ellenborough. These instructions, it should be noted, were based on an earlier understanding between Shah Shuja' and Ranjit Singh. It said that the first 'should deliver up the sandal-wood gates at the shrine of the Emperor Mahmood, – being the same which were brought from Somnat, in India, when that destroyer smote the idol, and the precious stones fell from his body.'[24] They apparently thought that these doors were the gates of the Temple of Somnath, plundered by Mahmud some eight hundred years before![25] On 19 September Nott entered Kabul, just a few days after the arrival of Pollock and his 20,000 men from Jalalabad. For some days the British troops plundered the town and many Afghans were executed. Parts of the bazaar were demolished.

The British finally withdrew from Kabul on 12 October. With them went Fath Jang and his uncle, the blind Zaman Shah. Fath Jang's younger brother, Shahpur, was left on the throne, but he was soon replaced by Muhammad Akbar and sent back to India where he joined his brother.

Twelve days before the British finally left Kabul, on 1 October 1842, Lord Ellenborough proudly proclaimed:[26]

> Our victorious army bears the gates of the temple of Somnath in triumph from Afghanistan, and the despoiled tomb of Sultan Mahmud looks upon the ruins of Ghazni. The insult of eight hundred years is at last avenged. The gates of the temple of Somnath, so long the memorial of your humiliation, are become the proudest record of your national glory, the proof of your superiority in arms over the nations beyond the Indus.

22 Fath Jang surrendered to the British on 1 September, at Gandamak.
23 The evacuation was assisted by Agha Khan Mahallati and his troops. He was the ancestor of the present-day leader of the Isma'ilis (Agha Khan IV).
24 Burnes 1834: I, 175.
25 These gates are now in the National Museum, New Delhi, after having collected dust in Agra for more than a century.
26 Sykes 1940, II:59.

The Second Reign of Dust Muhammad Khan

After their debacle the British were now convinced that Dust Muhammad Khan was the only Afghan leader who could keep the country
under some form of control and thus protect the northwestern gate-
ways to India against the Russians. The Amir was thus allowed to
return to his country, but he only did so after first sending four of his
sons in advance, apparently to support his eldest son, Muhammad
Akbar, but there may also have been some concern as to Akbar's
loyalty. All went well, however, and Dust Muhammad Khan, as *Amir-
i Kabir*, re-entered Kabul to occupy the throne which he had been
forced to vacate in the autumn of 1839.

His most famous son was the above mentioned Muhammad Akbar
Khan, the hero of the war against the British. He was young, ambitious, anti-British and full of vigour after his successes in driving out
the *ferenghi*. Following the restitution of the Muhammadzay to the
Kabul throne he wanted to invade the Indian subcontinent. His father
withheld him from doing so, but all this did not improve relations
between the two, especially when the British annexed Sind in 1843.
Before the animosity between father and son could come to a head,
however, Akbar Khan suddenly died, in February 1847, aged 29.
Soon rumours spread that the jealous Dust had poisoned his popular
son.[27]

Whatever the feelings of his subjects, Dust Muhammad remained
in control. During the twenty years of his second reign, between 1843
and 1863, he succeeded in gaining effective command over many
parts of the country that had slipped away from central control in
previous years. From 1845, and especially after 1849, he organized
a series of campaigns north of the Hindu Kush.[28] Most of the towns
in Lesser Turkistan had been virtually independent for many years,
although most of them owed allegiance to the Kabul chiefs since the
time of Ahmad Shah Durrani. The various towns were ruled by
Özbek chiefs or *Amir*s. Important places were, and are, Qunduz in
the east, Tashqurghan (now known as Khulm) and Haybak (modern
Samangan) further to the west; Mazar-i Sharif and Balkh along the
Balkhab; and in the west the four towns of Maymana, Sar-i Pul,
Andkhuy and Shibarghan.

In 1849, Muhammad Akram Khan, one of Dust Muhammad
Khan's sons, occupied Balkh. Akram Khan was made governor and

---

27 Sykes 1940:63 tells that a Hindu doctor poisoned him when he was about to
arrest his father and claim the throne.
28 Grevemeyer 1982, Holdsworth 1959, Lee 1996.

upon his death in 1852 he was suceeded by a half-brother, Muhammad Afzal Khan. Afghan control spread gradually, and by 1863, when Dust Muhammad Khan died, only the district of Maymana in the northwest and Badakhshan in the northeast of the country were still independent of Kabul rule. In the south, Dust Muhammad Khan managed to subdue two important Ghalji tribes, namely the Hotaki and Tokhi, northeast of Qandahar. The town of Qandahar itself was regained in November 1855, after the death of his half-brothers, Mihrdil Khan and Kohandil Khan, in March and August of the same year.

Dust Muhammad appointed many of his sons as governors of the various provinces. Ghulam Haydar became the governor of Qandahar in September 1856, and his full brother Sher ʿAli Khan was appointed governor of Kabul, after having been governor of Ghazni. They collected the revenue and also had their own military following. In fact, they were virtually independent. Leaving his sons in virtual control of their provinces was an integral part of Dust Muhammad Khan's policy. It was a balancing act between, on the one hand, using his many sons as the respected and feared governors of the subject lands, and on the other hand the risk of his sons revolting against Kabul rule. On another level, Dust Muhammad may have relished the idea of his sons watching each other, thinking twice before individually revolting against their father.

Throughout his reign, the relations with the British slowly improved. This was the time of the so-called 'Masterly Inactivity' of the British Indian authorities, although Peshawar fell into British hands in 1849 when they defeated the Sikhs. The existing borders were recognized by both parties in the Anglo-Afghan Treaty of Peshawar, which was signed on 30 March 1855. The signators were Sir John Lawrence, by that time the highest British official in the northwest of the Indian subcontinent, and Ghulam Haydar, the heir apparent of Afghanistan. Relations between Afghanistan and British India were further strengthened with the Anglo-Afghan Treaty of Friendship, which was signed on 26 January 1857.

The new rapprochement between Afghanistan and British India was instigated by new Iranian threats from the west. In 1856 the Persians under Nasir ad-Din Shah (*r.* 1848–96) occupied Herat, which up till then had been governed by an Afghan governor who was independent of Kabul control. The British feared that a war between Iran and Afghanistan would ultimately lead to further Russian advances, and they were now convinced that they needed a strong Afghanistan to secure the British Indian borders. The Treaty of 1857 included a large subsidy to the Amir and the provision of weapons. It furthermore allowed for a British legation under Major H. B. Lumsden to be established in Qandahar, to keep a close eye on what would happen in Herat. In addition, non-European representatives were established in Kabul.

The Persian occupation of Herat ultimately led to a three-month war with England, as a result of which the Persians were forced to retreat, although the new Barakzay governor of the town, a nephew of Dust Muhammad Khan, still recognized the Iranian Shah as his overlord. However, the British were in no position to put further pressure on the Shah, because of their own dire situation in India caused by the Indian Mutiny. This general uprising in India against British rule, which started in May 1857, was a real test of Afghan–British relations. Although put under pressure from all Afghan sides to occupy Peshawar and advance further west, Dust Muhammad Khan managed to keep Afghanistan out of the conflict. This saved the British position in the northwest of the Indian subcontinent, and also led to further British confidence in the Amir.

For some years, until 1860, the Persians maintained a strong presence in the Northwest of Afghanistan. When the Persians finally withdrew, after having tried to subdue the Tekke Türkmen in Marw and the city-state of Maymana, they left a vacuum, which on 27 May 1863 led to Dust Muhammad Khan finally taking Herat. Some weeks later, on 9 June, he died.[29] If one Afghan leader may be accredited with the completion of the state of Afghanistan as we know it today, it certainly must by Dust Muhammad Khan. Much of his work would be undone in the years to follow, but in 1880 his grandson, Amir 'Abd al-Rakhman Khan, could build upon a tradition that had been firmly established by his grandfather, both among the Afghans and among the British, Persians and Russians.

Yet it should be realized that the incorporation of the north of the country and of Herat in the west were not welcomed by all sections of the local population. The spread of Kabul control was in fact an extention of Pashtun control. In the north, the spread of central authority led to the fall of the Özbek leaders and the imposition of Pashtun rule upon the local population, mostly Özbek or Tajik. In the west, the new Pashtun rulers of the Sunnite creed came to dominate a Persian-speaking, mainly Shi'ite population. A Hungarian traveller, the famous Arminius Vámbéry, who reached Herat some two months after its fall described the feelings of despair of the Heratis.[30]

29 He was buried at Herat near the Gazirgah.
30 Vámbéry 1864; see also Marvin 1885:45.

Sher ʿAli

After the death of three of his 27 sons, namely Akbar Khan (1847), Ghulam Haydar (1858) and Akram Khan (1852), Dust Muhammad Khan had appointed one of his younger sons, Sher ʿAli Khan, born in 1823, as his successor. He was the full brother of Muhammad Akbar Khan and Ghulam Haydar, and the son of Dost Muhammad's favourite wife, Bibi Khadija, who herself belonged to an important Durrani family. Yet it was only to be expected that many other sons of Dust Muhammad Khan would contest Sher ʿAli's accession to the Kabul throne.

Main opposition came from the side of two sons born by a Bangash wife. The Bangash are a Pashtun tribe, presently living in Pakistan, south of Peshawar, who never played an important role in Afghan history. Their status was therefore fairly low. The two brothers were Muhammad Afzal Khan, born in 1811, and Muhammad Aʿzam Khan, born in 1818. In fact, Muhammad Afzal Khan was Dust Muhammad's eldest son, but no doubt because of the relatively humble origins of his mother, his father did not accept him as heir-apparent. Both brothers held important positions in North Afghanistan during Dust Muhammad Khan's lifetime, and when the Amir died, the two brothers rebelled against their half-brother and started years of fratricidal warfare. At first they were unsuccessful. The younger brother, Aʿzam Khan, was defeated and forced to flee to India, while the elder brother was thrown into prison. However, this was not the end of the story, for in 1866 Muhammad Afzal's son, called ʿAbd al-Rahman Khan, defeated Sher ʿAli and put his father on the throne. Afzal Khan's reign was, however, of short duration, since he died on 7 October 1867 and he was succeeded by his full brother, Aʿzam Khan. However, in January 1869 Sher ʿAli, with the help of his son, Yaʿqub Khan, and with financial assistance from the British, returned to Kabul and regained the throne. Aʿzam fled to Iran where he died in October of the same year, while ʿAbd al-Rakhman Khan was forced to flee to Mazar-i Sharif and eventually even further north.[31] Sher ʿAli's position was now secure.

Sher ʿAli regained the Kabul throne at a time of rapid Russian advances in South Central Asia. In 1865 the Russians had taken Tashkent; in 1868 they occupied Samarqand, and in 1869 Bukhara became a vassal state of the Russians. Sher ʿAli feared for this

---

31 Eventually he arrived in Tashkent, which was held by the Russians under General Kaufmann.

increased Russian influence and asked for a meeting with the British viceroy. This resulted in the Ambela Conference of March 1869 with the Governor-general, Lord Mayo. The Afghans asked British assurances of assistance in case of a Russian attack on Afghanistan. The Amir also wanted the support of the British for his son and intended successor, ʿAbd Allah Jan. The British, however, did not want to give any hard assurances. This was still the time of the Masterly Inactivity and they did not want to interfere directly in Afghan affairs. However, they promised to provide the Amir with financial and military support. Furthermore, they decided upon the demarcation of Kabul rule, thus making sure where Russia ended and Afghanistan began. Negotiations were started with the Russians, and in 1873 both parties agreed on the Amu Darya as the northern boundary of Afghanistan.[32] The year before, General Frederic Goldsmid had toured Sistan at the invitation of both Persia and Afghanistan in order to mediate in their border dispute. The outcome, however, was rather disappointing to Afghanistan. The so-called Goldsmid Award allocated Sistan east of the Hilmand to Afghanistan and west of the Hilmand to Iran. In this way, Afghanistan lost the most fertile part of the area. As a result, the relationship between the Amir and the British went sour again.

In the following years Sher ʿAli instigated some internal reforms. Land revenue was collected in cash and no longer partly in kind. He also tried to stop the delegation of tax collecting to the governors. Contrary to his father, he was less inclined to delegate power to his sons. The payment of the regular troops was also changed, and they were all paid in cash, directly, and no longer by the villages where they were garrisoned. Moreover, the soldiers were provided with uniforms. In this way, a standing army was created of some 56,000 men, most of them Ghaljis. There were also other attempts at modernization. Modern rifles were being made in Kabul, and stamps were printed for the postal service between Kabul and Peshawar (1871). There were even two newspapers being circulated in Kabul.

Yet, dynastic problems continued to haunt Afghan politics. A bitter strife developed between Sher ʿAli and his son, Muhammad Yaʿqub Khan. In 1870, he fled to Persia with his full brother, Muhammad Ayyub Khan. Father and son were reconciled after Yaʿqub Khan had occupied Herat in 1871, but in 1874, when Sher ʿAli appointed another son, ʿAbd Allah Jan (AD 1862–78), as heir apparent, Yaʿqub Khan was thrown into a Kabul prison where he would remain until 1879. His brother Ayyub Khan failed in his attempt to help his

32 The so-called Granville–Gorchakoff Agreement.

brother, and was forced to return to Persia. When the British tried to intercede in favour of Ya'qub Khan, the Amir regarded this as another example of the negative British influence in the region.

The Second Anglo-Afghan War

In 1874 Benjamin Disraeli became Prime Minister in England, with Lord Salisbury as Secretary of State for India. They ended the period of Masterly Inactivity along the Afghan border. Up till then, the British had refused to give hard guarantees of military assistance in case of a Russian attack on the country. By the mid-1870s, however, British fears of Russian influence in the region were growing. In 1873 the Russians took Khiva, south of the Aral Sea, and in 1876 they occupied the Emirate of Khokand. It was clear that they would soon descend upon the Türkmen north of Iran and Afghanistan, and this would bring them within easy reach of Herat.

When the Governor-General, Lord Northbrook, refused to demand from Sher 'Ali the stationing of British observers in Herat, he was replaced in 1876 by Lord Lytton, an advocate of the so-called Forward Policy. He stated:[33]

> Afghanistan is a state far too weak and barbarous to remain isolated and wholly uninfluenced between two great military empires . . . We cannot allow (Sher 'Ali) to fall under the influence of any power whose interests are antagonistic to our own.

These aggressive words were soon followed by action. On 8 December 1876 the British occupied Quetta, close to Qandahar, and turned it into a military base. In the same year, Queen Victoria was proclaimed Empress of India, thus stressing Britain's commitment to its Indian possessions. Sher 'Ali still refused British residents in Afghanistan, and negotiations, in which Afghanistan demanded British guarantees of military assistance, dragged on.

The situation became even more explosive in 1878. In the spring of that year, Russian troops marched to the gates of Istanbul and the British fleet was ordered to anchor in the Sea of Marmora. An all-out war between the two superpowers seemed imminent, and Russian troops in Central Asia prepared for a march on Afghanistan and India. However, the Congress of Berlin averted a world war, and also averted Afghanistan being drawn into a confrontation between the two European superpowers. However, before the Treaty of Berlin was

---

33 Gregorian 1969:111–12. See also Olesen 1995:25.

signed, preparations had been made for the expected confrontation
in the East, and some of these could not be stopped.

On 22 July 1878, there arrived in Kabul, apparently out of the
blue, a Russian envoy sent by the Russian General Kaufmann in
Tashkent. His name was General Stolietov. His presence in Kabul
greatly embarrassed Sher 'Ali, and the British even more strongly
demanded permission to send a mission to Kabul. When the Amir
did not answer the British,[34] they sent General Neville Chamberlain
with a small force to the British–Afghan border west of Peshawar.
Chamberlain and his escort of some 1,000 men were subsequently
refused entry to the country, upon which the British set an ultima-
tum. When the Afghans did not react, the Second Anglo-Afghan war
had started.

On 21 November 1878, British troops entered Afghanistan and
they occupied Kabul on 8 January.[35] Sher 'Ali fled to the north
without receiving any assistance from the Russians, and soon died
near Balkh, on 21 February 1879.

> And yet when I think of Shir Ali as he lies in his sepulchre low,
> How he died betrayed, heart broken, 'twixt infidel friend and foe,
> Driven from his throne by the English, and scorned by the Russian,
>   his guest,
> I am well content with the vengeance, and I see God works for the
>   best.[36]

Ya'qub Khan, released from prison, took his father's place and he
and his commander-in-chief went to the British who camped at Gandamak, to sign the so-called Gandamak Treaty, on 26 May 1879.[37]
In this Treaty of 'eternal peace and friendship' Afghanistan relin-
quished the right to pursue an independent foreign policy and
allowed for a permanent British mission to be stationed in Kabul. In
return, the British guaranteed support against any attacks from
outside and provided the Amir with an annual subsidy.[38] Furthermore, some districts presently along the Pakistani side of the border

---

34   On 17 August, Sher 'Ali lost his son and heir-apparent, 'Abd Allah Jan.
35   For this war, see especially *The Second Anglo-Afghan War* 1908. See also
Trousdale 1984. On the same day that the British captured the fortress of 'Ali
Mashhad in the Khaybar Pass, another Russian, Colonel Grodekoff, rode into Herat
(Marvin 1885:296).
36   From Sir Alfred Lyall's *The Amir's Soliloquy*.
37   As told by Sykes (1940, II:113), both men wore Russian uniforms.
38   The other signatory was Louis Cavagnari, who as a result of the Treaty
could go to Kabul. The Treaty was ratified by Lord Lytton, the Viceroy, on 30 May
1879.

were handed over to the British for administrative purposes, although they formally remained part of Afghanistan.[39]

The British resident, Major Louis Cavagnari, entered Kabul on 24 July 1879. They occupied buildings inside the Bala Hisar, but all their precautions were in vain, because Cavagnari and his entourage were killed on 3 September of the same year by a large mob of Afghans. This heralded the march of General Sir Frederick Roberts (1832–1914)[40] on Kabul, which he soon put under his harsh rule. The Bala Hisar of Kabul was destroyed, and Ya'qub Khan fled to India, where he died in 1923.[41]

In the winter and spring that followed, the British in Afghanistan again came under heavy pressure. They were soon confined to the Sherpur cantonment in Kabul, where they withstood, at great cost, a massive attack on 23 December.[42] The British realized they were trapped, and they soon sought for a way out, not only because of the military problems they faced, but also because of the immense costs. However, at first they did not know anyone who would be suitable to lead Afghanistan without handing the land over to the Russians. The solution to their problems announced itself the following year.

In 1880, 'Abd al-Rahman Khan, born in Kabul in 1844 and the son of Afzal Khan, returned from exile among the Russians in Tashkent and Samarqand. The British soon regarded him as the powerful princeling that they had been looking for, and in the spring of 1880 they paved the way for his elevation to the Afghan throne. To smooth his accession they even fought a number of battles with opponents of the newcomer, especially against the Ghaljis south of Kabul.[43] Finally, on 20 July, at Charikar north of Kabul, 'Abd al-Rahman Khan announced himself as the new Amir. The British recognized him willingly, and they did so at a public meeting in Kabul, on 22 July. He was hailed as the 'Amir of Kabul and its dependencies'.[44] Apparently the British wanted to limit the new Amir's

---

39   These districts included Pishin, northwest of Quetta; Sibi, southeast of Quetta, and the Kuram valley, south of Peshawar. Sibi and Pishin were formally annexed by the British in 1887.

40   He was the son of General Sir Abraham Roberts, the commander of the forces of Shah Shuja' during the First Anglo-Afghan war.

41   For years after, however, until the early twentieth century, the Afghan rulers in Kabul feared his return and accused many a man of being his spy.

42   The Afghan resistance was led by two legendary Afghan heroes, Muhammad Jan and Mulla Mushk-i 'Alam.

43   This included the battle fought by General Stewart against the Ghaljis, with some Durrani support, at Ahmad Khel on 14 April 1880.

44   Later changed into 'Amir of Afghanistan and its Dependencies'.

Illustration 15   *The cemetery of Maywand (photograph: author, autumn 1978).*

land to just part of Afghanistan, leaving local princes to rule other sections.

However, the problems for the British were not over. On 27 July of the same year, the Afghans under Muhammad Ayyub Khan, who had proclaimed himself Amir of Herat, defeated a British force of some 2,500 men under General Burrows at Maywand, close to Qandahar. About one thousand British troops were killed (Ill. 15).[45] The situation for the British in and around Qandahar was critical, especially when Ayyub Khan laid siege to Qandahar. The British asked for assistance from Kabul, which resulted in a forced march by General Roberts, in which a distance of some 500 km was bridged within a month. The famous march ended in a decisive battle on 1 September near Qandahar, in which the Afghans were defeated.

A change at Westminster, in which the liberal Gladstone replaced Disraeli, also meant a different British policy as to Afghanistan. The war in Afghanistan had been very costly and the number of troops involved was very high. Lord Ripon replaced Governor-General Lytton, and the decision was made to strengthen Afghanistan, and not to let it fall apart as planned by the previous government. Kabul was evacuated in August 1880, while Qandahar was left in April of the following year.

45   One of the better-known wounded Englishmen was Dr Watson, the friend of Sherlock Holmes.

17

The Dynasty of Amir ʿAbd al-Rahman Khan

In the summer of 1880 the British acknowledged ʿAbd al-Rahman Khan as the Amir of Kabul and its dependencies.[1] In turn, on the basis of the Treaty of Gandamak of 1879, they finally gained the right to establish a permanent mission in Kabul and other places, although the legations were manned by Indian (and Muslim) staff, rather than British. The British at the same time guaranteed material support, including weaponry, and a steady income in the form of an annual subsidy. They also promised, as the Afghans had for so long wished they would do, to interfere in case the Russians would attack the country. For the young and energetic ʿAbd al-Rahman Khan, the road was now open to extend his power and strengthen central authority, with the financial backing of the British and without fear of foreign intervention. Much work had to be done, however, since the Second Anglo-Afghan War had led to a sharp decline in the country's economy and Kabul's authority had suffered considerably, in favour of the power of the traditional tribal and religious leaders (Ill. 16).[2]

For the next twenty years, Afghanistan under the 'Iron Amir' passed through a period of drastic changes. The power of the local and religious leaders was drastically curtailed and foreign contacts were kept to a minimum. Afghanistan was almost completely isolated from the rest of the world and the few foreigners that were allowed access were virtually treated as spies. At the same time, the Amir's ruthless policy led to the full consolidation of Kabul control within the modern boundaries of the country. Before he died in 1901, he had become Afghanistan's undisputed leader and the succession by his son, Habib Allah, was not contested.

---

1 For the 'Iron Amir', see also Gregorian 1969 and Hasan Kakar 1979. There is also the Amir's autobiography (ed. Sultan Muhammad Khan 1900). Interesting for their portrayal of Afghanistan and the Amir are Gray 1895 and Wheeler 1895.
2 Compare Gregorian 1969:126.

Illustration 16   *Drawing of an Afghan, c.AD 1858, by L. E. Duhousset.*

Consolidating Power

The first real challenge to the position of ʿAbd al-Rahman Khan came in 1881. Muhammad Ayyub Khan, son of Sher ʿAli and therefore a cousin of ʿAbd al-Rahman, managed to defeat a military column in the south of the country, which was headed by the Amir's general, Ghulam Haydar Orakzay Charkhi.[3] Ayyub Khan subsequently captured Qandahar in August of the same year, soon after the British had evacuated the city. He was supported by religious leaders who accused the new Amir of being a British agent. This indeed was a serious accusation in a country that twice had been overrun by the British, against someone who in everyone's eyes had become Amir with active British support. However, the new Amir acted immediately and decisively and took Qandahar the following month. Ayyub Khan fled and eventually, in 1888, settled in India, like so many of his family before him. He died in Lahore in 1914. At about the same time as his army took Qandahar, other troops of the Amir led by ʿAbd al-Quddus Khan captured Herat.[4] Most of the larger towns of Afghanistan were now in the hands of the Amir.

---

3   He later was appointed commander-in-chief of the Afghan army, and he died in 1898.

4   For ʿAbd al-Quddus, who would still be in active service during the third Anglo-Afghan war in 1919, see Adamec 1997:9.

To further strengthen his position, the Amir used British subsidies to build up a regular army. He did so because he realized very well that without an army under his command he would stand no chance against the powerful Pashtun tribes and their regular levies. He also continued earlier attempts by his predecessors to organize an independent administration that was under his control and free from interference from the side of the Pashtun tribes and his own extensive family. The bureaucracy in Kabul, which was virtually non-existent when Amir ʿAbd al-Rahman Khan came to the throne in 1880, grew enormously during his reign, and by the end included almost all the departments of any contemporary state administration. This, of course, also meant that he needed the money to pay for all these civil servants, for the British subsidy did not suffice. A firm grip on taxation thus was another objective of the Amir's policies, which again brought him into conflict with the Pashtun tribes that for long had been used to a special position as regards the other, non-Pashtun subjects.

His general aim was to create a new system of dependencies, whereby the ruling groups (tribal leaders, royal family and clergy) no longer depended for their position on their own following, but on the state (and the Amir). To somehow placate the traditional leaders, he installed a consultative body (Pashto: *Loya Jirga*) that consisted of members of the royal clan, tribal leaders and representatives of the Islamic clergy. Next to that, there was a Supreme Council that acted as a cabinet of ministers. Yet it was very clear that these two bodies were advisory councils and that all power lay with the Amir.

The provinces were no longer governed by his sons or other family members, as in the case of his predecessors. He thus further limited the power of his own royal clan, although at the same time the men and women of his own Muhammadzay clan received a state subsidy, thus guaranteeing their support for their kinsman-leader in Kabul.[5] The provincial governors were mostly soldiers themselves who also commanded the provincial garrison, and thus occupied a very powerful position. They were in the main responsible for the levying of taxes and the rounding up of conscripts for the army and their transfer to Kabul. Their power, however, was restricted by the Amir and his growing corps of administrators in the capital who kept well informed about what was going on in the provinces. Instead of being semi-independent rulers, as in previous years, the provincial governors thus became true middlemen in the administration of the country.

5   See A. Ghani, in Olesen 1995:67.

Islam as Legitimizing Factor

In 1880 Amir ʿAbd al-Rahman Khan, by accepting the stipulations of the Gandamak Treaty, conceded the right to conduct an independent foreign policy to the British. However, this did not mean that he could not play off the British against the Russians, and his policy as towards the two superpowers of those days could be described as a careful juggling act. This policy, however, was complicated by the fact that he also had to mediate between his subjects' deep aversion against the British and the simple fact that the British were the most powerful force in the region and a source of income and weaponry for the Amir. He thus needed British support, but at the same time, in order to hold his position within his own country, he had to profess an anti-British, almost xenophobic policy. He consequently continued to oppose the British, especially in the affairs along the borderlands, although he also had other reasons to do so. He regarded the continuing British encroachments into the Pashtun borderlands, by building roads and railways and by extending their administration into tribal lands, as an unwarranted infringement upon his own rights.[6] ʿAbd al-Rahman, like his predecessors and successors, remained a Pashtun, and the continuing expansion of British influence to the west, deep into Pashtun land, was difficult to accept.

The Amir was also a politician and he realized very well that an external enemy could be a boon. It was even better when there were two enemies. In his opposition to the British, and to a lesser degree the Russians, he therefore used the concept of *jihâd*, 'holy war', which firmly linked his rule to Islam. Consequently all his internal opponents could be branded as unwilling to join in the *jihâd* against the two powerful Christian neighbouring states, and hence as un-Islamic. In 1891, he accordingly asked all his followers to swear an oath of allegiance on the Qur'an. In this way the Amir strengthened his own position and legitimacy, not by way of tribal confirmation as in the case of his predecessors, but by professing his adherence to Islam and by linking Islam to the independence of Afghanistan.[7] He thus consciously used Islam to strengthen the position of himself and of the State, and to weaken the influence of the traditional power blocks.

---

6 Between 1875 and 1900, the British built railways that connected Quetta (and the Afghan border town of Chaman) and Peshawar with the Indian network. In the years to follow the Afghan frontier post at Landi Kotal (beyond the Khaybar) west of Peshawar was also connected.
7 Compare Olesen 1995:61–93.

The above policy included a paradox, for to substantiate the claim that his rule was sanctioned by Islam he had to strengthen the role of Islam in his government and administration. At the same time, however, he was keenly aware that the traditional religious establishment constituted an impediment to his plans of strengthening the role of the state. To solve this problem, the Amir followed a policy that brought many of the institutions of Islam under the wings of his government. He set up a uniform legal system all over the country, based on Islamic law (*Shariʿa*). This system was meant to replace tribal, customary law that up to then was prevalent. *Shariʿa* law was to be administered by government-appointed and government-paid religious judges. Furthermore, the judges were instructed to pass judgement on the basis of classic authorities, and not following their own interpretation and understanding. Later in his reign, the Amir decided to go a step further. He ordered that secular and state-appointed judges should deal with criminal and political cases. In this way the power of the religious groups was even further curtailed.

He also limited the power of the clergy in other ways. Religious endowments, often used to support the Islamic clergy, reverted to the state, and many of the clergy were given a state salary. In this way they were made dependent on the state, rather than on private income. He also ordered that only mullas (priests) with sufficient knowledge should receive a state subsidy. And only those who passed a test would receive a royal diploma and could wear a white turban; all others were ordered to wear a coloured headdress.[8]

The expansion of state control in religious matters also led to more state involvement in education. The Amir founded a royal *madrasa* (religious school) in Kabul and ordered the compilation of various religious handbooks and pamphlets that were distributed all over the country. Special religious officers were appointed to check on the people whether they adhered to the tenets of Islam. All in all, the position of Islam in Afghanistan was strengthened, but that of the traditional, religious leaders was drastically weakened. Islam was made subservient to the State.

Internal Imperialism

The Amir's building up of a central government and his policy of breaking with many aspects of traditional life, led to a large series of uprisings. Hence the Amir's reign is marked by many military campaigns throughout the country. The American Afghanistan specialist,

8   Olesen 1995:73–4.

Louis Dupree, referred to this period as that of Internal Imperialism.[9] The suppression of the revolts often went together with great bloodshed. His rule, in general, was harsh.[10] According to his own words, he was responsible, by 1894, for the death of some 120,000 of his subjects.[11] The Pashtun tribe of the Shinwaris near Jalalabad was defeated after a series of campaigns that continued throughout the 1880s. In order to discourage any Shinwari from revolting again, the heads of those who were killed were heaped up in two huge towers.[12] Another serious revolt broke out among the Ghaljis. Many of them resented the rise to power of the Amir, whom they still regarded as an upstart with a British background. They preferred Muhammad Yaʿqub Khan, the son of Sher ʿAli, who had been forced to abdicate by the British in 1879 and who had retired to India. The Ghaljis were initially led by Din Muhammad, also called Mushk-i Alam ('Scent of the World'), a fervently anti-British mulla living among the Ghaljis of Ghazni. He had become famous in Afghanistan during the Second Anglo-Afghan War. When ʿAbd al-Rahman Khan tried to limit his powers this religious leader stirred up the Ghaljis. He died in 1886, but his son, called ʿAbd al-Karim Andar, continued the rebellion. The revolt was put down at huge costs in 1886 and 1887.

The Amir strengthened his position in the north by gaining control of the town of Maymana in 1884, the last of the Turkistan towns to fall to the Afghans in the late nineteenth century. The Amir subsequently, in 1888, defeated his rebellious cousin Muhammad ʿIshaq Khan, whom the Amir had earlier appointed governor of the North.[13] The Hazaras in Central Afghanistan were harshly treated and finally and completely brought under control in 1893. The cruelties committed by the Pashtun army and tribal levies are well remembered by the Hazaras and constitute one of the main reasons for the continuing animosity between both ethnic groups. Another major campaign was that against the Kafirs in Kafiristan. When their country was finally subjugated in the winter of 1895/1896, it was subsequently called Nuristan, 'Land of Light'.

As discussed earlier, the Amir also ordered large-scale migrations of Pashtuns from the south and east to lands north of the Hindu Kush. The migrants were mainly Ghaljis. In this way, he weakened the Ghaljis south of the Hindu Kush, while at the same time creating a force in the north that was dependent upon him and would

---

9   Dupree 1980:417.
10   Compare also Martin 1907, who describes life in Afghanistan around the turn of the century.
11   Mousavi 1998:113.
12   Compare Mousavi 1998:112.
13   He was the son of Amir Muhammad Aʿzam Khan, ʿAbd al-Rahman Khan's uncle.

constitute a powerful Pashtun presence among the Özbeks and Tajiks.

When he became Amir, many of the borders of Afghanistan were still disputed. When he died in 1901, British and Russian boundary commissions had established and charted almost all the outer boundaries of the country. This did not go without struggle. In 1884 the Tsarist forces had defeated the Türkmen of the Marw oasis, and they subsequently occupied all the land north of Iran and Afghanistan. The following months constituted a period of great anxiety in London (the famous 'Merwousness'): would the Russians continue their advances to the south, towards Herat? In the following year, the crisis came to a head. In April, Russian troops under General Alikhanov threatened some 500 Afghan soldiers led by General Ghaws ud-Din Khan, who were stationed in the district of Panjdih, along the Murghab river between Herat and Marw. War seemed imminent. In the end, British officers stationed in Panjdih remained neutral and did not participate in the ensuing fighting. They merely looked on while the Afghans were driven away. All this happened while ʿAbd al-Rahman Khan was on a state visit to India, in the company of the Viceroy, Lord Dufferin. The fall of Panjdih did not diminish the tension, since the British feared for a further Russian advance upon Herat. British military advisers to the Afghan army, in fear of Russian advances, asked for the pulling down of the famous *Musallâ* complex north of the old town of Herat, since these buildings obstructed the line of fire from the city ramparts. Only six minarets and the mausoleum of Gawharshad now remain of this magnificent Timurid complex.[14] In the end the destruction of the buildings proved unnecessary, for the Russians refrained from moving on Herat. In 1887, a treaty was signed whereby Panjdih was officially declared Russian territory and the present northwestern border of Afghanistan, from the Hari Rud to the Amu Darya, was acknowledged. Herat remained an Afghan town.[15] In 1895, the boundary along the Amu Darya itself, in the north of the country, was officially confirmed in the so-called Pamir Agreement, and the Amu Darya was accepted as the boundary line between both countries.[16]

14 Nine minarets remained after the demolition of the buildings. Three minarets collapsed in 1931 and 1951 during earthquakes. Since 1979, further damage has occurred.
15 For the position of Herat in British eyes, see Malleson 1880 and Yate 1888b:23–43.
16 This meant that the district of Darwaz, south of the river, was ceded by Tsarist Russia to Afghanistan, while Shughnan, across the river, was handed over to the Russians.

Around that time, in 1893, the eastern border of the country was delineated along the so-called Durand Line, named after Sir Henry Mortimer Durand, at that time the foreign secretary of the government of British India. This border cuts straight through tribal lands of various Pashtun groups and has remained a source of tension between Afghanistan and its eastern neighbour state to this very day.[17] It in fact confirmed most of the stipulations of the Treaty of Gandamak, concluded in 1879. But it also laid down the furthest possible extent of British control, and in this way the Amir could be satisfied, since it brought to an end the continuing British advances to the west, deeper and deeper into Pashtun land.[18]

Amir ʿAbd al-Rahman Khan had five wives. With one of these he had two sons, named Habib Allah, born in 1871 in Samarqand, and Nasr Allah, born in 1874. Nasr Allah was sent to Britain in 1895 to represent his father, who at that time was seriously ill. The Amir and his sons, now Afghanistan had been brought under their firm rule, wanted complete independence from Britain. The Amir, via his son, thus asked for direct representation in London, and probably also a British ambassador in Kabul. The British refused and decided that all communication between Kabul and London should continue to go via the Government in India. Hence, Nasr Allah's visit came to nothing, although he was received with all splendour. The failure of Nasr Allah's visit did not enhance relations between the two countries, and undoubtedly led to Afghan involvement in a large-scale rising of the Pashtun tribes east of the Durand Line in 1897.

The Afghans in the Early Twentieth Century

The Amir died on 1 October 1901. He was buried opposite the royal palace (the *Arg*), which he had ordered to be built along the left bank of the Kabul river in the centre of modern Kabul, to replace the Bala Hisar that was destroyed in 1879.[19] He left a prison population in

17   For the text of the Treaty, see Sykes 1940, II:352–4.
18   Whether or not this Line was intended as an international boundary remains open to various interpretations. The Amir fought a hard bargain: he managed to receive a much larger annual subsidy from the British, plus more weapons and ammunition. Much of the Pashtun land east of the Durand Line never passed under direct British, or Pakistani rule, but remained autonomous (political) agencies, generally known as the Tribal Areas.
19   The Amir's mausoleum used to be one of his palaces. It was completed as a mausoleum by his son, Habib Allah. It now stands in the Zarnegar Park, in the centre of Kabul, close to the *Arg* and another palace, namely that of one of the Amir's younger wives. For Kabul, see also Hahn 1964/5.

Kabul of some 20,000 people.[20] His eldest son, Habib Allah Khan, was proclaimed Amir two days after his father's death, on 3 October.[21] In previous years he had gained much experience in the administration of the country, and he was married to a daughter of one of the leading religious scholars in the country.[22] He was thus well placed to assume the leadership of Afghanistan.

His father had established a firm central authority and the borders of the country were deliniated and internationally recognized. Habib Allah was thus in the position carefully to relax the harsh rule of his father. This he did, and the religious leaders of the country, whose power had been suppressed during the previous years, were given back some of their former privileges. He also permitted many refugees who under his father had been forced to leave the country, to return. These included the Tarzi family and that of the Musahiban, both of whom in later years would take prominent roles in the country's development. The army was won by a salary increase, while the tribes were placated by the installation of a special Council to deal with tribal affairs. The religious leaders were won over by the establishment of another Council with the special task of checking whether official policy was in accordance with Islam.

The British in the meantime tried to renegotiate the terms of their agreement with his father. The Viceroy of India at that time, Lord Curzon (1899–1905), invited the young Amir to discuss the agreements previously concluded with Amir ʿAbd al-Rahman Khan. Habib Allah refused to go. Louis W. Dane, foreign secretary of the government of India, subsequently came to Kabul to discuss the matter.[23] Habib Allah seems to have presented, to the surprise of the British, military plans for an attack on Russia, which at that time was involved in a war with Japan (1904–5). The British were even invited to extend their railway from Quetta into Afghanistan and along the Hilmand to near Herat.[24] These plans came to nothing, but in the end Habib Allah won, and on 21 March 1905 the British recognized him as 'Independent King of the State of Afghanistan and its Dependencies'. The British also paid the arrears of subsidy that they had stopped paying in 1901. Foreign policy, however, was still

---

20   Compare Mousavi 1998:113.
21   His mother was a concubine of Amir ʿAbd al-Rahman Khan, called Gulriz, who came from Badakhshan.
22   Olesen 1995:94.
23   At that time Curzon was in London for consultations; his place in India was temporarily taken by Lord Ampthill.
24   Sykes 1940, II:219–20. It should be noted that in 1903 the British started to build a railroad from Quetta to the west, towards Iran. It was completed in 1916.

conducted via British India, and Afghanistan did not gain its full independence.

Habib Allah started a series of reforms and he further introduced the country to Western technology. Louis Dupree rather disparagingly tells that he was 'more enamoured with mechanical gadgetry than with the social, political, and economic mechanics of change'. Such a statement seems unfair. During his reign, the first modern hospital was built and the first hydroelectric plant. The first telephone line between Kabul and Jalalabad was established in 1910. He built new roads and he clearly saw the benefits of large-scale education, contrary to his father, who regarded education as only appropriate for 'noble' minds. In 1903 he established in Kabul the first Western-style centre for secondary education, the Habibiyya College, and he also opened the doors of a military college. While Indians ran the Habibiyya College,[25] the military academy was led by Turkish officers. In 1913, the Department of Education was opened, and in 1914 he established a Teacher Training Centre. In doing so he laid the foundations of modern education in the country. Another legacy of Amir Habib Allah is the western-style palace park at Paghman, west of Kabul high in the mountains.[26]

In January 1907 he and a following of some 1,100 men and women went to India to meet the new Viceroy, Lord Minto (1905–10). He was received in great style at Agra, where he was bestowed the Grand Cross of the Order of the Bath. In Lahore he visited the Islamic College, where he adviced the students: 'acquire knowledge! acquire knowledge! acquire knowledge!'.[27] He was even introduced to Freemasonry, although this was rather to the displeasure of his followers. All augured well for the future, however, until in the same year, on 31 August, the British and Russians, unknown to the Afghans concluded the Anglo-Russian Convention. This more or less officially ended the Great Game, but also divided Iran in respective spheres of influence and allowed Russian commerce special opportunities in Afghanistan, equal to those enjoyed by British traders, although Russia recognized that the country lay outside its sphere of interest.[28] The Amir never agreed to the provisions of the Convention and the intended appointment of Russian and British commercial agents in Kabul never took place.

---

25   In the 1920s its curriculum was more based on the French system. After the Second World War it was run by Americans.
26   It was later turned into a sanatorium. Nearby is also a triumphal arch erected by Aman Allah to commemorate his victory over the British in 1919, and the summer palace of Zahir Shah.
27   Pennell 1909:141.
28   For the text of the treaty as of relevance to Afghanistan, see Sykes 1940, II:356–7.

Liberalization

During Habib Allah's reign, one of the most prominent Afghans of the century came to the fore. This was Mahmud Beg Tarzi, who lived from 1865 to 1933. He was the son of the poet and writer, Ghulam Muhammad Tarzi (1830–1900) and grandson of Rahmdil Khan, one of the (half-) brothers of Dust Muhammad Khan and *sardâr* of Qandahar.[29] His father was forced to leave the country in 1881 when ʿAbd al-Rahman Khan was installed as the new ruler in Kabul. He travelled with his family to the Middle East, where he received a pension from the Ottoman caliph, ʿAbd al-Hamid (*r.* 1876–1909).

Mahmud Tarzi was born in Ghazni and joined his father into exile. He served for the Ottomans in Damascus, but returned in 1903 after his father's death and that of ʿAbd al-Rahman Khan. Tarzi was a great advocate of independence and reform and greatly influenced by the ideals of pan-Islamism. He followed in the footsteps of the great reformer, Sayyid Jamal ud-Din Afghani (1838–97), who stressed that Islam could only survive if it could rid itself of corrupt dictators and ignorant priests. Jamal ud-Din Afghani, it is generally accepted, was Iranian by birth, although he did live for some time in Afghanistan.[30] His pen-name may well reflect the accepted idea among Muslim intellectuals in the nineteenth century that Afghanistan, being one of the few Muslim states not under direct western control, was an example for a Muslim revival. Afghani indicated that selective borrowing from western culture would help the world of Islam in stemming the tide of growing western influence.

In this way Tarzi stressed the importance of modernization. He also argued that in order to strengthen Islam, the believers had to support the state, since it was the state that could promote reforms. He thus underlined the importance of nationalism. He consequently led the growing group of civil servants and others in Afghanistan whose interest was vested in the State and who objected to xenophobia and the aversion to outside influences. He received high government posts during the reigns of Habib Allah and the latter's son and successor, Aman Allah. His importance in Afghanistan is reflected in the family connections between himself and the ruling clan. One of his daughters, called Surayya, married Aman Allah and another daughter married Aman Allah's brother, ʿInayat Allah.[31]

29 *Tarzi* means 'stylist'.
30 He was (re)buried in Kabul, although he died in Istanbul. Compare Keddie 1972.
31 Their mother was Tarzi's second wife, of Syrian origin. A third daughter of Tarzi married another son of Habib Allah (Dupree 1980:456) while in exile.

Tarzi applauded the defeat of the Russians during the Russo-Japanese war of 1904–5, and he also welcomed the Chinese Revolution of 1910. In 1911 he started a Persian-language bimonthly journal, called the *Sirâj al-Akhbâr-i Afghâniyya* ('Torch of the News of Afghanistan'). The newspaper was eventually closed down in 1918 when Tarzi's anti-British points of view and his ideals of pan-Islamism became too much of an embarrassment to the Amir. However, he remained in high favour, especially when his father-in-law Aman Allah came to the throne in 1919. He was Minister of Foreign Affairs between 1919 and 1922 and again between 1924 and 1927.[32]

A Mission from Germany

During the First World War, the Afghan establishment was torn between sympathy for the Germans and a realistic appraisal of the power of the British. The Amir himself tended to prefer a policy of strict neutrality, but his brother Nasr Allah and his son ʿInayat Allah supported a group, which included the anti-British Mahmud Beg Tarzi, that wanted to wage war on Britain. They found support among the Pashtun tribes along both sides of the Durand Line, which around this time were influenced by religious leaders who preached a holy war against the British. Although the Afghan government did not officially support them, indirectly some influential leaders in Kabul provided weapons and money.[33] In this way, the First World War brought to light two forces in Afghanistan that constituted a threat to the position of the Amir. On the one hand there was the Kabul-based intelligentsia, influenced by the pan-Islamic ideals of Afghani and Mahmud Tarzi. This group was basically nationalistic, securely linked to the State, and not directly averse to western ideas and technology. On the other hand there were the Pashtuns in the borderlands, rather xenophobic, who were influenced by traditional religious leaders and primarily intent on carrying out a *jihâd* against the British and on preserving their own identity and traditions.

In the early months of the war the Germans managed to gain, from (Turkish) Mesopotamia, much influence in neighbouring Iran.[34] Following the declaration by the Caliph in Istanbul of *jihâd* against the Allies, a mission of Turkish and German representatives was sent, via Iran, to Afghanistan. In the autumn of 1915, Habib Allah was thus

---

32 He eventually left the country when Aman Allah abdicated in 1929. He died in Istanbul in 1933, a disappointed man.
33 Olesen 1995:103.
34 Compare Hopkirk 1994.

confronted with the unsolicited visit by a group of German and Turkish officers who had travelled from Mesopotamia, across Iran, to Afghanistan. The group included Werner Otto Von Hentig and Oskar Von Niedermeyer. They hoped that the Amir would obey the call of the Turkish caliph to conduct a holy war against the British and their allies. They were accompanied by two Indian nationalists and a Turkish mission headed by Kazim Beg. The party was politely welcomed in Herat when it arrived there at the end of August. When, however, at the end of September the group finally arrived in Kabul, it was at first virtually put under house arrest in the royal summer villa built by Amir 'Abd al-Rahman Khan at the *Bâgh-i Bâbur*, outside of Kabul. The Amir for the first time formally received the mission a month later, on 26 October.

After months of meetings, a draft treaty with the Germans was written, which included the fantastic German promise of 100,000 rifles and enormous sums of money. Furthermore, Germany would support Afghanistan in any possible manner if the Amir waged war on British India. However, the Treaty was never ratified and the British managed to convince the Amir that he would be very unwise in joining the opposite camp. The Mission left Kabul in May 1916.[35]

Many of his subjects did not accept Habib Allah's decision to remain neutral. His position was further weakened when the British hardened in their refusal to grant full independence. It is still unclear what really happened, but on 20 February 1919 he was murdered, during a hunting trip in Laghman. He was buried in nearby Jalalabad.

Aman Allah (*r.* 1919–1929)

Habib Allah had four wives and more than thirty concubines, and some fifty children.[36] Upon his death, his entourage in Jalalabad proclaimed the late Amir's brother, Nasr Allah Khan, as the new ruler. He was supported by Habib Allah's eldest son, Sardar 'Inayat Allah, and many other members of the family. He also had the support of the conservative sections of society, including many of the tribes and the clergy. He was generally regarded as the man who supported the borderland Pashtuns in their demand for a war with British India and who had assisted them with money and weapons. He had always taken a strong anti-British position, and had strenuously opposed his

35   Although the two Indian nationalists and Kazim Beg remained in the country.
36   Compare Dupree 1980:430.

brother's policy of neutrality. His aversion to the British was perhaps partly caused by his experiences in England when he visited the country as his father's representative in 1895. When his brother was killed in 1919, he was therefore widely held to have been involved in the plot.

However, Sardar Aman Allah, the third son of Habib Allah and aged 29, was at the time governor of Kabul. He commanded the *Arg* and the Treasury, always an asset in times of troubles. He was an advocate of the 'modernist' faction, but without the direct links with the Pashtun tribes of his uncle. He accused his uncle of being a usurper and an accomplice in the murder of his father. Perhaps even more convincing, he offered the army higher pay. The army subsequently supported Aman Allah, who was proclaimed Amir in Kabul on 25 September. Nasr Allah Khan was arrested three days later and he died shortly afterwards after having been sentenced to life imprisonment. ʿInayat Allah was also imprisoned but soon released after he had sworn loyalty to the new Amir.

Aman Allah was born in 1892 and married to Surayya, the daughter of Mahmud Beg Tarzi. Within a few months Aman Allah had secured his position, ably assisted by his father-in-law and by his Prime Minister, ʿAbd al-Quddus, the general of his grandfather. As soon as he had ascended the Afghan throne, the new Amir demanded a revision of the earlier agreements with Britain that stopped Afghanistan from conducting an independent foreign policy. In doing so he was driven, not only by nationalist feelings and the knowledge that he had to convince the Pashtun tribes that he was a 'good' Pashtun, but also by the opinion that a stance should be taken to defend Islam against the ever-growing influence of the West. By 1918 Turkey and the former Ottoman empire were defeated by the Allies and for a large part occupied by Allied forces. Afghanistan was one of the few Islamic countries that were still relatively independent of western powers.

Britain was slow in answering Kabul's demands and could not stop the Afghans from starting the Third Anglo-Afghan War when Aman Allah declared a *Jihâd*. War started in full on 4 May 1919 after a number of minor skirmishes. For the first time in this part of the world, aeroplanes played an important role. British plains bombed buildings in Jalalabad and, on 24 May, also Kabul (the Amir's palace). Fighting was, however, limited. The British, after their experiences in the First World War, did not want another long struggle, while on the other hand the Afghans were no real match to the British troops. An important event, however, which would have important repercussions, occurred when one of the Afghan generals, called Nadir Khan, almost succeeded in taking the British fortress of Thal in the Kuram valley, southwest of Peshawar. In doing so he acquired great fame among the Pashtuns, which would eventually help him in ascending the Afghan throne in 1929.

The war did not last long. An armistice was declared on 2 June, and the British conceded to most of the Afghan wishes when they signed the Treaty of Rawalpindi on 8 August of the same year. The Amir was the national hero and received the epithet *Ghâzi*. The succeeding Anglo-Afghan Treaty of 22 November 1921 confirmed many of the agreements made in 1919 and allowed for the establishment of diplomatic missions in Indian and Afghan towns, and a legation in London and Kabul. However, the Durand Line of 1893 was reaffirmed. The Amir also lost the annual subsidy that his predecessors had received from the British and that had given them a certain degree of autonomy as regards the traditional leaders.

Opening Up of the Country

While the Afghans and British were still negotiating the terms of the Treaty, an Afghan delegation visited Moscow and a number of European capitals, and also travelled to the United States. The activities of the mission were opposed by the new British Minister of Foreign Affairs, Lord Curzon, the former Viceroy. He feared a growing Bolshevik influence in the country, but the Afghans persevered and with the signing of the Anglo-Afghan Treaty they were officially free to conduct their own external affairs. In 1921, Treaties of Friendship were signed with the Soviet Union, Turkey, Italy and Persia, in 1922 followed by a similar treaty with France. Within the context of Aman Allah's defence of the Islamic world and within the spirit of pan-Islamism, Afghanistan recognized Turkey as the guide of Islam and custodian of the Islamic caliphate in March 1921.[37]

The first British ambassador to Afghanistan was Major Francis Humphrys, who arrived in Kabul in March 1922. In 1923, ambassadors were exchanged with France. Mahmud Beg Tarzi, Aman Allah's father-in-law, was appointed as the first Afghan ambassador in Paris. The French were also given a thirty-year monopoly to carry out archaeological work in the country.[38] In 1922, the two famous French archaeologists, Alfred Foucher and André Godard, arrived in Kabul and soon started work at Bamiyan.

---

37 The situation changed, however, when in the spring of 1924 the Caliphate was abolished.

38 The Délégation Archéologique Française en Afghanistan. The agreement was extended for another thirty years in 1952.

Aman Allah also supported the opposition in South Central Asia against the Bolsheviks. This opposition, led by the *Basmachis* as they were called by the Soviets, continued into the 1930s. Their struggle was already lost, however, by the end of 1922 when General Enwer Pasha (1881–1922), the former Turkish wartime leader who had joined the Basmachis, was killed by the Bolsheviks.[39] Aman Allah eventually gave refuge to Mir ʿAlim, last Amir of Bukhara, when he fled his country.[40] Yet, the Afghan position was somewhat ambiguous. In 1919 official contacts had already been established with the Bolshevik leaders in Moscow. Two years later, in 1921, Aman Allah signed the above-mentioned Treaty of Friendship with the Soviet Union, the first foreign state to do so.[41] In 1926 he subsequently concluded a Treaty of Neutrality and Non-Agression with the Soviet Union.

As a symbol of new times, Aman Allah also ordered the construction of a new administrative capital, to the southwest of Kabul. It was called Dar al-Aman (*Dâr al-Amân*, 'Abode of Safety/Peace'), and included the municipality offices and a huge Parliament building.[42] A narrow-gauged railway line connected the site with the centre of Kabul.[43]

The First Constitution

In April 1923, Afghanistan received its first written constitution (generally called the *Nizâmnâme*).[44] It was clearly inspired by the ideas of Mahmud Tarzi and it tried to turn Afghanistan into a modern nation-state, without however officially breaking its links with Islam. Of great importance was the fact that according to the new constitution the monarchy was no longer based on divine will or tribal decisions, but on the will of the people of Afghanistan. Article 4 accordingly stated that it was the nation of Afghanistan that gave its support to the King and his successors, out of gratitude for the

39   Another Turkish wartime leader, Jamal Pasha, also came to Afghanistan, in October 1920. He left again in September 1921 and was subsequently killed by an Armenian in Tiflis, July 1922.
40   He died in Kabul in 1956.
41   This Treaty included the establishment of a Soviet embassy in Kabul and Soviet consulates in the major Afghan towns (but, as agreed upon later, not in Ghazni and Qandahar). It also stipulated an annual Soviet subsidy to Afghanistan and the return to Afghanistan of Panjdih. None of these promises ever materialized.
42   Partly destroyed by fire in 1969, and later used to house the Ministry of Defence.
43   Soon after construction the project was abandoned. In 1978 the engine could still be seen in Dar al-Aman.
44   For discussion of this Constitution, see Olesen 1995:120–6.

services rendered by the King to the nation. The constitution also listed the rights and duties of the ruler and his subjects. All subjects, whether Muslims or not, were equal; they were citizens of the state of Afghanistan. They were given the right to receive free education. Forced labour, slavery and torture were abolished and freedom of the press was ensured.

In this way the new constitution officially broke with the age-long ideas of tribal affiliation and the Muslim community (*umma*). All Afghans, men and women, were citizens of the state, with equal rights. This rule did not only affect the position of the Pashtuns and others within their own ethnic group, but also the traditional dominance of the Pashtuns as regards the other ethnic entities. The Pashtuns were no longer, at least on paper, the rulers of the country. While Amir 'Abd al-Rahman Khan used Islam to overcome the opposition from the side of the tribal leaders, his grandson thus went a step further. He used western ideas of popular consent to build up a secular state, although without immediately antagonizing the religious establishment. To placate the mullas, the constitution stipulated that Islam was the official religion of Afghanistan, and the name of the Amir, as Defender of the Faith, was to be mentioned at all religious sermons. The King furthermore pledged that he would rule according to the constitution and according to Islamic law (*Shari'a*).

According to the Constitution, a Consultative Council of State (*Hay'at-i Shawrâ-yi Dawlat*) was established, made up of elected and appointed members. Together with King and ministers they constituted the legislative body. There was also a Senate (*Darbâr-i A'la*) made up of high officials and other important people selected by the King. Consultative Councils were set up in the provinces, but the King selected its members. There was no longer place for a *Loya Jirga*, or tribal meeting, although in 1924 and in 1928 the Amir called for such a gathering in order to endorse his policies. Yet, in spite of all these reforms, the ruler still wielded absolute power. He appointed ministers and was chairman of cabinet meetings.

Aman Allah's reforms did not meet with everyone's approval. Some of the most fervent opponents were Fazl Muhammad and his successor, Fazl Omar, the leaders of the Mujaddidi family. Since the early twentieth century, this family constituted one of the most influential religious families in the country. They are the descendants of the Sufi reformer Shaykh Ahmed Sirhindi, who lived in the late sixteenth and early seventeenth centuries in Mughal India. One of his descendants came to Afghanistan in the early nineteenth century and established a Sufi centre in the Shor Bazar of Kabul, hence the title of their leader, the *Hazrat Sâhib* of *Shor Bazâr*. The Mujaddidis still constitute the leading family of the Naqshbandiyya Sufi groups in East Afghanistan, and in the 1980s they headed an important resistance group against the Soviet Union.[45]

Although opposed by some traditional religious leaders, it was clear that Aman Allah did not want to separate the State from Islam. He was a devout Muslim himself, and his father-in-law, Mahmud Tarzi, was a pan-Islamist who basically wanted to reform and strengthen Islam with the help of a modernized, strong nation-state. Yet the main principle of the constitution, namely the break with the idea of the Muslim community (*umma*), proved a great obstacle. The outbreak of the Khost rebellion in 1924 led to another *Loya Jirga*, in July of the same year, at which the Amir had to make various concessions. This time the *Loya Jirga* consisted of representatives from all ethnic groups in the country. This by itself already meant a break with the past, since the *Loya Jirga* that in 1923 had approved of the new Constitution only included the representatives from the Pashtun tribes in the east and south of the country. The Amendments to the Constitution, introduced during this meeting, consequently included the obligation for Hindus and Jews to wear distinctive clothing and pay a special tax (the *jizya*). The religious leaders also forced the king to accept the stipulation that the Hanafi school of Islam was proclaimed as the official school. Provisions for higher education for women were also cancelled. The king furthermore had to accept that a Council of Islamic Scholars would decide whether new laws were in accordance with Islamic law.

Growing Opposition

In March 1924, a serious revolt broke out among the Pashtun Mangal tribe in Khost, along the borders with British India. They rebelled against the series of reforms instigated by the king. They felt that these measures interfered far too much with their own life and traditions. The Mangal were led by ʿAbd Allah Akhundzada Kharoti, also called *Mulla-i Lang*, and Mulla ʿAbd al-Rashid. They were later supported by ʿAbd al-Karim, a (slave-born) son of Muhammad Yaʿqub Khan, the former Amir of the country.[46] The rebels were joined by the Sulayman Khel and ʿAli Khel tribes. The revolt consti-

---

45 The Naqshbandiyya was established at Bukhara by Baha' al-Din Naqshbandi (AD 1318–89). The Naqshbandiyya Sufis in the west and north of the country follow the Hazrat of Karukh (near Herat). For mysticism in Afghanistan, see also Wieland-Karimi 1998.

46 According to Dupree (1980:449), this assistance was not appreciated by all of the rebels and the subsequent disagreements did much to diminish their strength.

tuted a serious threat to Aman Allah's position and a test whether he could still count on the support of the army, in spite of all the reforms he had announced. In order to deal with the problem, he proclaimed a holy war and, as recounted earlier, presented various concessions to his 1923 Constitution. Aman Allah received the support he needed and the rebels were finally defeated in January 1925. The leaders of the revolt were arrested and executed.

In 1926, Aman Allah assumed the title of King.[47] This title had not been used in Afghanistan since the days of the Sadozay rulers, the last of whom was Shah Shuja'. In spite of the uprising in Khost, he felt, probably correctly, that he still had the support of large segments of society, in particular among the Pashtuns. Many Afghans understood the need for education and also sympathized with the pan-Islamic ideas of the king and his family. Furthermore, they remembered him as the hero who defeated the British in 1919. However, support was gradually growing thin, and the general opinion could easily turn against Aman Allah. This happened when Aman Allah decided to leave the country for a long tour abroad.

From December 1927, Aman Allah and his wife visited Egypt, Italy, France, Germany, Britain, Russia, Turkey and Iran. In Turkey the Afghan king was received by Kemal Atatürk, and in Iran the royal party was welcomed by Reza Shah. Both of these autocratic rulers, it should be reminded, were engaged in a radical transformation and westernization of their country. His experiences abroad convinced Aman Allah that progress in Afghanistan was going too slowly. Upon his return in July 1928, Aman Allah summoned a *Loya Jirga* and he announced further reforms, all aimed at further secularization of Afghan society. He informed his audience that a representative parliament would be established, elected by all adult men. He also announced a conscription of all men for the army. He furthermore proclaimed that from March 1929, men in Kabul, and visitors to Kabul, should wear western dress and western hats. Women need no longer go veiled. Finally, all boys and girls should receive education.

Aman Allah's announcements were a bridge too far. Almost immediately widespread revolts broke out among the conservative Islamic clergy and the tribes. Tension in the capital rose even higher when Fazl Omar Mujaddidi was arrested and the chief religious judge of Kabul and others were executed. However, the real threat to Aman Allah's position did not come from circles in his capital, but from outside.

---

47   This was part of a series of symbolic changes. In the same year, Aman Allah also decided to change the monetary unit of the country. The rupee was replaced by the Afghani.

In November 1928 the Shinwaris revolted and they destroyed the royal winter palace in Jalalabad, close to the mausoleum of Amir Habib Allah. This event set the example for other groups. Soon the Kohistanis and Kohdamanis from north of Kabul carried out attacks on government representatives. The regular army rapidly disintegrated when many soldiers joined the rebels. On 14 January 1929, Aman Allah was forced to resign and he passed the crown on to his brother, ʿInayat Allah. When the latter could not hold his position, Aman Allah again proclaimed himself king.[48] He did so in Qandahar, with the support of large numbers of Durrani tribesmen, but his subsequent drive up from Qandahar to Kabul, together with Hazara warriors, failed, partly due to opposition from Ghalji tribesmen who had never liked him and his family anyhow. On 23 May 1929 he fled to India, never to return to his country.[49]

Muhammad Nadir Shah (1929–1933)

The Kohistanis and Kohdamanis (from the Kohistan and Kohdaman areas north of Kabul) who drove Aman Allah out of Kabul were led by a man called Habib Allah Kalakani.[50] He was a Tajik from just north of the capital, with a somewhat checquered career as soldier, highwayman and tea seller. His main power was his charismatic personality; his weakness the fact that he was a Tajik and not a Pashtun, and that he was of humble origins. He was popularly called *Bachcha-i Saqaw*, 'son of a water carrier', while his adherents entitled him 'Amir Habib Allah Ghazi, Servant of the Religion of the Messenger of God'. He took Kabul on 16 January and two days later he was proclaimed Amir, four days after the (first) abdication of Aman Allah.

As soon as Habib Allah Kalakani was installed as the new leader in Kabul, most of the reforms instigated by Aman Allah were cancelled. The schools and courts were again run by clerics and no longer by government officials. Conscription was abolished and women were again forced to wear all-concealing veils. Museums and libraries, symbols of modernization, were sacked. Many adherents

---

48   A British aeroplane took ʿInayat Allah to Peshawar on 18 January 1929. He ended his life in Tehran as guest of Reza Shah and his son. He died in 1946.
49   He died on 26 April 1960 after many years of exile in Italy and Switzerland. He was eventually buried in Jalalabad, next to his father. His wife Surayya, the daughter of Mahmud Tarzi, died eight years later and was also buried in Jalalabad, next to her husband.
50   See Poullada 1973 and Stewart 1973.

and relatives of Aman Allah were killed, including two of his brothers.

Not much is known about Bachcha-i Saqaw and about his rule. In later years his name became the symbol of mismanagement. Since he was a Tajik and the country after 1929 was again run by Pashtuns, it is difficult to separate fact from fiction. There are reports that he and his government actively assisted the anti-Soviet forces in Uzbekistan and Tajikistan. However, all this remains rather vague, and the role of the Soviet Union in his downfall, in the autumn of the same year, is unknown. The Soviets certainly profited from it, since Bachcha-i Saqaw cooperated with Ibrahim Beg, the *Basmachi* leader, while Nadir Shah, when he came to power in October of the same year, proved to be a pragmatist who refused to be drawn into the still-continuing conflict along the northern borders of the country. He ruthlessly forced many of the *basmachis* who had sought refuge in Afghanistan, back across the border into the hands of the Soviets.[51]

Bachcha-i Saqaw's ascent to power was a great shock to the Pashtun tribes, and from the beginning it was clear that they would never acknowledge him, in spite of the obviously conservative policy that Bachcha-i Saqaw followed. In the Jalalabad region, the Pashtun tribes elected someone called ʿAli Ahmad Khan as king. He had been an important official under Habib Allah and Aman Allah and the president of the Afghan delegation to the Rawalpindi Peace Conference in 1919. However, he was soon taken prisoner by Bachcha-i Saqaw's troops and taken to Kabul where he was executed by canon in July 1929.

The main Pashtun push against the regime in Kabul came from the side of the Musahiban family. They included General Muhammad Nadir Khan, the hero of the Third Anglo-Afghan War, and his five brothers and half-brothers, namely Muhammad ʿAziz Khan, Muhammad Hashim Khan, Shah Wali Khan (a brother-in-law of Aman Allah), Shah Mahmud and Muhammad ʿAli Khan. The most important of the brothers was Muhammad Nadir Khan, who was born in 1883 at Dehra Dun, India, as the son of Sardar Muhammad Yusuf Khan and grandson of Sardar Yahya Khan. The family was therefore also known as the Yahya Khel. They descended from Sultan Muhammad Khan (1795–1861), the *sardâr* of Peshawar and (half-) brother of Dust Muhammad Khan, and were thus related to the family of Aman Allah. Furthermore, in the female line Nadir Khan was related to the Sadozay who ruled Afghanistan between 1747 and 1826.

When his grandfather was allowed to return to Afghanistan in the early 1900s, Nadir Khan followed him. He embarked on a military

---

51   In 1931 he signed a Pact of Non-Agression with the Soviets.

career and was eventually appointed commander-in-chief of the Afghan army. He was probably included in the group around Nasr Allah that opposed Habib Allah's policy of neutrality during the First World War.[52] His siege of Thal during the Third Anglo-Afghan War gave him much credit among the borderland Pashtuns. He opposed the constitution of 1923 and voluntarily went to France, first as ambassador (where he replaced Mahmud Tarzi), but later, because of illness, he remained there as a private person. He returned to the area early in 1929 when he heard that Aman Allah had abdicated. He knew that he could find support among the borderland Pashtun tribes. The British did not stop him from reaching the Afghan border; they were alarmed by the apparent chaos in Afghanistan.[53] Once in the borderlands Nadir Khan was joined by his brother, Shah Mahmud, who had defected as governor under Bachcha-i Saqaw. Other brothers also joined him, and he furthermore received the support of the Hazrat of Shor Bazar and his Mujaddidi family, the clan of religious leaders from Kabul.

Nadir Khan received widespread support from the tribal Pashtuns, especially the Mahsuds and Waziris from east of the Durand Line. On 10 October 1929, after a number of unsuccessful attacks, his army headed by his brother Shah Wali captured Kabul and arrested Bachcha-i Saqaw. The tribal army of Nadir Khan proclaimed him king,[54] and on 3 November, Bachcha-i Saqaw was executed together with his brother and other leaders.

A New Constitution

In October 1931, Muhammad Nadir proclaimed a new constitution (the *Usulnâme-i Asâsi*), which would remain in force until 1964. Basically it was very similar to the constitution of 1923, but at the same time it confirmed the status quo after 1929. It acknowledged the position of Nadir Shah and his family and tried to placate just about all the relevant segments of Afghan society, including the religious establishment, the Pashtun tribes and their traditional leaders, and the middle class modernists (and civil servants) in the capital. Many stipulations were ambiguous, and left real power to the king.

The constitution conferred the kingship of Afghanistan upon Nadir Shah and his family. It was stated that this was done '(I)n

---

52   His cousin, and a son of Asaf Khan, called Ahmad Shah, commanded the body-guard of Habib Allah when he was murdered in February 1919.
53   Olesen 1995:173.
54   A *Loya Jirga* confirmed his kingship in September, 1930.

appreciation of the devotion shown and services rendered by His Majesty the Ghazi Muhammad Nadir Shah Afghan, in obtaining the independence and deliverance of the land of Afghanistan . . .' The constitution stated that the King appointed the Prime Minister, sanctioned the appointment of ministers, was commander of the army, approved (or not) measures put forward by the National Council, and was entitled to dismiss ministers.

Hanafi Islam was again, as in the Amendments to the 1923 Constitution, mentioned as the state religion, at the cost of other schools of Islamic thought, and in particular that of the Shiʿites. All legislation was made dependent on *Shariʿa*. Religious judges were given full autonomy, although the King retained the right of final appeal.[55] Religious and secular courts remained to exist side by side.[56]

Reference was made to the *Loya Jirga* as a consultative body that approved the initial establishment of the National Assembly. According to a separate law, the *Loya Jirga*, consisting of the tribal and other traditional leaders of the country, should convene at least once every three years. No extra taxes would be levied or, although this was not directly stated, any changes made to the constitution without the consent of the *Jirga*. In this way the tribal element was officially reintroduced into Afghan politics. Recruitment for the army was also left to the tribal chiefs or councils, and they remained in command of their levies. In addition, many tribes were exempted from taxation and taxes, thus securing their support for the king.[57]

Legislative powers were invested in the King, the Senate (*Majlis-i A'yân*) with twenty or more members who were appointed for life by the King, and the National Assembly (*Majlis-i Shawrâ-yi Milli*), which included 106 people.[58] They were elected for a period of three years, theoretically by votes from all adult Afghan men and women, although it was later stipulated that according to Islamic law women had no right to vote. There was also again a religious advisory group (*Jamiʿyyat al-ʿUlamâ*), which was a national council charged with the responsibilty to check whether any law or other government regulation was in accordance with Islamic law.

The Constitution contained a number of stipulations that showed that Nadir Khan was also aware of the influence of Kabul's 'modernists'. The Constitution guaranteed freedom of the press (although

---

55   In this way the clergy, and indirectly the king, gained control of the borderland tribes (Gregorian 1969:305, Olesen 1995:179).
56   The jurisdiction of these two types of courts was ill-defined, which gave rise to much confusion.
57   Olesen 1995:180.
58   The establishment of this Council had already been announced at the 1928 *Loya Jirga*.

the government kept a close eye on the 'Islamic' value of publications). Education was again made compulsory for children and state schools remained under the supervision of the government. Government *madrasa* were also opened, in order for the judicial system to find recruits with sufficient training under state control. These schools competed with the private *madrasa*. On the other hand, the constitution allowed any Afghan to teach religious values, thus again placating the religious establishment.

The constitution of 1931 confirmed the situation that had arisen after the events of 1929. Many outward measures taken or announced by Aman Allah were cancelled, including those with respect to veiling, polygamy and girls' schools. Nadir Shah also ordered that the consumption of alcohol should be severely punished. The outward symbols of policy have always been important in Afghanistan, and Nadir Shah fully understood this point. The tribal and religious leaders regained much of their former influence, but the provisions in the constitution were not always clear-cut, and the king and the State retained much of their importance. The regulations for the election of the *Majlis* were not included in the constitution and for many years to come, at least until 1964, it remained an advisory council. Subsequently, with all power blocks in Afghanistan somehow satisfied, a gradual process could start of further integration of local and religious interests into the affairs of the State. Aman Allah's policies had failed because they were implemented too quickly and without the sufficient backing of a powerful army. It would take almost thirty years before the Prime Minister of Afghanistan, and a nephew of Nadir Shah, would allow his wife to be publicly seen without a veil.

18

Changing Afghanistan

In spite of his harsh rule, opposition to Nadir Shah was never completely wiped out. He had made too many enemies and there were still many adherents of the ousted family of Aman Allah and Mahmud Tarzi. On 6 June 1933, Nadir Shah's brother Muhammad ʿAziz Khan, the Afghan ambassador to Germany, was murdered in Berlin. Some months later, on 8 November 1933, Muhammad Nadir Shah himself was assassinated while visiting a school in Kabul.[1] Both killings were generally linked to a long feud between the Musahiban brothers and the Charkhi family. The Charkhis were followers of Amir Aman Allah and they were the sons of Ghulam Haydar Orakzay Charkhi, the general of ʿAbd al-Rahman Khan. They were the staunchest opponents to the Musahiban family. Nadir Shah executed two of the brothers on a charge of treason, in 1932 and 1933 respectively. A third brother, Ghulam Siddiq Charkhi, was married to a daughter of Mahmud Tarzi, and therefore belonged to the family of Amir Aman Allah. He was Minister of Foreign Affairs under Aman Allah in 1928 and was subsequently sent to Berlin as ambassador. With the fall of Aman Allah he was removed from his post, but remained in Europe until his death in 1962.[2] Whether he was directly involved in the murder in Berlin of Muhammad ʿAziz Khan, in 1933, remains unknown.

After the death of Nadir Shah the feud between the Charkhis and the Musahiban did not spread any further. The brothers and half-brothers of Nadir Shah formed a united front and they acknowledged Nadir's son, Zahir Shah, as the new king. The prestige and influence of the Musahiban brothers were clearly sufficient to ensure a smooth transition. At the time of his father's death, Zahir Shah was only

---

1 Nadir Shah was buried in a mausoleum on the Tepe Maranjan, in the east of Kabul close to the Bala Hisar.
2 Adamec 1997:126.

19 years old. His father had trained him for his future work and Zahir Shah had served as Minister of Defence and Minister of Education.[3]

For many years after his accession to the throne, the young king was being supervised by his uncles. At first, Sardar Muhammad Hashim Khan (1886–1953) remained as Prime Minister, a function that he fulfilled since 1929, and he was the virtual ruler of the country until 1946. The cabinet that was installed after Nadir's death also included Shah Mahmud, another Musahiban brother, who was Minister of Defence. Another important cabinet member was Fazl Ahmad Mujaddidi, the brother-in-law of Fazl Omar, the Hazrat of Shor Bazar. He was Minister of Justice and later became Chairman of the Senate. The government in this way reflected the close cooperation between the Musahiban brothers and the traditional religious establishment.

Muhammad Hashim Khan continued the autocratic rule of his brother, although newspapers went on with the discussion of the role of Islam and Western thought in Afghan society. In 1946, after World War II, he was replaced as Prime Minister by his brother, Shah Mahmud Khan (*Ghazi*). Under his rule there was some further political relaxation and more liberalization of the press. This process culminated during the elections of 1949, when a large number of reformists could enter the Seventh ('Liberal') Parliament and soon afterwards a number of new press laws allowed for the publication of some independent and semi-independent newspapers. When, however, criticism in the papers and other media against the establishment and especially against the royal family became too pronounced, the government clamped down on its critics and by 1952 arrested many of its opponents.

The New Urban Middle Class

The new urban middle class of educated civil servants, military and others who supported the demand for more democratization in 1949 found its origin in the developments of the preceding decades. In the years after 1933, Afghanistan had passed through many changes. The 1931 Constitution had in fact been a step back, and the religious and tribal leaders regained part of their former importance. Yet, at the same time the state's role became more and more prominent and

---

3 At the time of writing of this book, he is still alive and his name is still circulating among Afghans and foreign diplomats as a possible way out of the continuing crisis in the country.

spread to various parts of public life that hitherto had remained outside the state and within the sphere of local customs. Religious leaders were incorporated into the state system; state sponsored secondary education, both secular and religious, was made available for many students, and secular courts dealing with civil cases were opened in various provincial capitals.

Consequently, a growing number of Afghan people were made dependent on the state, as civil servants, soldiers and officers, students, or otherwise. The rapidly expanding bureacracy and military could at first relatively easily absorb the newly educated elite. The state, and not the tribe, was increasingly being accepted as the social and political context of the individual. This, among others, was reflected in a growing number of studies and popular works that emphasized the ancient background and its importance of the Afghan (Pashtun) state. The origins and antiquity of Pashto were widely proclaimed. In 1936, Pashto was made into the national language, although both Pashto and Persian were still labelled the official languages of the country. From 1938, government officials were required to speak Pashto. The growing role of Pashto also reflected the increased importance of the Pashtuns in the administration of the country. Before that time, the so-called Farsiwans, the Persian-speaking part of the population, formed the administrative backbone of the country. Within the same context, but many years later (in 1958), Persian as spoken in Afghanistan was officially named *Dari*, to indicate its specifically Afghan character.[4]

A growing awareness of the state was also brought about by archaeological work in the country. The Kabul Museum in the former Municipality Building in Dar al-Aman officially opened its doors in 1931.[5] Since the 1920s French archaeologists had unearthed and studied the remains of Afghanistan's past, and the Kabul elite used these finds to promote their self-identity. Since the ancient remains mostly dated to Afghanistan's pre-Islamic past, archaeological work was generally used by those who wanted to promote a secular Afghanistan, rather than an Islamic Afghanistan.

The role of the state also penetrated deeply into economic life. From the early 1930s, the government actively supported the export of the famous karakul (Persian lamb) skins from the northwest of the country. The National Bank (*Bânk-i Milli*) was opened in 1934 and a system was developed whereby the state participated for 40 or 45 per cent in joint-stock companies. In the north of the country, especially around Qunduz, huge cotton estates were being

4 Olesen 1995:205.
5 Dupree, Dupree and Motamedi 1974.

established.[6] A negative effect, however, was the increase of imports, which reduced the chances of local producers. In addition, since land taxes remained low, rich merchants tended to invest in landed property, which in many areas created further stratification of society and a lessening of traditional regional and tribal ties.

After World War II

Afghanistan remained neutral during World War II, although Allied influence was strong. German and Italian residents in Afghanistan were expelled, at the request of Britain and the United States.[7] When the war ended, it was evident that dramatic political changes were about to take place in the Indian subcontinent. August 1947 saw the withdrawal of the British and the establishment of India and Pakistan. In the months preceding this momentous event, strong irredentist feelings arose in Afghanistan as to the inclusion of the land of the Pashtuns east of the Durand Line. The Afghan government wanted that the predominantly Pashtun population of the Northwest Frontier Province, along their eastern borders in British India, was given the choice whether to join with Afghanistan, to become independent, or to join with Pakistan or India. The British refused to do so, and in the end the Pashtuns were simply asked whether they wanted to join with India or Pakistan. The outcome was predictable, and the NWFP was united with Pakistan. Yet this did not solve the so-called Pashtunistan issue, which would haunt relations between Afghanistan and Pakistan for many years to come.

The establishment of new states in the Indian subcontinent led to a completely new strategic situation and coincided with the start of the Cold War between the United States and its allies, and the Soviet Union. From the start, the Americans showed no inclination to include Afghanistan into their sphere of influence. They had traditionally been rather averse to close relations with the country, and diplomatic relations had only been established in 1934. The American government held the opinion that the Soviets should be stopped along the Pakistani borders, and not along the northern boundaries of Afghanistan. This did not mean that western aid did not reach the

6 Cotton became the *spinzar* ('white gold') of Afghanistan, as it did in the nearby Soviet republics.
7 One man who during World War II finally received permission to enter Afghanistan was Sir Mark Aurel Stein, the intrepid explorer of 'India Chinese Turkestan Persia and Iraq' (according to the text on his grave stone). He died, aged 81, on 26 October 1943, soon after entering Afghanistan and was buried at the Christian cemetery in Kabul.

country, but it was relatively little as compared to what was received by neighbouring countries. In fact, this American policy ran parallel to the traditional Afghan policy of neutrality and was not really contested by the Kabul government.

The Premiership of Muhammad Dawud Khan

A major change in Afghan politics occurred on 20 September 1953. On that day, Muhammad Dawud Khan, with the palace's consent, replaced Shah Mahmud as Prime Minister.[8] This episode marked the transition in power from the generation of Nadir Shah and his brothers, to that of their children, namely the king himself and two of his cousins, Dawud Khan and his brother, Najm Khan.

Dawud was the son of Muhammad 'Aziz, the half-brother of Nadir Shah, who was murdered in Berlin in 1933. He was born in Kabul in 1909 and received his education in Kabul, at the Amaniyya College, and in Paris. He joined the army in 1931 and was promoted to major-general the following year. Between 1939 and 1947 he was Commander of the Central Forces and in the government of his uncle, Shah Mahmud, he was in 1947 appointed Minister of Defence and then, after a brief interlude, Minister of the Interior (1949–50). He was a supporter of the reformists who for a short period after 1949 had been allowed to broadcast their demands. Dawud wanted to break with orthodox Islamic elements, which he saw as an impediment to further progress. He was aware, however, that in order to realize his plans to modernize the country, he would need strong and loyal military support. He thus started building up the army.

To modernize the army, Dawud needed foreign help. The United States at that time pursued a policy of large-scale support to Pakistan, and only limited help to Afghanistan. In 1954, Pakistan accordingly concluded the Mutla Security Pact with the United States, and in 1955 joined the Baghdad Pact, which included Turkey, Iraq, Iran and Pakistan, and which later changed into the CENTO (Central Treaty Organization). With Pakistan thus being firmly cemented to the anti-communist alliances led by America, the international position of Afghanistan became more and more complex, especially since the Pashtunistan issue continued to dominate the relations with Pakistan. In 1955, this even briefly led to a mobilization of the Afghan army. In this way, the Afghan government felt forced to ask the Soviet Union for assistance.

8   Shah Mahmud died in 1959.

While the Americans kept a relatively low profile in Afghanistan, the Soviet Union subsequently showed great interest in its poor southern neighbour. In December 1955, Nikita Khrushchev and Nikolai Bulganin, returning from a highly successful trip to India, visited Kabul and Prime Minister Dawud. They obviously were in league with India in trying to cause damage to Pakistan, which had become the new American ally in the region and the main foe of the Indians. The Soviet leaders thus made it clear that they were willing to support Afghanistan in its struggle with Pakistan about the Pashtunistan issue, and they offered large amounts of aid, including weapons. Dawud gladly accepted the offer. Soon thereafter, Soviet arms and arms instructors entered the country and many Afghans were sent to the Soviet Union for military training.

As so many developing nations at that time, and in imitation of the Communist countries, Afghanistan also developed a series of Five-Year Plans. The Soviet Union gave massive aid, but also western nations joined in. The first Five-Year Plan ran between 1956 and 1961 and was mainly aimed towards the building of roads and other infrastructure for communication. Soviet aid was mainly directed towards the north of the country, while the Americans carried out construction works in the south. For instance, the United States helped in building the airfield of Qandahar and the Arghandab dam, while the Soviets built the Salang Pass and Tunnel. Foreign aid also stimulated the exploitation of natural resources, such as the natural gas reserves near Shibarghan.

The Cold War and international rivalry were also reflected in the support given to Kabul University, officially established in 1946, and to other educational institutions in Kabul. The Soviet Union supported the Polytechnic Institute, which was opened in 1967, while the Americans backed the university faculties of agriculture, education and engineering.[9] The French were involved with law, while the Germans assisted with the faculties of science and economics. Al-Azhar University in Cairo was linked to the Kabul Faculty of Shari'a, opened in 1952.

Growing Unrest and the Pashtunistan Issue

In 1959 premier Dawud finally felt strong enough to confront the religious establishment. On 31 August of that year he allowed women

9 Ironically, Hafiz Allah Amin, the Marxist ruler of Afghanistan in 1979, was a student of the (American) branch of Kabul University, while Ahmad Shah Mas'ud, who was the main military opponent of the Soviets in the 1980s, was trained at the (Russian) Polytechnic.

to appear in public without a veil, and the women of the royal family were publicly seen without this garment. The last time this had occurred was in the reign of King Aman Allah, in the late 1920s. To the traditional tribes and mullas this event constituted a clear break with the past. Riots followed and acid was thrown at women. However, public opinion turned against the attackers, and Dawud won his first major battle with the religious establishment.[10]

In the same year, land tax was enforced in the Qandahar area, the traditional centre of the ruling Pashtun tribes. This ended a tradition that was more than 200 years old. The traditional landowners in the area and their followers showed a great deal of opposition, but eventually they had to give in. Revolts also broke out in Paktya among the borderland Pashtuns. They objected to roads being built into their secluded valleys, which they thought, constituted a threat to their traditional autonomy and way of life. The revolt was easily put down. Dawud's position seemed very strong indeed.

The unrest in the late 1950s may have been one of the reasons behind Dawud's decision to rekindle the ever-dormant Pashtunistan issue. Dawud realized very well that an attempt to recover the Pashtun lands east of the Durand Line would find massive support among the army and the rest of the Afghan population, and thus strengthen his own position. At an international level he was supported by the Soviet Union, which in May 1960 during another visit by Nikita Khrushchev had reiterated its support of Afghanistan's policy as regards the Pashtunistan issue. Thus, from mid-1960, tension between Afghanistan and Pakistan mounted again and both countries accused each other of border violations. In June 1961, King Zahir informed Parliament that the Pashtuns east of the Durand Line should have the right of self-determination. Two weeks later the Pakistani government retaliated by closing the border with Afghanistan for all nomads. In August, Pakistan also closed all Afghan consulates and trade offices in the country. On 3 September, Afghanistan in turn closed the borders with Pakistan and all trade and transfer of goods between the two countries came to a halt. The result was disastrous for Afghanistan. The closure of its borders with Pakistan plunged the country into a deep economic crisis. The Afghan government probably simply had not realized how dependent the country had become on Pakistan for its import and export. Since the roads between Afghanistan and Iran were unsuitable for large-scale transport, the country was consequently made ever more dependent on its mighty northern neighbour, the Soviet Union, which was only too willing to help. The crisis dragged on for two winters. Both parties were firmly

10   Olesen 1995:213.

entrenched in rhetoric and the situation seemed unsolvable. All the while the Afghans were suffering, and their import and export were made almost completely dependent on the Soviet Union.

The Liberal Constitution

On 9 March 1963, and to everyone's surprise, Dawud announced his resignation. In fact, he probably realized that this decision was the only solution to the Pashtunistan crisis. Muhammad Yusuf, the former Minister of Mines, succeeded him. His appointment meant a break with the past, since he was the first Prime Minister for many years who did not belong to the royal family. One of the first items on the new government's agenda was the relationship with Pakistan. Contacts with the Pakistani government were re-established, and in May 1963, with the Shah of Iran as mediator, both governments decided to normalize their relations.

The spring of 1963 marked another turning point in the history of Afghanistan. It was evident that Afghanistan was going to change. The atmosphere in the capital had altered. People in the streets of Kabul were convinced that a new era had started. They proved right. In the weeks following Dawud's resignation, announcements were made as to the drafting of a new constitution. For more than a year, various experts and committees discussed the future of the country, and in the end, on 9 September 1964, proposals were presented to a special *Loya Jirga*. Ten days later, the *Loya Jirga* approved the proposals, and on 1 October 1964, the king signed the new constitution. At the same time a new interim government was appointed, under Muhammad Yusuf, whose main task it was to prepare the general elections.

With its new constitution, Afghanistan became a constitutional monarchy. Article 1 stated that sovereignty belonged to the nation and was personified in the King (Article 6). Parliament manifested the will of the nation (Article 41). In sum, the new constitution made Afghanistan into a secular state. It put an end to a period in which the royal family played a key role in the administration of the country. In this way the constitution reflected the growing resentment against the settled establishment among the ever increasing groups of educated Afghans, many of whom were without employment and without any representation. Members of the royal family were barred from the positions of Prime Minister, Member of Parliament, or judge in the Supreme Court. The *Loya Jirga* even went a step further and demanded that no member of the royal family would head a political party, or renounce his titles in order to lead one.

The constitution guaranteed education, freedom of property, freedom of religion and of assembly. There was to be a free press and citizens were allowed to form political parties,[11] on condition that they did not violate Islamic law.

Parliament now consisted of a National Assembly (Pashto: *Wolesi Jirga*, 'People's Council') and a Senate (Pashto: *Meshrano Jirga*, 'House of Notables'). The Assembly would be formed by way of free and secret elections by all adult men and women. The Senate consisted of three groups: one third was appointed by the King; one third consisted of representatives from the 28 provincial councils, and one third of the Senators were elected from each of the provinces. The King retained the right to dissolve Parliament.

The first elections under the 1964 Constitution were held in August and September 1965 and the first session of the newly elected *Wolesi Jirga* took place on 14 October. The opening sessions of the National Assembly, however, soon developed into shouting matches between the various delegates. When on 25 October 1965 the decision was made to meet in closed session, demonstrations broke out in Kabul. Four days later, Yusuf resigned.[12] He was succeeded by Muhammad Hashim Maywandwal.[13]

Growing Discontent

The demonstrations of 1965 were the result of a long process. Throughout the 1950s and 1960s, socio-economic tensions in Afghanistan and especially in the capital Kabul, had increased. Education led to a growing number of young people who flocked from the countryside to the capital looking for work. They were dissatisfied with the leading role of the elite. As a result, many students and others turned to the political right (fundamentalism, Islamism) or the left (Marxism or Maoism). Others, of Pashtun descent, adopted Pashtun nationalism. The new constitution and the newly elected Assembly did not dramatically change the situation. As observed by many, the Members of Parliament (*wâkil*) in the 1965 Assembly were

11   The freedom to form political parties was never really implemented.
12   He was appointed ambassador to West Germany in 1966 and to Moscow in 1973. In 1994/1995 Mahmud Mestiri, the ambassador of Boutros Boutros-Ghali, the UN Secretary-General, mentioned his name as a possible Prime Minister.
13   Who also soon had to resign, in October 1967, because of ill health. He was succeeded as interim Prime Minister by 'Abd Allah Yaftali, and later by Nur Ahmad Etemadi (1967–71), 'Abd al-Zahir (1971–2), and Muhammad Musa Shafiq (1972–3). Maywandwal died in October 1973, either by suicide or murder, after he had been arrested by Dawud's police.

in general more conservative than the new middle classes in Kabul who had influenced the drafting of the new constitution. Furthermore, the king never ratified the proposed Act on Political Parties, apparently out of fear of thereby promoting the Marxist groups. The MP's therefore acted in general as (conservative) individuals and as middlemen between the Executive (ministers and high officials) and their own clientele.[14] The new urban classes in Kabul therefore did not regard themselves properly represented in Parliament.

At the same time, the exodus of young people to the towns and the growing influence of the state were rapidly leading to an opposition between the town and countryside. The urbanized elite was alienated from its roots in the country. Many of the young educated middle class were deeply disillusioned. On the one hand they were still attached to their rural background, and on the other hand they had been introduced to western, or at least urban norms and values. Many now replaced their former rock-solid belief in traditional values by equally unquestionable loyalty to other beliefs, such as Marxist or Islamist ideologies.

The Communist Party

On 1 January 1965, the year of the first general elections, Marxist Afghans founded the People's Democratic Party of Afghanistan (PDPA). One of the leading figures was Nur Muhammad Tarakki, a Ghalji Pashtun, who was made General-Secretary and who would later (in 1977) become the first Marxist president of the country. He was born in 1917, reportedly in a nomad family of the Tarakki tribe, in Ghazni Province. He worked for a time as translator for the US Information Service, but left his job in September 1963 to become a freelance writer.[15] Another prominent member from the very beginning was Babrak Karmal, the later president of Afghanistan (1980–6) during the Soviet occupation, who was made Deputy Secretary. Karmal was born in Kabul in 1929 and he was therefore some twelve years younger than Tarakki. Contrary to Tarakki, who allegedly came from a family of wandering Pashtuns south of Ghazni, Karmal grew up in a relatively wealthy Pashtun family in the capital. His father was a general in the Afghan army and served as governor in Paktya

14 Apart from the Political Parties Act, the King also refrained from signing the Provincial Councils Act and the Municipal Councils Act, although they were passed by Parliament.
15 Whether or not he received another income, from the side of the Soviet Union, see Magnus and Naby 1998:110.

Province. In the early 1950s he became a communist and adopted the name of *Kârmâl* ('friend of work').

For the 1965 elections, the PDPA stressed its policy of working towards a national front and a national democratic government. In reality, they were slavishly pro-Soviet. Babrak Karmal was elected to the 1965 Parliament (Tarakki was not!), together with two other members of the PDPA.[16] Right from the beginning they opposed the normal proceedings of the *Wolesi Jirga* and organized the series of demonstrations and riots in October 1965 that left at least three people dead and led to the resignation of Muhammad Yusuf.

By 1966, the Communist Party split up into two factions, which soon came to be called the Khalq and the Parcham.[17] The Khalq ('masses') faction was named after the newspaper that was published for the first time on 11 April 1966, by Nur Muhammad Tarakki, only to be banned six weeks later. This faction found its origins in Marxism and Pashtun nationalism, especially among the young educated, urbanized elite of the Ghaljis. They were very militant, 'driven by a suicidal and destructive lust for violence'.[18] The other faction, the Parcham ('Banner'), was named after the newspaper with the same name, which was published between March 1968 and July 1969 by Sulayman Layeq and Mir Akbar Khaybar. It included articles in Dari and Pashto, some of which written by Babrak Karmal. The faction was nicknamed the 'royal communist party', since Babrak Karmal, as MP, received official favours which the Khalq under Tarakki had to do without. It attracted students, civil servants, (mainly non-Pashtun) military personnel, and other members of the Pashtun, but Persianized Kabul intelligentsia, rather than the less sophisticated Pashtuns new to the city, who tended to follow the Khalqi ranks.

The Islamist Opposition

While many young Afghans, with vested interests in the state, turned towards Marxism, others turned towards Islam.[19] In doing so many of them consciously tried to break with the traditionalist groups that formed part of the establishment and in the main simply wanted to continue the situation as it was. Instead they wanted to establish a

16 An independent candidate who was also elected, Dr Anahita Ratebzad, joined the PDPA at a later date.
17 Compare Arnold 1983.
18 Roy 1990:34.
19 For these remarks, see especially Roy 1990.

'just' society based on a purified Islam. In pursuing this goal, they found support in the writings of a number of Muslim scholars in Egypt, Pakistan and other countries. These authors advocated a strict form of Islam in which there was no separation between Mosque and State, or between secular and religious law. They were thereby often strongly modernist, in using or applying Islam to modernize their society. They were strong advocates of social justice. They also wanted to liberate Islam from the past. They held the belief that all directions emanate from the Qur'an and the Shari'a, and that all later interpretations are additions without eternal value. This explains their opposition towards the traditional religious scholars who were generally more concerned with maintaining peace and order. Also, they held the view that power ultimately derived from God, and was passed on through the Islamic community to the ruler. Sovereignty was thus not vested in the people. Advocates of this movement are generally called Islamists; their main objective is the reformation of society, contrary to the aims of traditionalists and fundamentalists (those who want to return to the basic tenets of the Islam), who are more concerned with Islam itself, rather than with the state.

In Egypt the Islamist movement is represented by the Muslim Brotherhood (*Ikhwân al-Muslimun*, 'Society of Muslim Brethren'),[20] founded in 1929 by Hasan al-Banna' (1906–49) and in Pakistan by the *Jamâ'at-i Islâmi*, founded by Sayyid Abu 'l Al'a Mawdudi (1903–79). One of the most important early Islamist groups in Afghanistan was headed by Professor Ghulam Muhammad Niazi (1932–78).[21] His movement reportedly started in 1957 when he returned from Egypt from a period of study at the Al-Azhar University where he was deeply influenced by the Muslim Brotherhood. He later became Dean of the Theology Faculty of Kabul University. Among his students were Burhan ud-Din Rabbani and 'Abd ul-Rasul Sayyaf, both of whom would later head their own resistance parties in the war against the Soviet Union. Another member of the movement at that time was Gulb ud-Din Hekmatyar, who in later years would become the leader of the *Sâzmân-i Jawanân-i Musulmân* ('Organization of Muslim Youth') and in the late 1970s the leader of a resistance party against the communist regime in Kabul.[22]

There were many similarities between the leftist and Islamist parties in Afghanistan. These similarities not only relate to their

20 Hence the name Ikhwanis given to the Islamists in Afghanistan.
21 Niazi was arrested in 1974 by President Dawud. He was executed by the Tarakki regime in 1978.
22 In 1971, Rabbani succeeded Niazi as leader of the movement. The group henceforward became generally known as the *Jam'iyyat-i Islâmi-yi Afghânistân* ('Islamic Society of Afghanistan').

adherents, who often derived from the same social strata, but also to their methods and some of their concepts. They shared the same type of organization in cells of activists, a very militant outlook, radical black and white thinking, a belief in a revolution to change society, and the concept of a party to lead the masses. What they also shared, and what was still rather new in Afghanistan, was their acceptance of the idea of the State of Afghanistan, and their disapproval of any ethnic discrimination. What was the Revolution to the Marxists, was the *Jihâd* to the Islamists: the establishment of state power.

Muhammad Dawud Khan, President (1973–1978)

In the early 1970s the political and economic situation in Afghanistan and neighbouring lands changed dramatically. After the resignation of President Ayyub Khan of Pakistan in 1969, the United States' position in Pakistan was weakened, especially when the new Pakistani government started to seek contacts with China, at that time the Soviet Union's main enemy. The Soviet Union thereupon stirred up old animosities in the subcontinent, in order to further weaken Pakistan. In 1970, the Soviet Union concluded a treaty with India, the arch-enemy of Pakistan. In the next year, war broke out between India and Pakistan. East Pakistan became the independent state of Bangla Desh and General Yahya Khan of Pakistan was replaced by the populist, Zu 'l-Fiqar 'Ali Bhutto.[23] Pakistan was now seriously weakened while the position of the Soviet Union had become much stronger. It also meant that Pakistani influence in Afghanistan diminished, while that of the Soviets increased.

In the same years, severe famine swept through Afghanistan and discontent rose among the Afghans. Although the government of Prime Minister Muhammad Musa Shafiq (1972–3) managed to deal fairly adequately with the situation, tension in Afghanistan continued to grow. Whatever happened behind the scenes is unknown, but on 17 July 1973 the former Prime Minister Muhammad Dawud seized power while his cousin and brother-in-law, Zahir Shah, was in Rome for medical treatment. The Commander of the Central Forces, 'Abd al-Wali Khan, cousin and son-in-law of the king, was arrested.[24] The Prime Minister was pushed aside and on 24

23 It is reported that in 1971 the Soviet leaders suggested to King Zahir Shah that Afghanistan would join in carving up Pakistan. Afghanistan would receive all of Pashtunistan.
24 Born in 1924 as the son of Shah Wali Khan (Zahir Shah's uncle), he was educated at Sandhurst, England, and married a daughter of King Zahir Shah. He has lived in Italy since 1976.

August, Zahir Shah announced his abdication and since then has lived in Rome.[25]

Dawud was supported by the army and the Parcham faction of the Communist Party, among whom the Tajik commander of the air force, Major General ʿAbd al-Qadir. Dawud abolished the monarchy and proclaimed the Democratic Republic of Afghanistan. The Soviet Union and India recognized the new government two days after the coup. Dawud took the posts of President, Premier, Minister of Defence and Minister of Foreign Affairs. Four PDPA members were appointed in Dawud's government, and many other PDPA members, mostly of the Parcham faction, found their way into the higher echelons of Dawud's government and the military. In October 1975, ʿAbd al-Qadir was accordingly appointed Minister of the Interior. The change of government also led to a change in Afghanistan's position as towards Pakistan. Dawud took a much harder line about Pashtunistan[26] and an independence movement in Baluchistan, thereby again trying to win the support of the Afghan people and the Soviet Union. It would prove a dangerous and lethal game.

Dawud regarded the Islamist movement as his strongest enemy. In June 1974, he arrested 200 Islamic leaders in Kabul. Gulb ud-Din Hekmatyar and Rabbani fled to Pakistan while Niazi was put in prison. These developments in fact constituted the start of the war in Afghanistan that continues to the present day, for in July 1975, the Afghan Islamist leaders in Pakistan organized a series of revolts in Afghanistan against Dawud's regime. Many future leaders of the Afghan resistance took part in the uprisings, and thereby gained invaluable experience. However, this time the revolt failed completely and many of the Islamist leaders subsequently fell out and established their own opposition movements.

With the Islamist threat temporarily out of the way, Dawud no longer needed the Marxists and he subsequently tried to divest his administration of communist sympathizers. Dawud realized that the links between Afghanistan and the Soviet Union had become far too tight and that the traditional Afghan policy of neutrality needed to be restored. Furthermore, he knew that many communists and communist sympathizers occupied important places in his government and administration. In fact, he had appointed many of them himself.

---

25   His uncle, Shah Wali Khan, who took Kabul for his brother Nadir Khan in 1929, joined his nephew, and died in Rome in March 1977.
26   Dupree (1980:757) tells that on 17 July 1973 Dawud made his announcement in Pashto, and not in Dari.

In 1975, Dawud attended the funeral of King Faysal of Saudi Arabia and spoke in private with Zu 'l Fiqar 'Ali Bhutto of Pakistan. A rapprochement with Pakistan followed. Saudi Arabia and other Middle Eastern oil-states, grown rich following the 1973 Arab–Israeli war, were willing to support an anti-communist policy in Afghanistan. In this way, Dawud prepared the ground for a major change in his policies. He subsequently clamped down on the Marxist movement, both on the Parchamis and the Khalqis. The climax came on 30 January 1977 when a *Loya Jirga* convened by Dawud proclaimed a new constitution. This *Jirga* meant a clear break between Dawud and the PDPA, for PDPA members were banned from the *Loya Jirga* and had also been banned from assisting in drafting the new constitution.

The constitution was still clearly inspired by leftist supporters, but also tried to attract modernist and populist backing, since it stressed the opposition between the 'people' and the 'exploiters'.[27] Afghanistan was made into a one-party state, led by the *Hizb-i Inqelâb-i Milli* ('National Revolutionary Party'). The party selected the nominees for the National Assembly, the *Milli Jirga*. The President was nominated by the Party and elected by the *Loya Jirga*, which included the members of the *Milli Jirga* and various other high officials, many of whom appointed or at least under supervision of the President.

The new constitution also called for the nationalization of all large industries, banks, mineral resources and other important enterprises. Equal rights were granted to men and women, and all Afghans from the age of eighteen were given the right to vote. There was no longer a difference in the eyes of the law between Sunnites and Shi'ites. It also called for land reforms and the establishment of cooperatives. Yet, in spite of all these apparently 'progressive' and 'democratic' measures, the President retained absolute powers. He convened and dismissed the Assembly and he could veto any law it passed.

The new constitution was never fully implemented. The break between Dawud and the PDPA led to growing tension between Afghanistan and the Soviet Union. During his visit to Moscow in April 1977, Dawud and Brezhnev exchanged very angry words.[28] To the Soviets, Dawud had become an unreliable ally who with Arab money was rapidly being drawn into the western camp. It is likely that behind the scenes the Soviet Union now pressed for reconciliation between the two branches of the PDPA. As a result, in July 1977,

27 Olesen 1995:220.
28 Magnus and Naby 1998:121.

both factions of the communist party joined hands, with disastrous effects. Dawud had tried to use the Soviet Union to modernize his country without being incorporated by his powerful northern neighbour. The gamble had failed.[29]

29　Compare Ghaus 1988:194.

19

The Years of Communism

In early 1978, tension in Afghanistan was mounting.[1] Dawud's regime was trying to rid itself of its former Marxist supporters, but without much success. Ever since the official reunion of the Parcham and the Khalq, the communist party was working towards the overthrow of Dawud's regime. Next to Tarakki and Karmal, an important role was played by a Ghalji Pashtun named Hafiz Allah Amin. He was entrusted with the task of mobilizing the PDPA cadres within the military. He belonged to the Khalq faction and was originally a Ghalji Pashtun of the Kharoti tribe. His family derived from Paghman, west of Kabul. Born in 1929, he had spent most of his life in the capital. After further education in America he became a teacher in Kabul. He was known as a fervent Pashtun nationalist, but in the mid-1960s he converted to Marxism and in 1969 was elected in Parliament to represent Paghman. In the time of Dawud, he recruited many officers for the Khalq faction of the communist party.

At the same time, a Parchami man was working within the military as well. This was Mir Muhammad Akbar Khaybar, one of the founders of the communist party and a prominent ideologue. Born in 1925 in Logar, south of Kabul, he met Babrak Karmal when they were both in prison in the early 1950s, and ever since they remained very close.

In April 1978, on the eve of the so-called Saur Revolution, most of the Islamist leaders had fled abroad, to Pakistan. Dawud stood virtually alone, surrounded by people he could not trust. The fall of Dawud was sparked off by the assassination, on 17 April 1978, of Akbar Khaybar. The identity and background of the murderer have never been ascertained. Was he sent by Dawud? Or by one of his Marxist rivals? Whatever the case, a showdown between the PDPA

---

1 Giustozzi's study on Afghanistan between 1978 and 1992 was announced for March 2000, and could not be incorporated into this book.

Marxists and Dawud's followers was imminent. The Marxists organized demonstrations, and Khaybar's funeral was turned into a mass
rally against Dawud. In his turn, Dawud ordered the arrest of his
opponents, but the PDPA leader Nur Muhammad Tarakki managed
to escape and gave the go-ahead for a military coup. The fighting
broke out on 27 April (the 7th of the month of Saur).

A key actor in the coup was the Parchami General 'Abd al-Qadir,
Dawud's ally in 1973, who directed the air attacks on the palace.
Dawud was killed, together with many of his family, including his
brother, Sardar Muhammad Najm. The new leaders established a
Revolutionary Council that was initially headed by the two military
protagonists, Muhammad Aslam Watanjar and General 'Abd al-
Qadir. Watanjar was the man who led the attack on Dawud's palace.
Incidentally, he was also, just like 'Abd al-Qadir, a leading figure in
Dawud's coup of 1973.[2]

Subsequently the Revolutionary Council issued Decree No. 1,
which granted all power to Nur Muhammad Tarakki. He became
the President and Prime Minister of the Democratic Republic of
Afghanistan (Decree No. 2). He was assisted by two deputy PM's,
namely Babrak Karmal, of the Parcham faction, and Hafiz Allah
Amin of the Khalq faction, who also acted as Minister of Foreign
Affairs.

At first, the new government adhered in public to Islam. Official
speeches were commenced with the *Basmala* and the new leaders
attended the Friday prayers. Furthermore, minorities were given
various rights. Decree No. 4 promoted the 'development of literature,
education and publication in mother tongues of tribes and national-
ities.'[3] Soon more direct decrees and orders were issued. Decree No.
5 removed Afghan citizenship from the members of the former royal
family. In May 1978, the *jihâd* against illiteracy was declared. In
July of the same year, Decree No. 6 pronounced all pre-1973 debts
and mortgages cancelled and later debts were reduced. Decree No. 7
related to family regulations and marriage. Men and women were
given equal rights; the bride price was reduced to a token sum; forced
marriages were banned and a minimum age was declared for men
(18) and women (16). Decree No. 8, issued in late November 1978,
restricted ownership of land to a maximum.

2   On both occasions he was the first to drive his tank towards the palace. In 1990
he became Minister of Defence under Dr Najib Allah. He was a prominent Khalqi
member who was born in 1946 in a leading Ghalji family in Paktya province. In 1990
Najib Allah appointed him Minister of Defence, and he probably left the country
after Najib Allah's fall in 1992.
3   Adamec 1997:59.

At the same time, the new Marxist rulers emphasized other, more symbolic changes. On 19 October, a red flag replaced the traditional black-red-green flag of the country. Also around this time, the leaders dropped open professions regarding Islam. Symbolism was obviously very important. They were accordingly also keenly aware of the importance of propaganda. The newspapers from those days, including the English-language Kabul Times, read like one long eulogy of the new regime. The new leaders obviously realized the sad truth that in Afghanistan there was no clear-cut opposition between 'workers' and 'oppressors'. The workers (*kârgar*) therefore first had to be convinced of their deplorable fate and of the nastiness of their traditional leaders. All media had to be mobilized to convince the Afghans of the Truth.

Growing Unrest

Not everyone in Afghanistan accepted the new message and unrest was growing. A factor that contributed to the opposition among the non-Pashtun ethnic groups in Afghanistan was the fact that the elite of the PDPA was of Pashtun origin, and Pashto was increasingly being used as the main language of the country, at the cost of Dari. Continuing internecine strife between the two factions of the PDPA soon furthermore weakened the regime. The more moderate, and perhaps more worldly and intellectual Parchami leaders were gradually ousted from government. On 5 July 1978, Babrak Karmal was sent as ambassador to Czechoslovakia. On 17 August, Tarakki strengthened his position by assuming the tasks of Minister of Defence. One day later, ʿAbd al-Qadir, the prominent Parchami member and (ex-) Minister of Defence, was named as being involved in a coup against Tarakki and was arrested.[4] Within a week, other Parchami members of the government were arrested, including the prominent Hazara leader, Sultan ʿAli Keshtmand.[5]

Yet, in spite of a growing opposition both within and without the regime, a decision was made that would have very serious consequences for the future of the country. On 5 December 1978, the new regime concluded a twenty-year Treaty of Friendship and Co-operation with the Soviet Union. Article 4 of the Treaty stated,

---

4 He was freed from prison in 1980 and served as Minister of Defence between 1982 and 1985. With the fall of the Marxists he seems to have moved to Europe.
5 His death sentence was changed to 15 years' imprisonment. He was freed in 1980 and in 1981 became Prime Minister (1981–8). He now seems to live in England.

somewhat ominously, that both parties 'shall consult with each other and take, by agreement, appropriate measures to ensure security, independence and territorial integrity of the two countries'.

In Kabul much of the opposition focused on the Hazrat of Shor Bazar, of the Mujaddidi family. When the Tarakki regime felt more and more threatened, it took drastic action, and in January 1979 the Marxists arrested the Hazrat and almost all the other male members of his family. Almost 80 of them were subsequently, in secret, executed. The same winter also saw the first territorial gains of the resistance. The so-called Nuristan Front occupied most of Nuristan, and at the same time most of Hazarajat escaped from Kabul control, at the hand of the so-called Revolutionary Council of the Islamic Union of Afghanistan (generally called the *Shawrâ*), a traditional Hazara organization that combined various groups.

Relations with the United States were seriously disrupted in February 1979 following the death of Ambassador Adolf Dubs. He was killed in the Kabul Hotel during a rescue attempt after his kidnap by opponents to the Marxist regime. Up to that time the United States was still providing aid to Afghanistan. This was now stopped. The American government was already deeply involved in the events in neighbouring Iran, where in early 1979 the Shah was ousted and replaced by Ayatullah Khumayni. The Americans were becoming increasingly alarmed about a possible Soviet occupation of Afghanistan and their marching on to the warm waters of the Persian Gulf and the Indian Ocean, unopposed by anyone now the Iranians had turned against Washington. Yet, there was very little they could do.

The Islamic Revolution in Iran not only weakened America's position in this part of the world, it also strengthened the resistance against the Marxist regime in Kabul. In March 1979, a serious uprising broke out in Herat, close to the Iran border. This rebellion was instigated, among others, by Islamic leaders who after the Islamic Revolution in Iran had returned to Afghanistan. In the end large groups of Afghan military from Herat Province defected to the opposition. For a few days the town was in their hands, until it was taken again by a column from Qandahar, assisted by aeroplanes.

Hafiz Allah Amin

Meanwhile, within the regime, important changes took place. The growing unrest had undermined Tarakki's position. On 27 March 1979, Hafiz Allah Amin was appointed Prime Minister of a Government of National Deliverance and in the months to follow, Amin gradually extended his powers. His son was made chairman of the PDPA's youth organization, and his nephew was made head of the security services.

In the summer of 1979, however, the position of the communist regime in Kabul became almost untenable and Soviet involvement increased. In June, the Soviet army took over control of Begram airbase just north of Kabul. A popular uprising in Kabul on 3 August was quelled with much bloodshed, and a massive revolt of the military garrison of the Bala Hisar in Kabul, during the same month, could only be crushed after heavy bombing. Tarakki's position was now hopeless, and on 16 September 1979 Radio Kabul announced that President Tarakki had been replaced and succeeded by Prime Minister Hafiz Allah Amin. The radio also said that Tarakki was ill. An eery situation followed, until, on 9 October, Kabul Radio announced Tarakki's death. He was allegedly killed during a shoot-out between his adherents and those of Amin. Other sources report that Tarakki was strangled in the night of October 8/9 by Amin's followers.[6]

Under Russian pressure Amin tried to reconcile the opposing forces. On 9 October he published a list with the names of 12,000 people who had been executed by Tarakki's regime. He released political prisoners, invoked Allah in official speeches and allocated government funds for restoring mosques. On a military level he managed to defeat the resistance in Paktya, along the Pakistan border, although with much Soviet help and only very temporarily. Opposition against the Kabul regime, however, could no longer be stopped. Mass desertions from the army and continuing infighting among the communists severely weakened its position.

Moscow now became seriously alarmed about a possible failure of the Marxist revolution in Afghanistan. Apart from seriously undermining their own ideology, there were other reasons for worry. The Islamic Revolution in Iran stressed the strategic importance of Afghanistan, and the Moscow regime anticipated further American involvement in Iran. Their concern increased when Hafiz Allah Amin showed signs of trying to loosen the relationship with the Soviet Union.[7] In November 1979 Amin even asked for the recall of the Soviet ambassador, Alexandr Puzanov, an old hand in the country since 1972. He had to leave on 19 November 1979.

6 *The Truth about Afghanistan* 1980:87. This very interesting booklet was obligingly thrown at me by staff of the Soviet consulate in Amsterdam at Christmas Eve 1980.
7 He seems to have approached the United States for aid (Magnus and Naby 1998:127).

The Kremlin now made the fateful decision that military inter-vention in Afghanistan was inevitable. Soviet forces and civil ser-vants, under overall command of Marshall Sergei Sokolov, entered the country and took over crucial posts. The American government on 26 December reported the large-scale transfer of men and mate-rials from the Soviet Union to Afghanistan and especially to Kabul. On 27 December, the Soviet army took over military installations in Kabul and occupied the Dar al-Aman Palace, the residence of Hafiz Allah Amin. During the attack Amin himself, together with his nephew and head of the security services, Asad Allah Amin, were killed. To explain the invasion, the Soviet Union and the new Marxist Afghan regime declared that Amin had been a CIA spy.[8]

The Soviet Occupation

Babrak Karmal, back from his temporary exile in Moscow, was installed as the new president of Afghanistan. Together with Tarakki he had been one of the founders of the PDPA. While Tarakki became the leader of the Khalq faction, Babrak Karmal was the spokesman of the Parcham. Karmal was chosen in the 1965 Parliament, while Tarakki was not. After the Saur Revolution in 1978, he became Deputy Prime Minister under Tarakki, but he and his Parchami followers were soon brushed aside. After having served as ambas-sador to Czechoslovakia he was recalled to Kabul by the Tarakki regime, but wisely refused to return, and sought refuge in the Soviet Union.

He returned to Afghanistan together with the Soviet forces and was appointed President, Prime Minister, chairman of the Revolu-tionary Council and secretary-general of the Central Committee of the communist party. Another Parchami leader who came to the fore-front was Sultan 'Ali Keshtmand. He was a Hazara and another founding member of the PDPA. A follower of Babrak Karmal, he was sentenced to death during the purges in 1979, but Hafiz Allah Amin changed his sentence to fifteen years' imprisonment. After the Soviet invasion, he became deputy Prime Minister and Minister for Plan-ning, and a member of the Politbureau. In 1981 he was apppointed Prime Minister.[9] Within the constellation of Afghan politics, the ele-

8   He was accused of having tried to organize a coup d'état together with Hekmat-yar's *Hizb-i Islâmi* that should have taken place on 29 December 1979 (*The Truth about Afghanistan* 1980:91).
9   Much later, in 1990, he was appointed first Vice-President. After the fall of the regime he left for England.

vation of a Hazara to the post of Prime Minister was another reason for the Pashtuns to oppose the Marxist regime in Kabul.

At first the Khalq faction of the PDPA was also represented in the new government. This must have been done at the urgent request of the Soviet Union, who wanted to impose unity upon the PDPA. Deputy Prime Minister was Asad Allah Sarwari, head of the former AGSA, the secret police.[10] Other Khalqi members were Muhammad Gulabzoy, Minister of the Interior,[11] and Sherjan Mazduryar, Minister of Transport. In the summer of 1980, however, a large number of former associates of Hafiz Allah Amin were executed and the influence of the Khalq faction was drastically curtailed.

In order to win the people's favour and reconcile them with the presence of Soviet troops, Karmal ordered the release of all political prisoners. He also expressed his respect for Islam, family values, private ownership and other aspects of traditional life. The red flag of the Khalqis was replaced by traditional green. The interim constitution of 21 April 1980 guaranteed freedom of religion. At the same time, it firmly placed sovereignty with the people, without any reference to Islam as a legitimizing factor. In order to show a certain continuation, the *Loya Jirga* was made into the highest state authority. Next to the *Loya Jirga*, however, was the Revolutionary Council, which wielded real power. The people were supposed to express their revolutionary zeal in the PDPA, while the National Fatherland Front covered all groups, including the Islamic High Council.

The arrival of Soviet troops and the removal of Amin did not lead to a weakening of the opposition against the Marxist regime. Armed revolts broke out all over the country. In late February 1980, large demonstrations were held in Kabul, and the shops remained closed. The protests were supported, if not instigated by ʿAbd al-Majid Kalakani, the founder of the Maoist SAMA resistance party (*Sâzmân-i Âzâdibakhsh-i Mardom-i Afghânistân*).[12] The demonstrations stopped when Kalakani was arrested on 27 February.[13] The Soviet troops also encountered internal problems. At first Soviet forces included many soldiers from the Central Asian republics. The Soviet leaders obviously thought that these would more easily mix with the Afghans and be more readily accepted as 'elder brothers'. However, soon many men defected and the Soviets were forced to withdraw

10 Although not for long. The same year he was 'promoted' to the post of Ambassador in Mongolia.
11 And head of the Interior Forces.
12 He thus originated from the same village as *Bachcha-i Saqaw*, the Tajik leader of the country in 1929.
13 He was subsequently executed on 8 June.

the Central Asian soldiers. By mid-1980 most of the Soviet troops came from other republics. By early 1982, the total military presence of the Soviet Union in Afghanistan had risen to some 120,000, excluding civilian advisers.

International disapproval of the Soviet invasion of Afghanistan was widespread and clear. In January 1980 the Security Council and the General Assembly of the United Nations adopted resolutions that asked for an immediate withdrawal of all foreign troops from the country. Foreign ministers from the Islamic states mentioned the Soviet Union by name and deplored its 'aggression against the people of Afghanistan'. President Carter of the United States declared a grain embargo against the Soviet Union and very soon information was spread that Egypt and the United States were channelling weapons and ammunition to the *Mujâhedin*. In July 1980, some sixty countries boycotted the Moscow Olympics.

One of the means used by the Soviets and the Kabul regime to 'pacify' the country was the secret police. The KHAD (*Khedmât-i Ittilâʿat-i Dawlati*), was the direct successor of the AGSA[14] and the KAM[15] of Muhammad Tarakki and Hafiz Allah Amin respectively. The KHAD was established directly after Babrak Karmal's ascent to power. It was initially, until 1986, led by Dr Najib Allah, the future president of Afghanistan (1986–92). He was a Ghalji Pashtun married to a (Durrani) Muhammadzay, and a former bodyguard of Karmal. He was born in Kabul in 1947 and belonged to a fairly affluent family. In the mid-1960s he became a member of the PDPA and attached himself to the Parcham faction. He graduated from the Faculty of Medicine of Kabul University in 1975. When Tarakki became president of the country following the Saur Revolution, he was as so many other Parchamis removed from Kabul and appointed as ambassador to Tehran. He was soon recalled, however, but refused to return. He finally went back to Afghanistan together with Babrak Karmal to become the head of the secret police.

When in the mid-1980s the KHAD became a Ministry, its name was consequently changed to the WAD (*Wizârat-i Ittilâʿat-i Dawlati*). The KHAD/WAD not only controlled a large network of informers, but also the National Guard, which was reputed to be the best fighting force among the Afghan government troops. The Parcham thus controlled the KHAD/WAD and its National Guard, while Khalqis generally led the army.

---

14 Pashto: *Da Afghânistân da Gatay da Satanay Edâra* ('Afghanistan Security Service Department').
15 Pashto: *Da Kârgarano Amniyyati Muʿasasa* ('Workers' Security Institution').

Illustration 17   *The modern fortress and town of Ghazni. In the 1980s, the citadel was permanently occupied by Soviet and Afghan security forces, while the town itself was in the hands of the Mujahedin (photograph: author, summer 1982).*

Afghan Resistance

Throughout the war, resistance against the Kabul regime and the Soviet army was carried by two forces, namely the regional groups and the external parties. The regional groups mainly originated from local networks, either local, ethnic or religious. They were the groups doing the actual fighting. The external parties were led by the Islamist and traditional Islamic leaders who before and after 1979 had sought refuge abroad. Most of the Sunnite leaders resided in Peshawar, while the Shi'ites tended to live in Quetta (Pakistan), or in Iran. In spite of these basic differences, a process started from the very beginning whereby the internal and external forces amalgamated. One of the main reasons for this development, which in the end placed much power in the hands of the Afghan leaders outside of Afghanistan, was the fact that foreign aid for the Afghan resistance was mainly chan- nelled via Pakistan and the external resistance parties. The mass exodus of Afghans to Pakistan, some three million in total, also con- tributed to this development.[16]

Most of the Afghans fleeing to Pakistan were Pashtuns. They crossed the border and sought refuge with their kinsmen east of the Durand Line. Often, however, only the women and children would

16   Some two million Afghan refugees fled to Iran.

migrate, while the men would remain behind to fight the enemy. Vice versa, many Pashtuns from east of the border joined their kinsmen in Afghanistan. The border was open; Pakistani authorities did not prevent any crossing by the *Mujâhedin*, and in this way the Afghans always had a safe haven where they could find refuge and acquire weapons and ammunition.

In almost all cases, the opposition against the Soviet forces and the Marxist regime in Kabul, whether led by local commanders in the field or by religious leaders from outside the country, was based on Islam. Those who took up arms against the Kabul regime called themselves *Mujâhedin*, 'those fighting a *jihâd*'. They were defending Islam against the 'infidels', the Marxists. Within this broad context, however, the various groups of Mujahedin reflected a wide array of interpretations of Islam. There was not only the opposition between Shi'ites and Sunnites, but there were also groups that wanted to restore Afghanistan to what it used to be, or what they thought it used to be. These were the so-called traditionalists. Their leaders in the main originated from among the landed gentry.[17] There were also those who wanted to restore Islam to what it used to be, or what they thought it used to be. They wanted to liberate Islam from all later additions after the time of Muhammad and the first Caliphs. They wanted to read and re-read the ancient texts.[18] These were the so-called fundamentalists. Thirdly, there were the Islamists, who were among the first to oppose the Kabul establishment from the mid-1960s onwards. Like the fundamentalists, they wanted to restore Islam to what it was, according to them, in the time of Muhammad. In addition, however, very much like the Marxists themselves, they wanted to change the state of Afghanistan. Islam to them was an ideology, rather than a belief. Adherents of these various interpretations of Islam could be found among the six, and later seven, main Sunnite resistance parties in Peshawar, which from 1980 had been selected by the Pakistani government as mediators in the transfer of weapons and other assistance to the Afghan opposition.[19]

The seven groups included four Islamist parties:

- *Hizb-i Islâmi-yi Afghânistân* ('Islamic Party of Afghanistan') led by Gulb ud-Din Hekmatyar.
- *Hizb-i Islâmi-yi Afghânistân*, led by Mawlawi Yunus Khalis.
- *Ittihâd-i Islâmi barâye Azâdi-yi Afghânistân* ('Islamic Union for the Liberation of Afghanistan') led by 'Abd al-Rasul Sayyaf.

17 Compare Roy 1990:3.
18 Compare Roy 1990:3–6.
19 Mainly via the Pakistani Inter-Services Intelligence, headed by General 'Abd al-Rahman Akhtar (1979–87), and then by General Hamid Gul.

Illustration 18 *Propaganda poster from 1980, the year of the Moscow Olympics and the first year of the Soviet occupation of Afghanistan (collection: author).*

- *Jam'iyyat-i Islâmi-yi Afghânistân* ('Islamic Society of Afghanistan') of Professor Burhan ud-Din Rabbani.

Furthermore there were three more traditionalist Islamic groupings, mainly Pashtun in composition:

- *Harakat-i Inquilâb-i Islâmi-yi Afghânistân* ('The Islamic Revolutionary Movement of Afghanistan') led by Mawlawi Muhammad Nabi Muhammadi.

- *Jabha-yi Najât-i Milli-yi Afghânistân* ('National Liberation Front of Afghanistan') of Sibghat Allah Mujaddidi.
- *Mahaz-i Milli-yi Islâmi-yi Afghânistân* ('National Islamic Front of Afghanistan'), led by Sayyid Ahmad Gaylani.

At the beginning of the war with the Soviet Union, the traditionalist/fundamentalist party of Mawlavi Muhammad Nabi Muhammadi was by far the largest and most important. It was supported by clergy and *madrasa* students, mostly of Pashtun origin. It also received some support from the Pashtun tribes along the Pakistani border. Nabi Muhammadi was born in 1921 in Logar, south of Kabul, and educated at various religious schools. In 1965 he was elected into Parliament and remained a fierce opponent of communist influence in the country. He fled to Pakistan after the Marxist coup of 1978. His resistance party was rather loosely organized and mainly included the traditionalist groups. Over the years, however, the role of this party diminished, and by the late 1980s the main political and military forces opposed to the regime and the Soviet occupation were the two parties of Gulb ud-Din Hekmatyar and Burhan ud-Din Rabbani.

Gulb ud-Din Hekmatyar was born in 1947 at Imam Sahib, near Qunduz, in the north of the country. He is a Kharoti Ghalji and thus belongs to the same Pashtun tribe as Hafiz Allah Amin, the Marxist President in 1979. He was for a very brief period a student of the Polytechnic in Kabul, and after joining the Islamist camp he spent time in prison in the early 1970s for the murder of a Maoist student. He founded the *Hizb-i Islâmi-yi Afghânistân* in 1976 after he was forced to flee to Peshawar during the reign of Muhammad Dawud. Hekmatyar was opposed to local leaders, local mullas and Sufis (Islamic mystics). He wanted to establish an Islamic state based on Islamic law. He was by far the most radical and ruthless of the Afghan leaders against the Marxist regime. The *Hizb-i Islâmi* of Gulb ud-Din Hekmatyar, in spite of its record of obstructing the activities of other resistance groups, throughout the war with the Soviet Union received the largest amount of foreign help. The group was the favourite of the *Jamâ'at-i Islâmi*, the influential Islamist movement in Pakistan, and of the Pakistani Inter-Service Intelligence that organized all foreign aid to the Mujahedin.

The other main resistance party was the *Jam'iyyat-i Islâmi-yi Afghânistân* of Professor Burhan ud-Din Rabbani. He is a Tajik born in Fayzabad, in 1940. He was strongly influenced by the ideas of Mawdudi and the Egyptian Muslim Brotherhood. Over the years, however, he became more moderate, also towards Shi'ites. His power base is a network of sufis and clerics, mainly in the north and west of the country, while his Tajik origins helped him in building up a large following in the northeast of the country. Rabbani was strongly supported by two regional commanders, namely Ahmad Shah Mas'ud, who has his headquarters in the Panjshir valley, and Muhammad Isma'il, who fought in Herat and the rest of West Afghanistan.

Ahmad Shah Mas'ud is perhaps the best-known resistance commander in Afghanistan. He was born in 1956 and in the mid-1970s took part in the active resistance against President Dawud. His successful defence of the Panjshir valley against numerous Soviet attacks in the 1980s made him known as the 'Lion of the Panjshir'. He often received foreign journalists, which of course also helped in spreading his name and fame abroad. Apart from the military successes that he achieved during the war he also built up a parallel administrative organization. Ever since the early 1980s Ahmad Shah Mas'ud has been a bitter enemy of Gulb ud-Din Hekmatyar. Many times their forces have clashed, both before and after the Soviet withdrawal.[20]

The other resistance parties played a minor role. The *Hizb-i Islâmi* of Mawlani Yunus Khalis split off from Hekmatyar's party in 1979. Yunus Khalis's following was much smaller than that of Hekmatyar, and more or less restricted to the Pashtun lands along the Peshawar-Kabul highway and in Paktya. This group was less radical than its namesake and more willing to listen to and cooperate with other parties. Yunus Khalis, born in 1919, remained however a strong supporter of Islamist ideals.

The last Islamist party is the *Ittihâd-i Islâmi barâye Azâdi-yi Afghânistân*. This party was formed by 'Abd al-Rasul Sayyaf, born in Paghman west of Kabul in 1946. He was educated at Al-Azhar University in Cairo and later became lecturer in Kabul. He was arrested in 1975 while about to board an aeroplane to study law at George Washington University. He survived the 1979 prison massacres because of kinship with Hafiz Allah Amin. After his release in January 1980, he came to Peshawar and was elected spokesman of the Islamic Union for the Liberation of Afghanistan, a loose coalition of all Afghan resistance parties in Peshawar. When his two-year period of office ended, he refused to step down and was forced to leave. He subsequently established his own organization, but retained

---

20 In June 1989, a number of *Jam'iyyat* commanders of Mas'ud were killed by Sayyid Jamal, a commander of Hekmatyar's *Hizb-i Islâmi*. Jamal was later in the year arrested and executed by Mas'ud's forces.

the name of the umbrella group. Because of his background he acquired large funds from Arab sources. Sayyaf again came to the fore when in 1985 the resistance parties formed the Islamic Alliance of Afghan Mujahedin. Sayyaf was made chairman, and Mujaddidi was made his deputy.

One of the more traditionalist parties was the *Jabha-yi Najât-i Milli-yi Afghânistân*. This group was led by a prominent member of the Mujaddidi family, namely Sibghat Allah Mujaddidi. He strove for the establishment of a traditional Islamic state. His party's support was closely linked to that of the Mujaddidi family itself, among the Naqshbandiyya Sufi movement in East Afghanistan. Sibghat Allah Mujaddidi was born in 1925 and educated in Kabul and Cairo. He was imprisoned between 1959 and 1964 for being involved in a plot to kill the Soviet leaders and in the 1970s he was forced to leave Afghanistan and he settled in Denmark. After the Russian invasion he went to Peshawar to chair the National Liberation Front.

Finally there is the *Mahaz-i Milli-yi Islâmi-yi Afghanistan*, led by Sayyid Ahmad Gaylani. He was born in 1932 as the son of Sayyid Hasan Gaylani, who in 1905 moved from Baghdad to Afghanistan and became the leader of the Qadirite Sufi community in the area.[21] Sayyid Ahmad Gaylani, who received religious training at the Faculty of Theology of Kabul University, took over the leadership in 1964. He is married to a granddaughter of King Habib Allah. His party is no doubt the most liberal and secular of all the Peshawar parties and in favour of a return of Zahir Shah. It asks for a clear separation of legislative, executive and judicial powers, free elections and a free press. The followers of Gaylani are mainly found among the borderland Ghalji Pashtuns and the Pashtuns of Wardak, north of Ghazni.[22]

From the very beginning of the war, the resistance parties in Pakistan have tried, mostly under outside pressure, to form an alliance. In January 1980, immediately after the Soviet invasion, this led to the aforementioned Islamic Union for the Liberation of Afghanistan, headed by 'Abd al-Rasul Sayyaf. It included five of the main parties, but not Hekmatyar's *Hizb-i Islâmi*. The Union soon disintegrated, but it was reformed in 1985 under the name of the Islamic Alliance of Afghan Mujahedin. It included all the seven main

21 The Qadiriyya fraternity derives from Baghdad and was introduced into the tribal zone from India.
22 Sufism among the Pashtun border tribes has often taken the form of Maraboutism (compare Roy 1990:38–44). This means that it is not the relationship between pupil and teacher (*murid* and *pir*), as in orthodox Sufism, but between a clan or tribe and the *pir* that is essential. Maraboutism applies to both the followers of Gaylani (Qadiriyya) and (partly) also those of Mujaddidi (Naqshbandiyya).

resistance parties. Yet the effect of these alliances was negligible, and merely served to broadcast a united front to the outside world.

The Hazaras

The Hazaras took a completely different position. Traditionally they constitute the poorest segment of Afghan society and over the years, Pashtun nomads and others had driven them deep into the mountains of Central Afghanistan. The Marxist coup of 1978 and the subsequent decline of Kabul authority in the countryside led to the semi-independence of the Hazaras. In September 1979, Hazara leaders subsequently founded the Revolutionary Council of the Islamic Union of Afghanistan (*Shawrâ-yi Ittifâq-i Inqilâb-i Islâmi-yi Afghânistân*), generally called the *Shawrâ* ('Council'). Its president was Sayyid ʿAli Beheshti and its military leader was Sayyid Muhammad Hasan Jagran ('major'). Their centre was in Ghur Province, in and around Waras, and in the Behsud area north of the Dasht-i Nawar.

Beheshti was born in Bamiyan, in the centre of Afghanistan, and trained in Iraq. He represented the traditional Shiʿite leaders of the Hazaras. At first the *Shawrâ* occupied a strong position, the more so since the Marxist regime and the Soviets hardly ever ventured into Hazarajat. Beheshti could set up a civil administration, collect taxes, and in general act as the leader of an independent country. In the early 1980s however, opposition from the side of other groups, supported by revolutionary Iran and including many Hazaras from Iran, seriously weakened the *Shawrâ*. The opposition included the *Sâzmân-i Nasr-i Afghânistân* ('Victory Organization of Afghanistan'), which was headed by Hojatoleslam Mir Husayn Sadeqi and ʿAbd al-ʿAli Mazari, and the *Sâzmân-i Pâsdârân-i Jihâd-i Islâm* ('Organization of the Guardians of the Islamic *Jihâd*'), led by Ustad Akbari. Both groups, and many others, wanted to imitate Iran and establish an Islamic state headed by Shiʿite clergy. They thus, contrary to Behesthi, advocated an independent Hazarajat. They also adhered to a very anti-Pashtun policy. In the spring of 1984 the opposition had become so strong that they could drive the *Shawrâ* from Waras, the stronghold of Beheshti. Beheshti eventually joined Burhan ud-Din Rabbani, while the other Shiʿite parties in 1990 united into the *Hizb-i Wahdat-i Islâmi* ('Islamic Party of Unity'), with ʿAbd al-ʿAli Mazari of the *Nasr* as chairman.[23]

---

23 Mazari was born in 1946 near Mazar-i Sharif in the north of the country. He enjoyed religious training in Iran and Iraq.

Negotiations

Between 1980 and 1988 the Soviet forces in Afghanistan and the Kabul regime fought a cruel war with the Afghan Mujahedin. To many observers it was clear from the very beginning that neither party would ever manage to completely defeat the other. The Soviet army and the government troops were entrenched in the main cities and at other fortified places, while the Mujahedin dominated the countryside. While the Soviets and Kabul troops were often capable of briefly occupying certain parts of the country outside the cities, their place was taken by their opponents the moment the last Soviet tank left the region. And while the Soviet army and Kabul troops could draw on the apparently limitless reserves of the Soviet Union, the Mujahedin could fall back on their safe havens in Pakistan and Iran and accept the ever increasing stockpiles of weaponry sent from the United States, China and the Middle East. A diplomatic solution seemed the only way out.

International negotiations between Pakistan and the Kabul government started in Geneva in June 1982. The two parties were seconded by the United States and the Soviet Union respectively. The Mujahedin did not directly participate. The talks focussed on the question how to end the external involvement in Afghanistan and how to establish permanent peace. The negotiations dragged on for a long time. The Soviets at first wanted a period of four years before withdrawing their troops, but an immediate stop of foreign aid to the Mujahedin. Their position and that of United States hardly changed for three years. However, when in March 1985 Michail Gorbachev became Secretary-General of the Communist Party of the Soviet Union, the Russian position relaxed.

Apart from the time-table, another problem arose, namely the fact that the Mujahedin would never participate in a new government together with Babrak Karmal. To forestall this problem, Babrak Karmal was made to resign and he was replaced by Muhammad Najib Allah, the head of the Afghan Secret Police, on 4 May 1986. All the time military pressure on the Soviets and the Kabul regime increased, not in the least by the introduction among the Mujahedin of Stinger and Blowpipe anti-aircraft missiles.

Prompted by the Soviet Union, Najib Allah embarked on a policy of national reconciliation. On 15 January 1987, he unilaterally declared a ceasefire for a period of six months and presented a number of proposals aimed at a reconciliation of all opposing parties. In answer to these proposals, a general meeting took place of field commanders of the resistance. It took place in Ghur province in July

1987 and was called together by Isma'il Khan, the *Jam'iyyat* resistance leader in Herat province.[24] The resistance leaders decided to reject Najib Allah's proposals, the ceasefire collapsed, and so did the Commission for Reconciliation that had been set up by Najib Allah. Also his invitation to the three traditional resistance parties in Peshawar to join his government was not heeded. Foreign aid to the resistance had in the meantime gone up to some $1,300 million, mainly provided by the United States and Saudi Arabia. The resistance parties now knew they were winning the war, and there was no need to accept any of Najib Allah's proposals.

However, Najib Allah continued his policy of reconciliation. In November 1987, at a *Loya Jirga* held in Kabul and attended by more than 1800 delegates, Najib Allah declared a new constitution, which dropped the adjective of 'Democratic' from the official name of the country. A two-chambered parliament was established. The members of the *Wolesi Jirga* were to be directly elected, while those of the Senate were either directly elected or appointed by the President. The *Loya Jirga*, it was stipulated, expressed the will of the people. It also stated that Islam was the state religion and it provided room for a multi-party system. In January 1988, a selective amnesty was announced for those Mujahedin who had been sentenced *in absentia*.[25]

In the meantime, new proposals were put forward in Geneva, which limited the proposed period of Soviet withdrawal. The negotiations resulted on 14 April 1988 in the signing of the so-called Geneva Accords by Afghanistan, Pakistan, the Soviet Union and the United States. It stated that the Soviet Union would withdraw from Afghanistan within nine months. Both sides also made promises to stop all external assistance to the Kabul regime and to the Mujahedin after the Soviet withdrawal and to assist in the safe return of the Afghan refugees to their country.

In April 1988, on the eve of the first stages of Soviet withdrawal, elections were held in (Kabul-controlled) Afghanistan for the newly established Parliament. The PDPA lost its majority position, and on 26 May 1988, Najib Allah appointed a new Prime Minister, Muhammad Hasan Sharq, who replaced Sultan 'Ali Keshtmand. Muhammad Hasan Sharq had acted as deputy Prime Minister under President Dawud and was (as far as is known) never a member of the PDPA. His appointment further illustrated Najib Allah's attempt to widen his power base. In November of the same year, Najib Allah moved his Minister of the Interior, Muhammad Bashir

---

24 Magnus and Naby 1998:153.
25 Apparently including Ahmad Shah Massud.

Gulabzoy, a veteran Khalqi leader, to the post of ambassador in Moscow.

On the Eve of Soviet Withdrawal

In February 1988, the spokesman of the Islamic Alliance of Afghan Mujahedin, Pir Sayyid Ahmad Gaylani, declared that the Alliance would not be bound by the proposed Geneva Accords since it was not included in the negotiations. Gaylani furthermore announced plans to form an Interim Government. In June of the same year, the interim government took office. It was chaired by Ahmad Shah, an American-educated member of Sayyaf's party. However, the Interim Government never really worked; the traditional antagonism between the resistance parties in Peshawar continued, and also the Hazaras opposed the (minor) role they were to play in the proposed government. In the end, the Hazaras formed their own alliance, the *Hizb-i Wahdat*. The position of the Mujahedin was furthermore complicated when in August 1988 their staunch supporter, President Zia ul-Haq of Pakistan, was killed.

In December 1988, the Afghan resistance leaders headed by Professor Rabbani travelled to the Saudi city of Taif in order to meet Yuri Vorontsov, the Soviet ambassador in Kabul. A full Soviet withdrawal from Afghanistan was now imminent, and all parties realized that the thus created vacuum might lead to chaos and much further bloodshed in the country. The meeting focused on the question whether power in Kabul could be transferred in an orderly manner. The discussions, however, were fruitless: the resistance saw no further role for Najib Allah and his party in the new government in Kabul, while the Soviets did not want to sacrifice Najib Allah and his followers. The stage was now set for a chaotic and bloody end to the Marxist regime, and a long period of internecine strife thereafter.

20

After the Soviets

The Soviet army completed its withdrawal from Afghanistan on 14 February 1989. On that day the last Soviet forces headed by General Boris Gromov crossed the Amu Darya. According to reliable estimates, some 750,000 Soviet military served in Afghanistan since 1979. Official Soviet figures tell that 13,310 Soviet soldiers were killed, 35,478 wounded and 311 were missing.[1] The war in Afghanistan coincided with the rise of Gorbachev in the mid-1980s and his policy of *glasnost* and *perestroika*, which brought about radical changes in Soviet society and ultimately led to the collapse of the Soviet Union in 1991. It is difficult to gauge to what degree the war in Afghanistan contributed to these dramatic developments.

In recent years, many books have been published, also in Russia, that deal with the Soviet occupation of Afghanistan.[2] What strikes the reader each time is the boredom and lack of commitment on the side of the Soviet military, especially among the lower ranks. They apparently lacked any understanding of their presence in that wild and inhospitable country. They did not believe what Soviet propaganda told them; in fact, they did not believe anything. All they knew was that most of the Afghans hated them. Even the Afghan army and the communist administrators in Kabul could not be trusted. Many 'communist' Afghans in Kabul had close relatives who were fighting with the *Mujâhedin*, and in this way vital information passed to the resistance. To the Soviet soldiers Afghanistan was a quagmire, or in other words, it was the Soviet's Vietnam.

Three quarters of a million men shared these traumatic experiences and returned to their homes in the Soviet Union. Their accounts of the horrors that they experienced were told and retold all over the Soviet empire. It would perhaps be too much to say that the Afghan

---

1 Adamec 1997:16, 403. See also Arnold 1993.
2 Compare the following website: www.cfcsc.dnd.ca/links/milhist/afgf

Mujahedin brought about the fall of the Soviet Union, but they certainly demoralized the Soviet people and ridiculed the Soviet army. They drained the Soviet treasury, caused great diplomatic damage and undermined the Soviet leaders' confidence in their own Marxist–Leninist ideology.

And what was the impact on Afghanistan and the Afghans? Apart from all the people being killed, mamed, driven from their homes or otherwise afflicted, the sad truth has since come to light that the defeat of the Kabul regime also meant the defeat of the state of Afghanistan. The war in the 1980s wiped out most of the bureaucrats and intelligentsia, who were either killed or forced to move abroad. Their places were taken by resistance leaders and others who represented special interest groups, either ethnically or religiously determined, and who were more inclined to promote their own interests and those of their following, than building up an independent state apparatus. This process of desintegration of Afghanistan started during the war in the 1980s, but continued rapidly after the Soviet withdrawal.

The Interlude

Soviet material support for the Kabul regime continued after the last Soviet soldier left the country, and so did foreign assistance to the Mujahedin. Najib Allah tried to survive by dropping most of the Marxist symbols of his government and by a general policy of 'divide and rule'. Militia were armed and paid for, and various warlords were richly rewarded by the Kabul regime. On the other side, the resistance parties in Peshawar came to some sort of agreement as to the formation of yet another Interim Government, the composition of which was announced on 23 February 1989. Sibghat Allah Mujaddidi was appointed as (acting) President and 'Abd ul-Rasul Sayyaf as (acting) Prime Minister.[3]

In early March 1989, just some weeks after the last Soviet soldier had left the country, the Mujahedin mounted a large offensive against Najib Allah's forces in Jalalabad. Optimism reigned supreme amongst the resistance parties in Peshawar and among their Pakistani and American supporters. They not only expected the immediate fall of Jalalabad, but also the subsequent total collapse of the Marxist regime. Western journalists flocked *en masse* to Kabul to witness the

---

3   From the beginning this Interim Government was opposed by the Shi'ite groups. Sayyid Ahmed Gaylani refused a post in the government, but later accepted the function of Supreme Judge.

downfall of the Marxists and the triumphant entry of the Mujahedin. No doubt the Americans hoped for a replay of the North Vietnamese victorious entry into Saigon in 1974. What actually happened afterwards was a total disaster for the anti-Najib Allah forces.

The siege of Jalalabad was organized by the resistance parties and their foreign sponsors in Peshawar, but most of the local commanders were opposed to these plans right from the beginning. They realized that the Mujahedin were not yet ready for traditional warfare, especially since they would lack any backing from the air. They were right. Within a few weeks the Mujahedin were forced to retreat, with heavy losses. Lack of coordination, internecine fighting and heavy bombing of their positions by Najib Allah's airforce led to a total defeat. Najib Allah remained in power in Kabul and was now even stronger than before.

That was not all. The Interim Government collapsed when in the autumn of the same year Hekmatyar withdrew his support. Fortunately for the Mujahedin, however, Najib Allah's power was slowly being eroded by defections. In March 1990, Shahnawaz Tanay, a Khalqi general, chief of staff of the armed forces since 1986 and Minister of Defence between 1988 and 1990, defected to Hekmatyar's party and staged a coup against Najib Allah, which failed. Many Khalqis now left the sinking ship and joined the resistance, especially Hekmatyar's *Hizb-i Islâmi*, while many Parchami defectors tended to side with Rabbani's *Jam'iyyat-i Islâmi*.

But Najib Allah hang on, still supported by Soviet arms and money. In June 1990, the name of the PDPA was changed into the Homeland Party (*Hizb-i Watan*) and the party dropped all remaining Marxist ideology. At the same time, Najib Allah evacuated a series of districts, although he remained in control of most of the major cities.

After the winter of 1990/1991, the resistance regrouped and in March 1991 they took the town and district of Khost, along the Pakistan border. Najib Allah's days were now numbered, although it was again the Soviet Union that would directly influence events in the country: in August 1991 a group of hardliners in Moscow tried to take control of the rapidly disintegrating Soviet Union. Their failure led to the definitive collapse of the Soviet empire in the same year, and consequently Soviet/Russian support for the Kabul regime evaporated. The Marxist regime in Afghanistan still managed to survive the winter of 1991/1992, but this was more due to the weakness of the resistance than to the strength of the regime.

The crunch came in March 1992 when a group of northern militia leaders rebelled against Najib Allah. The insurgents included General ʿAbd al-Rashid Dostum and Sayyid Mansur Nadiri. Dostum was the leader of the Jawzjan militia that was formed by the Kabul regime in 1988 and that consisted in the main of Özbeks from the north and northwest of the country. His troops fought in various parts of Afghanistan in support of the Marxist regime, and for his support of the regime he was even awarded the title of 'Hero of the Republic of Afghanistan'. His defection meant a great blow to Najib Allah. Sayyid Mansur Nadiri, the other leader who defected, was the son of Sayyid Nadir Shah Husayn, or simply Sayyid-i Kayan, who used to be the head of the Isma'ili community in Afghanistan.

Together the rebels took Mazar-i Sharif, and soon the north of Afghanistan was lost to the Kabul regime. The two northern leaders subsequently joined with Ahmad Shah Mas'ud from the Panjshir valley, and in April 1992 they managed to occupy Kabul, which effectively fell on 25 April. Najib Allah fled to the UN compound and the Marxist regime completely collapsed. Most of the weaponry fell into the hands of the various resistance groups, including more than two hundred fighter aircraft and hundreds of tanks and artillery pieces.[4]

Three days later, on 28 April, Sibghat Allah Mujaddidi, as President of the Interim Government, arrived from Peshawar. For the following two months he was President of Afghanistan on the basis of the so-called Peshawar Accord of 24 April 1992.[5] Under this agreement, which was concluded in the absence of Gulb ud-Din Hekmatyar and also without the Hazara *Hizb-i Wahdat*, a two-month interim government was set up in Kabul under Sibghat Allah Mujaddidi. It was further stipulated that a four-month interim government led by Professor Burhan ud-Din Rabbani would succeed him. A 'Council of Solution and Pact' would then form an interim government for eighteen months, during which time general elections would be organized.

But whatever the intentions of the Peshawar Accord, the truth was that in the spring of 1992 the Afghan capital Kabul was in the hands of non-Pashtun groups. Tajiks, Özbeks and Isma'ilis dominated the streets. The Pashtun groups, including Hekmatyar's *Hizb-i Islâmi*, could only watch. Mujaddidi's own group, the *Jabha-yi Najât-i Milli-yi Afghânistân*, was unwilling and also too weak to disarm the militias now controlling Kabul. Mas'ud and his allies did not want to leave Kabul for fear of Hekmatyar's *Hizb-i Islâmi*. Mujaddidi did not trust Hekmatyar either, since the latter had allegedly shortly before tried to blow up his aeroplane. When on 28 June 1992 Mujaddidi handed over the presidency to Professor Rabbani, his military leader

4 Kamal Matinuddin 1999:48–9.
5 For its text, see Kamal Matinuddin 1999:233–6.

Ahmad Shah Mas'ud was soon in control of most of Kabul. By that time, fighting had already started between Mas'ud's forces and those of Hekmatyar, but also between the *Hizb-i Islâmi* of Hekmatyar and the forces of General Dostum. Rabbani and Mas'ud seemed to be in the ideal position to extend their own influence. However, they never succeeded in doing so.

Rabbani's Government

Rabbani's government was hampered from the very beginning, not only by external foes, but also by internal problems. First there was the strife between Ahmad Shah Mas'ud and his experienced warriors on the one side, and the Peshawar-trained administrators of Rabbani. Secondly, ethnic tension arose between the Mujahedin of Mas'ud, mostly originating from the Panjshir valley, and those of Rabbani, from Badakhshan. Thirdly, there was the growing influence of Isma'il Khan, who called himself Amir and officially belonged to the *Jam'iyyat* of Rabbani. He managed to set up an efficient organization in Herat and western Afghanistan, and this area soon became the most thriving part of the country, quite contrary to the devastation in and around Kabul. Rabbani's main problem, however, was the external opposition to his government.

From late 1992, the forces of Rabbani and Mas'ud were under attack from an ever changing coalition of former resistance parties and other groups. The continuous fighting cost the lives of thousands of Afghans and seriously undermined the prestige of the Mujahedin. The main protagonists, apart from Rabbani's *Jam'iyyat*, were Hekmatyar and his *Hizb-i Islâmi*, the Özbek militia of General Dostum[6] and the Shi'ite *Hizb-i Wahdat* of 'Abd al-'Ali Mazari. All this time Rabbani refused to give up his presidency, although he should have done so by the end of October 1992, as stipulated by the Peshawar Accord. The continuous fighting destroyed much of Kabul and drove thousands of Kabulis out of their city. Outside of Kabul, a series of local warlords established their own positions, mainly along highways in order to levy taxes and harass travellers. The situation in Qandahar was particularly bad. Only Isma'il Khan in Herat and General Dostum in Mazar-i Sharif managed to keep their part of the country under control. The situation seemed hopeless, until in the summer of 1994 a new force appeared on the scene. This group consisted of religiously strongly motivated Pashtuns from the south of the country.

---

6   His following was organized into a party called the *Junbish-i Milli-yi Islâmi*.

The Taliban Rise to Power

By 1994 Pakistan was actively trying to establish a safe and direct route of communication with the newly established Central Asian republics. For Pakistan there were only two options: the route via Kabul and the Salang Pass, or the route via Qandahar and the Herat corridor. At that time, the situation in and around Kabul was utterly chaotic. Gulb ud-Din Hekmatyar, in spite of all the assistance he had been given by the Pakistanis, could not take the capital. In fact, instead of occupying the city and driving out the Tajiks, he could only destroy it by continuous artillery and missile attacks. The respect that he had enjoyed among many Afghans had evaporated.

Pakistan thus opted for the southern route. In the summer they appointed a Pakistani official to head a permanent mission in Herat. In mid-September this Mission was installed by Isma'il Khan, Rabbani's governor in Herat. In late September, high-level Pakistani officials made an overland journey through South and West Afghanistan to South Central Asia and China, and returned via the Karakorum Highway. The situation seemed favourable for further probing, and on 20 October the Pakistanis took ambassadors from the United States, China, Japan and a number of European countries to visit Herat.

In late October the Pakistani government went a step further and sent a large convoy from Quetta in Pakistan, via Qandahar and Herat to Central Asia. The Pakistani government made sure that the press was well-informed about this journey, which should have coincided with the Pakistani's Prime Minister's visit to Turkmenistan. What happened subsequently is still unclear. The convoy was stopped just outside Qandahar by local warlords. They did so apparently on their own initiative, but there may also have been instructions from Kabul, since Rabbani had protested against the plans of the Pakistanis and had told the Pakistani government that he, as President of Afghanistan, had not given permission. Whatever really happened, soon afterwards the convoy was recaptured by a rather new group of men, the Taliban, who shortly before had captured some border posts along the Pakistani border.

According to Taliban sources, the movement started in the summer of 1994 with a small group around Mulla Muhammad Omar Akhund, who was born in 1961 in the Panjway district west of Qandahar, and later moved with his family to Uruzgan Province, north of Qandahar. He is reported to be of Ghalji origin, of the Hotak tribe.[7] During the war with the Soviet Union he fought with a local

---

7   According to Kamal Matinudin 1999:222–3.

commander for the *Harakat-i Inquilâb-i Islâmi-yi Afghânistân* of Malawi Muhammad Nabi Muhammadi, and later for the *Jam'iyyat-i Islâmi* of Professor Rabbani. He is also said to have fought for the *Hizb-i Islâmi* of Yunus Khalis. During the war against the Soviet Union he lost an eye, and therefore received the nickname *rund*, 'one-eyed'.

The first public appearance of the Taliban, as reported by Taliban and Pakistani sources, occurred in September or October 1994, when they took the border post of Spin Baldak from the *Hizb-i Islâmi* troops of Gulb ud-Din Hekmatyar. At about the same time, they are reported to have captured Hekmatyar's arms depot of Toba Achakzay nearby. The depot, it was later reported, contained some 80,000 Kalashnikov assault rifles. Did all this really happen?

Whether it did or not, by the beginning of November the Taliban were sufficiently organized and armed to attack those that had captured the Pakistani convoy. The Taliban were victorious, and soon after, on 5 November, they occupied nearby Qandahar. Government forces under Mulla Naqib Akhundzade, nominally under command of Profesor Rabbani, laid down their arms without a fight. Other warlords in and around Qandahar also gave up. Soon the Taliban in Qandahar received visits from Pakistani and American officials, including John Monjo, the American ambassador to Pakistan.[8]

In the succeeding weeks, the Taliban occupied the provinces of Uruzgan north of Qandahar and Zabul to the northeast. The Taliban clearly made use of the great resentment among the population against the warlords and their following. But the Taliban, as widely reported, also used large sums of money to win the hearts and pockets of their opponents. Resistance was offered in the west by the troops of Ghaffar Akhundzade (murdered in Quetta in March 1998), of the Durrani 'Alizay tribe and fighting lasted until mid-January 1995.

The Taliban then moved north. Taj Muhammad, commander of Ghazni, allied himself with the Taliban when he came under attack of Hekmatyar's troops. Thus Ghazni fell in January 1995. The Taliban forces then joined with troops of Rabbani and Nabi Muhammadi to repulse a subsequent counter-attack from the side of the *Hizb-i Islâmi*. Pushed away from Ghazni, Hekmatyar and his troops were later, in late February 1995, also driven away from the environs of Kabul and from his headquarters at Charasyab, 25 km south of Kabul. Hekmatyar was forced to flee to Sarobi, east of the capital. In early 1995, the Taliban and Rabbani thus cooperated in pushing Hekmatyar out of the way. This left Rabbani temporarily in a very strong position. However, he still showed no signs whatsoever of

relinguishing his presidency, which did not endear him to his other
opponents, namely the Hazaras, Isma'ilis and Özbeks, many of whom
felt forced to join with the Taliban and oppose Rabbani's troops.
In this way, 'Abd al-'Ali Mazari, the leader of the Hazara *Hizb-i
Wahdat*, and Nabi Muhammadi and his troops linked up with the
Taliban and soon fighting started along the frontline in southwest
Kabul. Here the Taliban experienced their first defeat. By 19 March,
Mas'ud took Charasyab, and in the evening he was in complete
control of Kabul and its environs. The defeat of Rabbani's opponents
also led to the collapse of their alliance. Mazari was arrested by the
Taliban and subsequently killed.[9]

Although pushed back from south of Kabul, the Taliban continued
their move to the northwest, towards Herat. After changing successes,
whereby Muhammad Isma'il Khan in mid-August 1995 succeeded in
moving close to Qandahar, the Taliban hit back and took Shindand
airbase on 3 September and Herat on 5 September. Isma'il Khan fled
to Iran. Rabbani in Kabul now openly accused Pakistan of supporting the Taliban. The following day, the Pakistani embassy in Kabul
was looted.[10] Iran also expressed its concern about the advance of
the (Sunnite) Taliban, and the new republics of South Central Asia
and Russia raised similar feelings.

In 1996, the Taliban continued their advances. In June they took
Chagharan, the capital of Ghur province in the centre of Afghanistan
and defeated Rabbani's governor. In doing so they were assisted by
the other opponents of Rabbani, General Dostum and his Özbeks,
and the *Hizb-i Wahdat*, which in spite of Mazari's death had again
joined with the Taliban. The Taliban and their followers slowly
encroached upon Kabul, which was bombed furiously throughout
the year. On 11 September 1996, Jalalabad was taken,[11] and on 26
September Mas'ud ordered a withdrawal from Kabul, upon which
the Taliban entered the capital.

With the Taliban in Kabul, coalitions changed. Rabbani, Dostum
and 'Abd al-Karim Khalili, the new leader of the *Hizb-i Wahdat*, now
decided to join forces, and not without initial success. Mas'ud's military soon forced their way back to the northern outskirts of Kabul.
In the winter, however, Mas'ud's troops were pushed back again. For
the succeeding years, the plains north of Kabul would be the scene
of constant battle between Mas'ud and the Taliban.

9   Mazari was buried in Mazar-i Sharif. He was succeeded by 'Abd al-Karim Khalili,
who managed to oust his rivals Ustad Akbari and Muhammad Asef Muhsini from
Bamiyan in October 1995.
10   This was the old British embassy in Karte Parwan.
11   Until that time this area was controlled by a *shawrâ* led by Yunus Khales and
Hajji 'Abd al-Qadir.

The occupation of Kabul was the climax of the Taliban's operations. Within days of entering Kabul, a number of decrees were announced that especially affected the position of women: girls' schools were closed, women were forbidden to work outdoors and they could no longer walk the streets by themselves. There were also bans on music and music cassettes, kites and homing pigeons. Men were forced to grow beards. None of these decrees were new. They had been in force in Qandahar and Herat since the Taliban occupied these cities. However, since Kabul was a more cosmopolitan town, with a majority of non-Pashtun inhabitants, and with many foreign observers and NGOs, the black-turbaned Taliban widely came to be regarded, correctly or not, as a group of religious fanatics who were keen on taking the country back to the Middle Ages. The murder of Najib Allah and his brother, Shahpur Ahmadzay, by the Taliban,[12] immediately after their taking of the town, also led to serious doubts as to the true nature of the Taliban movement.

Taliban Ideology

The name of the Taliban is derived from *Tâlib*, the Arabic word for a religious student.[13] Most of the Taliban were educated at private religious schools along the Afghan–Pakistan border. These schools had sprung up in large numbers following the Soviet invasion in 1979 and the mass exodus of Afghan refugees to Pakistan. The curriculum of these schools is very traditional, emphasizing the study of the Qur'an in all aspects. Since the start of the war in 1979, thousands of students, mostly Afghans but also Pakistani Pashtuns, have attended these schools. The schools are strongly influenced by the *Jam'iyyat-i 'Ulamâ'-i Islâm*, a movement in Pakistan headed by Mawlana Fazlur Rahman. This movement stresses a strict following of the rules and regulations of Islam, and in particular of the Hanafi Sunni branch. It also harbours strong anti-Shi'ite feelings and a deep sense of social egalitarianism. Within this movement, the *'Ulamâ'* (body of religious scholars) plays an important role, since it can interpret and apply Islamic law, the *Shari'a*.

The Taliban are also influenced by ideas that emanate from Saudi Arabia. During the war against the Soviet Union, Saudi Arabia was

12 Although the two brothers may have been murdered by ex-Khalqi adherents of the Taliban movement (Maley 1998:2). Kamal Matimuddin (1999:224) tells that Najib Allah was murdered on the orders of Mulla Muhammad Rabbani, a senior aid to Omar, out of revenge for the killing by Najib Allah of his brother.

13 For the Taliban, see Gohari 1999; Kamal Matinuddin 1999; Maley 1998. See also the webpage: www.afghan-ie.com

one of the main donors of the Mujahedin. There were also many volunteers from Saudi Arabia and other Arab countries. One of these was the now well-known Osama bin Laden, a Saudi millionaire who founded the so-called House of Auxiliaries, which organized recruitment and the financing of volunteers. The volunteers and the Saudi sponsors introduced new ideas, often strongly Wahhabite, into Afghanistan and particularly among the Pashtuns. Both the Wahhabites, with their insistence on a puritanical Islam, and the influence exercised by the *Jam'iyyat-i 'Ulamâ'-i Islâm*, brought about a change in the political arena of Afghanistan. Islamic law became the rallying point, rather than the Islamic state as sought after by the Islamists.

It is difficult to characterize the Taliban. They do not seem to be very concerned about traditional values and traditional kinship relationships. In this way they reflect a clear break with the past. The fact that most of their leaders derive from refugee camps would explain this point. Instead, they accept the *Shar'ia* as the only law code. They all follow a leader, Muhammad Omar, whom in April 1996 they recognized as the *Amir al-Mu'minin*, 'Commander of the Faithful'. They also want to change the world, or at least their world, and they show strong tendencies towards a theocracy. Moreover, they stick to a literal interpretation of the Qur'an. All these aspects would characterize the Taliban as fundamentalist.[14] Yet, the Taliban outlook on life would best be described as parochial.

Taliban and the US

Even since the fall of Najib Allah, the US government appears to have lost interest in Afghanistan. Washington simply does not want to become embroiled in the Afghan quagmire, although it continues to provide funds to the United Nations relief agencies and Non-Governmental Organizations (NGOs) that channel food and other aid to Afghanistan. In most aspects America at first simply followed the official policy of Pakistan, including Pakistan's covert support for the Taliban from mid-1994 onwards.

At an international level, however, there are still certain factors that force Washington to keep an eye on the developments in this part of the world. The emergence of new republics in the former Soviet Union, including Turkmenistan, Uzbekistan and Tajikistan, brought with it the problem that these countries for their import and export remain dependent on Russia. In Cold War terms this is an

14   Compare Maley 1998:18–19.

undesirable situation for Washington. The opening up of new routes from the new republics to the coast of the Indian Ocean is therefore of great urgency. This urgency became even more pressing when large reserves of natural oil and gas were discovered in Turkmenistan.[15] The oil and gas could only be exported to the west either via Russia; via the Caspian Sea; via Iran, or via Afghanistan. Since the route via the Caspian Sea would be expensive and would anyhow involve another series of new states in the Caucasus, and since the Americans at that time were still unwilling to have anything to do with Iran, the proposed pipelines via Afghanistan constituted a welcome option. In this context, although apparently without direct official American involvement, it was no coincidence that in 1996 the American firm of UNOCAL and the Saudi Delta Oil company signed a two billion dollar contract with the Taliban and with Turkmenistan. This contract included the construction of gas and oil pipelines from Turkmenistan, via Taliban controlled Afghanistan, to Pakistan.[16] For the time being, however, the plans came to nothing. In fact it is Iran that has won the tug of war. The Iranian (and European) railway network is, since 1996, linked to that of Central Asia. The roads between Central Asia and the Iranian port of Bandar ʿAbbas have been improved, and Turkmenistan has signed an agreement that will lead to the building of a pipeline via Iran to the west.

In November 1997, the US government broke with its former policy as regards the Taliban. Minister of State, Madeleine Albright, in clear terms condemned the Taliban for their abuse of human rights. The American government was also very disappointed with the increase of the opium and heroine production in the country. In fact, according to the CIA factbook, Afghanistan has become the second largest exporter of opium and opium-related products, after Burma. Another point of disagreement between the United States and the Taliban was the fact that the Taliban had given refuge to the Saudi millionaire and terrorist Osama Bin Laden, and refused to extradite him.

The May 1997 Developments

After the winter of 1996/1997, war in Afghanistan continued. The Taliban were now in control of almost all the south of the country.

---

15 During the war the Soviet Union constructed pipelines from Uzbekistan to Begram airbase north of Kabul, and from Turkmenistan to Shindand airbase, south of Herat.
16 Magnus and Naby 1998:190. See also the map in Kamal Matinuddin 1999:145.

Rabbani and Mas'ud controlled the northeast, and Dostum the north. Dostum's position was destined to be the first to fall.

The northern Özbek warlord, 'Abd al-Rashid Dostum, had been the undisputed lord of North Afghanistan for many years. Changing sides a number of times in previous years, and having fought with the Taliban against Rabbani for a long time, in the end he had become one of the few remaining opponents of the Taliban. His forces were estimated at some 50,000 men, and his weaponry included fighter aircraft and tanks. Internationally he was supported by all the opponents of the Taliban, including Iran, Russia and India. In addition, his area bordered on the newly independent republic of Uzbekistan. He issued his own currency and he also ran an airline (Balkh Air), and for all intents and purposes was the leader of an independent country, yet he ran his country as a fairly liberal dictator. Women could walk the streets unveiled; alcohol was freely sold, and cinemas showed Indian films. Yet, his position was clearly not strong enough to withstand the Taliban.

On 14 May 1997, an official called 'Abd al-Rahman Haqqani was shot dead in Mazar-i Sharif. He belonged to the group of adherents of General 'Abd al-Malik Pahlavan,[17] the official foreign spokesman of Dostum, but also one of his opponents. The killing of Haqqani, which was soon blamed on Dostum, led to a deal between the Taliban and general Pahlavan. The agreement was made on 19 May, no doubt with the active support of the Pakistani government. The forces of General 'Abd ul-Malik Pahlavan together with the Taliban advanced upon Mazar-i Sharif, and on 24 May Dostum was forced to flee the country. On the following day Taliban troops entered the town. Dostum had by then fled to Turkey. Pakistan, Saudi Arabia and the United Arab Emirates almost immediately recognized the Taliban as the *de facto* rulers of Afghanistan. After taking Mazar, the Taliban advanced further west and also took Qunduz, along the borders with Badakhshan, thus also forcing Rabbani to leave the country. Afghanistan now seemed to be completely controlled by the Taliban.

Within hours of the Taliban entering Mazar, they informed the local population that they wanted to fully control the town, and to establish the same type of Islam as they had forced upon the towns of Kabul, Qandahar and Herat. For many Uzbeks and Hazaras this was too much. On 28 May fighting broke out again and many Taliban were killed in the streets of Mazar.[18] Their main opponents

17 Pahlavan is generally held responsible for handing over Isma'il Khan to the Taliban. Isma'il Khan escaped from Taliban captivity in the spring of 2000.
18 Some 3,000 Taliban, taken prisoner by General Malik's forces, were reported to have been killed (Kamal Matinuddin 1999:109).

were the Hazara forces of the Shi'ite *Hizb-i Wahdat* and the Isma'ili Shi'ites under Nadari. Both Shi'ite groups had little to expect from the Sunnite Taliban. General Malik, shortly before appointed Deputy Foreign Minister for the Taliban, changed sides again and also rebelled against the Taliban. In the end thousands of Taliban died, either in fighting or by execution. Many Pakistanis also died. At the same time large groups of Taliban, who had moved north from Kabul, via the Salang tunnel, to Mazar-i Sharif, were trapped when Ahmad Shah Mas'ud cut off their retreat route.

Subsequent Developments

In the autumn of 1997 fighting continued in the north of Afghanistan and north of Kabul. Before the winter started, most of the Taliban had been forced from the north, and Dostum could return to Mazar-i Sharif. Ahmad Masud and his Panjshiri forces re-occupied the plains north of Kabul and controlled the strategic Salang Pass. The Taliban had clearly suffered a major set-back.

Renewed fighting took place in 1998 and in August the Taliban finally took Mazar-i Sharif. During the same year they occupied the Bamiyan Valley in Central Afghanistan. The only opponent left was now Ahmad Shah Mas'ud in Badakhshan and the Panjshir Valley. By the spring of 2001, the military situation has hardly changed. Ahmad Shah Mas'ud still controls much of the northeast of the country, while the Taliban dominate the rest. The suffering of the Afghan population continues. In 1998, thousands of people were killed in the northeast of the country following a series of earthquakes, and severe droughts in recent years have led to the death of thousands of people and new waves of refugees. The situation has become even more pressing following a large-scale isolation of the country because of the Taliban's assistance to Osama bin Laden. In 1999, the United Nations imposed sanctions on Afghanistan, including a flight embargo. This measure was tightened in December 2000 when an arms embargo was imposed and all Taliban overseas assets were frozen. By early 2001, the situation in and around Afghanistan had become more desperate than ever before. The continuing drought and the endless fighting, combined with the international boycott, led to thousands of people being killed and hundreds of thousands fleeing the country. To restore their power among the Afghans and to show the world they were still in control, the Taliban resorted at the end of February to an act of state-sponsored vandalism, namely the destruction of all pre-Islamic monuments in the country, including the Bamiyan statues. The parochialism of the Pashtun Taliban leaders in Kabul and Qandahar was made very clear. In early March 2001, archaeological remains all over the country were deliberately destroyed. The international outcry was deafening, but did the politicians and media ever hear the voice of the starving Afghan refugees?

Epilogue: Six Years On

Since the completion of the hardback edition of this book, in early 2001, the political landscape of the Middle East and Southwest Asia has changed dramatically. The events of 9/11 led to the fall of the fundamentalist Taliban regime of Afghanistan and the installation of Hamid Karzai as president of a pro-Western government. However, the initial optimism of most Afghans turned into disappointment and disillusionment, and a great fear of the future. The problems facing the country are manifold: a spreading insurrection from the side of the Neo-Taliban, suicide attacks, the 'collateral damage' caused by American and ISAF forces,[1] kidnappings, corruption among Afghan officials, and opium production. The main problem, however, is the inability of the Afghan government and its Western sponsors to develop a clear and consistent policy for Afghanistan's security and development.

Further to that, many internal problems are aggravated by developments in neighbouring states, especially along Afghanistan's eastern borders with Pakistan. The long-standing policy of the Pakistani establishment to support Islamic parties, dating back to at least the 1980s, contributed to the rise of an almost autonomous, Islamic fundamentalist 'Talibanistan' in Pakistan's Northwest Frontier Province and Baluchistan and the creation of a safe haven for many of the opponents to Hamid Karzai's government.

---

1 A recent report by the SENLIS Council (November 2007, 'Stumbling into Chaos. Afghanistan on the Brink') has suggested that a force of some 80,000 men will be needed to guarantee stability and security in Afghanistan. The current force of 47,000 men (December 2007) is deemed too small, and in military terms this translates into the massive use of airpower and consequent 'accidents'.

The Fall of the Taliban

On 11 September 2001, 19 terrorists, most of whom had Saudi Arabian nationality, hijacked four airplanes in the United States. They were acting on the command of Osama bin Laden, at that time still enjoying the hospitality of the Afghan Taliban regime. Two of the planes destroyed the World Trade Center in New York; another hit the Pentagon in Washington, while the fourth crashed into a field in Pennsylvania before it could reach the White House. Some 3,000 people were killed. The United States under President George W. Bush reacted furiously and declared a 'war on terror'. When it was established that the al-Qaida network was behind the attacks, the United States decided to destroy this organization. Together with a large number of other countries, and with the approval of the United Nations, the United States subsequently started to build up military and diplomatic pressure on the Taliban regime in Afghanistan to hand over Osama bin Laden.

Pakistan played an important role. In 1994 the country had been instrumental in the rise of the Taliban and it had remained one of the few nations to officially recognize the regime.[2] Furthermore, Pakistan's military forces and its intelligence agencies, most important of which was the (military) Inter-Services Intelligence (ISI), solidly backed the Afghan fundamentalist leaders right to the very end and forged strong personal links that would last to the present day. But over the years the Pakistani government had also realized that the Taliban were not always willing to follow Pakistan's advice. Another worrying factor was the growing influence of the movement of al-Qaida under Osama bin Laden, who in 1996 had arrived in Afghanistan after his forced evacuation from Sudan. Al-Qaida brought with it a growing internationalist, jihadist aspect to the developments in Afghanistan. Even more alarming to the Pakistani authorities was the way in which the Pashtun Taliban regime in Afghanistan affected the Pakistani Pashtuns living along the borders. In all, some of the Pakistani leaders came to regard the Afghan Taliban as a possible threat to the state of Pakistan itself. The Pakistani leader, General Pervez Musharraf, who came to power on 12 October 1999, thus was given the chance after 9/11 to stop this development with American assistance. Hence Pakistan's traditional policy of assistance to the Taliban was stopped, at least officially. Many high Pakistani officials, military and civil, were relocated, and

---

2   Together with Saudi Arabia and the United Arab Emirates.

Pakistani politicians who sympathized with the Taliban were placed under house arrest or simply arrested.

The Pakistani government could not convince the Taliban leadership that it would be removed by force if it did not agree to hand over Osama bin Laden. It was thus clear that the Taliban regime had to be destroyed before Bin Laden could be arrested and his training camps in Afghanistan dismantled. The Americans and their most important partner, Great Britain, therefore decided to put more pressure on the Taliban and to speed up their removal. The Afghan opponents to the Taliban in the northeast of the country, mainly Tajiks who were united with the Uzbeks and Hazaras in the so-called Northern Alliance, received massive military assistance. They had been in disarray following the assassination of their veteran leader, Ahmad Shah Massud, on 9 September, two days before the attacks on the US.[3] Western help soon strengthened their position. In addition, an attempt was made to disengage some of the Pashtuns from the Taliban. Hamid Karzai, later president of the country, was sent to his tribal lands north of Qandahar, in Uruzgan Province, to stir up the local population against the Taliban. Another was Abdul Haq, a Mujahid leader from the 1980s, who returned to Afghanistan from his exile in Pakistan. However, he was arrested by the Taliban late October, somewhere to the south of Kabul, and killed.

Soon the majority of the Afghans, including the Pashtuns, realized that America and the Western world, together with Pakistan, had made up their minds to replace the Taliban and would not accept any different outcome. A growing number of local Pashtun commanders, who up until then had supported the Taliban, started to change sides in order to defend their own and their followers' interests. To them the outcome was clear. Who could resist American power? They turned against the Taliban and sided with traditional Pashtun leaders, including Hamiz Karzai, who had never showed much appreciation of the Taliban. These traditional leaders consequently gained more importance in Afghan politics.

Early October the Americans and British started the bombardment of Taliban units, thus increasing the pressure on their opponents. On 9 November the Northern Alliance managed to occupy the town of Mazar-i Sharif and soon afterwards they controlled almost all of the north of the country. Herat, in the west of Afghanistan, fell on 12 November, and Kabul, in the east, was occupied one day later. The following day, on 14 November, the Taliban evacuated the town of

---

3 Ahmad Shah Massud was killed by two followers of Osama bin Laden who pretended to be journalists. They carried stolen Belgian passports.

Jalalabad, along the borders with Pakistan. On 26 November the northern town of Kunduz fell to the Alliance, the only town in the north that so far had remained occupied by the Taliban. Shortly before Kunduz was occupied by the Northern Alliance, a mass evacuation of Pakistani supporters of the Taliban had prevented embarrassment on all sides. The only large town that now remained in Taliban hands was Qandahar in the far south of the country, but this city was evacuated on 7 December. Most of the Taliban leaders, including Mulla Omar, left the town before it fell to their opponents. In the meantime, Osama bin Laden and most of his immediate following had also managed to escape. They all found sanctuary in Pakistan, although this was denied at the time by the Pakistani authorities.

Afghan and foreign leaders met early in December 2001 on the Petersberg, near Bonn, Germany, to discuss future developments in Afghanistan. Hamid Karzai, the Pashtun leader from South Afghanistan, was asked to become president. In later years it was argued that the Petersberg conference should have included delegates from the defeated Taliban. However, at the time it would have been almost impossible to find an acceptable representation of the former Afghan leadership, and it would also have been impossible to convince the other Afghans that they should negotiate with the hated Taliban.

Moderate Optimism

In the early summer of 2002 there was very little sympathy left for the Taliban. Foreigners walking the streets of Qandahar, the former centre of the ousted Taliban, were openly told that Mulla Omar, the Taliban leader, should be arrested as soon as possible and hanged. In fact, this was the story that could be heard everywhere in Afghanistan. The Afghans were full of expectations and looking forward to Western help and an end to a war that had gone on for more than 20 years.

Since those euphoric days much has happened, both positively and negatively. Zahir Shah, the ex-king of Afghanistan who in 1973 was pushed aside by his cousin Dawud Khan, returned to Afghanistan on 18 April 2002.[4] In June 2002 a Loya Jirga was convened with more than 1,500 representatives from all over the country. The Jirga concluded with the confirmation of Hamid Karzai as president and the

---

4   He died in Kabul on 23 July 2007.

formation of a new interim government. In December 2003 and January 2004 another Loya Jirga was organized, with more than 500 delegates. This time they discussed proposals for a new constitution, which would guarantee a democratic Afghanistan with general elections and equal rights to all Afghans. After the proposals were accepted, on 3 January 2004, presidential elections were held on 9 October 2004. Hamid Karzai was elected by almost 60 per cent of the voters. Parliamentary elections followed on 18 September 2005. At the end of this process, late 2005, Afghanistan had a constitution, an elected national parliament and provincial councils, and an elected president. In addition, health care had drastically improved, some six million Afghan children could now go to school, the large roads connecting the main cities of the country had been repaired, and the Afghan government could call upon a national army of some 30,000 military.

Growing Problems

The national elections of September 2005 proceeded relatively well. However, at that time there were already some developments that showed a deteriorating situation in the country. In the south and east of Afghanistan the number of people partaking in the parliamentary elections was relatively small, sometimes as low as 25 per cent of those allowed to vote. This low percentage contrasted with the high number of voters in the north and west of the country. One of the main reasons for the poor showing was the deteriorating security situation. From 2003 onwards, the Taliban had regrouped in Pakistan and was slowly encroaching from the border areas into the southern and eastern provinces of the country.[5] It seems as if this development went very much unnoticed at first by the outside world.[6] In November 2007, the situation in the north and west was still relatively stable, but in the south and east it had become worse. Suicide attacks and other incidents occurred almost on a daily basis. In 2007, more than 6,300 people lost their lives and there were some 140 suicide attacks.

5   Giustozzi (2007:5) tells how in 2003 the Taliban eliminated much of the government structures in Zabul and eastern Paktika, immediately along the Pakistani borders.
6   Most American attention had turned west, towards Iraq. Sadam Hussain was removed in 2003. The Americans, however, sent to Kabul an ambassador who was well acquainted with the area, Zalmay Khalilzad.

Afghanistan's government is therefore still dependent for its security on an international military coalition of some 40,000 troops, led by NATO and with a mandate of the United Nations. In addition, there are some 8,000 military, mainly American, who are in Afghanistan within the context of the so-called War on Terror (named Operation Enduring Freedom in Afghanistan). The NATO-led troops, known as the International Security Assistance Force (ISAF), are primarily focussed on supporting the Afghan government. Operation Enduring Freedom is engaged with the fight against Taliban and al-Qaida elements. It may be clear that the line between both operations tends to get blurred, contributing to a diminished efficiency of the foreign troops in Afghanistan.

One of the main dilemmas facing the Afghan government and the Western powers is the extent to which security and development policy in Afghanistan should be decentralized. The Afghan government has inherited a Soviet-style centralized rule. However, decisions made in Kabul are not always appreciated in the countryside and many governors and police chiefs have been appointed to regions where they enjoyed no local support. Without support from a national army or a national police force, these officials, whatever their qualities and stance against incompetence and corruption, simply missed the power to enforce new policies. On the other hand, the appointment of local leaders often contributed to corruption, cronyism, and tensions between the various ethnic groups of a region. Since late 2001, government policy has shifted various times between the two policies. To date, the Afghan government seems to prefer strengthening local leaders, who have a strong position in their district. It remains to be seen, however, whether these local appointees will not lead to further disenchantment among various groups, and hence drive them into the hands of the opposition.

Pashtun Complaints

The nowadays hotly contested parts of Afghanistan, in the south and east of the country, are predominantly inhabited by Pashtuns. They are the traditional rulers of the country. From the mid-eighteenth century they provided the kings and amirs of Afghanistan. Some of the Pashtuns started the Taliban movement in 1994, and they brought almost all of the country under their control. The Pashtuns constitute the largest minority of the country, with some 40 per cent of the population. The president of the country, Hamid Karzai, is Pashtun, and so was Zahir Shah, the ex-king of the country.[7] However, Hamid Karzai had to share power with others, often non-Pashtuns, and many Pashtuns do not appreciate this. Shortly after the fall of the Taliban, the Transitional Government included many representatives from non-Pashtun minorities, especially Tajiks, who in the preceding years had suffered considerably at the hands of the Pashtun Taliban. For many Pashtuns the present situation, which they perceive as a threat to their traditionally dominant position, is a defeat. Such feelings can be, and are, used politically. A good example is Gulb ud-Din Hekmatyar. He is one of the major opponents of the present Afghan government. A consistent feature of his policy is his use of Pashtun nationalism. He uses nationalist feelings among the Pashtuns, especially those from the northeast of the country, to realize his own ambitions. He is the Mujahed leader who in 1994 ordered the bombardment of Kabul, which in the end killed some 25,000 people. He did so with the help of some of the Pashtuns who after the fall of the communist leader, Najibullah, did not accept the fact that Kabul had fallen into the hand of Tajiks and Uzbeks.

But apart from hurt pride among many Pashtuns, there are of course other factors that have led to the present negative developments in Afghanistan. In contrast to the north and part of the west of the country, the south and east have benefited relatively little from the government change in 2001. Because those parts have remained relatively unsafe, development in the area has been slow. Foreign and Afghan aid workers could not, and did not want to, work in the south. Poverty, a lack of government control and corrupt officials led to a dramatic increase of resentment and armed insurgence, but also to a huge increase in opium production. In the early days of the Taliban, some 91,000 hectares of land were used for poppy cultivation. But in 2006 the total surface used for poppy growing had risen to 165,000 hectares, of which the largest part was in South Afghanistan. In that year, Afghanistan provided 92 per cent of the world production of opium. Most of this opium is now processed into heroin in Afghan laboratories. Those Afghans who make vast amounts of money by poppy cultivation, opium production and trafficking are unlikely to welcome a spread of government control.

Then there is the religious dimension. Almost 30 years of civil war have created a prevalent atmosphere in many parts of Afghanistan in which religion, and in particular fundamentalist Islam, is playing an

---

7   From 2002 he lived, as the 'Father of the Nation', in the presidential palace, the former royal palace, together with Hamid Karzai.

important role. Before the war, religious life in Afghanistan was to a great degree directed by Sufi leaders with a more introspective approach. Since then, the general uprooting of society has given rise to a new brand of religious leaders, deeply influenced by the Deobandi school and Wahhabitism.[8] It has been argued that the spread of the insurgency in recent years has been to a great extent facilitated by the village mullas in the Pashtun countryside.[9] After the fall of the Taliban they had lost much of their influence. They could now, with the help of the insurgents, reclaim their former position.

Problems of the Pakistani Pashtuns

But perhaps the most important factor in the deterioration of the security situation in parts of Afghanistan is the influence of its neighbour states. Until recently, Western politicians and military seem to have focussed on the situation in the country itself. However, as said earlier, Afghanistan is not an island, and in particular the more than 2,000 km border with Pakistan is rapidly becoming a nightmare for the supporters of the Karzai government. A Dutch officer stated in 2006 that the fighting in the south of the country was like mopping up while the floodgates were open. His remark was not really appreciated by his superiors, but he was right. The Pakistani government cannot, and most of time does not want, to act against the Taliban bases in Pakistan. The Pakistani establishment has long understood that Islamic fundamentalism had turned into a threat to the existence of the Pakistani state, but the fall of the Taliban in Afghanistan, in 2001, made the position of Pakistan rather complicated. The Pakistani population is by and large very anti-Western. The two Pakistani provinces bordering Afghanistan, namely the Northwest Frontier Province and Baluchistan, were led, until late 2007, by a fundamentalist, anti-Western government. Most of the people living here are Pashtuns. Directly along the Afghan border, formally inside the Northwest Frontier Province, there are furthermore some autonomous districts, the so-called Federally Administered Tribal Areas (FATAs), where the Pashtun population resists any interference from outside, including from the Pakistani government. These Pashtuns, now influenced by fundamentalist forces in the region, are staunchly nationalistic and regard Western presence in Afghanistan as an occupation of 'their' Pashtun land. In 2005 and 2006, the

8   Giustozzi 2007:45.
9   Giustozzi 2007:43–6.

Pakistani army agreed to a ceasefire in two FATAs, namely South and North Waziristan respectively, in which the Pakistani army promised not to interfere in local affairs, while the Waziristan leaders promised not to assist Taliban and al-Qaida forces. It soon happened, however, that Waziristan was turned into a training ground for the opposition in Afghanistan. After July 2007, both agreements in Waziristan collapsed, and fighting ensued.

Sleeping with the Devil

Finally there is the international dimension. For many Muslims the Western presence in the Middle East, as in Iraq and Afghanistan, but also the Israel/Palestine drama, are proof of the Western attempt to undermine Islam and to suppress Muslims all over the world. Many Afghans, therefore, find it hard to accept that their security is dependent on the same military power that elsewhere in the world flushes the Quran down the toilet. 'Sleeping with the devil' is an expression that is often used in Afghanistan. Many Afghans realize very well that without the American military umbrella the country would soon relapse into civil war, but the American presence remains hard to accept.

The Pakistan Nightmare

Since the occupation by Pakistani security forces of the Red Mosque in the capital Islamabad, in July 2007, President Musharraf has taken a clear stand against growing fundamentalism, which is becoming dominant among the Pashtuns along the borders with Afghanistan. But since that time it has also become evident that the Pakistani army faces some very serious problems. The Pashtun fundamentalists have established themselves in North and South Waziristan, two FATAs south of Peshawar, but also in the Swat valley north of the provincial capital. Fighting between Pakistani troops and insurgents has recently led to many casualties, and also to many Pakistani military being captured by the fundamentalists. It must be rather disquieting for the Pakistani military command to hear that their men sometimes surrender in large numbers to the Pakistani Taliban, without putting up a fight. The deteriorating situation in Pakistan, but also Musharraf's troubled relationship with the judiciary, led him to declare a state of emergency on 3 November 2007. The future of Pakistan has thus become very uncertain. The nightmare of the establishment of an autonomous Pashtunistan along both sides of the border is slowly becoming a distinct reality. Such a state would be under the control of the fundamentalists and the internationally operating al-Qaida, and financially supported by opium production. This would be an unacceptable development, for the Pakistani authorities and for the Afghanistan government and their Western sponsors.

The Neo-Taliban

The Taliban movement that leads the insurgency in Afghanistan is different from the Taliban of the 1990s.[10] In the early days the leaders of the Taliban showed a certain parochialism in their views on the world and seemed primarily focussed on a rigid application of their brand of the *Shari`ah*. The 'Neo-Taliban' make use of modern techniques and methods to achieve their goals. They show some degree of flexibility in their control of the population, and see no qualms in using photographs and films, rigorously banned from Afghanistan in the 1990s, for propaganda purposes. It is not clear, however, to what degree the internationalist jihadist movement of al-Qaida has affected the Neo-Taliban ideology, and whether the Taliban leaders see their insurgency as part of the worldwide struggle against 'the Christian and Jewish crusaders', or prefer to focus on Afghanistan. This question also relates to the relationship between the Neo-Taliban and the al-Qaida network. In early 2007, there was sustained fighting in Waziristan between al-Qaida units and apparently Neo-Taliban fighters, who forced many of the al-Qaida men to leave the area. There have also been rumours that Taliban men sometimes resent the ruthless approach by the foreign fighters among the insurgents in Afghanistan. It may be certain that the use of suicide attacks was introduced to Afghanistan by foreign, Jihadist specialists.

The ethnic element is also important. Traditional opposition between the Nurzai and Achakzai Durranis led to a generally pro-government attitude of the latter. The Kakar and the Tarin, most of whom live in the east across the border, also show a markedly pro-Taliban attitude.[11]

---

10 It is impossible to obtain an accurate idea of their numerical strength. Various figures would suggest some 15,000 to 20,000 men in Afghanistan, including some 2,000 foreign (al-Qaida) fighters (compare Giustozzi 2007:35).
11 Giustozzi 2007:48. Mulla Dadullah, a prominent Taliban field commander in South Afghanistan who was killed in early 2007, was a Kakar (Ghurghusht).

Towards an Autonomous Afghania?

Then there is the Pashtunistan issue. Since the creation of Pakistan in 1947, the Pakistani establishment has been wary of any resurgent nationalist feelings among the militant Pashtuns in the Northwest Frontier Province. The Pakistani government has been especially afraid of any Afghan involvement in stirring up nationalist feelings, which could eventually lead to the breaking up of Pakistan. To counter this possibility, the Pakistani leaders have consistently tried to use Islam as the all-incorporating feature for all the ethnic groups in the country, including the Pashtuns. This successful policy led eventually to strong fundamentalist feelings among the Pashtuns, and strong anti-Western feelings and support for the Pashtun insurgents in neighbouring Afghanistan. But it also led to opposition against the Pakistani government, which since late 2001 has officially supported the Americans and which time and again is forced to interfere in the FATAs along the border. Fundamentalism and nationalism now seem to come together. In the summer of 2007, the provincial government of the Northwest Frontier Province suggested a new name for the province, namely Afghania.[12] Afghan is the traditional name for the Pashtuns, and the choice of the name Afghania, by a fundamentalist provincial government, would suggest that the nightmare of fundamentalism and nationalism uniting is becoming a reality.

Careful Policies

Between 9 and 12 August 2007, a general meeting was organized in Kabul between delegates from the Pashtun districts along both sides of the border. In his speech at the conclusion of the meeting, President Musharraf of Pakistan admitted that Pakistan was part of the Afghan problem, and that both countries should try to find a way out of the impasse. The meeting also led to the establishment of a committee of 50 people, from both countries, to talk with representatives of the opposition. Whether this will actually work out is still unclear. But President Hamid Karzai stated on 29 September that representatives of the Taliban could receive ministerial posts, provided they accept the Afghan constitution. Perhaps these are movements

---

12 The ending–ia is of course a Western feature, apparently unknown to the Peshawar legislators.

towards a better future for Afghanistan. After all, the people of Afghanistan will have to rebuild their country themselves, and this will never be possible without including all levels and segments of Afghan society. The Western military cannot stay in Afghanistan. However, again, much will depend on the situation in neighbouring Pakistan.

Bibliography

Selected Books and Articles on Afghanistan, Published after 2000

Allen, Charles, *God's Terrorists: The Wahhabi Cult and the Hidden Roots of Modern Jihad* (London, 2006).

Bleaney, C. H. and M. A. Gallego, with a foreword by Willem Vogelsang, *Afghanistan: A Bibliography* (Leiden and Boston, 2006).

Burke, Jason, *On the Road to Kandahar: Travels through Conflict in the Islamic World* (London, 2006).

Chayes, Sarah, *The Punishment of Virtue* (London, 2007).

Emadi, Hafizullah, *Culture and Customs of Afghanistan* (Westport, 2005).

Gannon, Kathy, *I is for Infidel. From Holy War to Holy Terror: 18 Years inside Afghanistan* (New York, 2005).

Girardet, Edward and J. Walther, *Afghanistan: Crosslines Essential Field Guide* (Geneva, 2004).

Giustozzi, Antonio, *Koran, Kalashnikov and Laptop: The Neo-Taliban Insurgency in Afghanistan* (London, 2007).

Griffin, Michael, *Reaping the Whirlwind: The Taliban Movement in Afghanistan* (London, 2001).

Haqqani, Husain, *Pakistan: Between Mosque and Military* (Washington, 2005).

Johnson, Chris and Jolyon Leslie, *Afghanistan: The Mirage of Peace* (London, 2005).

Macdonald, David, *Drugs in Afghanistan: Opium, Outlaws and Scorpion Tales* (London, 2007).

Omrani, Bijan and Matthew Leeming, *Afghanistan: A Traveler's Companion and Guide* (Hong Kong, 2005).

Rashid, Ahmed, *Taliban* (London, 2000).

Stewart, Rory, *The Places in Between* (London, 2005).

Vogelsang, Willem, The ethnogenesis of the Pashtuns, in: Warwick Ball and Leonard Harrow (eds), *Cairo to Kabul. Afghan and Islamic Studies* (London, 2002), pp. 228–35.

Vogelsang, Willem, Dressing for the future in ancient garb: The use of clothing in Afghan politics, *Khil'a* 1, 2005, pp. 123–38.

Zahab, Mariam Abou and Olivier Roy, *Islamist Networks: The Afghan-Pakistan Connection* (London, 2004).

Selected Books and Articles on Afghanistan,
Published before 2000

'Abd al-Karim 'Alawi, *Târikh-i Ahmad* (Lucknow, 1266).

Abdurrahman, *The Life of Abdur Rahman, Amir of Afghanistan*, edited by Sultan Mohammed Khan (2 vols, London, 1990; reprint, Karachi, 1990).

Adamec, L. W., *Afghanistan 1900–1923* (Berkeley, 1967).

Adamec, L. W., *Historical and Political Gazetteer of Afghanistan* (6 vols, Graz, 1972–85).

Adamec, L. W., *Who is Who in Afghanistan* (Graz, 1975).

Adamec, L. W., *Historical Dictionary of Afghanistan*. Second edition (London, 1997).

Ahmed, Akbar S., *Millennium and Charisma among the Pathans* (London, 1976).

Ahmed, Akbar S., *Pukhtun Economy and Society* (London, 1980).

Alder, G. J., *British India's Northern Frontier* (London, 1963).

Alder, G. J., *Beyond Bokhara. The Life of William Moorcroft. Asian Explorer and Pioneer Veterinary Surgeon, 1767–1825* (London, 1985).

Allchin, B. and R. Allchin, *The Rise of Civilization in India and Pakistan* (Cambridge, 1982).

Allchin, B. and N. Hammond (eds), *The Archaeology of Afghanistan, from the Earliest Times to the Timurid Period* (London, 1978).

Allchin, F. R. and K. R. Norman, Guide to the Aśokan inscriptions, *South Asian Studies* 1, 1985, pp. 43–50.

Allchin, R., B. Allchin, N. Kreitman and E. Errington (eds), *Gandharan Art in Context. East–West Exchanges at the Crossroads of Asia* (New Delhi, 1997).

Allen, T., *Timurid Herat* (Wiesbaden, 1983).

Amiet, P., Bactria and Elam, in: G. Ligabue and S. Salvatori, *Bactria. An Ancient Oasis Civilization from the Sands of Afghanistan* (Venezia, 1988), pp. 159–88.

Amin, Hamidullah and G. B. Schultz, *A Geography of Afghanistan* (Omaha, 1976).

Anderson, E. W. and N. H. Dupree (eds), *The Cultural Basis of Afghan Nationalism* (London, 1990).

Anderson, J., Tribe and community among the Ghilzay Pashtun, *Anthropos* 70, 1975.

Andrews, P. A., The White House of Khorasan: The felt tents of the Iranian Yomut and Goklen, *Iran, Journal of the British Institute of Iranian Studies* 11, 1973, pp. 93–110.

Anthony, D. W. and N. B. Vinogradov, Birth of the chariot, *Archaeology* 48, 2, 1995, pp. 36–41.

Arbeitsgemeinschaft Afghanistan und Deutsches Orient-Institut (eds), *Bibliographie der Afghanistan-Literatur* 1945–1967 (2 vols, Hamburg, 1968, 1969).

Arlinghaus, J., *The Transformation of Afghan Tribal Society: Tribal Expansion, Mughal Imperialism and the Roshaniyya Insurrection 1450–1600* (Ph.D. thesis, Duke University, 1988).

Arnold, A., *Afghanistan's Two-Party Communism: Parcham and Khalq* (Stanford, 1983).

Arnold, A., *The Fateful Pebble: Afghanistan's Role in the Fall of the Soviet Empire* (Novato, 1993).

Askarov, A., The beginning of the Iron Age in Transoxania, in: A. H. Dani and V. M. Masson (eds), *The Dawn of Civilization: Earliest Times to 700 BC* (History of Civilizations of Central Asia, vol. I.) (Paris, 1992, second impression, 1996), pp. 441–58.

Asimov, M. S., *L'archéologie de la Bactriane ancienne* (Paris, 1985).

Asimov, M. S., with C. E. Bosworth (eds), *The Age of Achievement: AD 750 to the End of the Fifteenth Century* (History of Civilizations of Central Asia, vol. IV) (Paris, 1998).

Atkinson, J., *The Expedition into Afghanistan: Notes and Sketches Descriptive of the Country* (London, 1842).

Auberger, J., *Ctesias. Histoires de l'Orient* (Paris, 1991).

Aubin, J., L'ethnogénèse des Qaraunas, *Turcica* 1, 1969, pp. 65–94.

Aubin, J., Réseau pastoral et réseau caravanier. Les grand'routes du Khurassan à l'époque mongole, *Le Monde Iranien et l'Islam* 1, 1971, pp. 105–30.

Auboyer, J., *The Art of Afghanistan* (London, 1968).

Azoy, W. G., *Buzkashi. Game and Power in Afghanistan* (University of Pennsylvania Press, 1982).

Babur, *Babur-Nama*, translated by A. S. Beveridge (London, 1922; reprint: Lahore, 1979). See also *Le Livre de Babur (Mémoires de Zahiruddin Muhammad Babur de 1494 à 1529)*, trans. J.-L. Bacqué-Grammont (Paris, 1980); and *The Baburnama. Memoir of Babur, Price and Emperor.* Translated and edited by Wheeler M. Thackston (New York, 1996).

Back, M., *Die sassanidischen Staatsinschriften* (Tehran and Liege, 1978).

Bacon, E., The inquiry into the history of the Hazara Mongols of Afghanistan, *Southwestern Journal of Anthropology* 7, 1951.

Badian, E., Alexander at Peucelaotis, *Classical Quarterly* 37, 1, 1987, pp. 117–28.

Bahari, E., *Bihzad. Master of Persian Painting* (London/New York, 1996).

Bailey, H. W., Iranica, Bulletin of the School of Oriental Studies 1943, XI, pt. 2.

Bailey, H. W., L'Harahuna, in: *Asiatica. Festschrift Friedrich Weller* (Leipzig, 1954), pp. 13–21.

Bailey, H. W., Languages of the Saka, in: *Handbuch der Orientalistik*, Erste Abteilung, Band IV, Abschnitt 1 (Leiden/Köln, 1958), pp. 131–54.

Bailey, H. W., North Iranian problems, *BSOAS* 42, 1979.

Bailey, H. W., Asiani and Pasiani, *Bulletin of the Asia Institute* 7, 1993, pp. 9–10.

Baker, P. H. B. and F. R. Allchin, *Shahr-i Zohak and the History of the Bamiyan Valley, Afghanistan* (Oxford, 1991).

Ball, W. (with the cooperation of J.-C. Gardin), *Archaeological Gazetteer of Afghanistan/Catalogue des sites archéologiques d'Afghanistan* (Paris, 1982).

Ball, W. (with the cooperation of J.-C. Gardin), Kandahar, the Saka and India, in: R. Allchin and B. Allchin (eds), *South Asian Archaeology 1995* (Cambridge, 1997), pp. 439–50.

Balland, D., Vieux sédentaires Tadjik et immigrants Pachtoun dans le sillon de Ghazni (Afghanistan Oriental), *Bull. de l'Ass. des Géogr. Français* 417–18, 1974, pp. 171–80.

Balland, D., Afghanistan: Political History, *Encyclopaedia Iranica* I, 1985, pp. 547–58.

Balland, D., Nomadic pastoralists and sedentary hosts in the Central and Western Hindukush Mountains, Afghanistan, in: N. J. R. Allan, G. W. Knapp and Ch. Stadel (eds), *Human Impact on Mountains* (Totowa, 1988), pp. 265–76.

Balland, D., Contraintes écologiques et fluctuations historiques de l'organisation territoriale des nomades d'Afghanistan, *Production pastorale et société* 11, 1982, pp. 55–67.

Balland, D. and A. de Benoist, Nomades et semi-nomades Baluch d'Afghanistan, *Revue géographique de l'Est* 22, 1982, pp. 117–44.

Barber, E. W., The Mummies of Ürumchi: Did Europeans migrate to China 4,000 Years Ago? (London, 1999).

Barfield, T. J., *The Central Asian Arabs of Afghanistan. Pastoral Nomadism in Transition* (Austin, 1981).

Barfield, T. J., *The Perilous Frontier. Nomadic Empires and China, 221 BC to AD 1757* (Oxford, 1989).

Barnett, R.D., The art of Bactria and the Treasure of the Oxus, *Iranica Antiqua* 8, 1968, pp. 34–53.

Barthold, W., *An Historical Geography of Iran*. Edited with an introduction by C. E. Bosworth (Princeton, 1984).

Bartholomae, Chr., *Altiranisches Wörterbuch* (Strasbourg, 1904; reprint Berlin/New York, 1979).

Beal, S., *Si-Yu-Ki. Buddhist Records of the Western World. Translated from the Chinese of Hiuen Tsiang AD 629* (London, 1884; reprint New Delhi, 1983).

Beal, S., *The Life of Hiuen-Tsiang by the Shaman Hwui Li* (new, second edition, London, 1911).

Beckwith, C. I., *The Tibetan Empire in Central Asia* (Princeton, 1987).

Bellew, H. W., *From the Indus to the Tigris. A Narrative of a Journey through the Countries of Balochistan, Afghanistan, Khorassan and Iran, in 1872* (London, 1873).

Bellew, H. W., *The Races of Afghanistan: being a brief Account of the principal natives inhabiting that country* (Calcutta and London, 1880; reprint Graz, 1973).

Bellew, H. W., *An Inquiry into the Ethnography of Afghanistan* (Woking, 1891; Graz, 1973).

Benveniste, E., edits d'Aśoka en traduction grecque, *JA*, 1964, pp. 137–57.

Benveniste, E., A. Dupont-Sommer and C. Caillat, Une inscription indo-araméenne d'Aśoka provenant de Kandahar (Afghanistan), *JA*, 1966, pp. 437–70.

Benveniste, E., Que signifie Vidêvdât?, in: M. Boyce and I. Gershevitch (eds), *W.B. Henning Memorial Volume* (London, 1970), pp. 37–42.

Berg, G. van den, *Minstrel Poetry from the Pamir Mountains* (Leiden, 1997).

Bernard, P., Fouilles d'Ai Khanoum, campagnes de 1971, *Comptes-rendus de l'Académie des Inscriptions et Belles-lettres*, 1972, pp. 605–32.

Bernard, P., The Greek kingdoms of Central Asia, in: János Harmatta (ed.), *The Development of Sedentary and Nomadic Civilizations: 700 BC to AD 250* (History of Civilizations of Central Asia, vol. II) (Paris 1994, 1996), pp. 99–129.

Bernard, P., L'Aornos bactrien et l'Aornos indien. Philostrate et Taxila: Géographie, mythe et réalité, *Topoi* 6, fasc. 2, 1996, pp. 475–530.

Bernard, P., F. Grenet and C. Rapin, De Bactres à Taxila, *Topoi* 7, 1996, pp. 457–530.

Berve, H., *Das Alexanderreich auf prosopographischer Grundlage* (München, 1926).

Biddulph, H., Shah Shujah's force, *Journal of the Society for Army Historical Research* 20, 1941, pp. 65–71.

Biddulph, J., *Tribes of the Hindoo Koosh* (Calcutta, 1880).

Bikerman, J., *Institutions de l'empire Seleucide* (Paris, 1938).

Al-Biruni, *Alberuni's India*. Trans. E. Sachau (London, 1888; second edition, 1910).

Biscione, R., Dynamics of an early South Asian urbanization: the First Period of Shahr-i Sokhta and its connections with Southern Turkmenia, in: Norman Hammond, *South Asian Archaeology* (London, 1973), pp. 105–18.

Biswas, A., *The Political History of the Hunas in India* (Delhi, 1973).

Bivar, A. D. H., The inscriptions of Uruzgan, *JRAS*, 1954, 3–4.

Bivar, A. D. H., The absolute chronology of the Kushano-Sasanian governors in Central Asia, in: J. Harmatta, *Prolegomena to the Sources on the History of Pre-Islamic Central Asia* (Budapest, 1979), pp. 317–32.

Blanc, J.-C., *L'Afghanistan et ses populations* (Paris, 1976).

Bloch, J., *Les inscriptions d'Aśoka* (Paris, 1950).

Bombaci, A., Ghazni, *East and West* 1957, pp. 247–59.

Bopearachchi, O., *Monnaies gréco-bactriennes et indo-grecques, Catalogue raisonné* (Paris, 1991).

Bosworth, A. B., *Conquest and Empire. The Reign of Alexander the Great* (Cambridge, 1988).

Bosworth, C. E., *The Ghaznavids. Their Empire in Afghanistan and Eastern India, 994–1040* (Edinburgh, 1963; reprint: New Delhi, 1992).

Bosworth, C. E., *The Islamic Dynasties. A Chronological and Genealogical Handbook* (Edinburgh, 1967).

Bosworth, C. E., *Sîstân under the Arabs: From the Islamic Conquest to the Rise of the Saffârids (30–250/651–864)* (Rome, 1968).

Bosworth, C. E., *The Medieval History of Iran, Afghanistan and Central Asia* (London, 1973).

Bosworth, C. E., *The Later Ghaznavids. Splendour and Decay. The Dynasty in Afghanistan and Northern India, 1040–1186* (Edinburgh, 1977; reprint: New Delhi, 1992).

Bosworth, C. E., *The History of the Saffarids of Sistan and the Maliks of Nimruz (247/861 to 949/1542–3)* (Costa Mesa, New York, 1994).

Bosworth, C. E., The Ghaznavids, in: M. S. Asimov and C. E. Bosworth (eds), *History of Civilizations of Central Asia* IV (Paris, 1998), pp. 95–117.

Bosworth, C. E., with G. Doerfer, Khaladj, *The Encyclopaedia of Islam*, vol. 4, 1978.

Bosworth, C. E. and G. Clauson, Al-Xwârazmi on the Peoples of Central Asia. Parts 1–2. *JRAS*, 1965.

Bourgeois, J. and D. Bourgeois, *Les seigneurs d'Aryana: Nomades contrabandiers d'Afghanistan* (Paris, 1972).

Boyce, M., *A History of Zoroastrianism*, vol. I (1975; 1989); vol. II (1982); vol. III (with F. Grenet) (1991) (Leiden).

Bowman, R. A., *Aramaic Ritual Texts from Persepolis* (Chicago, 1970).

Brandenburg, D., *Herat: Eine Timuridische Hauptstadt* (Graz, 1977).

Brandenstein, W. and M. Mayrhofer, *Handbuch des Altpersischen* (Wiesbaden, 1964).

Brentjes, B., *Der Knoten Asiens. Afghanistan und die Völker am Hindukush* (Leipzig, 1983).

Briant, P., *Etat et pasteurs au Moyen-Orient ancient* (Cambridge, 1982).

Briant, P., *L'asie centrale et les royaumes proche-orientaux du premier millénaire* (Paris, 1984).

Briant, P., *Histoire de l'Empire Perse. De Cyrus à Alexandre* (Paris, 1996).

Broadfoot, J. S., Reports on Parts of the Ghilzai Country, and on Some of the Tribes in the Neighbourhood of Ghazni, *The Royal Geographical Society, Supplementary Papers* 1, 3, 1885.

Bruce, C. E., *Notes on the Ghilzai and Powindah Tribes* (Peshawar, 1929).

Brunt, P. A., *Arrian. History of Alexander and Indica* (Cambridge, Mass. and London, 1976, 1983).

Buist, G., *Outline of the Operations of British Troops in Scinde and Afghanistan* (Bombay, 1843).

Bulliet, R. W., *The Camel and the Wheel* (Cambridge, Mass., 1975).

Bundahishn. Edited by T. D. Anklesaria (Bombay, 1908).

Burnes, A., *Travels into Bokhara and a Voyage on the Indus* (London, 1834; reprint: New Delhi, 1992).

Burnes, A., *Cabool: Being a Personal Narrative of a Journey to, and Residence in That City, in the years 1836, 7, and 8* (1842; reprint: Lahore, 1961; Graz, 1973).

Burnham, D. K., *Warp and Weft. A Textile Terminology* (Ontario, 1980).

Burrow, T., The proto-Indoaryans, *Journal of the Royal Asiatic Society*, 1973, pp. 123–40.

Byron, R., *The Road to Oxiana* (London, 1937).

Campbell, R. and M. E. L. Mallowan, The inscriptions of Assurbanipal, *Liverpool Annals of Archaeology and Anthropology* 20, 1933, pp. 96–109.

Caroe, O., *The Pathans. 550 BC–AD 1957* (London and New York, 1958 and 1964; reprint: Karachi, 1973 and 1986).

Carratelli, G. Pugliese and G. Garbini, *A Bilingual Graeco-Aramaic Edict by Aśoka* (Rome, 1964).

Casal, J.-M., *Fouilles de Mundigak* (2 vols, Paris, 1961).

Casimir, M. J. and B. Glatzer, Shah-i Mashad, a recently discovered madrasah of the Ghurid period in Garcistan (Afghanistan), *East and West* 21, 1971, pp. 53–68.

Cattenat, A. and J.-C. Gardin, Diffusion comparée de quelques genres de poteries charactéristiques de l'époque achéménide sur le plateau iranien et en Asie centrale, in: J. Deshayes (ed.), *La plateau iranien et l'Asie centrale des origines à la conquête islamique* (Paris, 1977), pp. 225–48.

Cazelles, H., Sophonie, Jérémie et les Scythes en Palestine, *Revue Biblique* 74, 1967, pp. 24–44.

Centlivres, P., *Un bazaar d'Asie Centrale* (Wiesbaden, 1972).

Centlivres, P., Les Uzbeks du Qattaghan, *Afghanistan Journal* 2, 1975, pp. 28–36.

Centlivres, P., L'histoire récente de l'Afghanistan et la configuration interethnique dans le Nord-Est de l'Afghanistan, *Studia Iranica* 5, 2, 1976, pp. 255–67.

Centlivres, P., La nouvelle carte ethnique de l'Afghanistan, *Les Nouvelles d'Afghanistan* 47, 1990, pp. 4–11.

Centlivres, P., with M. Centlivres-Demont, Frontières et phénomènes migratoires en Asie centrale: Le cas de l'Afghanistan de 1880 à nos jours, in: M. Centlivres-Demont (eds), *Migrationen in Asien. Abwanderung, Umsiedlung und Flucht* (Bern, 1983), pp. 83–114.

Centlivres, P., with M. Centlivres-Demont, Et si on parlait de l'Afghanistan? (Paris, 1988).

Chadwick, N. and V. Zhirminski, *Oral Epics of Central Asia* (Cambridge, 1969).

Chavannes, E., *Documents sur les Tou-kiue (Turcs) Occidentaux* (St Petersburg, 1903).

Christian, R., *A History of Russia, Central Asia and Mongolia, vol. I. Inner Asia from Prehistory to the Mongol Empire* (Oxford, 1998).

Christensen, A., *L'Iran sous les Sassanides* (Copenhagen, second edition, 1944).

Christensen, P., *The Decline of Iranshahr. Irrigation and Environments in the History of the Middle East, 500 BC to AD 1500* (Copenhagen, 1993).

Christol, A., Les édits grecs d'Aśoka: étude linguistique, *Journal Asiatique*, 1983, pp. 25–42.

Clifford, M. L., *The Land and People of Afghanistan* (New York, 1973).

Conolly, A., *Journey to the North of India. Overland from England, through Russia, Persia and Affghaunistaun* (2 vols, London, 1834).

Cordovez, D. and S. Harrison, *Out of Afghanistan: The Inside Story of the Soviet Withdrawal* (New York, 1995).

Cribb, J., Gandharan hoards of Kushano-Sassanian and Late Kushan coppers, *Coin Hoards* 6, 1981.

Cribb, J., Dating India's earliest coins, *South Asian Archaeology 1983*, Janine Schotsmans and Maurizio Taddei (eds) (Naples, 1985), pp. 535–54.

Cribb, J., Numismatic evidence for Kushano-Sasanian chronology, *Studia Iranica* 19, 1990, pp. 151–93.

Cribb, J., The Heraus coins: their attribution to the Kushan king Kujula Kadphises, c. AD 30–80, in M. Price, A. Burnett and R. Bland (eds), *Essays in Honour of Robert Carson and Kenneth Jenkins* (London, 1993), pp. 107–34.

Cunningham, A., *Ancient Geography of India* (Calcutta, 1924).

Curiel, R. and G. Fussmann, *Le trésor monétaire de Qunduz* (Paris, 1965).

Curiel, R. and D. Schlumberger, *Trésors monétaires d'Afghanistan* (Paris, 1953).

Curtis, J. A., Reconsideration of the cemetery at Khinaman, Southeastern Iran, *Iranica Antiqua* 23, 1988, pp. 97–124.

Curtis, J. A., with V. Sarkhosh, R. Hillenbrand and M. Rogers (eds), *The Art and Archaeology of Ancient Persia. New Light on the Parthian and Sasanian Empires* (London, 1998).

Czeglédy, K., Zur Geschichte der Hephthaliten, in: J. Harmatta (ed.), *From Hecataeus to Al-Huwârizmî. Bactrian, Pahlavi, Sogdian, Persian, Sanskrit, Syriac, Arabic, Chinese, Greek and Latin Sources for the History of Pre-Islamic Central Asia* (Budapest, 1984), pp. 213–17.

Daffinà, P., Gli heretici Chi-to e la divinità di Zâbul, *Rivista degli Studi Orientali* 37, 1962.

Daffinà, P., *L'immigrazione dei Sakâ nella Drangiana* (Rome, 1967).

Daftary, F., *The Isma'ilis. Their History and Doctrines* (New York, 1990).

Dagens, B., M. Le Berre and D. Schlumberger, *Monuments préislamiques d'Afghanistan* (Paris, 1964).

Dales, G. F., Archaeological and radiocarbon chronologies for protohistoric South Asia, in: N. Hammond (ed.), *South Asian Archaeology* (London, 1973), pp. 157–69.

Dalton, O. M., *The Treasure of the Oxus with Other Objects from Ancient Persia and India* (London, 1905).

Dani, A. H., Pastoral-agricultural tribes of Pakistan in the post-Indus period, in: A. H. Dani and V. M. Masson (eds), *The Dawn of Civilization: Earliest Times to 700 BC* (History of Civilizations of Central Asia, vol. I) (Paris, 1992 and 1996), pp. 395–419.

Dani, A. H. and P. Bernard, Alexander and his successors in Central Asia, in: János Harmatta (ed.), *The Development of Sedentary and Nomadic Civilizations: 700 BC to AD 250* (History of Civilizations of Central Asia, vol. II) (Paris, 1994, 1996), pp. 67–97.

Dani, A. H. and V. M. Masson (eds), *The Dawn of Civilization: Earliest Times to 700 BC* (History of Civilizations of Central Asia, vol. I) (Paris, 1992, second impression, 1996).

Dani, A. H. and B. A. Litvinsky, The Kushano-Sasanian kingdom, in: B. A. Litvinsky (ed.), *The Crossroads of Civilizations, AD 250 to 750* (History of Civilizations of Central Asia, vol. III) (Paris, 1996), pp. 103–18.

Dani, A. H., B. A. Litvinsky and M. H. Zamir Safi, Eastern Kushans, Kidarites in Gandhara and Kashmir, and Later Hephthalites, in: B. A. Litvinsky (ed.), *The Crossroads of Civilizations, AD 250 to 750* (History of Civilizations of Central Asia, vol. III) (Paris, 1996), pp. 163–83.

Davary, G. D. and H. Humbach, *Eine weitere aramäoiranische Inschrift der Periode des Aśoka aus Afghanistan* (*Abhandlungen der Akadamie der Wissenschaften und der Literatur in Mainz*, 1, 1974, pp. 1–16).

Davies, C. C., *The Problem of the North-West Frontier, 1890–1908. With a Survey of Policy since 1849* (Cambridge, 1932; reprint: London, 1975).

Davis, R. S., The Palaeolithic, in: F. R. Allchin and N. Hammond, *The Archaeology of Afghanistan* (London, 1978), pp. 37–70.

Davis-Kimball, J., et al. (eds), *Nomads of the Eurasian Steppes in the Early Iron Age* (Berkeley, 1995).

Delloye, I., *Des femmes d'Afghanistan* (Paris, 1980).

Dhorme, E. Les peuples issus de Japhet d'après le chapitre X de la Génèse, *Syria* XIII, 1932, pp. 28–49.

Diakonoff, I. M., Media, in: *Cambridge History of Iran*, II, 1985, pp. 36–148.

Diakonoff, I. M., On some supposed Indo-Iranian glosses in cuneiform languages, *Bulletin of the Asia Institute* 7, 1993, pp. 47–9.

Diver, M., *The Hero of Herat* (London, 1912).

Diver, M., *The Judgement of the Sword* (London, 1924).

Doerfer, G., *Lexik und Sprachgeographie des Chaladsch* (Wiesbaden, 1987).

Dollot, René, *L'Afghanistan: histoire, description, moeurs et coutumes, folklore, fouilles* (Paris, 1937).

Dor, R. and C. D. Naumann, *Die Kirghisen des afghanischen Pamir* (Graz, 1978).

Dorn, *History of the Afghans* (London, 1829–56; 1965).

Dupree, L., The retreat of the British Army from Kabul to Jalalabad in 1842: history and folklore, *Journal of the Folklore Institute* 4, 1, 1967, pp. 50–74.

Dupree, L., *Afghanistan* (Princeton, 1973; revised edition, 1980).

Dupree, L., Afghanistan: Ethnography, *Encyclopaedia Iranica* I, 1985, pp. 495–501.

Dupree, L. and L. Albert (eds), *Afghanistan in the 1970s* (New York, 1974).

Dupree, N. H., *The Road to Balkh* (Kabul, 1967).

Dupree, N. H., *An Historical Guide to Afghanistan* (Kabul, second edition 1977).

Dupree, N. H., with L. Dupree and A. A. Motamedi, *The National Museum of Afghanistan. A Pictorial Guide* (Kabul, 1974).

Durand, A., *The Making of a Frontier* (London, 1900).

Edelberg, L. and S. Jones, *Nuristan* (Graz, 1979).

Eden, Emily, *Up the Country* (London, 1866).

Edwards, David B., *Heroes of the Age: Moral Fault Lines on the Afghan Frontier* (Berkeley and Los Angeles, 1996).

Eilers, W., Das Volk der Makâ vor und nach den Achâmeniden. Befund – Herkunft – Fortleben. *Archäologische Mitteilungen aus Iran*. Ergänzungsband 10, 1983, pp. 101–19.

Einzmann, Harald, *Religioses Volksbrauchtum in Afghanistan* (Wiesbaden, 1977).

Elfenbein, J., A Periplus of the 'Brahui Problem', *Studia Iranica* 16, 1987, fasc. 2, pp. 215–33.

Elias, N., *Report of a Mission to Chinese Turkestan and Badakhshan* (Calcutta, 1886).

Elphinstone, Hon. Mountstuart, *An Account of the Kingdom of Caubul and its Dependencies in Persia, Tartary, and India, Comprising a View of the Afghan Nation and a History of the Dooraunee Monarchy*, 3 vols (London, 1815; reprint Graz, 1969; and reprint Karachi, 1972).

Engels, D. W., *Alexander the Great and the Logistics of the Macedonian Army* (Berkeley, 1978).

Enoki, K., On the nationality of the Ephthalites, *Memoirs of the Research Department of the Toyo Bunko*, 18, 1959, pp. 1–158.

Enoki, K., On the date of the Kidarites (I–II), *Memoirs of the Research Department of the Toyo Bunko, The Oriental Library*, no. 27, 1969, 1–26, and vol. 28, 1970, pp. 13–38.

Enoki, K., Some remarks on Chieh-shi, *East and West* 27, 1977, 1–4.

Enoki, K., with G. A. Koshelenko and Z. Haidary, The Yüeh-chich and their migrations, in: János Harmatta (ed.), *The Development of Sedentary and Nomadic Civilizations: 700 BC to AD 250* (History of Civilizations of Central Asia, vol. II) (Paris, 1994, 1996), pp. 171–89.

Enriquez, C. M., *The Pathan Borderland* (Calcutta and Simla, 1910).

Errington, Elizabeth and Joe Cribb (eds), *The Crossroads of Asia. Transformation in Image and Symbol in the Art of Ancient Afghanistan and Pakistan* (Cambridge, 1992).

Ettinghausen, Richard and Oleg Grabar, *The Art and Architecture of Islam* (New Haven and London, 1987, 1994).

Eyre, V., *The Military Operations at Cabul* (fourth edition, London, 1843).

Eyre, V., *The Kabul Insurrection of 1841–42* (London, 1879).

Fairservis, Walter A., *The Roots of Ancient India. The Archaeology of Early Indian Civilization* (second, revised edition, Chicago and London, 1975; first edition, 1971).

Ferdinand, K., Nomad expansion and commerce in Central Afghanistan. A sketch of some modern trends, *Folk* 4, 1962, pp. 123–59.

Ferdinand, K., Nomadism in Afghanistan, with an appendix on milk products, in: L. Földes (ed.), *Viehwirtschaft und Hirtenkulture* (Budapest, 1969), pp. 127–60.

Ferrier, J. P., *Caravan Journeys and Wanderings in Persia, Afghanistan, Turkistan, and Baluchistan (with Historical Notices of the Countries lying between Russia and India)* (London, 1857; reprint: Delhi, 1967; Westmead, 1971).

Ferrier, J. P., *History of the Afghans* (trans. London, 1858).

Fischel, W. J., The Jews of Central Asia (Khorasan) in mediaeval Hebrew and Islamic literature, *Historia Judaica* VII, 1945, pp. 29–50.

Fischer, K., Zur Lage von Kandahar an Landverbindungen zwischen Iran und Indien, *Bonner Jahrbücher* 167, 1967, pp. 129–232.

Fischer, K., D. Morgenstern and V. Thewald (eds), *Nimruz. Geländebegehungen in Sistan 1955–1973 und die Aufnahme von Dewal-i Khodaydad 1970* (2 vols, Bonn 1974/1976).

Fisher, W. B., *The Land of Iran* (*Cambridge History of Iran*, I; Cambridge, 1968).

Forbes, A., *The Afghan Wars, 1839–1842 and 1878–1880* (London, 1892).

Forster, G., *A Journey from Bengal to England through the Northern Part of India, Kashmir, Afghanistan and Persia and into Russia by the Caspiansea* (London, 1798).

Forstner, M., Ya'qub b. al-Lait und der Zunbil, *Zeitschnift der Deutschen Morgenländischen Gesellschaft*, CXX/1, 1970, pp. 69–83.

Foucher, A., *La vieille route de l'Índe de Bactres à Taxila* (Paris, 1942).

Francfort, H.-P., *Les fortifications en Asie centrale de l'âge du bronze à l'époque kouchane* (Paris, 1979).

Francfort, H.-P., *Fouilles d'Ai Khanoum* (Paris, 1984).

Francfort, H.-P., *Fouilles de Shortughai* (Paris, 1989).

Francfort, H.-P., (ed.), *Nomades et sédentaires en Asie centrale: Rapports de l'archéologie et d'ethnologie* (Paris, 1990).

Frank, A. G. and B. K. Gills (eds), *The World System: From Five Hundred Years to Five Thousand* (London and New York, 1992).

Franz, E., Zur gegenwärtigen Verbreitung und Gruppierung der Turkmenen in Afghanistan, *Bässler Archiv, Beiträge zur Völkerkunde* 20, 1972, pp. 191–239.

Franz, E., Ethnographischen Skizzen zur Lage der Turkmenen in Afghanistan, *Orient* 13, 1972, pp. 175–84.

Fraser, J. B., *The Kuzzilbash. A Tale of Khorasan* (3 vols, London, 1828).

Fraser, P. M., The son of Aristonax at Kandahar, *Afghan Studies* 2, 1979, pp. 9–21.

Fraser, P. M., *Cities of Alexander the Great* (Oxford, 1996).

Fraser-Tytler, Sir W. K., *Afghanistan* (third edition, London, 1967).

Frye, Richard N., *The Golden Age of Persia* (London, 1975).

Frye, Richard N., *The History of Ancient Iran* (München, 1984).

Frye, Richard N., *The Heritage of Central Asia* (Princeton, 1996).

Fuchs, W., *Huei-ch'ao's Pilgerreise durch Nord-West Indien und Zentral-Asien um 726* (Berlin, 1938).

Fussman, G., *Atlas linguistique des parlers dardes et kafirs. I. Cartes. II. Commentaire* (Paris, 1972).

Fussman, G., with Le Berre, *Monuments bouddhiques de la région de Caboul* (Paris, 1976).

Fussman, G., with J.-C. Gardin and O. Guillaume, *Surkh Kotal en Bactriane*, vol. II (Paris, 1990).

Fussman, G., L'Indo-Grec Ménandre, *Journal Asiatique* CCLXXXI, 1–2, 1993, pp. 61–137.

Fussman, G., L'inscription de Rabatak et l'origine de l'ère saka, *Journal Asiatique* 286, 2, 1998, pp. 571–651.

Gandha Singh, *Ahmad Shah Durrani: Founder of Modern Afghanistan* (Bombay, 1959).

Gankovsky, Yu. V., The Durrani Empire, in: *Afghanistan: The Past and Present* (Moscow, 1981), pp. 76–98.

Gardin, J.-Cl., L'archéologie du paysage bactrien, *Comptes-rendus de l'Académie des Inscriptions et Belles-Lettres*, 1980, pp. 480–501.

Gardin, J.-C. and P. Gentelle, Irrigation et peuplement dans la plaine d'Ai Khanoum de l'époque achéménide à l'époque musulmane, *Bulletin de l'Ecole Française d'Extrême Orient* 66, 1976, pp. 59–99.

Gardin, J.-C. and P. Gentelle, (ed.), *L'archéologie de la Bactriane ancienne* (Paris, 1985).

Gentelle, P., *Prospections archéologiques en Bactriane Orientale (1974–1978). Vol. I. Données paléografiques et fondements de l'irrigation* (Paris, 1989).

Gershevitch, I., Sissoo at Susa (O. Pers. Yakâ = Dalbergia Sissoo Roxb.), *Bulletin of the School of Oriental Studies* 19.2, 1957, pp. 317–20.

Gershevitch, I., Ad 'Sissoo at Susa', *Bulletin of the School of Oriental and African Studies* 21.1, 1958, p. 174.

Gershevitch, I., The well of Baghlan, *Asia Minor* NS 12, 1966, pp. 47–55.

Gershevitch, I., Gershevitch, Old Iranian literature, in: *Handbuch der Orientalistik*, I.4.2.1 (Leiden, 1968), pp. 1–30.

Gershevitch, I., Nokonzok's well, *Afghan Studies* 2, 1979, pp. 55–73.

Gershevitch, I., (ed.), *The Cambridge History of Iran, vol. 2. The Median and Achaemenian Periods* (Cambridge, 1985).

Gervers-Molnar, V., *The Hungarian Szür: An archaic mantle of Eurasian origin* (Toronto, 1973).

Geurts, M. M. M. and M.-J. Valentijn, *Afghanistan* ('s Gravenhage, 1980).

Ghaus, Abdul Samad, *The Fall of Afghanistan: An Insider's Account* (Washington, 1988).

Ghirshman, R., *Les Chionites-Hephthalites* (Paris, 1948).

Ghirshman, R., *Iran* (Harmondsworth, 1954).

Ghirshman, R., *L'Iran et la migration des Indo-Aryens et des Iraniens* (Leiden, 1977).

Gibb, H. A. R., *The Arab Conquests in Central Asia* (New York, 1923; reprint New York, 1970).

Gignoux, Ph. and B. A. Litvinsky, Religions and religious movements – I, in: B. A. Litvinsky (ed.), *The Crossroads of Civilizations, AD 250 to 750* (History of Civilizations of Central Asia, vol. III) (Paris, 1996), pp. 403–20.

Giustozzi, Antonio, *War, Politics and Society in Afghanistan 1978–1992* (London, 2000).

Glatzer, B., *Nomaden von Gharjistân. Aspekte der wirtschaftlichen, sozialen und politischen Organisation nomadischer Durrânî-Paschtunen in Nordwestafghanistan* (Wiesbaden, 1977).

Glatzer, B., *The Travels of Ibn Battuta* (Cambridge, 1958–62).

Gleig, G., Sale's Brigade in Afghanistan (London, 1861).

Gnoli, Gh., *Richerche storiche sul Sîstân antico* (Rome, 1967).

Gnoli, Gh., More on the Sistanic hypothesis, *East and West* 27, 1977, pp. 309–20.

Gnoli, Gh., *Zoroaster's Time and Homeland. A study on the origins of Mazdeism and related problems* (Naples, 1980).

Göbl, R., *Dokumente zur Geschichte der Iranischen Hunnen in Baktrien und Indien* (Wiesbaden, 1967).

Göbl, R., *Münzprägung des Kushanreiches. System und Chronologie der Münzprägung des Kushanreiches* (Vienna, 1984).

Gohari, M. J., *Taliban Ascent to Power* (Oxford, 1999).

Golombek, L., Abbasid mosque at Balkh, *Oriental Art* 15, 1969, pp. 173–89.

Golombek, L., *The Timurid Shrine at Gazur Gah* (Toronto, 1969).

Gommans, J. J. L., *The Rise of the Indo-Afghan Empire, c.1710–1780* (Leiden, New York and Köln, 1995).

Gratzl, K. (ed.), *Hindukusch. Österreichische Forschungsexpedition in den Wakhan* (Graz, 1970).

Gray, J. A., *My Residence at the Court of the Ameer* (1895).

Greenwood, Lt., *Narrative of the Late Victorious Campaign in Afghanistan Under General Pollock* (London, 1844).

Gregorian, V., *The Emergence of Modern Afghanistan: Politics of Reform and Modernization 1880–1946* (Stanford, 1969).

Grenet, F., Mithra et les planètes dans l'Hindukush central: essai d'interprétation de la peinture de Dokhtar-i Nôshirvân, in: R. Gyselen (ed.), *Au carrefour des religions. Mélanges offerts à Philippe Gignoux* (Bures-sur-Yvette, 1995), pp. 105–19.

Greussing, K. and J.-H. Grevemeyer (eds), *Revolution in Iran und Afghanistan* (Frankfurt am Main, 1980).

Grevemeyer, J.-H., *Herrschaft, Raub und Gegenseitigkeit. Die politische Geschichte Badakhshans 1500–1883* (Wiesbaden, 1982).

Grey, C. and H. Garrett, *European Adventurers of Northern India: 1785–1849* (Lahore, 1929).

Grimes, B. F. (ed.), Ethnologue. Languages of the World. Thirteenth edition (Dallas, 1996).

Grötzbach, E. (ed.), Neue Beiträge zur Afghanistanforschung (Liestal, 1988).

Grötzbach, E., *Afghanistan. Eine geographische Landeskunde* (Darmstadt, 1990).

Gyselen, R., *La géografie administrative de l'empire sassanide* (Paris, 1989).

Habberton, *Anglo-Russian Relations Concerning Afghanistan: 1837–1907* (Urbana, 1937).

Hackim, R. and Ahmad Ali Kohzad, *Légendes et coutumes Afghanes* (Paris, 1953).

Hahn, H., *Die Stadt Kabul (Afghanistan) und ihr Umland* (Bonn, 1964–5).

Hakemi, A., *Catalogue de l'exposition, Dessert de Lut* (Tehran, 1972).

Hakemi, A., with M. Sajjedi, Shahdad excavations in the context of an oasis civilization, in: G. Ligabue and S. Salvatori (eds), *Bactria. An Ancient Oasis Civilization from the Sands of Afghanistan* (Rome, 1988), pp. 141–57.

Hamilton, A., *Afghanistan* (London, 1906).

Hammond, T., *Red Flag over Afghanistan* (Boulder, 1984).

Harlan, J., *A Memoir of India and Afghanistan* (Philadelphia, 1842).

Harlan, J., *Central Asia: Personal Narrative of Josiah Harlan, 1823–1841* (London, 1939).

Harmatta, J., The emergence of the Indo-Iranians: the Indo-Iranian languages, in: A. H. Dani and V. M. Masson (eds), *The Dawn of Civilization: Earliest Times to 700 BC* (History of Civilizations of Central Asia, vol. II) (Paris, 1992, 1996), pp. 357–78.

Harmatta, J., Languages and scripts in Graeco-Bactria and the Saka kingdoms, in: János Harmatta (ed.), *The Development of Sedentary and Nomadic Civilizations: 700 BC to AD 250* (History of Civilizations of Central Asia, vol. II) (Paris, 1994a, 1996), pp. 397–416.

Harmatta, J., Languages and literature in the Kushan empire, in: János Harmatta (ed.), *The Development of Sedentary and Nomadic Civilizations: 700 BC to AD 250* (History of Civilizations of Central Asia, vol. II) (Paris, 1994b; 1996), pp. 417–40.

Harmatta, J., Religions in the Kushan Empire, in: János Harmatta (ed.), *The Development of Sedentary and Nomadic Civilizations: 700 BC to AD 250* (History of Civilizations of Central Asia, vol. II) (Paris, 1994c, 1996), pp. 313–29.

Harmatta, J. (ed.), *The Development of Sedentary and Nomadic Civilizations: 700 BC to AD 250* (History of Civilizations of Central Asia, vol. II) (Paris, 1994, 1996).

Harmatta, J. and B. A. Litvinsky, Tokharistan and Gandhara under Western Türk rule (650–750), in: B. A. Litvinsky (ed.), *The Crossroads of Civilizations, AD 250 to 750* (History of Cvilizations of Central Asia, vol. III) (Paris, 1996), pp. 367–401.

Hart, L. W., *Character and Costumes of Afghaunistan* (London, 1843).

Haughton, J., *Char-ee-kar and Service there with the 4th Goorkha Regiment (Shah Shooja's Force) in 1841: An Episode of the First Afghan War* (London, 1879).

Hasan Kakar, H., *Government and Society in Afghanistan: The Reign of Amir Abd-al Rahman Khan* (Austin, 1979).

Havelock, H., *Narrative of the War in Affghanistan in 1838–1839* (London, 1840).

Hayat Khân, *Hayâti Afghâni* (London, 1874; Lahore, 1981).

Heathcote, T. A., *The Afghan Wars, 1839–1919* (1980).

Helms, S. W., Excavations at 'the City and the Famous Fortress of Kandahar, the Foremost Place in all of Asia', *Afghan Studies* 3–4, 1982, pp. 1–24.

Helms, S. W., *Excavations at Old Kandahar in Afghanistan 1976–1978. Stratigraphy, Pottery and Other Finds* (Oxford, 1997).

Henning, W. B., An astronomical chapter of the Bundahishn, *Journal of the Royal Asiatic Society*, 1942, pp. 229–50.

Henning, W. B., The Aramaic inscription of Asoka found in Lampâka, *Bulletin of the School of Oriental and African Studies* 13, 1949–50, pp. 80–8.

Herberg, W., Topografische Feldarbeiten in Ghor. Bericht úber Forschungsarbeiten zum Problem Jam-Feroz Koh, *Afghanistan Journal* 3, 1976, pp. 57–69.

Herrmann, G., Lapis lazuli: the early phases of its trade, *Iraq* 30, 1968, pp. 21–57.

Herzfeld, E., *Kushano-Sasanian Coins* (Memoirs of the Archaeological Survey of India, vol. 38) (Calcutta, 1930).

Hiebert, F. T., Chronology of Margiana and Bactria in the Bronze Age, *Information Bulletin of the International Association for the Study of the Cultures of Central Asia*, vol. 19, 1993, pp. 136–48.

Hiebert, F. T., *Origins of the Bronze Age Oasis Civilization in Central Asia* (Cambridge, Mass., 1994).

Hiebert, F. T., with C. C. Lamberg-Karlovsky, Central Asia and the Indo-Iranian borderlands, *Iran* 30, 1992, pp. 1–15.

Hill, D. and O. Grabar, *Islamic Architecture and its Decoration AD 800–1500.* (London, 1967).

Hiro, D., *Between Marx and Muhammad. The Changing Face of Central Asia* (London, 1994).

Holdich, T. H., *The Indian Borderlands 1880–1900* (London, 1901).

Holdich, T. H., *The Gates of India* (London, 1910).

Holdsworth, M., *Turkestan in the Nineteenth Century* (Oxford, 1959).

Holt, F. L., *Alexander the Great and Bactria: The Formation of a Greek Frontier in Central Asia* (Leiden, 1988).

Holt, F. L., *Thundering Zeus. The Making of Hellenistic Bactria* (Berkeley, Los Angeles, London, 1999).

Honigmann, E. and A. Maricq, *Recherches sur les Res Gestae Divi Saporis* (Brussels, 1953).

Hookham, H., *Tamburlaine the Conqueror* (1962).

Hopkirk, P., *The Great Game. On Secret Service in High Asia* (London, 1990).

Hopkirk, P., *On Secret Service East of Constantinople. The Plot to Bring Down the British Empire* (London, 1994).

Hough, W., *A Narrative of the March and Operations of the Army of the Indus in the Expedition to Affghanistan in the Years 1838–1839* (London, 1841).

Hudud al-ʿÂlam. The 'Regions of the World', a Persian Geography 372 AH *982* AD. English translation and commentary by V. Minorsky (London, 1937; second edition, 1970).

Hui-li, *The Life of Hsuang-tsang* (Peking, 1959).

Huldt, B. and E. Jansson (eds), *The Tragedy of Afghanistan* (London, 1988).

Hulsewé, A. F. P. and M. A. N. Lowe, *China in Central Asia. The Early Stage: 125* BC–AD *25* (Leiden, 1979).

Humbach, H., *Baktrische Sprachdenkmäler* (Wiesbaden, 1966).

Humbach, H., Puspapura = Pešâwar, *MSS* 23, 1968, pp. 45–8.

Humbach, H., Die aramäische Aśoka-Inschrift vom Laghman-Fluss, *Indologen-Tagung 1971* (Wiesbaden, 1973), pp. 161–9.

Humbach, H., Die baktrische Ära der Tochi-Inschriften, in: W. Eilers (ed.), *Festgabe deutscher Iranisten zur 2500 Jahrfeier Irans* (Stuttgart, 1971), pp. 74–9.

Humbach, H., The Tochi inscriptions, *Studien zur Indologie und Iranistik* 19, 1994, pp. 137–56.

Humbach, H., with P. O. Skaervo, *The Sasanian Inscription of Paikuli* (Wiesbaden, 1980).

Humlum, J., *La géographie de l'Afghanistan* (Copenhagen, 1959).

Hyatt, J. P., The peril from the north in Jeremiah, *Journal of Biblical Literature* 59, 1940, pp. 449–513.

Itô, Gikyô, A new interpretation of Aśokan inscriptions, Taxila and Kandahar I, *Studia Iranica* 6, 1977, pp. 151–61.

Itô, Gikyô, Aśokan inscriptions, Laghmân I and II, *Studia Iranica* 8, 1979, pp. 175–84.

James, M. R., *The Apocryphal New Testament* (Oxford, 1924).

Janata, A., Die Bevölkerung von Ghor. Beitrag zur Ethnographie und Ethnogenese der Chahar Aimaq, *Archiv für Völkerkunde* 17–18, 1962/1963, pp. 73–156.

Janata, A., Beitrag zur Völkerkunde Afghanistans, *Archiv für Völkerkunde* 29, 1975, pp. 7–36.

Janata, A., Constituents of Pashtun ethnic identity. The Jaji case, *Studia Iranica* 16, 1987, pp. 201–14.

Jarrige, J.-F., Die frühesten Kulturen in Pakistan und ihrer Entwicklung, in: *Vergessene Städte am Indus. Frühe Kulturen vom 8. bis 2. Jahrtausend* (Mainz am Rhein, 1987), pp. 50–66.

Jarrige, J.-F., Der Kulturkomplex von Mehrgarh (Periode VIII) und Sibri. Der 'Schatz' von Quetta, in: *Vergessene Städte am Indus. Frühe Kulturen vom 8. bis 2. Jahrtausend* (Mainz am Rhein, 1987), pp. 102–11.

Jarrige, J.-F., with M. Hassan, Funerary complexes in Baluchistan at the end of the third millennium in the light of recent discoveries at Mehrgarh and Quetta, *South Asian Archaeology 1985* (Riverdale, 1989).

Jarrige, J.-F., with M. Santoni, *Fouilles de Pirak* (2 vols, Paris, 1979).

Jentsch, Ch., *Das Nomadentum in Afghanistan: Eine geographische Untersuchung zu Lebens- und Wirtschaftsformen in asiatischen Trockengebiet* (= *Afghanische Studien* 9, 1973).

Jettmar, K. (ed.), in collaboration with Lennart Edelberg, *Cultures of the Hindu Kush. Selected papers from the Hindu-Kush cultural conference held at Moesgård 1970* (Wiesbaden, 1974).

Jettmar, K. (ed.), *Die Religionen des Hindu Kush* (Stuttgart, 1975).

Jones, S., *An Annotated Bibliography of Nuristan (Kafiristan) and the Kalash Kafirs of Chitral* (Part I) (Copenhagen, 1966).

Jones, S., Nuristan: Mountain communities in the Hindu Kush, *Afghan Studies* 1, 1978, pp. 79–92.

Kakar, H. K., *Afghanistan: A Study in Internal Political Development, 1880–1896* (Kabul, 1971).

Kakar, H. K., *Government and Society in Afghanistan. The Reign of Amir Abd al-Rahman Khan* (Austin, 1977).

Kakar, M. H., *Afghanistan. The Soviet Invasion and the Afghan Response, 1979–1982* (Berkeley, Los Angeles, New York, 1995).

Kalter, J., *The Arts and Crafts of Turkestan* (London, 1984).

Kamal Matinuddin, *The Taliban Phenomenon. Afghanistan 1994–1997* (Oxford, 1999).

Kammenhuber, A., *Die Arier im Vorderen Orient* (Indogermanische Bibliothek, Reihe 3, Untersuchungen) (Heidelberg, 1968).

Kaye, J., *History of the War in Afghanistan* (third edition, 3 vols, London, 1874).

Keddie, N. R., *Sayyid Jamal ad-Din 'al-Afghani': A Political Biography* (Berkeley, 1972).

Kent, R. G., *Old Persian. Grammar, Texts, and Lexicon* (second edition, New Haven, 1953).

Kervran, M., La mosque des 'neuf coupoles' à Balkh, in: La Bactriane de Cyrus à Timour (Tamerlan), *Dossiers d'Archéologie* 247, 1999, p. 35.

Kessler, M., Ivan Viktorovich Vitkevich (1806–1839): A Tsarist agent in Central Asia, *Central Asian Collectanea* 4, 1960.

Khazanov, M. A., *Nomads and the Outside World* (Cambridge, 1984; Madison, 1994).

Khan, D., Wakhan in Historical and Political Setting, *Regional Studies* 4, pt. 2, 1986, pp. 3–54.

Khoury, P. S. and J. Kostiner, *Tribes and State Formation in the Middle East* (Berkeley, 1992).

Khwaja Nimatullah b. Khwaja Habibullah al-Harawi, *Tarikh-e Khan Jahani wa Makhzan-e Afghani* (vols I–II, Dacca, 1960–92).

Kieffer, Ch. M., Wardak, toponyme et ethnique d'Afghanistan, in: *Monumentum H. S. Nyberg* I (Leiden, 1975), pp. 475–83.

Kieffer, Ch. M., La maintenance de l'identité ethnique chez les Arabes arabophones, les Ôrmur et les Parâcî en Afghanistan, in: E. Orywal (ed.), *Die ethnischen Gruppen Afghanistans* (Wiesbaden, 1986), pp. 101–64.

Kipling, R., *Kim* (London, 1901).

Klimburg, M., *Afghanistan. Das Land im historischen Spannungsfeld Mittelasiens* (Wien, 1966).

Klimburg, M., with A. Janata, *Nuristan. Gläubige und Kafiren im Hindukush (Afghanistan)* (Wien, 1990).

Klimburg-Salter, D., *The Kingdom of Bamiyan* (Naples and Rome, 1989).

Klinkott, M., *Islamische Baukunst in Afghanisch-Sistan. Mit einem geschichtlichen Überblick von Alexander dem Grossen bis zur Zeit der Safawiden-Dynastie* (Berlin, 1982).

Klochkov, L. S., Signs on a potsherd from Gonur (on the question of the script used in Margiana), *Ancient Civilizations from Scythia to Siberia*, vol. 5, no. 2, 1998, pp. 165–75.

Klochkov, L. S., Glyptics of Margiana. The principles of the description and classification, *Ancient Civilizations from Scythia to Siberia*, VI, 1–2, 1999, pp. 41–59.

Knight, F. E., *Where Three Empires Meet* (London, 1895).

Kohl, P. C., *Central Asia. Palaeolithic Beginnings to the Iron Age/L'Asie centrale. Des origines à l'âge du fer* (Paris, 1984).

Kohl, P. C., The ancient economy, transferable technologies and the Bronze Age world-system: a view from the north-eastern frontier of the ancient Near East, in: M. Rowlands, M. T. Larsen, and K. Kristiansen (eds), *Centre and Periphery in the Ancient World* (Cambridge, 1987), pp. 13–24.

König, F. W., *Die Persika des Ktesias von Knidos* (Graz, 1972).

Kopecky, L.-M., The Imami Sayyed of the Hazarajat: The maintenance of their social elite position, *Folk* 24, 1982.

Koshelenko, G. A. (ed.), *Arkheologiya SSSR. Drevneishie Gosudarstva Kavkaza i Srednej Azii* (Moscow, 1985).

Koshkaki, M. B. al-din Khan, *Qataghan et Badakhshân*, trad. par M. Reut (3 vols, Paris, 1979; orginal version: Kabul, 1923).

Kraus, W., *Afghanistan. Natur, Geschichte und Kultur, Staat, Gesellschaft und Wirtschaft* (Tübingen and Basel, 1972; revised version: 1975).

Krawulsky, D., *Horâsân zur Timuridenzeit nach dem Târîh-e Hâfez-e Abrû (verf. 817–823 h.) des Nallâh ʿAbdallâh b. Lutfallâh al-Hvâfi genannt Hâfez-e Abrû*, 2 vols (Wiesbaden, 1984).

Kristensen, A. K. G., *Who were the Cimmerians, and where did they come from?* (Copenhagen, 1988).

Kuhrt, A. and S. Sherwin-White (eds), *Hellenism in the East: The Interaction of Greek and non-Greek Civilizations from Syria to Central Asia after Alexander* (Berkeley, 1987).

Kulke, H., Die Lapislazuli-Lagerstätte Sare Sang (Badakhshan). Geologie, Entstehung, Kulturgeschichte und Bergbau, *Afghanistan Journal* 3, 1976, pp. 43–56.

Kussmal, F., Badaxshan und seine Tagiken, *Tribus* 14, 1965, pp. 711–99.

Labourt, J., *Le christianisme dans l'empire Perse* (Paris, 1904).

Lal, M., *Life of the Ameer Dost Muhammed Khan of Kabul* (2 vols, London, 1846).

Lamberg-Karlovsky, C. C. and M. Tosi, Shahr-i Sokhta and Tepe Yahya: tracks on the earliest history of the Iranian Plateau, *East and West* 23, 1973, pp. 21–53.

Lane Fox, Robin, *Alexander the Great* (London, 1973).

Lazard, G., F. Grenet and C. de Lamberterie, Notes bactriennes, *Studia Iranica* 13, 1984, pp. 199–232.

Lecoq, P., *Les inscriptions de la Perse achéménide. Traduit du vieux perse, de l'élamite, du babylonien et de l'araméen, présenté et annoté* (Paris, 1997).

Lee, J. L., *The 'Ancient Supremacy'. Bukhara, Afghanistan & the Battle for Balkh, 1731–1901* (Leiden, New York and Köln, 1996).

Leriche, P., *La Bactriane de Cyrus à Timour (Tamerlan): les fabuleux trésors de l'Oxus* (Dijon, 1999).

Leriche, P., 'Bactres', in: P. Leriche, *La Bactriane de Cyrus à Timour (Tamerlan): les fabuleux trésors de l'Oxus* (Dijon, 1999), pp. 28–35.

Le Strange, G., *The Lands of the Eastern Caliphate. Mesopotamia, Persia and Central Asia from the Moslem Conquest to the Time of Timur* (Cambridge, 1905; third reprint, London, 1966).

Levi, P., *The Light Garden of the Angel King. Journeys in Afghanistan* (1972; revised version Harmondsworth, 1984).

Levi, S. and E. Chavannes, Voyages des pèlerins bouddhistes: L'itinéraire d'Ou-kong, *Journal Asiatique* 6, 1895.

Lezine, A., Hérat. Notes de voyage (I), *Bulletin d'études orientales* 18, 1963/64, pp. 127–45.

Ligabue, G. and S. Salvatori, *Bactria. An Ancient Oasis Civilization from the Sands of Afghanistan* (Venice, 1989).

Littauer, M. A. and J. H. Crouwel, *Chariots and Related Equipment from the Tomb of Tut'ankhamûn* (Oxford, 1985).

Litvinsky, B. A., Cities and urban life in the Kushan kingdom, in: János Harmatta (ed.), *The Development of Sedentary and Nomadic Civilizations* (History of Civilization of Central Asia, vol. II) (Paris, 1994, 1996), pp. 291–312.

Litvinsky, B. A., The Hephthalite Empire, in: B. A. Litvinsky, Zhang Guandda and R. Shabani Samghabadi (eds), *The Crossroads of Civilizations: AD 250 to AD 750* (History of Civilizations of Central Asia, vol. III) (Paris, 1996), pp. 135–62.

Litvinsky, B. A., with Igor R. Pichikjan, Gold plaques from the Oxus Temple (Northern Bactria), *Ancient Civilizations from Scythia to Siberia*, vol. 2, no. 2, 1995, pp. 196–220.

Litvinsky, B. A., with L. T. P'yankova, Pastoral tribes of the Bronze Age in the Oxus Valley (Bactria), in: A. H. Dani and V. M. Masson (eds), *The Dawn of Civilization: Earliest Times to 700 BC* (History of Civilizations of Central Asia, vol. I.) (Paris, 1992, 1996), pp. 379–94.

Litvinsky, B. A., with M. I. Vorobyova-Desyatovskaya, Religions and religious movements – II, in: B. A. Litvinsky, Zhang Guand-da and R. Shabani Samghabadi (eds), *The Crossroads of Civilizations: AD 250 to AD 750* (History of Civilizations of Central Asia, vol. III.) (Paris, 1996), pp. 421–48.

Litvinsky, B. A., with Zhang Guand-da and R. Shabani Samghabadi (eds), *The Crossroads of Civilizations: AD 250 to ad 750* (History of Civilizations of Central Asia, vol. III) (Paris, 1996).

Lockhart, L., *Nadir Shah: A Critical Study Based upon Contemporary Sources* (Cambridge, 1938).

Lockhart, L., *The Fall of the Safavi Dynasty and the Afghan Occupation of Persia* (Cambridge, 1958).

Lohuizen – de Leeuw, J. E. van, *The Scythian Period* (Leiden, 1949).

Longworth Dames, M., Afghanistan, *Encyclopaedia of Islam*.

Luckenbill, D. D., *Ancient Records of Assyria and Babylonia*, vol. I. (Chicago, 1926).

Lukonin, V. G., Kushano-Sasanidskie monety, *Epigrafica Vostoka* 18, 1967.

Lukonin, V. G., Political, social and administrative institutions, taxes and trade, *Cambridge History of Iran*, vol. 3/1, 1983.

Lyonnet, B, *Prospections archéologiques en Bactriane Orientale (1974–1978). Vol. 2. Céramique et peuplement du chalcolithique à la conquête arabe* (Paris, 1997).

McAlpin, D., Proto-Elamo-Dravidian: The evidence and its implications, *Transactions of the American Philosophical Society* 71, 1981, pt.3.

McChesney, R. D., *Waqf in Central Asia* (Princeton, 1991).

MacDowall, D. W., The Shahis of Kabul and Gandhara, *Numismatic Chronicle* 7th series, no. 8, 1965, pp. 189–224.

MacDowall, D. W., Pre-islamic coins in Kandahar museum, *Afghan Studies* 1, 1978, pp. 67–77.

MacDowall, D. W., Pre-Islamic coins in Herat museum, *Afghan Studies*, 2, 1979, pp. 45–53.

MacDowall, D. W., The successors of the Indo-Greeks at Begram, in: J. Schotsmans and M. Taddei (eds), *South Asian Archaeology 1983* (Naples, 1985a), pp. 555–66.

MacDowall, D. W., Two Azes hoards from Afghanistan, *South Asian Studies* 1, 1985b, pp. 51–5.

MacDowall, D. W., Der Einfluss Alexanders des Grosen auf das Münzwesen Afghanistans und Nordwest-Indiens, in: Jakob Ozols und Volker Thewalt, *Aus dem Osten des Alexanderreiches. Völker und Kulturen zwischen Orient und Okzident. Iran, Afghanistan, Pakistan, Indien* (Köln, 1984), pp. 66–73.

MacDowall, D. W. and M. Taddei, The Early Historic Period: Achaemenid and Greeks, in: F. R. Allchin and N. Hammond, *The Archaeology of Afghanistan* (London, New York and San Francisco, 1978), pp. 187–229.

MacGregor, *Central Asia* (3 vols, Calcutta, 1871).

Mackay, S., *The Iranians. Persia, Islam and the Soul of a Nation* (Harmondsworth, 1998; first edition: 1996).

McLachlan, K. and W. Whittacker, *A Bibliography of Afghanistan* (Cambridge, 1983).

MacLean, F., *Eastern Approaches* (London, 1949).

McMahon, A. A., The southern borderlands of Afghanistan, *Journal of the Royal Geographical Society*, April 1897.

Macmunn, G., *Afghanistan from Darius to Amanullah* (London, 1929).

MacNicoll, A. and W. Ball, *Excavations at Kandahar 1974 and 1975* (Oxford, 1996).

Macrory, P., *Signal Catastrophe* (London, 1966).

Macrory, P., *The Fierce Pawns* (Phildelphia, 1966).

Magnus, R. H. and E. Naby, *Afghanistan. Mullah, Marx and Mujahid* (Boulder, 1998).

Majumdar, N. G., The Bajaur casket of the reign of Menander, *Epigraphica Indica* 24, 1937, pp. 1–8.

Maley, W. (ed.), *Fundamentalism Reborn? Afghanistan and the Taliban* (London, 1998).

Malleson, G. B., *History of Afghanistan, from the Earliest Period to the Outbreak of the War of 1878* (London, 1879).

Malleson, G., *Herat* (London, 1880).

Mallory, J. P., *In Search of the Indo-Europeans. Language, Archaeology and Myth* (London, 1989).

Mandersloot, G., *Firozkohi. Een Afghaans reisjournaal* (Rotterdam, 1971).

Manz, B. F., *The Rise and Rule of Tamerlane* (Cambridge, 1989).

Marco Polo, *Travels*, edited by Sir Henry Yule (London, 1903). See also: *The Travels of Marco Polo*, translated and with an introduction by Ronald Latham (Harmondsworth, 1958).

Maricq, A., Res Gestae Divi Saporis, *Syria* 35, 1958, pp. 295–360.

Maricq, A., with G. Wiet, *Le minaret de Djam. La découverte de la capitale des sultans Ghorides (XIIe–XIIIe siècles)* (Paris, 1959).

Marquart, J., *Erânshahr nach der Geographie des Ps Moses Xorenac'i* (Berlin, 1901).

Marquart, J., *A Catalogue of the Provincial Capitals of Êrânšahr* (Rome, 1931).

Marquart, J., *Wehrot und Arang* (Berlin, 1938).

Marquart, J., with J. J. M. de Groot, Das Reich Zâbul und der Gott Zûn vom 6.-9. Jahrhundert, *Festschrift Eduard Sachau* (ed. G. Weil) (Berlin, 1915), pp. 248–92.

Marsden, P., *The Taliban. War, Religion and the New Order in Afghanistan* (Karachi, 1998).

Marshall, J., *Taxila* (3 vols, Cambridge, 1953).

Martin, F. A., *Under the Absolute Amir* (London, 1907).

Marvin, Ch., *Merv, the Queen of the World, and the Scourge of the Man-stealing Turcomans* (London, 1880).

Marvin, Ch., *Reconnoitring Central Asia. Pioneering Adventures In the Region Between Russia and India* (London, 1885; reprint New Delhi, 1996).

Masson, Ch., *Narrative of Various Journeys in Balochistan, Afghanistan, and the Panjab Including a Residence in Those Countries from 1826 to 1838* (3 vols. London, 1842; reprint: Karachi, 1974, Graz, 1975).

Masson, Ch., *Narrative of a Journey to Kalat, including an Account of the Insurrection at that Place in 1840; and a Memoir of Eastern Balochistan* (London, 1843; reprint Karachi, 1977).

Masson, Ch., *Legends of the Afghan Countries, in verse; – with Various Pieces, Original and Translated by Charles Masson, etc.* (London, 1848).

Masson, V. M., *Drevnezemledel'cheskaya kul'tura Margiani* (Moscow, 1959).

Masson, V. M., The Bronze Age in Khorasan and Transoxania, in: A. H. Dani and V. M. Masson (eds), *The Dawn of Civilization: Earliest Times to 700 BC* (History of Civilizations of Central Asia, vol. I.) (Paris, 1992a, second impression, 1996), pp. 225–45.

Masson, V. M., The decline of the Bronze Age civilization and movements of tribes, in: A. H. Dani and V. M. Masson (eds), *The Dawn of Civilization: Earliest Times to 700 BC* (History of Civilizations of Central Asia, vol. I.) (Paris, 1992b, second impression, 1996), pp. 337–56.

Masson, V. M., with V. I. Sarianidi, *Central Asia. Turkmenia before the Achaemenids* (London, 1972).

Maxwell-Hyslop, K. R., Dalbergia Sissoo Roxburgh, *Anatolian Studies 33*, 1983, pp. 67–72.

Maxwell-Hyslop, K. R., A comment on the finds from Khinaman, *Iranica Antiqua 23*, 1988, pp. 129–38.

Mayrhofer, M., *Die Indo-Arier im alten Vorderasien* (Wiesbaden, 1966).

Mayrhofer, M., *Die Arier im Vorderen Orient. Ein Mythos?* (Wien, 1974).

Mayrhofer, M., *Iranisches Personennamenbuch. Band I. Die altiranischen Namen* (Wien, 1979).

Meadow, R. H., A chronology for the Indo-Iranian borderlands and southern Baluchistan 4000–2000 BC, in: D. P. Agrawal and A. Ghosh (eds), *Radiocarbon and Indian Archaeology* (Bombay, 1973), pp. 190–204.

Melikian-Chirvani, A. S., Eastern Iranian architecture: a propos of the Ghurid parts of the Great Mosque of Heart, *Bulletin of the School of Oriental and African Studies 33*, 1970, pp. 322–7.

Melikian-Chirvani, A. S., L'évocation littéraire du bouddhisme dans l'Iran musulman, *Le monde iranien et l'Islam* II, 1974, pp. 1–72.

Metcalf, B. D., *Islamic Revival in British India: Deoband, 1860–1900* (Princeton, 1982).

Michaud, R. and S., *Caravanes de Tartarie* (Paris, 1977).

Miller, C., *Khyber: British India's North West Frontier* (New York, 1977).

Mitchener, M., *Indo-Greek and Indo-Scythian Coinage* (London, 1976).

Millard, A. R., The Scythian problem, in: J. Ruffle et al. (eds), *Glimpses of Ancient Egypt: Studies in Honour of H.W. Fairman* (Warminster, 1979), pp. 119–122.

Minorsky, V., The Turkish dialect of Khalaj, *Bulletin of the School of Oriental Studies* 10, 1940.

Mishra, Y., *The Hindu Shahis of Afghanistan and the Punjab,* AD 865–1026 (Patna, 1972).

Mohammed Ali, *A New Guide to Afghanistan* (Kabul, 1958).

Mohan Lal, *Travel in the Punjab, Afghanistan and Turkistan to Balkh, Bokhara and Herat* (London, 1846; reprint: Calcutta, 1977).

Mohan Lal, *Life of the Amir Dost Mohammad Khan* (2 vols, 1846).

Monchi-Zadeh, D., *Topografisch-Historische Studien zum Iranischen Nationalepos* (Wiesbaden, 1975).

Morgan, D., *The Mongols* (Oxford, 1986).

Morgenstierne, G., *An Etymological Vocabulary of Pashto* (Oslo, 1927).

Morgenstierne, G., 'Pashto', 'Pathan' and the treatment of the r + sibilant in Pashto, *Acta Orientalia* 18, 1940, pp. 138–44.

Morgenstierne, G., G. Neu-iranische Sprachen, in: *Handbuch der Iranistik,* Iranistik, Linguistik (Leiden/Köln, 1958), pp. 155–78.

Morgenstierne, G., Languages of Nuristan and surrounding regions, in: K. Jettman (ed.), *Cultures of the Hindu Kush* (Wiesbaden, 1974), pp. 1–10.

Morgenstierne, G., The languages of Afghanistan, *Afghanistan Quarterly* 20, pp. 81–90.

Morgenstierne, G., The linguistic stratification of Afghanistan, *Afghan Studies* 2, 1979, pp. 23–33.

Moorcroft, W. and G. Trebeck, *Travels in the Himalayan Provinces of Hindustan and the Panjab; in Ladakh and Kashmir; in Peshawar, Kabul, Kunduz and Bokhara; from 1819–1825,* edited by H. H. Wilson (2 vols, London, 1841; reprint Delhi, 1971).

Morris, James, *Heaven's Command. An Imperial Progress* (London, 1973).

Mousavi, S. A., *The Hazaras of Afghanistan: An Historical, Cultural, Economic, and Political Study* (Richmond, 1998).

Mukherjee, B. N., *The Disintegration of the Kushâna Empire* (Varanasi, 1976).

Naby, E., The Uzbeks in Afghanistan, *Central Asian Survey* III, 1, 1984, pp. 1–21.

Narain, A. K., *The Indo-Greeks* (Oxford, 1957).

Nâzim, M., *The Life and Times of Sultân Mahmûd of Ghazni* (Cambridge, 1931).

Newby, E., *A Short Walk in the Hindu Kush* (London, 1958).

Newell, R. S., *The Politics of Afghanistan* (Ithaca, 1972).

Niedermayer, O. von, and E. Diez, *Afghanistan* (Leipzig, 1924).

Ni'matullah, Khwaja Ni'matullah b. Khwaja Habibullah al-Harawi, *Târikh-e Khân Jahâni wa Makhzan-e Afghâni.* (published in Dacca, 1960–92). A translation is by Dorn (1829–36; reprint London and Santiago de Compostella, 1965; Karachi, 1976).

Nöldeke, Th., *Tabari: Geschichte der Perser und Araber zur Zeit der Sasaniden* (1879; reprint Leiden, 1973).

Noelle, C., *State and Tribe in Nineteenth-Century Afghanistan. The Reign of Amir Dost Muhammad Khan (1826–1863)* (Richmond, 1997).

Norman, K. R., Notes on the Greek version of Aśoka's Twelfth and Thirteenth Rock edicts, *Journal of the Royal Asiatic Society* 1972, pp. 111–18.

Norris, J., *The First Afghan War: 1838–1842* (Cambridge, 1967).

Nyrop, R. S. and D. M. Seekins (eds), *Afghanistan: A Country Study* (Washington, 1986).

O'Kane, B., *Timurid Architecture in Khurasan* (Costa Mesa, 1987).

Olesen, A., The Sheikh Mohammadi – A marginal trading community in East Afghanistan, *Folk* 27, 1985, pp. 115–46.

Olesen, A., Peddling in East Afghanistan: Adaptive strategies of the peripatetic Sheikh Mohammadi, in: A. Rao (ed.), *The Other Nomads: Peripatetics in Cross-Cultural Perspective* (Cologne, 1987), pp. 35–63.

Olesen, A., *Afghan Craftsmen. The Cultures of Three Itinerant Communities* (London, 1994).

Olesen, A., *Islam and Politics in Afghanistan* (Richmond, 1995).

Olufsen, O., *Through the Unknown Pamirs* (London, 1904).

Orywal, E., *Die Baluc in Afghanisch-Sistan. Wirtschaft und sozio-politische Organisation in Nimruz, SW-Afghanistan* (Berlin, 1982).

Orywal, E., *Afghanistan – Ethnische Gruppen 1:2, 5 Mio* (TAVO Blatt A VIII 16. Wiesbaden, 1983).

Orywal, E., *Die ethnischen Gruppen Afghanistans. Fallstudien zu Gruppenidentität und Intergruppenbeziehungen* (Wiesbaden, 1986).

Parpagliolo, M. T. S., *Kâbul: The Bâgh-i Bâbur* (Rome, 1972).

Pedersen, G., *Afghan Nomads in Transition. A Century of Change among the Zala Khân Khêl* (Copenhagen, 1994).

Pennell, T. L., *Among the Wild Tribes of the Afghan Frontier. A Record of Sixteen Years' Close Intercourse with the Natives of the Indian Marches* (London, 1909).

Periplus Maris Erythraei, translated and edited by G. B. Huntingford (London, 1980).

Phillips, E. D., The Scythian domination in Western Asia: Its record in history, scripture and archaeology, *World Archaeology* IV, 2, 1972, pp. 129–38.

Piankova, L. T., Le Tadjikistan méridional au Bronze tardif, *Découverte des civilisations d'Asie Centrale* (Les Dossiers d'Archéologie No. 85), 1993, pp. 70–5.

Pichikyan, I. R., Rebirth of the Oxus Treasure: Second part of the Oxus Treasure from the Miho Museum Collection, *Ancient Civilizations from Scythia to Siberia* IV, 4, 1997, pp. 306–83.

Piotrowicz, L., L'invasion des Scythes en Asie antérieure au VIIe siècle av. J. C., *Eos* 32, 1929, pp. 473–508.

Planhol, X. de, *Kulturgeographische Grundlagen der islamischen Geschichte* (Zürich und München, 1975).

Poladi, H., *The Hazaras* (Stockton, 1989).

Posch, W., *Baktrien zwischen Griechen und Kushan. Untersuchungen zu kulturellen und historischen Problemen einer Übergangsphase. Mit einem textkritischen Exkurs zum Shiji 123* (Wiesbaden, 1995).

Possehl, G., *Scientific Dates for South Asian Archaeology* (Philadelphia, 1990).

Pottinger, G., *The Afghan Connection. The Extraordinary Adventures of Major Eldred Pottinger* (Edinburgh, 1983).

Potts, T., *Mesopotamia and the East. An Archaeological and Historical Study of Foreign Relations 3400–2000* BC (Oxford, 1994).

Pougatchenkova, G. A., Dal'verzin Tepe-Hozdo. La première capitale des Kouchans, *Dossiers d'Archéologie* 247, 1999, pp. 58–61.

Poullada, L. B., *Reform and Rebellion in Afghanistan, 1919–1929. King Amanullah's Failure to Modernize a Tribal Society* (Ithaca, 1973).

Poullada, L. B., The Wu-sun and Sakas and the Yüeh-chih migration, *Bulletin of the School of Oriental and African Studies* 33, 1970, pp. 154–60.

Puri, B. N., The Kushans, in: János Harmatta (ed.), *The Development of Sedentary and Nomadic Civilizations: 700* BC *to* AD *250* (History of Civilizations of Central Asia, vol. II) (Paris, 1994a, 1996), pp. 247–63.

Puri, B. N., The Sakas and Indo-Parthians, in: János Harmatta (ed.), *The Development of Sedentary and Nomadic Civilizations: 700* BC *to* AD *250* (History of Civilizations of Central Asia, vol. II) (Paris, 1994b, 1996), pp. 191–207.

Radermacher, H., Historische Bewässerungssysteme in Afghanisch-Sistan. Gründe für ihren Verfall und Möglichkeiten ihrer Reaktivierung, *Zeitschrift für Kulturtechnik und Flurbereinigung* 16, pp. 65–77.

Raja Anwar, *The Tragedy of Afghanistan: A First Hand Account* (London, 1988).

Rao, A., Note préliminaire sur les Jat d'Afghanistan, *Studia Iranica* 8, 1979, pp. 141–9.

Rao, A., *Les Gorbat d'Afghanistan. Aspects économiques d'un groupe itinérant 'Jat'* (Paris, 1982).

Rao, A., Peripatetic minorities in Afghanistan, in: A. Rao (ed.), *The Other Nomads: Peripatetic Minorities in Cross-cultural Perspective* (Cologne, 1987).

Rao, G. K., R. Pinder-Wilson and W. Ball, The stupa and monastery at Guldarra. Report on the British Institute's preservation programme, *South Asian Studies* 1, 1985, pp. 79–88.

Rapin, C., La trésorerie du palais hellénistique d'Aï Khanoum. L'apogée et la chute du royaume grec de Bactriane, *Fouilles d'Aï Khanoum* VIII (Paris, 1992).

Rathjens, C., Der afghanische Hindukush, *Jahrbuch der Österr. Alpenvereins* 1955, pp. 116–21.

Rathjens, C., Karawanenwege und Pässe im Kulturlandschaftswandel Afghanistans seit dem 19. Jahrhundert, in: *Festschrift H. v. Wissmann* (Tübingen, 1962), pp. 209–21.

Rathjens, C., *Das Klima*, in: W. Kraus, *Afghanistan* (Tübingen and Basel, 1975), pp. 32–41.

Rattray, J., *The Costumes of the Various Tribes, Portraits of Ladies of Rank, Celebrated Princes and Chiefs, Views of Principal Fortresses, and Interior of the Cities and Temples of Afghaunistan* (London, 1848).

Raunig, W., Einige Bemerkungen zu Verkehr und Handelstendenzen in der afghanischen Provinz Badakhshan, in: J. Schneider (ed.), *Wirtschaftskräfte und Wirtschaftswege. Festschrift H. Kellenbenz* (Stuttgart, 1978). Vol. IV, pp. 549–83.

Raverty, Major H. G., *Notes on Afghanistan and Part of Baluchistan: Geographical, Ethnological and Historical* (London, 1888).

Rawlinson, Major H., Report on the Dooranee Tribes [dated 19 April 1841] (Appendix III in MacGregor, *Central Asia*, vol. II, Calcutta, 1871).

Redard, G., *Afghanistan* (Zurich, 1974).

Ridgway, R. T. I., *Pathans* (Peshawar, 1983).

Rizvi, S. A. A., *History of the Dar al-Ulum Deoband* (Deoband, 1980).

Robert, L. De Delphes à l'Oxus, inscriptions grecques nouvelles de la Bactriane, *Comptes Rendus de l'Académie des Inscriptions et Belles-lettres*, 1968, pp. 416–67.

Roberts, Fieldmarshal Earl, *Forty-One Years in India* (London, 1911).

Robertson, G. S., *The Kafirs of the Hindu-Kush* (London, 1896; reprint: London and New York, 1970; Karachi, 1974).

Robinson, J. A., *Notes on the Nomad Tribes of Eastern Afghanistan* (New Delhi, 1935; reprint Quetta, 1978).

Rolle, R., *Die Welt der Skythen. Stutenmelker und Pferdebogner: Ein antikes Reitervolk in neuer Sicht* (Luzern and Frankfurt, 1980).

Rosenfield, J. M., *The Dynastic Arts of the Kushans* (Berkeley and Los Angeles, 1967).

Roskoschny, H., *Afghanistan und seine Nachbarländern* (Leipzig, 1885).

Ross, F. E. (ed.), *Central Asia. Personal Narrative of General Josiah Harlan, 1823–1841* (London, 1939).

Roux, J.-P., *L'Asie centrale. Histoire et civilisations* (Paris, 1997).

Roy, O., *Islam and Resistance in Afghanistan* (second edition; Cambridge, 1990).

Roy, O., *The Failure of Political Islam* (Cambridge, Mass., 1994).

Rowland, B., *The Art and Architecture of India. Buddhist, Hindu, Jain* (1953, 1967, third revised edition, Harmondsworth, 1970).

Rowlands, M., Larsen, M. T. and Kristiansen, K. (eds), *Centre and Periphery in the Ancient World* (Cambridge, 1987).

Rubin, B. R., *The Fragmentation of Afghanistan. State Formation & Collapse in the International System* (New Haven and London, 1995).

Rubin, B. R., *The Search for Peace in Afghanistan. From Buffer State to Failed State* (New Haven and London, 1995).

Sale, Lady Florentia, *A Journal of the Disasters in Afghanistan, 1841–2* (London, 1843).

Salvini, Mirjo, *Geschichte und Kultur der Urartäer* (Darmstadt, 1995).

Santoni, M., Sibri and the South Cemetery of Mehrgarh, *South Asian Archaeology* (Cambridge, 1984), pp. 52–60.

Sarianidi, V., *Raskopki Tillya-tepe v severnom Afghanistana* (Moscow, 1972).

Sarianidi, V., *Drevnie Zemledel'cy Afganistana* (Moscow, 1977).

Sarianidi, V., *L'or de la Bactriane. Fouilles de la nécropole de Tillia-Tépé en Afghanistan septentrional* (Leningrad, 1985).

Sarianidi, V., *Die Kunst des Alten Afghanistan. Keramik, Siegel, Architektur, Kunstwerke aus Stein und Metall* (Leipzig, 1986).

Sarianidi, V., Khram i Nekropol' Tillyatepe (Moscow, 1989).

Sarianidi, V., Food-producing and other Neolithic communities in Khorasan and Transoxania: Eastern Iran, Soviet Central Asia and Afghanistan, in: A. H. Dani and V. M. Masson (eds), *The Dawn of Civilization: Earliest Times to 700 BC* (History of Civilizations of Central Asia, vol. I.) (Paris, 1992, second impression, 1996), pp. 109–26.

Sarianidi, V., Margiana in the Ancient Orient, *Information Bulletin of the International Association for the Study of the Cultures of Central Asia* 19, 1993, pp. 5–28.

Sarianidi, V., New discoveries at ancient Gonur, *Ancient Civilizations from Scythia to Siberia*, vol. 2, no. 3, 1995, pp. 289–310.

Sarianidi, V., *Margiana and Protozoroastrism* (Athens, 1998).

Said Amir Arjomand, *The Shadow of God and the Hidden Imam* (Chicago, 1984).

Scarcia, G. and M. Taddei, The Masjid-i Sangi of Larvand, *East and West* 23, 1973, pp. 89–108.

Scharlipp, W.-E., *Die frühen Türken in Zentralasien* (Darmstadt, 1992).

Schinasi, M., *Afghanistan at the Beginning of the Twentieth Century* (Naples, 1979).

Schippmann, K., *Grundzüge der Geschichte des Sasanidischen Reiches* (Darmstadt, 1990).

Schippmann, K., *Lashkari Bazar, Une résidence royale ghaznévide et ghoride. I A. L'architecture* (Paris, 1978).

Schippmann, K., with M. Le Berre et G. Fussman, *Surkh Kotal en Bactriane*. Vol. I (Paris, 1983).

Schmitt, R., *Compendium Linguarum Iranicarum* (Wiesbaden, 1989).

Schoff, W. H., *Parthian Stations of Isidore of Charax* (Philadelphia, 1914).

Schurmann, H. F., *The Mongols of Afghanistan; An Ethnography of the Môghols and Related Peoples of Afghanistan* (The Hague, 1962).

Scott, D. A., Ashokan missionary expansion of Buddhism among the Greeks (in Northwest India, Bactria, and the Levant), *Religion* 15, 1985, pp. 131–41.

Sedlar, J. W., *India and the Greek World: A Study in the Transmission of Culture* (Totowa, 1980).

Shaffer, J. G., The later prehistoric period, in: F. R. Allchin and N. Hammond (eds), *The Archaeology of Afghanistan* (Cambridge, 1979), pp. 71–186.

Shahrani, M. N., *The Kirghiz and Wakhi of Afghanistan: Adaptation to Closed Frontiers* (Seattle, 1979).

Shaked, S., Notes on the new Aśoka inscription from Kandahar, *Journal of the Royal Asiatic Society*, 1969, pp. 118–22.

Sherratt, A., Plough and pastoralism: aspects of the secondary products revolution, in: I. Hodder, G. Isaac and N. Hammond (eds), *Patterns of the Past* (Cambridge, 1981), pp. 261–305.

Sherwin-White, S. and A. Kuhrt (eds), *From Samarkhand to Sardis: A New Approach to the Seleucid Empire* (Berkeley, 1993).

Shimo, H., The Qaraunas in the historical materials of the Ilkhanate, *Memoirs of the Research Department of the Toyo Bunko* 35, 1977, pp. 131–81.

Simonetta, A. M., A new essay on the Indo-Greeks. The Sakas and the Pahlavas, *East and West* 9, 1958, pp. 154–83.

Sims-Williams, N., A note on Bactrian chronology, *Bulletin of the School of Oriental and African Studies* 48, 1985, pp. 111–16.

Sims-Williams, N., Eastern Iranian languages, *Encyclopaedia Iranica* VII/6, 1996, pp. 649–52.

Sims-Williams, N., A Bactrian God, *Bulletin of the School of Oriental and African Studies* 60, 1997a, pp. 336–8.

Sims-Williams, N., *New Light on Ancient Afghanistan. The Decipherment of Bactrian* (An inaugural lecture delivered on 1 February 1996) (London, 1997b).

Sims-Williams, N., Further notes on the Bactrian inscription of Rabatak, with an appendix on the names of Kujula Kadphises and Wima Taktu in Chinese, in: N. Sims-Williams (ed.), Proceedings of the Third European Conference of Iranian Studies held in Cambridge, 11th to 15th September 1995 (Wiesbaden, 1998), pp. 79–92, Pls. 9–12.

Sims-Williams, N., with J. Cribb, A new Bactrian inscription of Kanishka the Great, *Silk Road Art and Archaeology* 4, 1996, pp. 75–142.

Singer, A., Ethnic origins and tribal history of the Timuri of Khurasan, *Afghan Studies* 3–4, 1982, pp. 65–76.

Singh, G., *Ahmad Shah Durrani: Father of Modern Afghanistan* (New Delhi, 1959).

Sinor, D. (ed.), *The Cambridge History of Central Asia* (Cambridge, 1990).

Sircar, D. C., *Studies in the Geography of Ancient and Medieval India* (Delhi, 1971; 1997 second and revised edition).

Si-Yu-Ki, *Buddhist Records of the Western World*. Translated from the Chinese of Hiuen Tsiang AD 629, by Samuel Beal (London, 1884; reprint New Delhi, 1983).

Sliwinski, M., *Afghanistan 1978–87. War, Demography and Society* (Central Asian Survey, Incidental papers, no. 6; London, 1988).

Snoy, P. Nuristan and Mungan, *Tribus* 14, 1965, pp. 101–48.

Sourdel-Thomine, J., L'art gûride d'Afghanistan à propos d'un livre récent, *Arabica* VII, 1960, pp. 273–80.

Spain, J. W., *The Way of the Pathans* (London, 1962).

Spain, J. W., *The Pathan Borderland* (The Hague, 1963, reprint Karachi, 1985).

Spuler, B., *Die Mongolen in Iran* (Leiden, 1985).

Stack, S. C., *Herat: A Political and Social Study* (Ph.D. diss., University of California, Los Angeles, 1975).

Staviskij, B. Ja., *La Bactriane sous les Kushans. Problèmes d'histoire et de culture* (Paris, 1986).

Stein, A., Zur Geschichte der Shâhis von Kâbul, *Festgruss an Rudolf von Roth* (Stuttgart, 1893), pp. 1–10.

Stein, A., A Chinese expedition across the Pamirs and Hindu Kush 747 AD, *Indian Antiquary* 52, 1923, pp. 98–103, 139–45, 173–7.

Stein, A., *An Archaeological Tour in Gedrosia* (Calcutta, 1931a).

Stein, A., On the Ephedra, the Hûm plant, and the Soma, *Bulletin of the School of Oriental Studies* 6, 2, 1931b, pp. 501–14.

Stein, A., *Archaeological Reconnaissances in North Western India and South-Eastern Iran* (London, 1937).

Steul, W., *Pashtunwali. Ein Ehrenkodex und seine rechtliche Relevanz* (Wiesbaden, 1981).

Stewart, R. T., *Fire in Afghanistan, 1914–1929: Faith, Hope and the British Empire* (New York, 1973).

Stocqueler, J. H., *Memorials of Afghanistan 1838–1842* (Calcutta, 1843).

Sulimirski, T., Scythian antiquities in Western Asia, *Artibus Asiae* 17, 1954, pp. 282–318.

Sultan Mahomed Khan (ed.), *The Life of Abdur Rahman, Amir of Afghanistan* (2 vols London, 1900).

Sundermann, W., Zur frühen missionärischen Wirksamkeit Manis, *Acta Orientalia Academiae Scientiarum Hungaricae* 24, 1 and 3, 1971.

Sykes, P., *A History of Afghanistan* (2 vols, London, 1940; reprint: Lahore, 1979; New Delhi, 1981).

Szabo, A. and T. J. Barfield, *Afghanistan. An Atlas of Indigenous Domestic Architecture* (Austin, 1991).

Szemerenyi, O. Four Old Iranian Ethnic Names: Scythian – Skudra – Sogdian – Saka (Vienna, 1980).

Szuppe, Maria, *Entre Timourides, Uzbeks et Safavides. Questions d'histoire politique et sociale de Hérat dans la première moitié du XVIe siècle* (Paris, 1992).

Tapper, N., The advent of Pashtun Maldars into Northwestern Afghanistan, *Bulletin of the School of Oriental and African Studies* 36, 1973, pp. 167–70.

Tapper, N., Nomadism in modern Afghanistan: asset or anachronism?, in Dupree and Talbot (eds), *Afghanistan in the 1970s* (New York/London, 1974), pp. 126–43.

Tapper, N., Abd al-Rahman's North-West Frontier: The Pashtun colonisation of Afghan Turkistan, in: R. Tapper (ed.), *The Conflict of Tribe and State in Iran and Afghanistan* (Beckenham, 1983), pp. 233–61.

Tapper, R. (ed.), *The Conflict of Tribe and State in Iran and Afghanistan* (Beckenham, 1983).

Tardieu, M., La diffusion du Bouddhisme dans l'empire Kouchan, l'Iran et la Chine, d'après un Kephalaion manichéen inédit, *Studia Iranica* 17, 1988, fasc. 2, pp. 153–82.

Ta'rikh-i Sistan (ed. by Bahar) (Tehran, 1953). Trans. M. Gold (Rome, 1976).

Tarn, W., *The Greeks in Bactria and India* (second edition, Cambridge, 1951). A third, revised edition was published by Frank Holt (Chicago, 1984).

Tate, G. P., *Seistan. A Memoir on the History, Topography, Ruins, and People of the Country* (4 parts, 3 vols, Calcutta, 1910).

Thackeray, E. T., *Views of Kabul and Environs from pictures taken by the Photograph School of Bengal Sappers and Miners* (London, 1881).

Thapar, R., *Aśoka and the Decline of the Mauryas* (Oxford, 1961).

Tomaschek, W., *Über die ältesten Nachrichten über den Skythischen Norden* I, *SBWAW* 116, 1888.

Tosi, M., Excavations at Shahr-i Sokhta, *East and West* 19, 1969, pp. 283–386.

Tosi, M., *Prehistoric Sistan*, vol. I. (Rome, 1983).

Tosi, M., S. Malek Shahmirzadi and M. A. Joyenda, The Bronze Age in Iran and Afghanistan, in: A. H. Dani and V. M. Masson (eds), *The Dawn of*

Civilization: Earliest Times to 700 BC (History of Civilizations of Central Asia, vol. I.) (Paris, 1992; second impression 1996), pp. 191–223.

Tosi, M. and R. Wardak, The Fullol hoard: a new find from Bronze Age Afghanistan, *East and West* 22, 1972, pp. 9–17.

Töttösy, C., The name of the Greeks in ancient India, *Acta Orientalia Academiae Scientiarum Hungaricae* 3, 1956, pp. 301–18.

Toynbee, A. J., *Between Oxus and Jumna* (London, 1963).

Troxell, H. A. and W. F. Spengler, A hoard of early Greek coins from Afghanistan, *American Numismatic Society Museum Notes* 15, 1969, pp. 1–19.

Trousdale, W. (ed.), *The Gordon Creeds in Afghanistan. 1839 and 1878–1879* (London, 1984).

The Truth about Afghanistan, compiled by Y. Volkov et al. (Muscow, 1980).

Upasak, C. S., *History of Buddhism in Afghanistan* (Varanasi, 1990).

Urban, Mark L., *War in Afghanistan* (New York, 1988).

Vaggione, R. P., Over all Asia? The extent of the Scythian domination in Herodotus, *Journal of Biblical Literature* 92, 1973, pp. 523–30.

Vambéry, A., *Travels in Central Asia* (London, 1864).

Varenne, Jean, *Zoroastre, le prophète de l'Iran* (Paris, 1996).

Vigne, G. T., *A Personal Account of a Visit to Ghuzni, Kabul and Afghanistan* (London, 1843).

Vogelsang, W. J., Early historical Arachosia in South-east Afghanistan, Meeting-place between East and West, *Iranica Antiqua* XX, 1985, pp. 5–99.

Vogelsang, W. J., Four short notes on the Bisutun text and monument, *Iranica Antiqua* 21, 1986, pp. 121–40.

Vogelsang, W. J., Indian antics. A reply to P. Bernard, *Studia Iranica* 17, 1988a, 2, pp. 253–8.

Vogelsang, W. J., A period of acculturation in ancient Gandhara, *South Asian Studies* 4, 1988b, pp. 103–13.

Vogelsang, W. J., Gold from Dardistan. Some comparative remarks on the tribute system in the extreme Northwest of the Indian subcontinent, in: P. Briant and C. Herrenschmidt (réd.), *Le tribut dans l'empire Perse. Actes de la Table ronde de Paris 12–13 Décembre 1986* (Paris, 1989), pp. 157–71.

Vogelsang, W. J., Gandharans, Bactrians, and Scythians: Who was who in the sixth century BC?, in: T. S. Maxwell (ed.), *Eastern Approaches. Essays on Asian Art and Archaeology* (Delhi, 1992a), pp. 1–15.

Vogelsang, W. J., *The Rise and Organisation of the Achaemenid Empire. The Eastern Iranian Evidence* (Studies in the History of the Ancient Near East, vol. III. Leiden, New York and Köln, 1992b).

Vogelsang, W. J., Medes, Scythians and Persians: The rise of Darius in a North-South perspective, *Iranica Antiqua* XXXIII, 1998, pp. 195–224.

Vogelsang, W. J., The sixteen lands of Vidêvdât I. Airyân'm Vaêjah and the homeland of the Iranians, *Persica* XVI, 2000, pp. 49–66.

Vogelsang-Eastwood, G. M., *Tutankhamun's Wardrobe* (Rotterdam, 1999).

Walser, G., 1985, Die Route des Isidorus von Charax durch Iran, *Archäologische Mitteilungen aus Iran* NS 18, pp. 145–56.

Weinbaum, M., *Pakistan and Afghanistan: Resistance and Reconstruction* (Boulder, 1994).

Wheeler, S., *The Ameer Abdur Rahman* (1895).

Whitteridge, G., *Charles Masson of Afghanistan. Explorer, archaeologist, numismatist and intelligence agent* (Warminster, 1986).

Widengren, G., Xosrau Anosurvan, les Hephthalites et les peuples turcs, *Orientalia Suecana* 1, 1952.

Wieland-Karimi, A., *Islamische Mystik in Afghanistan: die strukturelle Einbindung der Sufik in die Gesellschaft* (Heidelberg, 1998).

Wiesehöfer, J., *Ancient Persia* (London, 1996).

Wiebe, D., *Stadtstruktur und Kulturgeographischer Wandel in Kandahar und Südafghanistan* (Kiel, 1978).

Wilber, D. N., *Afghanistan* (New Haven, 1962).

Wilke, F., Das Skythenproblem im Jeremiahbuch, *Alttestamentische Studien für Rudolf Kittel* (Leipzig, 1913), pp. 222–54.

Wilson, H. H., *Ariana Antiqua. A Descriptive Account of the Antiquities and Coins of Afghanistan: With a Memoir of the Buildings Called Topes, by C. Masson Esq.* (1841; reprint Delhi, 1971).

Wirth, G. and O. von Hinüber (eds and trans.), *Arrian. Der Alexanderzug. Indische Geschichte, Greek and German* (Munich and Zürich, 1985).

Wolski, J., *L'empire des Arsacides* (Louvain, 1993).

Wood, J., *A Journey to the Source of the River Oxus* (First edition: London, 1841. Second edition, with an essay on the geography of the valley of the Oxus by H. Yule: London, 1872. Reprint: Karachi 1976).

Wood, M., *In the Footsteps of Alexander the Great* (London, 1997).

Wutt, K., *Pashai. Landschaft, Menschen, Architektur* (Graz, 1981).

Xinru Liu, *Ancient India and Ancient China. Trade and Religious Exchanges* AD 1–600 (Delhi, 1994).

Yapp, M., Disturbances in eastern Afghanistan, 1839–41, *Bulletin of the School of Oriental and African Studies* 25, 3, 1962, pp. 499–523.

Yapp, M., Disturbances in western Afghanistan, 1839–41, *Bulletin of the School of Oriental and African Studies* 26, 2, 1963, pp. 288–313.

Yapp, M., The revolution of 1841–2 in Afghanistan, *Bulletin of the School of Oriental and African Studies* 27, 2 1964, pp. 333–81.

Yapp, M., *Strategies of British India: Britain, Iran and Afghanistan 1798–1850* (Oxford, 1980).

Yate, C. E., *Northern Afghanistan or Letters from the Afghan Boundary Commission* (Edinburgh/London, 1888).

Yate, C. E., *Khurasan and Sistan* (Edinburgh, 1900).

Yusuf, M. and M. Adkin, *The Bear Trap* (Lahore, 1992).

Zawadzki, S., *The Fall of Assyria and Median-Babylonian Relations in the Light of the Nabopolassar Chronicle* (Poznan and Delft, 1988).

Zeimal, E. V., The Kidarite kingdom in Central Asia, in: B. A. Litvinsky, *The Crossroads of Civilizations*, AD 250 to 750 (History of Civilizations of Central Asia, vol. III) (Paris, 1996), pp. 119–33.

Zürcher, E., The Yüeh-chih and Kaniska in Chinese sources, in: A. L. Basham, *Papers on the Date of Kaniska* (Leiden, 1968), pp. 346–90.

Index